Birnbaum's Country Inns and Back Roads, North America

A BIRNBAUM TRAVEL GUIDE

Alexandra Mayes Birnbaum
EDITORIAL CONSULTANT

Lois Spritzer
Editorial Director

Laura L. Brengelman
Managing Editor

Mary Callahan
Beth Schlau
Senior Editors

Jill Kadetsky
Editor

Patricia Canole
Gene Gold
Susan McClung
Associate Editors

Marcy S. Pritchard
Map Coordinator

Susan Cutter Snyder
Editorial Assistant

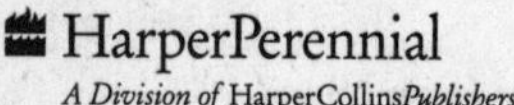
A Division of HarperCollins*Publishers*

ISSN 0749-2561 (Birnbaum Travel Guides)
ISSN 70-615664 (Country Inns and Back Roads, North America)
ISBN 0-06-278203-7 (pbk.)

96 97 98 99 ❖/RRD 5 4 3 2 1

Cover design © Drenttel Doyle Partners
Cover photograph © Bruce Wodder/The Image Bank

BIRNBAUM TRAVEL GUIDES

Bahamas, and Turks & Caicos
Bermuda
Canada
Cancun, Cozumel & Isla Mujeres
Caribbean
Country Inns and Back Roads
Disneyland
Hawaii
Mexico
Miami & Ft. Lauderdale
United States
Walt Disney World
Walt Disney World for Kids, By Kids

Writer/Editor

Suzi Forbes Chase

Contributing Editor

Nancy Cohen

Contents

New Hampshire

Vermont

Massachusetts

Upper South

California

Pacific Northwest, Alaska, and British Columbia

Foreword

A HarperCollins book since the early 1980s and now a member of the *Birnbaum Travel Guides* series, *Country Inns & Back Roads* is, we believe, a natural outgrowth and expansion of some of the information already found in *Birnbaum's United States* and *Canada* guidebooks—with a delightful difference. A geographic listing of our favorite getaways in the US and Canada, *Country Inns* is written especially for those who prefer small towns to big cities, cedar furnishings to chrome, and sylvan settings to spectacular skylines (although we list some special urban oases as well).

Obviously, our larger country books could not possibly cover the broad range of wonderful inns that dot the landscape across both countries. But here, in a book dedicated solely to chintz curtains, down comforters, grandfather clocks, and home-baked muffins, the breadth of our coverage has expanded greatly. All you need to do is select a destination, turn to the table of contents, and we'll do the rest.

We have organized this guide by region. Within each regional section, inns are listed alphabetically by state or province, then area, city, island, or town. Maps indicate major cities and have legends that point out, by number, towns in which our favorite inns are located. For example, if you'd like to visit Cape Cod, Massachusetts, you can see at a glance which places we recommend. An index listing the properties alphabetically by name is another easy-to-use resource.

As with the rest of the books in the *Birnbaum Travel Guides* series, no part of this text is carved in stone. In our annual revisions we will continue to refine, expand, and further hone our material to serve your travel needs better. Not surprisingly, we are inundated with mail from innkeepers from all parts of the country, whose properties are not included in this guide. Over the next year we will make every effort to visit these various properties with an eye toward their possible inclusion in a future edition of *Country Inns & Back Roads.* Likewise, we will continue to visit inns that are already included in this book, to ensure that our readers will find things much the same as (or better than) last year.

In addition to our own research, nothing is of greater value to us than your personal reaction to what we have written and your own experiences while staying in American and Canadian inns. Please write to us at 10 East 53rd Street, New York, NY 10022.

Northern New England and Quebec

NEW HAMPSHIRE

12. Chesterfield: CHESTERFIELD INN
13. Conway: DARBY FIELD INN
14. Francestown: INN AT CROTCHED MOUNTAIN
15. Hart's Location: NOTCHLAND INN
16. Henniker: MEETING HOUSE INN
17. Holderness: MANOR ON GOLDEN POND
18. Jackson: CHRISTMAS FARM INN; INN AT THORN HILL
19. North Sutton: FOLLANSBEE INN
20. Sugar Hill: SUGAR HILL INN
21. Sunapee: DEXTER'S INN AND TENNIS CLUB
22. Tamworth: TAMWORTH INN
23. Temple: BIRCHWOOD INN

VERMONT

24. Barnard: TWIN FARMS
25. Brandon: LILAC INN
26. Chittenden: TULIP TREE INN
27. Craftsbury Common: INN ON THE COMMON
28. Dorset: CORNUCOPIA OF DORSET
29. Goshen: BLUEBERRY HILL
30. Grafton: OLD TAVERN AT GRAFTON
31. Lower Waterford: RABBIT HILL INN
32. Ludlow: GOVERNOR'S INN
33. Manchester Village: 1811 HOUSE; INN AT ORMSBY HILL
34. Middlebury: SWIFT HOUSE INN
35. Newfane: FOUR COLUMNS INN
36. Shelburne: INN AT SHELBURNE FARMS
37. Simonsville: ROWELL'S INN
38. Stowe: EDSON HILL MANOR
39. Waitsfield: INN AT THE ROUND BARN FARM
40. Weathersfield: INN AT WEATHERSFIELD
41. West Dover: INN AT SAWMILL FARM
42. Wilmington: TRAIL'S END– A COUNTRY INN
43. Woodstock: JACKSON HOUSE

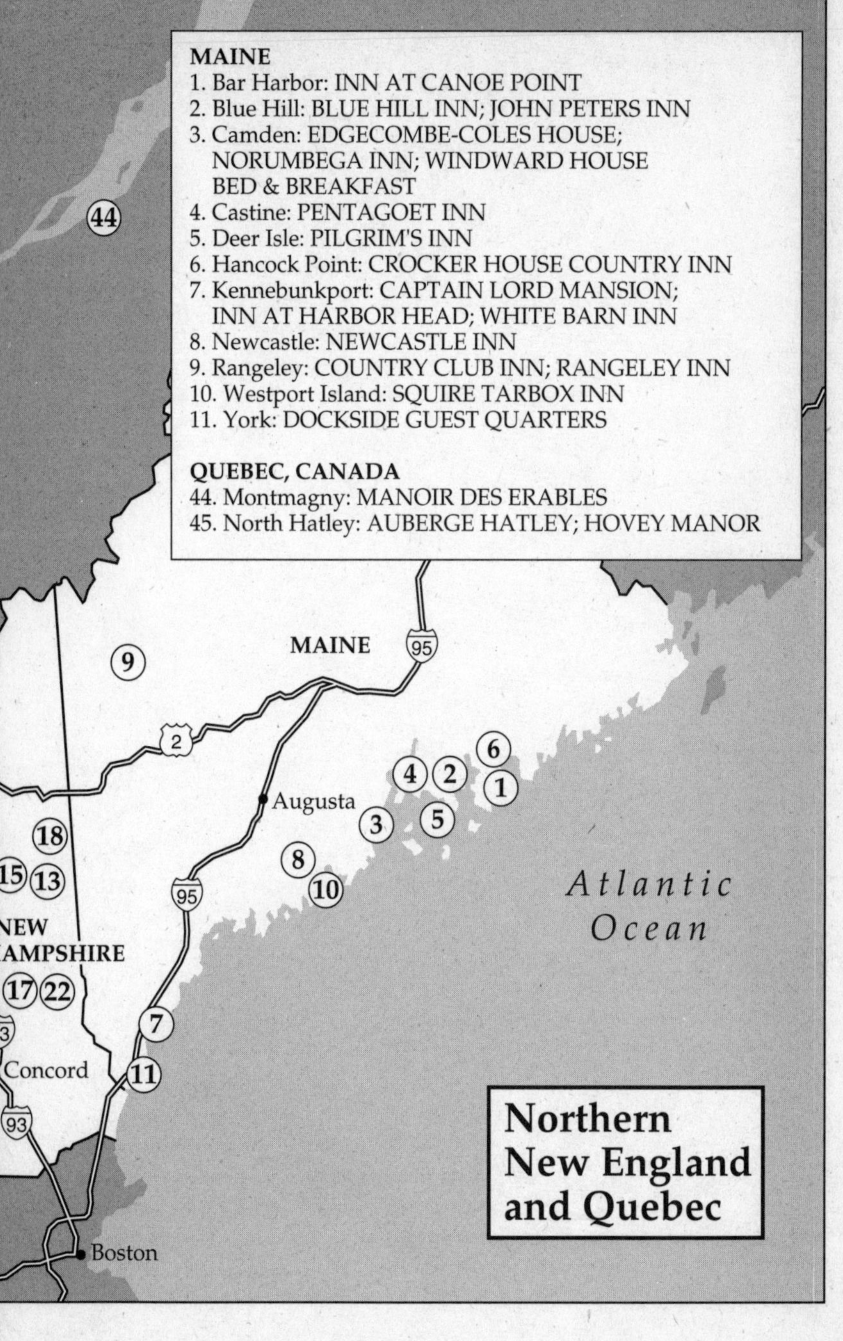
MAINE
1. Bar Harbor: INN AT CANOE POINT
2. Blue Hill: BLUE HILL INN; JOHN PETERS INN
3. Camden: EDGECOMBE-COLES HOUSE; NORUMBEGA INN; WINDWARD HOUSE BED & BREAKFAST
4. Castine: PENTAGOET INN
5. Deer Isle: PILGRIM'S INN
6. Hancock Point: CROCKER HOUSE COUNTRY INN
7. Kennebunkport: CAPTAIN LORD MANSION; INN AT HARBOR HEAD; WHITE BARN INN
8. Newcastle: NEWCASTLE INN
9. Rangeley: COUNTRY CLUB INN; RANGELEY INN
10. Westport Island: SQUIRE TARBOX INN
11. York: DOCKSIDE GUEST QUARTERS
QUEBEC, CANADA
44. Montmagny: MANOIR DES ERABLES
45. North Hatley: AUBERGE HATLEY; HOVEY MANOR
MAINE
Augusta
NEW HAMPSHIRE
Concord
Boston
Atlantic Ocean
Northern New England and Quebec

Northern New England and Quebec

Maine

INN AT CANOE POINT

BAR HARBOR, MAINE

As you drive down this property's curving, tree-lined driveway, with glimpses of water beyond, you know you're in for a treat. Then the *Inn at Canoe Point* appears—an oasis of tranquillity on two secluded acres at the edge of Frenchman's Bay.

This English Tudor–style inn was built as a family summer cottage in 1889 and remained a private residence until 1986, when it was purchased by Don Johnson and Esther Cavagnaro and fully renovated to welcome guests. The peace and quiet of this retreat is in marked contrast to the bustle of Bar Harbor, just 2 miles away.

Though its mood is relaxed, the inn also has an elegant air. In the public rooms the decor is a harmonious mixture of antiques and traditional furniture. The main entry hall/living room features a fireplace and a baby grand piano. A granite fireplace dominates one side of the *Ocean Room;* on the other is a panoramic view of Frenchman's Bay. Enjoy a full breakfast either in the *Ocean Room* or, in sunny weather, on the outside deck.

Specialties include cranberry-walnut pancakes, blueberry French toast, and spinach quiche.

The five guestrooms echo the inn's warm, casual style. Overlooking either the water or the rocky shoreline, all have modern bathrooms; some have private balconies. A decanter of wine awaits guests in each room. In the master suite, amenities include both a fireplace and a deck, while the *Garret Suite,* the inn's largest, takes up the entire third floor and includes a bedroom with French windows as well as a sitting room with a balcony.

The inn is a quarter mile from *Acadia National Park* and 2 miles from Bar Harbor, giving guests a choice of many local activities, including bicycling, hiking, whale watching and naturalist cruises, antiquing, and visiting art galleries.

INN AT CANOE POINT Box 216K, Bar Harbor, ME 04609 (phone: 207-288-9511). This cottage has five guestrooms with private baths and queen- or king-size beds. Open year-round. Rate for a double room (including full breakfast) *Memorial Day* through October: $135 to $235; rest of the year $90 to $165. No credit cards accepted. Not appropriate for children under 12. No pets. Nikki, a German shepherd, in residence. No smoking. Don Johnson and Esther Cavagnaro, innkeepers.

DIRECTIONS: Traveling north on I-95, take Exit 30 in Augusta to Route 3. Follow Route 3 (which becomes Route 1 and 3 shortly after Belfast) north. At Ellsworth continue on Route 3 another 15 miles south toward Bar Harbor. Drive a quarter mile past the entrance to *Acadia National Park,* and turn into the inn's driveway on the left.

BLUE HILL INN

BLUE HILL, MAINE

Blue Hill, a village of impressive houses on streets lined with majestic elm trees, is located on lovely Blue Hill Bay, on the east coast of the Penobscot peninsula. The *Blue Hill Inn,* commanding a prominent location in the center of this quaint village, has been a part of local history since 1840.

When Don and Mary Hartley purchased the inn, in 1987, they focused on maintaining its historic authenticity as they renovated it. The original slanting, pumpkin-colored pine floors have been polished and accented with Oriental carpets, and the two parlors feature 19th-century antiques, including an 1850 melodeon and an 18th-century English chest inlaid with rosewood and walnut. Easy chairs and comfortable sofas are grouped around the fireplace, which crackles throughout the winter.

The guestrooms, furnished with antiques and reproductions, are equally attractive. Four of the rooms have wood-burning fireplaces, and some of the bathrooms feature old-fashioned claw-foot tubs.

One of this hostelry's most popular attractions is its acclaimed restaurant. Dinner is a particularly wonderful affair, beginning with the "innkeeper's reception," featuring hors d'oeuvres, cocktails, and wine enjoyed around the fire in the parlor on chilly days or in the perennial garden in warm weather. Afterward comes an elaborate five-course meal (open to non-guests by reservation only) served in the formal dining room, which glows by the 20 candles of a 19th-century brass chandelier. The set menu changes daily but always begins with soup, followed by a sorbet, an entrée (perhaps salmon with ginger and lime, or guinea hen with champagne grapes), and a refreshing salad. Desserts might include a mint soufflé with bitter chocolate sauce or pears poached in red wine and cassis. An extensive wine list and a selection of fine ports round out the experience. A full breakfast is offered to guests each morning.

The inn's gardens abound with flowers and comfortable spots for reading and relaxing, including a lazy-day hammock. Don arranges sailing excursions—and even overnight sojourns in June—on the 54-foot pinky schooner *Summertime* (a replica of an 1830s mackerel fishing boat) or on a 30-foot Catalina sailboat. A canoe also is available. Guests enjoy exploring nearby *Acadia National Park* and the numerous craft shops and art galleries in the area.

BLUE HILL INN Union St., Rte. 177, PO Box 403, Blue Hill, ME 04614 (phone: 207-374-2844; fax: 207-374-2829). This historic inn has 11 guestrooms with private baths and twin, double, queen-, or king-size beds. Partially wheelchair accessible. Closed January and the first two weeks of December; restaurant closed Sunday through Thursday dinner from December through May. Rate for a double room (including full breakfast, dinner, and a 15% service charge) *Memorial Day* through October: $138 to $190; bed and breakfast only, November to *Memorial Day:* $92 to $155. Two-night minimum stay on weekends from *Memorial Day* through October and on holidays. MasterCard and Visa accepted. Not appropriate for children under 13. No pets. No smoking. Donald and Mary Hartley, innkeepers.

DIRECTIONS: Traveling north on I-95, take the Augusta exit to Route 3 east. Follow Route 3 east through Belfast to Bucksport. Four miles beyond Bucksport, turn onto Route 15 south toward Blue Hill. Follow Route 15 south for 8 miles to the inn sign (it's 4 7⁄10 miles from here). Leave Route 15 south at the sign (there's no road name), and the road soon merges with Route 177, which leads east to the inn. From Bangor take Route 15 south to Bucksport and follow signs to Route 177 east to the inn.

JOHN PETERS INN

BLUE HILL, MAINE

This property, an imposing Greek Revival mansion with a brick façade embellished by four Ionic columns, overlooks 25 acres on the tidal waters of Blue Hill Bay. In 1987, innkeepers Rick and Barbara Seeger renovated the main building (part of which was built in 1810 and part in 1910) and the carriage house (built in 1900). The inn is listed on the National Register of Historic Places.

In the library/living room, a baby grand piano and two large fireplaces create an elegant yet comfortable atmosphere. The broad porch, landscaped gardens, and outdoor pool beckon guests in summer. In the historic mansion itself are eight guestrooms; the carriage house has six more.

All of the bedrooms are charmingly furnished with country-style antiques and either genuine or reproduction Oriental rugs; many, also have fireplaces and decks or balconies with views of the bay or the countryside. The Seegers have used a color scheme of soft blues and greens throughout to create a peaceful atmosphere.

Breakfast, including juice, fresh fruit, and Barbara's homemade waffles or eggs, is served on bone china on an enclosed porch overlooking a picture-postcard scene of yachts in the harbor. If it's offered, be sure to try the lobster omelette with hollandaise sauce.

Among the area's numerous attractions are *Acadia National Park,* summer theater, and chamber music concerts.

JOHN PETERS INN **Peters Pt., PO Box 916, Blue Hill, ME 04614 (phone: 207-374-2116). This inn on Blue Hill Bay has 14 guestrooms with private baths and twin, queen-, or king-size beds. Wheelchair accessible. Closed November through April. Rate for a double room (including full breakfast): $95 to $150. MasterCard and Visa accepted. Not appropriate for children under 12. No pets. One dog in residence. No smoking. Barbara and Rick Seeger, innkeepers; Serena Williams, manager.**

DIRECTIONS: Traveling north on I-95, take Exit 30 in Augusta to Route 3. Follow Route 3 north to Belfast, then take Route 1 north to Bucksport. Four miles beyond Bucksport, turn south onto Route 15 to Blue Hill. In Blue Hill turn left onto Main Street. In half a mile bear right onto Route 176 east, and continue a half mile to the inn sign.

EDGECOMBE-COLES HOUSE

CAMDEN, MAINE

High on a hillside overlooking Penobscot Bay, this historic inn gracefully straddles the 19th and 20th centuries. The original section, dating back to 1800, was incorporated as a side wing when the main building was constructed in 1891. Restored in the 1980s, by innkeepers Terry and Louise Price, the entire house showcases a fine collection of 19th-century antique furnishings, Oriental rugs, and original oil paintings.

With sensational ocean views and a carved-wood fireplace, the living room is a popular place for guests to relax. The den, which also features a carved fireplace and a view of Penobscot Bay, contains the inn's extensive library; several interesting embroidered samplers hang on the walls.

The six guestrooms overlook the ocean, the forest behind the inn, or the well-landscaped gardens. Like the public areas, the bedrooms are furnished with 19th-century antiques and original art; four of them also have fireplaces.

Breakfast is a special ritual—and an ideal opportunity for guests to get to know one another. In the dining room, Louise sets the pub-style cherry table with her antique blue-and-white china (including Blue Willow and Phoenix patterns–there's even a set of child-size dishes). The menu changes daily, but dishes may include blueberry pancakes, "Dutch babies" (a cross between popovers and pancakes, served with butter and syrup), and pastries, as well as fresh fruit and juices. In winter, there's sure to be a fire blazing in the fireplace; summertime guests may choose to eat on the porch.

After breakfast you can take a leisurely bicycle ride through the charming village of Camden (bikes are provided by the inn) or go sailing, fishing, or hiking. Other nearby attractions include chamber music concerts and theatrical productions in summer.

EDGECOMBE-COLES HOUSE **64 High St., HCR 60, Box 3010, Camden, ME 04843 (phone: 207-236-2336; fax: 207-236-6227). This country mansion has six guestrooms**

with private baths, queen- or king-size beds, and telephones. Open year-round. Rate for a double room (including full breakfast): $80 to $180. Two-night minimum stay mid-July through August. Major credit cards accepted. Not appropriate for children under eight. No pets. Several dogs in residence. No smoking. Terry and Louise Price, innkeepers.

DIRECTIONS: Take I-95 north to Exit 22 (Brunswick/Bath), then follow Highway 1 north approximately 60 miles to Camden. Continue north on Highway 1 (High Street) for just over half a mile; the inn is on the left.

NORUMBEGA INN

CAMDEN, MAINE

Poised dramatically at the edge of Penobscot Bay, this inn lives up to its billing as "a castle to call home." Built in 1886, the structure was designed to resemble a Tudor castle, with dense stone walls and turrets that would look right at home on Great Britain's *Hampton Court Palace.* Converted to a bed and breakfast inn in 1984, the property is now owned by Murray Keatinge, who decorated it in an opulent but comfortable style, filling the rooms with exquisite Victorian antiques. The common rooms boast hand-carved oak walls and inlaid floors of maple and cherry. A baby grand piano dominates the living room, and the lounge features an antique billiards table, a favorite among guests. The verandah offers an expansive view of the inn's spacious lawns and the bay.

The 12 guestrooms and suites are unusually large; five have fireplaces, seven have decks or terraces, and one has a Jacuzzi. One of the most popular accommodations is the former library, which has been transformed into a suite with a mahogany balcony lined with bookshelves. This suite also features a king-size bed, a sitting room complete with a working fireplace, and breathtaking views across Camden Harbor. Even more impressive, however, is the *Penthouse Suite,* accessible by a private spiral staircase. The skylit suite has a king-size bed, a living room with fireplace, and a deck overlooking the harbor.

Every morning, manager Chris Shrum prepares a marvelous breakfast, served either in the dining room or, in summer, on the verandah. Among the specialties are crêpe-like pancakes topped with puréed raspberries and raspberry-flavored whipped cream. Though the inn does not offer a formal dinner, there's always a pot of homemade soup on the stove and a cookie jar filled with fresh-baked treats in the kitchen; in the evenings, an array of cheese, crackers, fruit, wine, and tea is laid out in the living room.

After breakfast, guests can partake of a number of activities, including playing badminton, croquet, or *bocci* on the grounds, exploring Camden by bicycle, or simply wandering around the three-and-a-half-acre landscaped gardens. There are museums, antiques shops, and opportunities to golf, sail, and hike nearby.

NORUMBEGA INN 61 High St., Camden, ME 04843 (phone: 207-236-4646; fax: 207-236-0824). A luxury inn on the coast of Maine, it has 12 guestrooms with private baths, king-size beds, and telephones. Open year-round. Rate for a double room (including full breakfast and evening refreshments): $135 to $450. Two-night minimum stay in summer. Major credit cards accepted. Not appropriate for children under seven. No pets. Smoking permitted in guestrooms only. Murray Keatinge, innkeeper; Chris Shrum, manager.

DIRECTIONS: Take I-95 north to Exit 22 (Brunswick/Bath), then Highway 1 north approximately 60 miles to Camden. The *Norumbega Inn* is a half mile north of the center of Camden on Highway 1, which becomes High Street.

WINDWARD HOUSE BED & BREAKFAST

CAMDEN, MAINE

Built in 1854, this stately Greek Revival clapboard house is on the National Register of Historic Places. It has been painted blue-gray with cream trim and burgundy windows and doors; colorful flower beds frame the front porch and deck. The property sits in the midst of Camden's historic district and overlooks the harbor.

Innkeepers Jon and Mary Davis have decorated the common rooms with Oriental rugs and original watercolors. The living room, featuring a soapstone fireplace, is a popular gathering place, especially in chilly weather; the library offers an extensive collection of books and the inn's only television set. Afternoon tea, cider, port, and sherry are served in the *Wicker Room,* a sitting room with a sweeping view of the illuminated English-style flower gardens, the herb and edible flower gardens, and the apple orchard. Soft music is piped throughout the inn's common areas.

The decor of the seven guestrooms shows a similar attention to detail. All are furnished with fine antiques, including desks and four-poster, canopy, or brass beds; three of the rooms have skylights. Warm quilts, fluffy bathrobes and luxurious baths with Crabtree & Evelyn toiletries complete the picture.

A typical breakfast may include fresh raspberries and bananas, French toast garnished with fresh peaches, toasted almonds, and peach butter, oatmeal muffins with cinnamon topping, and lemon-poppyseed bread.

Several fine restaurants, shops, and performing-arts venues are within walking distance, as are facilities for sailing, hiking, and cycling.

WINDWARD HOUSE BED & BREAKFAST 6 High St., Camden, ME 04843 (phone: 207-236-9656). This historic inn has seven guestrooms with private baths and double or queen-size beds. Closed November through April. Rate for a double

room (including full breakfast) May through June: $75 to $90; July through October: $85 to $145. Major credit cards accepted. Not appropriate for children under 10. No pets. One cat in residence. No smoking. Jon and Mary Davis, innkeepers.

DIRECTIONS: Take I-95 north to Exit 22 (Brunswick/Bath), then Highway 1 north approximately 60 miles to Camden. In Camden, Highway 1 becomes High Street; the inn is on the left across from the library.

PENTAGOET INN

CASTINE, MAINE

A quintessential New England village with tree-lined streets, a village green, and numerous restored Georgian and Federal houses, Castine is tucked away off the beaten track. The town was settled after the Revolutionary War by British Loyalists, who retained their allegiance to the crown rather than to the newly formed United States. Now very much a bit of Americana, Castine boasts one of Maine's best inns—the old-fashioned, Victorian *Pentagoet.*

Originally built in 1894 to house summer tourists, the inn was purchased by Lindsey and Virginia Miller in 1986. The adjacent annex dates back even earlier than the main house—it was erected in the late 1700s—and the *Pentagoet*'s decor reflects these two periods with a pleasant mix of 19th-century antiques, including wicker and walnut furniture in the main house and colonial and period pieces in the annex. The main house has 11 guestrooms decorated in Victorian style with lace curtains and floral wall-paper; the five bedrooms in the annex feature patchwork quilts, Windsor chairs, hooked rugs, and colonial sideboards. One of the suites in the annex has a fireplace.

The broad porch that nearly encircles the house is a favorite gathering place. With its wicker furniture, rocking chairs, and swings, it re-creates the mood of a Victorian summer by the seashore; snacks and iced tea are served here on summer afternoons. Another favorite spot is the library, which houses the Millers' extensive collection of books and an ornate Bosendorfer piano.

A pot of coffee (brewed from freshly ground beans) arrives at guests' doors each morning, and breakfast is served in the dining room shortly thereafter. Good entrée choices include scrambled eggs with cream cheese and chives and bread pudding with warm berry sauce. Homemade breads, bacon, juice, and coffee also are offered.

Dinner here is an elaborate, five-course treat, beginning with an "innkeeper's reception," with drinks and appetizers served in the library (often accompanied by live chamber music). Pentagoet lobster pie, the house specialty, is a menu staple, but other entrées vary daily. They may include sautéed scallops with lime-ginger seasoning or brandied buttered game hen with pecan stuffing. Dessert is always a homemade sweet, such as steamed cranberry pudding in butter sauce. Afterward guests can congregate in the library and enjoy fudge kisses and "Miss Lizzie's toddy," a drink named after the house's original owner that consists of coffee mixed with various liqueurs.

A wide range of activities is available, including visiting *Acadia National Park,* golf, tennis, swimming, shopping, and attending cultural events.

PENTAGOET INN Main St., PO Box 4, Castine, ME 04221 (phone: 207-326-8616; 800-845-1701 outside Maine; fax: 207-326-9382). This Victorian inn has 16 guestrooms with private baths and twin, double, queen-, or king-size beds. Closed from November through April. Rate for a double room (including full breakfast and dinner): $155 to $180; bed and breakfast: $130. MasterCard and Visa accepted. Not appropriate for children under 12. No pets. One tabby cat and one German shepherd in residence. No smoking. Lindsey and Virginia Miller, innkeepers.

DIRECTIONS: From I-95 north take Exit 30 in Augusta onto Route 3 and continue north to Belfast. In Belfast take Route 1 north. Three miles past Bucksport turn onto Route 175 south and follow it about 4 miles to Route 166. Continuing south on Route 166 toward Castine, watch for the *Maine Maritime Academy*'s sign and turn left there onto Main Street. The inn is on the right, on the corner of Perkins Street.

PILGRIM'S INN

DEER ISLE, MAINE

This inn has an ideal location on secluded Deer Isle, which juts into Penobscot Bay from the Blue Hill peninsula. Built in 1793 by a local entrepreneur, the Greek Revival–style building is listed on the National Register of Historic Places. The four-story, barn-red structure features a gambrel roof and several mullioned windows. The front of the house overlooks Northwest Harbor, and there is a millpond in back.

Stepping through the front door is like passing into another era. The common rooms, which include a library, gameroom, tap room, and living room, have a colonial feel to them, with eight-foot fireplaces, wood stoves, beehive ovens, brick walls, and pumpkin-colored pine floors. The warm, friendly atmosphere reflects the personalities of Jean and Dud Hendrick, who have owned the inn since 1982.

The 13 large guestrooms are decorated with fine colonial antiques and Laura Ashley fabrics. A separate two-story cottage near the harbor, complete with a kitchen, a living room with a fireplace, a dining room, and a bedroom, is also available for rent. Decorated in the same romantic style as the guestrooms, it's a perfect honeymoon hideaway—its rear deck affords splendid views, especially at sunset.

An attached barn houses the noteworthy dining room (open to nonguests), where jute mats cover the original wood floors. After a convivial cocktail hour with hors d'oeuvres, dinner is served. The menu changes nightly but always features local ingredients, including seafood, free-range chicken, fruit, and shiitake mushrooms from Deer Isle, as well as herbs, vegetables, and edible flowers from the hotel's own gardens. A full buffet breakfast is served to guests daily.

A small building behind the inn houses the *Rugosa Rose,* a shop featuring fine gifts made in Maine. For the more active, sailboat rental and instruction are available, as are bicycles for exploring the country roads. You also can arrange a trip to the serene Isle au Haut or a sea excursion to watch seals and dolphins at play in the ocean (the inn will pack a picnic lunch for you). *Acadia National Park* and the famed *Haystack School of Crafts* are both nearby.

PILGRIM'S INN Main St., Deer Isle, ME 04627 (phone: 207-348-6615). This colonial inn has one cottage and 13 guestrooms (eight with private baths) with twin, double, or queen-size beds. Limited wheelchair accessibility. Closed mid-October through mid-May. Rate for a double room (including full breakfast and dinner): $140 to $200. MasterCard and Visa accepted. Guestrooms in the inn are not appropriate for children under 10, but younger children are welcome in the cottage. No pets. One English springer spaniel, Mr. Beau Dandy, in residence. Smoking permitted in downstairs common rooms only. Jean and Dud Hendrick, innkeepers.

DIRECTIONS: From I-95 north take Exit 30 in Augusta to Route 3, then head north to Belfast. From Belfast, follow Route 1 north beyond Bucksport to the intersection with Route 15 south. Follow Route 15 south to Deer Isle Village and turn right onto Main Street. The inn is one block up the street on the left.

CROCKER HOUSE COUNTRY INN

HANCOCK POINT, MAINE

Hidden away on Hancock Point, three minutes' walk from Frenchman's Bay, this establishment is the sole remnant of a 19th-century village that served as the terminus of the Washington, DC–Bar Harbor railway line. Cobblestones quarried near here were used to pave the streets of Boston, New York, and Philadelphia.

The living room, with its wicker furniture, handmade needlepoint rug, abundant plants, and bright floral watercolors, offers a cheerful, comfortable atmosphere. The guestrooms are decorated in warm apricot and peach colors and accented by stenciled walls, locally made quilts, and needlepoint rugs. One room is equipped with a king-size, pencil-post pine bed with matching dresser. An adjacent carriage house offers two additional guestrooms, a spa, and a common room, where the inn's only television is located.

The popular, highly acclaimed dining room (open to non-guests) serves excellent continental dishes prepared by owner Rick Malaby, who was a chef in Washington, DC, before opening the inn in 1979. Sample entrées include fresh local scallops sautéed with mushrooms, scallions, garlic, and tomatoes and rack of lamb marinated in garlic and mustard with an herbed crust. A jazz pianist plays on Friday and Saturday evenings. A full breakfast is offered daily.

On the grounds guests can play croquet and go bicycling. Boat moorings are available, and boat rentals are possible in nearby Bar Harbor. Tennis, Mt. Desert Island, and *Acadia National Park* are close as well.

CROCKER HOUSE COUNTRY INN HC 77, Box 171, Hancock Point, ME 04640 (phone: 207-422-6806; fax: 207-422-3105). This rustic inn has 11 guestrooms with private baths and double, queen-, or king-size beds. Wheelchair accessible. Closed January through late April; open weekends only November and December. Rate for a double room (including full breakfast): $75 to $125. Major credit cards accepted. Not appropriate for children under four. Pets allowed by prior arrangement only. Smoking permitted in two guestrooms and in one dining room. Richard and Elizabeth Malaby, innkeepers.

DIRECTIONS: Traveling north on I-95, take Exit 30 in Augusta to Route 3. Follow Route 3 north to Belfast, then take Route 1 approximately 8 miles past Ellsworth. Turn right at the sign for Hancock Point and continue approximately 5 miles to the inn, which is on the right.

CAPTAIN LORD MANSION

KENNEBUNKPORT, MAINE

During the War of 1812, the British naval blockade made shipbuilding impossible for Captain Nathaniel Lord. Rather than allow his sailors to remain idle, he employed them to build him a magnificent house. Using wood intended for Lord's ships, they constructed a three-story, Federal-style mansion with elaborate arched doorways, plenty of fireplaces, soaring ceilings, wide-plank pine floors, and a suspended elliptical staircase. At the very top of the house is an octagonal cupola, a lookout point from which Captain Lord could view the daily activity on the Kennebunk River. Today, guests of the *Captain Lord Mansion,* now an upscale country inn, can do the same. Were the erstwhile captain to return, he'd feel right at home.

Beautifully restored by innkeepers Bev Davis and Rick Litchfield, this house has become one of Maine's showpieces. (Ask to see the photos Bev and Rick took of the restoration process—they're fascinating.) Painted

Jamestown yellow with white trim and surrounded by elegant gardens, the inn is listed on the National Register of Historic Places.

The uniqueness of the architecture is evident in the grand entrance hall with the unusual staircase; the inn also boasts the kitchen's original fireplace (which was used for cooking in colonial times). Today, the main gathering area is the living room, where tea, coffee, and homemade scones are offered every afternoon.

The 22 bedrooms are distributed between the mansion, an adjacent cottage called the *Captain's Hideaway,* and *Phebe's Fantasy,* an 1807 Federal home. Each is elegantly furnished with high-quality antiques and a canopied four-poster; 20 of the rooms also have fireplaces, and 10 have mini-refrigerators stocked with cold drinks. The most romantic accommodation is the *Captain's Room,* which has a double Jacuzzi in the opulent bathroom. (In keeping with the mansion's old-fashioned atmosphere, just two of the guestrooms have TV sets, though a third is available to all in a common room.)

Breakfast is served family-style, each day, at the two harvest tables in the large colonial kitchen. Abundant offerings include fresh fruit, homemade muffins, and a hot entrée—waffles, pancakes, or cheese strata (a soufflé-like dish made with cheese, eggs, milk, and herbs). A gift shop sells small antiques, local crafts, and souvenirs of the mansion.

Golf, tennis, bicycling, and the *Rachel Carson Wildlife Refuge* are all nearby, and whale watching trips can be arranged.

CAPTAIN LORD MANSION Green St., PO Box 800, Kennebunkport, ME 04046 (phone: 207-967-3141; fax: 207-967-3172). This historic inn has 22 guestrooms with private baths, double, queen-, or king-size beds, and telephones. Open year-round. Rate for a double room (including full breakfast and afternoon tea) January through mid-May: $85 to $149; mid-May through December: $149 to $275. Two-night minimum stay on weekends. Discover, MasterCard, and Visa accepted. Not

appropriate for children under six. No pets. Two cats in residence. No smoking. Bev Davis and Rick Litchfield, innkeepers; Rebecca Stevens, assistant innkeeper.

DIRECTIONS: Traveling north on I-95, take Exit 3 (Kennebunk). Take Route 35/9A and follow the signs through Kennebunk to Kennebunkport. Go over the drawbridge and take the first right onto Ocean Avenue. After five blocks turn left onto Green Street; the mansion is two blocks up on the left.

INN AT HARBOR HEAD

KENNEBUNKPORT, MAINE

For pure romance, it's hard to beat this lovely bed and breakfast establishment. Set in a rambling, gray-shingled country house affording a spectacular view of Cape Porpoise Harbor, the inn's seaside setting fosters the breezy, casual feeling of a rustic cottage. The public areas and guestrooms, however, are sophisticated, displaying the artistic talent of innkeeper Joan Sutter. The formal sitting room, for example, is appointed with Oriental rugs, a Chinese screen, and a sparkling crystal chandelier. Here, though, "elegant" doesn't mean "stuffy": Guests feel right at home snuggling into a wing chair by the fire or lying in the hammock watching boats and fishermen in the harbor.

All of the guestrooms (which have luxurious private baths) are furnished with antiques, down comforters and pillows, and stereos. The decor of each has been individually created by Joan, and her expressive murals grace many of the walls. For example, in the *Summer Suite* (which has a fireplace) hand-painted clouds drift across the ceiling over the king-size wicker bed; its elevated, cathedral-ceilinged bath has a Jacuzzi and commands a splendid ocean view. The *Harbor Suite* features a fireplace, a queen-size bed with a lacy canopy, as well as more of Joan's artwork—a trompe l'oeil mural in the sitting room, which also has a private balcony with a spectacular view—and a serene island mural with herons in the bedroom. Additional touches include a crystal decanter of complimentary sherry on the nightstand and nightly turndown service with Godiva chocolates left on the pillow.

Breakfast is served in the formal dining room on a mahogany table laid with gilt-edged Lenox china, lacy placemats, and linen napkins in sterling silver rings. Choices might include poached pears with Grand Marnier custard sauce or French toast stuffed with ricotta and cream cheese, covered with fresh fruit. Low-fat breakfasts also are available. Afternoon refreshments—wine, cheese, tea, cappuccino, and cookies—are served as well.

Activities in the area include basking on the beautiful beach (the inn provides passes and towels), golf, fishing, tennis, whale watching excursions, visits to historical museums, and shopping.

INN AT HARBOR HEAD 41 Pier Rd., Cape Porpoise, Kennebunkport, ME 04046 (phone: 207-967-5564 or 207-967-4873; fax: 207-967-8776). The inn has five guestrooms with private baths and queen- or king-size beds. Closed mid-December through mid-April. Rate for a double room (including full breakfast and afternoon refreshments): $120 to $250. Two-night minimum stay on weekends and holidays. MasterCard and Visa accepted. Not appropriate for children under 12. No smoking indoors. Joan and David Sutter, innkeepers.

DIRECTIONS: From I-95 traveling north, take Exit 3 and follow Route 35/9A to Kennebunkport. Make a left at the intersection of Routes 9 and 35. Cross the bridge and follow Route 9 east through Dock Square, then follow the signs to Cape Porpoise. Past the *Wayfarer* restaurant at the head of the cove, the inn is the eighth house on the right.

WHITE BARN INN

KENNEBUNKPORT, MAINE

With its picture-postcard scenery, Kennebunkport is the quintessential Maine village. This peaceful town—best known as former President George Bush's New England vacation spot—is the perfect setting for the *White Barn Inn.* The upscale retreat occupies several historic buildings—the oldest of them, the farmhouse and barn, dating to 1820—on three acres. Until 1988 the property was used as a boardinghouse, but it's taken a quantum leap forward; distributed among the various buildings, today, are 24 luxurious guestrooms, all outfitted with marble baths (several with whirlpools) and decorated with antiques or top-quality reproductions, fresh flowers, and English-style fabrics, including chintz. Many rooms have working fireplaces and TV sets hidden away in armoires, and several boast four-poster, canopy, or sleigh beds. The 13 guestrooms, in the main building, feature period furnishings whimsically hand-painted by a local artist. Nightly turndown service includes treats left on the nightstand—anything from strawberries dipped in chocolate to petits fours.

The restaurant (open to non-guests), in two high-ceilinged barns furnished with antiques, is one of the most highly acclaimed in New England. Candlelight plays across the polished floors and reflects in the china, crystal, and silver. The menu changes nightly but always features fresh local seafood and herbs and vegetables grown in the inn's gardens. The offerings might include a sandwich of lightly grilled Maine salmon and spinach with cabernet sauvignon mashed potatoes or native sea bass wrapped in a layer of potato "scales" with fennel, tomato, olives, and leeks, followed by a chocolate marquis tart with hazelnuts and Frangelico. A full breakfast and afternoon tea with port and brandy (both included in the room rate) are offered daily.

Boating, swimming, bicycling, golf, tennis, cross-country skiing, and browsing through Kennebunkport's antiques shops are all possible.

WHITE BARN INN **Beach St., PO Box 560C, Kennebunkport, ME 04046 (phone: 207-967-2321; fax: 207-967-1100). This historic inn has 24 guestrooms with private baths and double, queen-, or king-size beds, telephones, and air conditioning. Open year-round; restaurant closed January 3 through early February. Rate for a double room (including full breakfast and afternoon tea): $140 to $300. Two-night minimum stay on weekends; three nights holiday weekends. Major credit cards accepted. Not appropriate for children under 12. No pets. Smoking permitted in bar only. Laurence Bongiorno and Laurie Cameron, innkeepers.**

DIRECTIONS: From I-95 north take Exit 2 (Ogunquit/Wells). Follow Route 9 west to Route 35. Turn right onto Beach Street; the inn is a quarter mile up the street on the right.

NEWCASTLE INN

NEWCASTLE, MAINE

A bright green awning caps the entrance to this handsome, white clapboard, Federal-style inn. Erected in the 1850s as a carriage house, the building became an inn during the 1920s. About 70 years later, when Howard and Rebecca Levitan were seeking a classic New England country inn, they decided this was their dream house.

It's easy to see why. The *Newcastle* offers the perfect setting, on the banks of the Damariscotta River, near Pemaquid Beach. Every room commands a terrific view of the inn's lovely gardens, bright, in summer, with lupines and daisies, and some offer glimpses of the river beyond. The interior is decorated in a casual, elegant style, with wallpaper borders, stencils, and wainscoting. Some rooms have a Southwest theme and feature the Levitan's art collection. As this book went to press, the new owners were in the process of redecorating the entire inn.

The common rooms are comfortable and cozy; one of them, known as the *Stencil Room,* has a hand-stenciled floor complemented by oriental rugs. The living room has plush sofas and chairs grouped around a fireplace; there's an outside deck as well as a glassed-in porch furnished with antique wicker and stools and tables reminiscent of an old-fashioned ice-cream parlor. The *Briar Patch* is an intimate pub where Howard can be found chatting with guests in the evening.

Each of the 15 bedrooms features antique furnishings and a stereo; several have four-poster or canopy beds, fireplaces, and river views. All are decorated with colonial-style wallpapers and bed coverings.

Meals at the *Newcastle* are a special experience. Breakfast may include cinnamon chocolate cake, Grand Marnier French toast, fluffy lemon-zest pancakes, or raisin bread pudding with strawberries. Dinner, a rather formal affair (which also is open to non-guests), begins with hors d'oeuvres and cocktails in the common rooms. An hour later guests are led to the dining room, where a set menu is presented on handwritten cards. In the past, dinner has featured arugula and *porcini* risotto, roasted salmon with sun-dried tomato sauce, stuffed breast of duck with lingonberry turnovers, and white chocolate cheesecake with strawberry and Grand Marnier sauce. A selection of fine wines accompanies the meal.

The *Monhegan Island Maritime Museum,* hiking, bird watching, fishing, boating, swimming, and golf are nearby.

NEWCASTLE INN **River Rd., Newcastle, ME 04553 (phone: 207-563-5685; 800-83-BUNNY; fax: 207-563-1390). This inn on the Maine coast has 15 guestrooms with private baths and twin, double, or queen-size beds. Open year-round. Rate for a double room (including full breakfast and dinner): $125 to $225; bed and breakfast: $60 to $175. Discover, MasterCard, and Visa accepted. Not appropriate for children under 10. No pets. One dog on the premises. No smoking. Howard and Rebecca Levitan, innkeepers.**

DIRECTIONS: Follow I-95 north to Exit 22 (Bath/Brunswick/Coastal Route 1). Continue through Brunswick, Bath, and Wiscasset. Seven miles beyond Wiscasset turn right onto River Road and follow the signs to the inn, which is a half mile up the street on the right.

COUNTRY CLUB INN

RANGELEY, MAINE

If you want to escape to the great outdoors, this is just what the doctor ordered. A rustic lodge 2,000 feet above sea level, the *Country Club Inn* offers a breathtaking view of Rangeley Lake as well as a broad expanse of clear blue sky.

The inn is decorated, throughout, in a simple, comfortable style. The centerpieces of the living room are its soaring cathedral ceiling and two massive fieldstone fireplaces (not to mention the moose head); it's furnished with sofas and rocking chairs and supplied with plenty of jigsaw puzzles, books, and games. An adjacent pub with an outside deck is a popular place for guests to gather in the evenings. The 19 guestrooms have private patios with views of the inn's gardens, the lake, and the Saddleback Mountains.

The dining room has the same impressive views as the rest of the house. A full breakfast featuring eggs, French toast, or pancakes is served daily, and a typical dinner (also open to non-guests by reservation) might include roast duck Montmorency or filet mignon.

The inn's setting is ideal for a number of outdoor activities, including hiking the nearby Appalachian Trail, swimming in the inn's pool, playing horseshoes, volleyball, or croquet, boating on the lake, and teeing off at a nearby 18-hole golf course. In winter, you can ski or ride a snowmobile (which can be rented in town) along 100 miles of groomed trails in the area.

COUNTRY CLUB INN PO Box 680, Rangeley, ME 04970 (phone: 207-864-3831). In Maine's Saddleback Mountain Range, this lodge has 19 guestrooms with private baths and double, queen-, or king-size beds. Wheelchair accessible. Closed April through mid-May and mid-October through late December. Rate for a double room (including full breakfast and dinner): $148 to $164; bed and breakfast: $110; room only: $99. Major credit cards accepted. Children welcome. Pets allowed (additional charge of $10 per day). One dog in residence. Smoking permitted except in the dining room. Steve and Margie Jamison, innkeepers.

DIRECTIONS: From I-95 north take Exit 12 (Auburn) and follow Route 4 for 90 miles to Rangeley. From Rangeley continue to follow Route 4 for 1½ miles to the inn's driveway. Turn left at the sign and travel 1½ miles farther to the inn itself.

RANGELEY INN

RANGELEY, MAINE

This inn, an impressive blue clapboard building with a sweeping verandah, was built in 1907 as a summer resort. Now it does a thriving wintertime business as well. The front porch affords a peaceful haven for utter relaxation; the adjacent motor lodge has a stunning view of Haley Pond and the Saddleback Mountains. A bird sanctuary borders the property, so the patient ornithologist may well catch a glimpse of ducks, Canada geese, herons, and even a loon or two.

A comfortable, homey place, the *Rangeley Inn* is great for a family vacation, and has been ever since innkeepers Ed and Fay Carpenter took it over in the early 1970s. The furnishings are country-style—sturdy antique pieces made of oak or cherry. Guests can amuse themselves playing pool and board games in the TV room, and there's a barbecue area and a screened pavilion in the garden.

There are 51 guestrooms, including 15 in the newer motor lodge. All are decorated with country-style wallpapers, turn-of-the-century tables, chairs, and hope chests, and iron or brass beds. Several of the baths retain their original claw-foot tubs.

The dining room, with its ornate pressed-tin ceiling (it looks antique but was actually added by Ed), is painted a salmon color. Flowers accent the windows and tables. Breakfast and dinner are available to both guests and non-guests. The fare emphasizes local ingredients, especially blueberries (98% of the US crop is grown in Maine), and herbs grown in the inn's gardens flavor many dishes. Try the chicken sautéed in fresh blueberries, or enjoy an after-dinner glass of blueberry schnapps by the fire in the (circa 1877) pub.

It seems something fun always is happening here in summertime. The *Fiddlers' Contest,* which takes place in July, is a popular favorite, as is the town's *Sidewalk Art Show* and *Blueberry Festival* in August; several concerts and plays are held in the area as well. In addition, guests may enjoy guided sunrise canoe trips, moose watching, hiking, fishing, swimming, dogsled races, snowmobiling, and cross-country and downhill skiing in the nearby Saddleback Mountains.

RANGELEY INN Main St., PO Box 160, Rangeley, ME 04970 (phone: 207-864-3341; 800-MOMENTS; fax: 207-864-3634). This village inn and motor lodge in western Maine has 51 guestrooms with private baths and twin, double, or queen-size beds. Wheelchair accessible. Open year-round; dining room closed end of ski season to *Memorial Day* and November to *Christmas.* Rate for a double room: $69 to $109. Two-night minimum stay on winter weekends. Major credit cards accepted. Children welcome. Pets allowed by prior arrangement only. One cat in residence. Smoking permitted in guestrooms and the cocktail lounge. Fay and Ed Carpenter, innkeepers.

DIRECTIONS: From I-95 take Exit 12 (Auburn) and follow Route 4 north for 40 miles to Rangeley. The inn is at the southern end of the village on Route 4 (which becomes Main Street at this point).

SQUIRE TARBOX INN

WESTPORT ISLAND, MAINE

The *Squire Tarbox Inn* is not only a quaint New England inn, but also a fine restaurant, a goat farm, and a thriving local producer of *chèvre* (goat cheese). Its charming setting near Squam Creek provides a scenic feast of buttercups and lupines, country lanes, and birds—the perfect antidote to the hassles of city living.

Prior to opening the *Squire Tarbox Inn,* Karen and Bill Mitman worked at Boston's *Copley Plaza* hotel, and that experience stands them in good stead. They know how to create a friendly, welcoming atmosphere, and they are eager to show visitors around the farm.

The original building dates to 1763, but a clapboard, Federal-style main house was added by Squire Samuel Tarbox in 1825, to form one large, rambling, colonial farmhouse. The design blends the rustic wide-board construction of the 1700s with the wainscoting of the early 1800s. Listed on the National Register of Historic Places, the inn still has its original pumpkin-colored pine floors, carved moldings, hand-hewn beams, and a large hearth with an oven. A three-story barn with exposed beams contains three sitting rooms (two with fireplaces and one with a wood-burning stove). A screened deck off the main dining room is a pleasant place to sit in warm weather (binoculars are provided for bird watching). A player piano, an antique music box, colonial toys, and jigsaw puzzles depicting country scenes provide entertainment for guests.

The 11 guestrooms are decorated in country style—mahogany antiques, intricate handmade quilts, and braided rugs—and several have fireplaces or private balconies.

The food alone is well worth the trip to Maine. Dinner begins with a sampling of the inn's cheeses (which are sold locally and by mail order), accompanied by wine. A five-course meal is served nightly in the dining room, which is open to non-guests. The fare often features dairy products made on the premises; for example, whey buns (made from a recipe devised by Karen) always are served. Other dishes that might appear include *chèvre* ravioli, beef tenderloin with burgundy-mushroom sauce, swordfish with lemon-caper sauce, and dark chocolate mousse with Grand Marnier and whipped cream. A full breakfast of juice, fresh fruit, granola, homemade bread, oatmeal, and quiche is offered daily.

Activities off the inn's grounds include swimming at nearby beaches, sailing, bicycling, antiquing, and feasting on lobsters. The nearby *Maine Maritime Museum* holds many fascinations.

SQUIRE TARBOX INN Westport Island, RD 2, Box 620, Wiscasset, ME 04578 (phone: 207-882-7693). This inn and goat farm near Boothbay Harbor has 11 guestrooms with private baths and twin, double, queen-, or king-size beds. Closed November through April. Rate for a double room (including full breakfast and dinner): $105 to $220; bed and breakfast: $85 to $189. Two-night minimum stay required on weekends from July 15 to October 23. Major credit cards accepted. Not appropriate for children under 12. No pets. Various animals on the property include 14 goats, a horse, two donkeys, two cats, and several hens. No smoking. Karen and Bill Mitman, innkeepers.

DIRECTIONS: Take I-95 north to Exit 22 (Brunswick). Follow Route 1 north past the Bath bridge for 7 miles to Route 144. Turning south onto Route 144, continue for 8½ miles to Westport Island and the inn.

DOCKSIDE GUEST QUARTERS

YORK, MAINE

Harris Island is a serene haven of panoramic harbor vistas, fishing boats, and sandy beaches located across the York River from historic York Village. The *Dockside Guest Quarters,* composed of an 1880s homestead with broad porches and several contemporary multiunit cottages set amid landscaped lawns, fits neatly into that picture. The Lustys, who have run the inn for the past 40 years, have a seemingly endless supply of seafaring stories and anecdotes about the area.

In the original building, known as the *Maine House,* the living room is comfortably furnished with antiques, a fireplace, a TV set, board games, and books on maritime subjects and Maine history; there's also a sitting room.

The decor of the 21 guestrooms (distributed among the *Maine House* and the cottages) is nautical, with an eclectic mix of antiques and modern pieces; in addition, there are braided rugs, floral bedspreads, print wallpapers, and maritime artwork. All the rooms boast splendid ocean views.

Local seafood is the specialty at the *Restaurant-at-Dockside* (open to non-guests), set in a separate building. Even on the hottest summer days its porches overlooking the harbor pick up cool breezes. A "continental-plus" breakfast buffet with fresh fruit, muffins, bagels, and cereal is served in the *Maine House* to guests for a small additional charge.

The inn has facilities for croquet, volleyball, shuffleboard, badminton, fishing, canoeing, and boat trips, and the surrounding area offers a variety of other activities, including beachcombing, swimming, walking, shopping, whale watching cruises, and fishing expeditions. There are plenty of lawn chairs if you simply want to spend a lazy afternoon doing as little as possible. Guests also can explore nearby York Village, a National Historic District, as well as the charming New Hampshire town of Portsmouth.

DOCKSIDE GUEST QUARTERS PO Box 205, York, ME 03909 (phone: 207-363-2868; fax: 207-363-1977). This inn has 21 guestrooms and suites (19 with private baths) with twin, double, queen-, or king-size beds and TV sets. Open year-round; restaurant closed Mondays and from *Columbus Day* to *Memorial Day.* Rate for a double room: $65 to $150. Two-night minimum stay in July and August; three nights on holiday weekends. MasterCard and Visa accepted. Children welcome. No pets. Smoking permitted in a few of the guestrooms. Lusty family, innkeepers.

DIRECTIONS: From I-95 northbound take Exit 4 to US Route 1 south. At the first light turn left onto Route 1A, following it through the center of Old York Village. Turn onto Route 103 and travel across the York River Bridge to Harris Island. Take the first left after crossing the bridge, and watch for signs to the inn.

New Hampshire

CHESTERFIELD INN

CHESTERFIELD, NEW HAMPSHIRE

Built as a tavern in 1787, the *Chesterfield Inn* was later converted to a farmhouse. It sits on 10 hillside acres high above the Connecticut River, with panoramic views across to the Green Mountains of Vermont. Restored in 1984, the inn has been owned by Phil and Judy Hueber since 1987.

A beehive fireplace dominates the inn's sitting room, where a 20-foot cathedral ceiling and wraparound windows create a light and airy atmosphere; a brass chandelier adds an elegant touch.

Weathered barn boards and exposed beams highlight the architecture of the 13 spacious guestrooms and suites (nine of them in the main house and four in the *Johanna Wetherby Guest House*); each is furnished with period antiques, and many of the walls are hand-stenciled. All rooms have private baths and small refrigerators (honor bars) stocked with wines, waters, and imported beers. Many boast cathedral ceilings, fireplaces, balconies, or patios. Judy enjoys making quilts, and several examples of her handiwork adorn the rooms too.

The spectacular new dining room has a French country charm, plus wall-to-wall windows, affording views across the inn's gardens to the Connecticut River Valley and the Green Mountains. The room adjoins a parlor and a pretty outdoor terrace.

Superb meals are among the delights here. Breakfast, served on the sun porch or the terrace, may include Judy's fruit-filled crêpes or a summer vegetable custard. Dinner is a leisurely, multicourse affair. The menu boasts exotic twists, such as *chipotle* pork medallions with green apple sauce, or grilled swordfish with pineapple-ginger relish.

Nearby attractions include the *Marlboro Music Festival* (held in Marlboro, Vermont, in July or August), skiing, and hiking. When the pond freezes over, guests lace up their skates and take to the ice. Sleigh ride are offered at nearby farms.

CHESTERFIELD INN Rte. 9, Chesterfield, NH 03466 (phone: 603-256-3211; 800-365-5515; fax: 603-256-6131). Overlooking the Connecticut River, this inn has 13 guestrooms with private baths, double, queen-, or king-size beds, telephones, TV sets, and air conditioning. Wheelchair accessible. Open year-round; dining room closed Monday dinner. Rate for a double room (including full breakfast and tea): $115 to $170. Major credit cards accepted. Children welcome. Pets allowed by prior arrangement only. Two cats in residence. Smoking permitted in two guestrooms. Judy and Phil Hueber, innkeepers.

DIRECTIONS: From I-91 take Exit 3 to Route 9 east. Continue on Route 9 for 3 miles. The inn is on the left.

DARBY FIELD INN

CONWAY, NEW HAMPSHIRE

Reaching this inn is a true adventure. It sits atop a mountain, at the end of a dirt road that winds through a dense forest. The long journey leads to great expectations, and the *Darby Field Inn* does not disappoint.

The property, on eight acres at the edge of the *White Mountain National Forest,* has a lengthy history. A couple named Samuel and Polly Chase Littlefield first farmed this land in 1826, built a farmhouse in 1830, and eventually decided to take in boarders. By the 1940s the original house had become the common rooms of an inn called *Bald Hill Lodge.* At that time the barn and blacksmith shop were torn down to make way for a dining room and kitchen, and a swimming pool and a small ski lift were added. The house enjoys panoramic views of Mt. Washington (the highest point in New England), as well as Adams and Madison Mountains, with White Horse Ledge in the center. Not surprisingly, the scenery is one of the major reasons innkeepers Marc and Maria Donaldson bought the inn in 1979.

The 16 guestrooms, many of which boast lovely mountain views, are decorated in a homey country style. Several have antique four-poster beds with patchwork quilts or braided rugs, and most have private baths.

The dining room (open to non-guests at dinner) specializes in hearty meat dishes, including filet mignon, lamb chops, veal, and roast duck. Most of the vegetables come from the inn's own garden. Full breakfasts feature such creations as "heavenly hots"—thin, light, fluffy pancakes made with sour cream and served with pure maple syrup.

Twelve miles of groomed cross-country ski and hiking trails are located on the property, and the rugged, mountainous terrain in the area is ideal for exploration. Canoeing, golf, and tennis facilities are nearby. Guests also may choose to stay put, congregating in the convivial pub, relaxing in front of the massive stone fireplace in the living room, wandering the gardens, or swimming in the pool.

DARBY FIELD INN **Bald Hill, PO Box D, Conway, NH 03818 (phone: 603-447-2181; 800-426-4147; fax: 603-447-5726). This country inn in the White Mountains has 16 guestrooms (14 with private baths) with twin, double, queen-, or king-size beds. Closed several weeks in April. Rate for a double room (including full breakfast and dinner): $130 to $200; bed and breakfast: $90 to $160; children ages two to 12 (in parents' room): $20; children under two: free (parents must provide crib). Two-night minimum stay on weekends and during fall foliage season. Major credit cards accepted. No pets. One dog and one bird in residence. Smoking permitted in the pub only. Marc and Maria Donaldson, innkeepers.**

DIRECTIONS: From I-95 traveling north, take Exit 4 (Spaulding Turnpike). Follow Route 16 approximately 60 miles. Turn left onto Bald Hill Road at the inn sign, a half mile before the village of Conway. A mile farther turn right at the second inn sign, then continue 1 mile to the inn.

INN AT CROTCHED MOUNTAIN

FRANCESTOWN, NEW HAMPSHIRE

Built in 1822 as a farmhouse, this historic inn once served as a stop on the Underground Railroad, which helped slaves escape to Canada; a secret tunnel led from the cellar to the road. During the late 1920s it became a renowned farm, with prize-winning livestock, including sheep, cattle, horses, and Angora goats. Part of the house was destroyed by fire and rebuilt in 1935, but much of the original brick building still remains. John and Rose Perry purchased the inn in 1976 and have been improving it ever since.

On a 65-acre parcel of land, the inn offers a tranquil setting and a breathtaking view across the Piscataquog Valley. The decor is elegantly rustic—rich wood tones are accented with vivid, jewel-like colors and striking paintings, and flowers grace the public and private rooms. Its 13 cozy guestrooms are furnished with lovely antiques befitting a country estate. The house also has nine working fireplaces (five in the common rooms, four in guestrooms).

The two dining rooms (also open to non-guests) are warmed by the original old fireplaces, and the main one contains the built-in bookcases and books (including a history of the inn) from the old house. This room also has restful views across the manicured lawns and gardens.

In addition to her role of gracious hostess, Rose stars as the chef. Her artistry combines an eye for enticing presentation with creative use of well-matched fresh ingredients—many of the vegetables, herbs, and edible flowers she uses are grown on the grounds. The result is delectable continental fare fused with culinary elements from her native Singapore. Even the simple breakfast is well prepared and presented. Dinner, which is served Friday and Saturday nights, may include home-smoked salmon; mango or peach-tomato salsa; charcoal-broiled swordfish Indonesian, with fresh ginger, green pepper, and basil; and roast pork with a seasonal fruit sauce. For the less adventuresome, the menu includes more traditional entrées such as lamb chops with mint jelly. For desert, house specialties are a sinfully dense, dark chocolate mousse and a flavorful, not-too-sweet raspberry sherbet—order both. After dinner, guests usually congregate in the library/tavern for a nightcap in front of still another fireplace.

A mountainside swimming pool, a wading pool, and two clay tennis courts are on the grounds, an 18-hole golf course is nearby, and hiking paths (which double as groomed cross-country ski trails in winter) thread through the woods. The less athletically inclined can find entertainment at several of the area's cultural attractions, including the *Sharon Art Center, Peterborough Players, Monadnock Music Festival,* and *American Stage Festival.*

INN AT CROTCHED MOUNTAIN Mountain Rd., Francestown, NH 03043 (phone: 603-588-6840). This historic inn in southern New Hampshire has 13 guestrooms (eight with private baths) with twin, double, or queen-size beds. Wheelchair accessible. Closed April and November; dinner served Friday and Saturday nights only; breakfast available daily. Rate for a double room (including full breakfast and dinner): $120 to $140; bed and breakfast: $60 to $70 on weekdays; $100 to $120 on weekends. No credit cards accepted. Children welcome. Pets allowed ($5 additional charge per day). Two English cocker spaniels, Winslow and Lucy, in residence. Smoking allowed in tavern and sitting room. Rose and John Perry, innkeepers.

DIRECTIONS: From Boston follow Route 3 north through Nashua to 101A to Milford. In Milford take Route 13 to New Boston, then Route 136 to Francestown. From Francestown follow Route 47 for 2½ miles and turn left onto Mountain Road. The inn is a mile up the road on the right.

NOTCHLAND INN

HART'S LOCATION, NEW HAMPSHIRE

A unique feature of New Hampshire's granite-based terrain is the presence of rugged notches left from the last glacial age, from which the *Notchland Inn* gets its name. Just 10 miles from Mt. Washington, the highest peak in New England, the inn sits on a picturesque knoll in *White Mountains National Forest,* commanding a view of the Saco River and its valley. The grounds—400 acres laced with hiking and cross-country ski trails—touch the base of four mountains. The Davis Path, which leads to Mt. Crawford and, eventually, to the summit of Mt. Washington, starts just across the street. The property also boasts two swimming holes, a pond, and for warmer soaks, a hot tub located in a gazebo overlooking the pond.

Off a major highway, the inn has served travelers for more than 70 years. Dr. Samuel Bemis, a dentist and inventor, completed the English-style manor house in 1862, using native granite blocks and timber. The former *Mt. Crawford House,* an inn that was also on this property and dates to 1790, is now the dining room, while an 1852 schoolhouse contains two suites.

After being abandoned for many years, the inn has been painstakingly restored, its huge brick chimneys, embossed-tin ceilings, tiled fireplaces, and Gothic-style hardwood paneling carefully refurbished. One of the most unusual rooms is the *Stickley Room,* which was designed in the 1890s by architect and designer Gustav Stickley. It has six-foot-high wainscoting stained gray-green and a "Sheriff of Nottingham" fireplace (a Tudor-style hearth with a high, arched canopy of wrought iron). The simple lighting fixture was created by Stickley as well. In the music room, guests are encouraged to perform impromptu selections on the piano.

The seven guestrooms and four suites have their own fireplaces; tile floors and vanities in the bathrooms are recent additions. Bright and cheerful, the rooms are furnished with antiques from England and colonial America, accented by contemporary designer wall coverings and fabrics. The antique beds (two are four-posters) are strategically placed to showcase the incredible mountain views seen from most of the rooms.

Another entrancing aspect of this inn is its menagerie of animals. Coco, a friendly Bernese mountain dog, acts as official greeter; Dolly, the Belgian draft horse, takes guests on sleigh rides in winter and (sometimes) carriage rides in summer; and Mork and Mindy, miniature horses, like to frolic with D. C. and Sid, the llamas.

Dinners at the *Notchland* (open to non-guests) have achieved legendary status in local circles. The menu varies seasonally but always includes a choice of two soups, two appetizers, three entrées, and three desserts. Popular dishes include lightly curried butternut squash–and–sweet potato soup, chicken champagne, chocolate walnut tart, and a very lemon pie. A full breakfast featuring juice, fresh fruit, and an entrée (perhaps cinnamon almond French toast, an egg dish, or pancakes) is available to inn guests.

Mt. Washington's craggy granite cliffs, snow-fed streams, forests of pine, spruce, and fir, and crystalline air offer some of the most invigorating wilderness in the country—ideal for hiking, fishing, and other outdoor activities. For railroad buffs, the *Crawford Notch Line,* a scenic railroad that began operation in 1878, once again is winding its way along the trestles that connect the precipices to Crawford Notch, a spectacularly panoramic trip that passes right by the *Notchland Inn.* Nearby towns provide antiquing, and theatrical productions are staged in summer.

NOTCHLAND INN Hart's Location, NH 03812 (phone: 603-374-6131; 800-866-6131; fax: 603-374-6168). This historic inn near Crawford Notch has 11 guestrooms with private baths and queen- or king-size beds. Open year-round. Rate for a double room (including full breakfast and dinner): $160 to $250; bed and breakfast: $120 to $210. Two-night minimum stay on weekends; three nights on holidays and during fall foliage season. Major credit cards accepted. Not appropriate for children under 12. No pets. One dog, one cat, and several horses and llamas on the property. No smoking. Les Schoof and Ed Butler, innkeepers.

DIRECTIONS: Traveling north on I-93, take Exit 35 onto Route 3 to Twin Mountain. Turn right in Twin Mountain onto Route 302 east and travel 20 miles through Crawford Notch to the inn.

MEETING HOUSE INN

HENNIKER, NEW HAMPSHIRE

Located on five acres in the lovely Contoocook Valley and nestled at the base of *Pat's Peak* ski area, this property is a quiet retreat in a small rural village. The inn takes its name from a log meetinghouse, built in the 1760s, that sat at the base of Craney Hill, about a quarter mile away.

The inn's special personality is a reflection of its owners, June and Bill Davis, their daughter Cheryl, and her husband, Peter Bakke. They have decorated it in an eclectic style, with antiques that have been in both families for generations (such as the 1780 grandfather clock), hand-stitched needlework, and unique artwork.

Another unusual element of the decor is "The Sands of Time," a display of small, sand-filled plastic bags that hang from the walls of the restaurant, which is housed in a meticulously restored barn. The bags, contributed by hotel guests, contain sand from exotic spots around the world, including Mt. Everest and the floor of the Atlantic Ocean. Often the innkeepers receive bags from guests who haven't been here in years, evidence of people's attachment to this warm and friendly place.

The six guestrooms have wide-plank pine floors and antique colonial-era furnishings (including canopied and brass beds). The elegant decor is accented by floral chintz fabrics. Room amenities include a decanter of sherry and a basket of crackers.

A full breakfast is delivered in a picnic basket to guests' rooms, where it may be enjoyed in a leisurely fashion. The hot breakfast entrée is always a surprise, but some of the most popular are Meeting House Sunrise, a baked dish of ham, potatoes, fresh local vegetables, and cheese topped with an egg, or a baked French toast sandwich with fresh fruit and one of June's special syrups. A full dinner featuring hearty New England fare is served in the restaurant (which is open to the public). The evening might start with one of Bill's 14-ingredient bloody marys, then continue with such entrées as seared tuna with raspberry sauce or roast duck with apples and cashews. An interesting wine list is available.

For pampering, there's a hot tub and sauna. Guests enjoy walking through the inn's extensive herb and flower gardens, where they are delighted by the love poems Cheryl hand-painted on slates and placed among the flowers, and by the quaint birdhouses that Peter made by hand. Tennis, golf, downhill and cross-country skiing, antiquing, craft shops, water sports, and theaters are all nearby.

MEETING HOUSE INN 35 Flanders Rd., Henniker, NH 03242 (phone: 603-428-3228; fax: 603-428-6334). In south-central New Hampshire, this country inn has six guestrooms with private baths, double or queen-size beds, and air conditioning. Open year-round; restaurant closed Monday and Tuesday dinner. Rate for a double room (including full breakfast): $65 to $98. Two-night minimum stay on weekends in October and February and on holidays. Major credit cards accepted. Children welcome with advance notice. No pets. One cat, Grensil, in residence. No smoking. June and Bill Davis, Cheryl Davis Bakke, and Peter Bakke, innkeepers.

DIRECTIONS: Take I-89 west to Exit 5, then travel west on Route 9/202 to Route 114 south, continuing about 2 miles to the *Pat's Peak* sign. Turn right onto Flanders Road; the inn is a half mile up the hill on the right.

MANOR ON GOLDEN POND

HOLDERNESS, NEW HAMPSHIRE

If Squam Lake had not been so prominently showcased in the movie *On Golden Pond,* starring Katharine Hepburn and Henry Fonda, it might have remained in relative obscurity. Since the world found out about it, however, the lake has had no shortage of visitors—particularly in summer and fall.

There are many reasons to come to this delightful area. In summer, Squam Lake is ideal for swimming, fishing, and boating; in winter, ice fishing is popular; and, in fall, mirror images of the autumn foliage reflect in the water. An Englishman named Isaac Van Horn first discovered the pleasures of the area in 1903 and built an English-style manor house on a 14-acre parcel of land overlooking the water. In 1991, David and Bambi Arnold purchased the house and its outbuildings, a collection of rustic cottages, and ambitiously began renovating the property.

They have turned it into a first class hotel. The manor house is furnished throughout with period antiques, with a quintessentially British ambience. The upstairs library offers an extensive collection of books and jigsaw puzzles, as well as leather chairs with hassocks for relaxed reading. Downstairs are a second library (strikingly decorated with a table made from a bellows and several Beatrix Potter lamps) and a living room with hand-carved mahogany woodwork and a marble fireplace. On occasion, a pianist plays in the cozy *Three Cocks Pub,* which has a copper bar, copper-topped tables, and an old English pub sign.

All of the guestrooms are supremely comfortable, their private baths featuring the original pedestal sinks. Most rooms have wood-burning fireplaces; three have two-person whirlpool tubs. Done up in blue and white, the *Churchill Suite* has a light blue carpet and leaded windows, a canopied bed, a fireplace, an antique wardrobe closet, and a writing desk placed to capture views of the lake. The *Buckingham Suite* offers a canopied four-poster bed, a marble fireplace, a tapestry wall hanging, and a porch overlooking the water. The five two-bedroom cottages have a more rustic flavor and are ideal for families. All have kitchens and grassy yards; three have fireplaces.

The three dining rooms (open to the public) boast additional marble fireplaces. The formal evening meal features such entrées as rack of veal with berry-and-port sauce and pistachio-breaded rack of lamb with a red lentil compote. A full breakfast is served to inn guests.

On the grounds are a pool, tennis courts, a croquet lawn, a badminton court, and a sandy beach; the hotel has a number of canoes and boats for guests' use. Activities in the area include downhill and cross-country skiing, hiking, golf, horseback riding, and visiting *White Mountains National Forest* and the *Squam Lake Science Center.*

MANOR ON GOLDEN POND Box T, Rte. 3, Holderness, NH 03245 (phone: 603-968-3348; 800-545-2141; fax: 603-968-2116). Set in a manor house and several cottages, this inn offers 28 guestrooms and suites with private baths, twin, double, queen-, or king-size beds, and TV sets. Open year-round. Rate for a double room in the manor house (including full breakfast and dinner): $180 to $350; in cottages (by the week, with no meals included): $850 to $1,600. Two-night minimum stay on major holidays and in autumn. Major credit cards accepted. Children welcome in cottages; manor house not appropriate for children under 12. No pets. No smoking. David and Bambi Arnold, innkeepers.

DIRECTIONS: From I-93 traveling north, take Exit 24 in Ashland, then travel Highway 3 for 4 miles to Holderness. In Holderness cross the bridge and look for the sign to the inn, two blocks farther on the right.

CHRISTMAS FARM INN

JACKSON, NEW HAMPSHIRE

The inn's white clapboard farmhouse, built in 1777 on 14 acres of rolling land, is located on a country road at the base of the White Mountains. At first the green-shuttered house can be seen only in brief glimpses through a filter of large maple trees. Then it reveals itself—its long front porch decorated with hanging flower baskets and a row of green rocking chairs.

Sydna and Bill Zeliff purchased the house in 1976 with the idea of turning it into an inn. It had been called *Christmas Farm* since 1946, and they were quick to seize the Yuletide theme. Several of the 37 guestrooms are named for Santa's reindeer and elves, meals are served in the *Mistletoe Pub* and the *Sugar Plum Dining Room,* and the overall color scheme is red and green. In addition, the Zeliffs hold a *Christmas* celebration in July. Here, the holiday spirit lasts far beyond December.

There are guestrooms in the main house, in a 1778 saltbox, and in a barn. In addition, several two-bedroom cottages set in the woods are available for rent–each with its own fireplace, yard, and porch. The guestrooms and cottages are furnished with high-quality reproductions and decorated in Laura Ashley fabrics; several have four-poster or canopy beds and Jacuzzis.

The dining room, which affords a splendid view of the extensive flower gardens, serves well-prepared continental fare. Breads and rolls are baked on the premises. Typical entrées include sautéed pheasant breast with chicken sausage in a Grand Marnier and dried cranberry sauce, and grilled lamb chops that have been marinated in ginger and garlic and are served with a burgundy wine sauce. Be sure to leave room for the amaretto-soaked sponge cake served in a pool of raspberry sauce and topped with chocolate shavings. A full breakfast is also offered, and meals are open to non-guests.

Plenty of recreational activities are available. The inn's grounds boast a swimming pool, a putting green, horseshoes, shuffleboard, volleyball, table tennis, a children's play area, and a sauna. Golf, tennis, fishing, hiking, and cultural activities are also nearby.

CHRISTMAS FARM INN PO Box CC, Rte. 16B, Jackson, NH 03846 (phone: 603-383-4313; 800-HI-ELVES; fax: 603-383-6495). Located in the Mt. Washington Valley, this inn has 37 guestrooms with private baths, telephones, and twin, double, queen-, or king-size beds. Open year-round. Rate for a double room (including full breakfast and dinner): $136 to $190; children ages 12 to 18 (in their parents' room): $50; children ages two to 12: $25; children under two: free. Two-night minimum stay during school vacations, fall foliage season, and winter weekends. Major credit cards accepted. No pets. Smoking permitted in the pub and in some guestrooms. Sydna and Bill Zeliff, innkeepers.

DIRECTIONS: From I-95 traveling north, take Exit 4 (Spaulding Turnpike, which becomes Route 16). Take Route 16 for approximately 70 miles. Turn off onto Route 16A to Jackson. Continue across the covered bridge for a half mile. At the schoolhouse on the right, turn left onto Route 16B and travel a half mile. The inn is on the right.

INN AT THORN HILL

JACKSON, NEW HAMPSHIRE

Architecture and nature buffs alike will find much to occupy them at this grand country estate located on nine acres in northern New Hampshire. Designed by famed architect Stanford White, the estate's main house retains several features that are characteristic of his work, including leaded-glass sliding doors and a gambrel roof. The manmade beauty is matched by that of the natural show that unfolds before the broad front porch—whether you're watching nearby Mt. Washington become shrouded by dusk or enjoying the vivid colors of sunrise.

If Stanford White could see the *Inn at Thorn Hill* today, he'd undoubtedly feel right at home, as it has been faithfully restored by Jim and Ibby Cooper, who bought the place in 1992. White built the 14-room mansion in 1895 for Katherine Prescott Wormeley, a distinguished translator of the works of Balzac. Judging from the enormous rooms, she must have enjoyed lavish entertaining: The dining room seats 42, and the living room is so massive that it's now divided into three separate areas, where guests congregate to socialize or play board games. The smaller parlor contains the only television set, and the spacious drawing room has a Steinway baby grand piano and a soapstone wood stove.

The main inn's 10 guestrooms feature views of the mountains; they are individually decorated with Victorian antiques. Accommodations also are available in the adjacent *Carriage House,* whose 40-foot-long *Great Room* is highlighted by a fireplace, and in three cottages, each outfitted with a gas fireplace, Jacuzzi, and a deck or porch. These rooms, too, are tastefully decorated with period antiques.

The dining room (which is open to non-guests for dinner) is justifiably noted for its haute cuisine. Choices include an appetizer of sautéed veal sweetbreads with a balsamic, tomato, and basil sauce, and such entrées as sautéed medallions of pork served with green apple and potato pancakes and apple aioli, and grilled chicken breast served with red chili pumpkin-seed sauce and *crème fraîche.* Full breakfast and afternoon tea are offered as well.

The property offers many recreational facilities, including an Olympic-size pool and cross-country ski trails. In addition, the Coopers often host interesting special activities such as workshops on art, cooking, or quilt making. Off the grounds are major ski resorts, golf, hiking, and summer theater.

INN AT THORN HILL Thorn Hill Rd., Box A, Jackson, NH 03846 (phone: 603-383-4242; 800-289-8990; fax: 603-383-8062). This luxurious country inn has 19 guestrooms with private baths and twin, double, queen-, or king-size beds. Limited wheelchair access. Closed weekdays in April. Rate for a double room (including full breakfast, afternoon tea, and dinner): $140 to $275. Major credit cards accepted. Not appropriate for children under 12. No pets. No smoking. Jim and Ibby Cooper, innkeepers.

DIRECTIONS: From I-95 traveling north, take Exit 4 (Spaulding Turnpike), which becomes Route 16. Follow Route 16 for approximately 70 miles to Jackson. Once in the village, take Route 16A through the covered bridge to Thorn Hill Road and turn right. The inn is up the hill.

FOLLANSBEE INN

NORTH SUTTON, NEW HAMPSHIRE

Set in a distinctive, rambling farmhouse built in the 1840s, this inn is surrounded by three acres of land adjoining Kezar Lake. Four miles from New London, the *Follansbee* and the placid village of North Sutton have hosted visitors for more than a century. Some of this history is recorded in an album available to guests, which includes intriguing old photographs and post-cards depicting the inn and past guests, and nostalgic written accounts of childhood and honeymoon stays.

Owned by Dick and Sandy Reilein since 1985, the crisp white clapboard house has green trim and a broad front porch, accented with bright flowers in summer. Guests can sit in rockers, wicker chairs, or an old-fashioned swing and gaze at the peaceful lake, or watch the sunset reflected in the calm waters from a bench built into the sturdy dock.

The warm hospitality extended here makes you feel as if you're staying with old friends. The sitting room, paneled with weathered barn siding and furnished with overstuffed chairs, presents an inviting setting for socializing. The room is particularly pleasant in winter, when the wood-burning stove offers a respite from the chill. A second parlor contains another fire-place, comfortable seating, and a small service bar, which has an impressive selection of wines and local beers, as well as hot *kir* and cider in winter. In warm weather, fruit juice, tea, and soft drinks are offered on the front porch.

The public areas are reminiscent of a grandmother's attic, decorated with numerous folksy touches, including Reilein family mementos. Named after members of the Follansbee family and other local forebears, the 23 comfortable guestrooms feature low ceilings and country antiques. Only 11 of the rooms have private baths, but the shared baths are large. Several have old-fashioned claw-foot tubs.

In the morning, guests congregate in the spacious dining room overlooking the lake to enjoy homemade granola, yogurt, juice, and coffee, and then are invited to the kitchen to select from a hot buffet, which may consist of an egg soufflé, pancakes, or French toast. Dinner is served to guests with advance notice. A typical menu of flavorful, homestyle fare might include hearty tortellini vegetable soup; spinach salad with feta cheese, *tamari* dressing, and marinated vegetables; savory dill bread; Cornish game hens; and whipped chocolate cheesecake.

The inn has a small armada of boats, including two sailboards, a rowboat, a canoe, and a paddleboat. For a memorable afternoon, take a self-powered excursion to the small island in the middle of the lake and enjoy one of Sandy's picnic lunches as you soak up the sun. Stroll the scenic 3-mile path around the lake or take a bicycle ride on secluded roads. Fisherfolk can drop a line in the state-stocked waters for bass, perch, and pickerel. In winter, there is cross-country skiing on the miles of groomed trails along the adjacent 500-acres, which are part state park, part private property. Major downhill-skiing areas also are nearby.

A collection of early homestead buildings and farm implements are on display at nearby *Musterfield Farm*; visit in January for ice cutting and square dancing. The *Hay Estate*, former mansion and gardens of US statesman John Hay, and the *Indian Museum* at Mt. Kearsarge also make interesting excursions. The Reileins provide guests with information on other historic homes in the area as well.

FOLLANSBEE INN PO Box 92, North Sutton, NH 03260 (phone: 603-927-4221; 800-626-4221). On Lake Kezar near New London, this inn offers 23 guestrooms (11 with private baths) with twin, double, queen-, or king-size beds. Closed briefly in April and November. Rate for a double room (including full breakfast): $75 to $95. Two-night minimum stay on some weekends in rooms with private baths. MasterCard and Visa accepted. Not appropriate for children under 10. No pets. One English springer spaniel in residence. No smoking. Dick and Sandy Reilein, innkeepers.

DIRECTIONS: Located 90 miles from Boston. From I-89 north, take Exit 10. Turn left at the end of the ramp and follow signs to North Sutton, turning right onto Route 114 north. The inn is behind the white church, across Keyser Road from the lake.

SUGAR HILL INN

SUGAR HILL, NEW HAMPSHIRE

Built in 1789, the *Sugar Hill Inn* was originally the home of one of the many hardy American families who came to the White Mountains to farm. Traditional post-and-beam construction was employed for the house, and the massive rock fireplaces provided the principal source of heat; glowing pumpkin-colored pine planks, some as wide as 26 inches, were used for walls and floors. A working farm until the 1920s, the property became an inn in 1929, and over the years three cottages were added.

Jim and Barbara Quinn purchased the inn in 1986 and decorated it in colonial style. (Their daughter Kelly Ritarossi and her husband, Stephen, joined them as innkeepers in 1995.) The two charming common rooms have original fireplaces, and the living room contains a 1906 player piano where guests congregate for evening sing-alongs. In the small pub is another fireplace, a pine bar, and a piano that has been computerized to play CDs. The house's wide verandahs, filled with pots of flowers and white wicker furniture, are reminiscent of a gracious old Southern home.

The 10 guestrooms in the main inn and six cottage suites feature antique beds (most are either four-poster or canopy), hand-braided rag rugs, and handmade quilts. Barbara stenciled the walls according to original patterns found during the renovations. The suites have private decks or terraces and wood-burning fireplaces.

In the morning, guests awaken to the aroma of freshly baked muffins and brewing coffee. A full breakfast, which might feature walnut pancakes with fresh fruit, is served in the dining room. Every afternoon the parlor is set for tea, served from a silver service on a cart laden with scones, sweet rolls, and breads. In the evening the dining room (also open to non-guests by reservation) is infused with candlelight and music, as a flutist and pianist softly play in the background. Jim and Stephen are the chefs. The rack of lamb, crusted with herbs, mustard, and cream, is especially popular. A fine selection of wines is available.

The inn is located in the White Mountains, with downhill and cross-country skiing, tennis, concerts, the *Robert Frost Historic Home,* summer theater, golf, biking, and craft shows nearby. After a full day of activity, guests can use the powerful telescope on the verandah for stargazing.

SUGAR HILL INN Rte. 117, Sugar Hill, NH 03580 (phone: 603-823-5621; 800-548-4748; fax: 603-823-5639). This inn has 16 guestrooms with private baths and twin, double, queen-, or king-size beds. Closed April. Rate for a double room (including full breakfast, afternoon tea, and dinner): $183 to $229. Two-night minimum stay during fall foliage season. MasterCard and Visa accepted. Not appropriate for children under 10. No pets. No smoking. Jim and Barbara Quinn and Kelly and Stephen Ritarossi, innkeepers.

DIRECTIONS: Traveling north on I-93 from Boston, take Exit 38 and follow Route 18 north through Franconia. In Franconia turn left onto Route 117. The inn is half a mile up the hill on the right.

DEXTER'S INN AND TENNIS CLUB

SUNAPEE, NEW HAMPSHIRE

New Hampshire, in the summer, is a kaleidoscope of blue skies, green trees, and sunshine, while, in fall, the colors change to red and orange. On 20 acres overlooking Lake Sunapee, *Dexter's* is itself a palate of bright yellow clapboard, green shutters, and white trim, enhanced by expansive lawns and colorful flower beds.

Built in 1803, the Colonial Revival main house was part of a private estate until 1948. It has since been thoroughly restored and furnished with period reproductions. Frank and Shirley Simpson purchased the inn in 1969, and their daughter Holly and her husband, Michael Durfor, are now the innkeepers.

Popular gathering places for guests include the screened porch, with white wicker furniture and a ceiling painted to look like a tent, and the large family room at the back of the main inn, which doubles as a small bar at night. In the evening, guests enjoy cheese and crackers in the cozy library/living room, which has a fireplace and a piano and is furnished with comfortable love seats.

Each of the 19 guestrooms is carpeted and individually decorated with antiques or 1940s oak furniture; three have four-poster or canopy beds, and five are air conditioned. Most are reached by little hallways that zigzag through the wings of the main house, although several are located in the annex barn across the street. Next to the main house is the *Holly House Cottage,* which accommodates up to six guests in two bedrooms, and includes a living room with a fireplace and a fully-equipped kitchen.

The full breakfast might include eggs Benedict or a "Dex/Mex" omelette, and hearty country fare is served at dinner. Both meals also are open to non-guests. Dinner selections might include poached salmon, thick lamb chops, or chicken *piccata* and, for dessert, butterscotch-pecan pie or a chocolate-walnut torte. The cocktail lounge is a convivial place for after-dinner drinks.

As lovely as the inn interior is, one of the primary attractions at *Dexter's* is the variety of outdoor activities. There are three Plexipave tennis courts with a resident pro, a swimming pool, and various lawn games, such as horseshoes, shuffleboard, and volleyball. Guests who favor golf, hiking, or lake swimming will find opportunities nearby. Local attractions include live entertainment at *Sunapee Harbor Marine,* a maple syrup sap house, summer stock at the *New London Barn Playhouse,* and the *Saint-Gaudens National Historic Site*.

DEXTER'S INN AND TENNIS CLUB Stagecoach Rd., Box 703, Sunapee, NH 03782 (phone: 603-763-5571; 800-232-5571). Near Lake Sunapee, this country inn and tennis club has 19 guestrooms with private baths and twin, double, queen-, or king-size beds. Wheelchair accessible. Closed November through April (although the cottage may be available during the winter); dining room also closed Tuesday dinner. Rate for a double room (including full breakfast and dinner): $135 to $190; children under 12 (in parents' room): $35. Two-night minimum stay on weekends. Discover, MasterCard, and Visa accepted. Pets allowed in the annex and *Holly House Cottage* ($10 additional per night). No smoking except in lounge and on the porch. Michael Durfor and Holly Simpson-Durfor, innkeepers.

DIRECTIONS: Located 50 miles from Manchester, New Hampshire, and 100 miles from Boston. From I-89 north take Exit 12 to Route 11 west. Travel 5½ miles, turn left onto Winn Hill Road (which becomes Stagecoach Road), and continue another 2 miles. The main inn is on the right.

TAMWORTH INN

TAMWORTH, NEW HAMPSHIRE

Built as a hotel in 1833, this rambling Victorian structure is located on the Swift River and presides over three tranquil acres of manicured lawns and attractive gardens. The grounds owe their beauty to innkeeper Kathy Bender, a professional landscape architect, who, with her husband, Phil, purchased *Tamworth* in 1988.

The inn is a hub of activity, a gathering place for local residents as well as overnight visitors. Its many common rooms, including several porches, the popular dining room, a living room with a fireplace, the pub, and the pool patio, are open to the public. The library, however, lined with bookcases and containing a VCR with an extensive video collection, is reserved for overnight guests.

Guestrooms are decorated with quilts that have been hand-sewn by Kathy, as well as with antique furniture such as iron beds and painted dressers. Victorian fabrics and wallpapers have been used, and one of the rooms has a lovely mural painted by a previous guest who couldn't afford to pay his bill. Thoughtful amenities include baskets of toiletries, crystal water glasses, and fresh coffee delivered to the rooms every morning.

A buffet breakfast features such entrées as baked eggs or French toast. Dinner might include roast leg of lamb or roast duckling with cranberry glaze. The inn's specialty dessert, a profiterole, is a puff pastry filled with ice cream and topped with a gooey hot fudge sauce. Lighter fare is served in the *Tamworth Inn Pub,* where "World Famous Tamworth Chili" will warm you to your toes.

Local attractions include the historic *Barnstormer's Theatre* just across the lane, where eight productions are presented every summer. The actors often can be found by the pool or in the pub chatting with the guests before and after performances. Summertime sun worshipers bask in chaise lounges around the pool. For the more daring there's a swimming hole on the Swift River, and the inn can arrange canoe rentals. Fly fishing on the river is equally popular (equipment can be rented in town). The area also is renowned for its hiking and cross-country ski trails.

TAMWORTH INN Main St., PO Box 189, Tamworth, NH 03886 (phone: 603-323-7721; 800-NH-2-RELAX; fax: 603-323-7721). This inn has 15 guestrooms with private baths and twin, double, queen-, or king-size beds. The dining room is wheelchair accessible. Closed April. Rate for a double room (including full breakfast and dinner entrée—appetizer, dessert, and drinks are extra): $110 to $160; bed and breakfast: $85 to $130. Two-night minimum stay on some holiday weekends. MasterCard and Visa accepted. Not appropriate for children under seven. Pets allowed by prior arrangement ($5 per stay). Cats in residence. Smoking permitted in pub only. Phil and Kathy Bender, innkeepers.

DIRECTIONS: From I-95 north take Exit 4 (Spaulding Turnpike), which becomes Route 16. Follow Route 16 approximately 50 miles. Turn west onto Route 113 at Chocorua, and travel 3 miles to Tamworth. The inn is on the left in the center of town.

BIRCHWOOD INN

TEMPLE, NEW HAMPSHIRE

Tucked away near Mt. Monadnock, the village of Temple has changed little in 200 years. The grange hall, church, village store, Revolutionary-era cemetery, and old blacksmith shop are still intact. So is the *Birchwood Inn,* which is in the center of town. The present Federal-style brick building, along with the adjacent barn, was built as a tavern and inn about 1775. Owned since 1979 by Judy and Bill Wolfe, it is now listed on the National Register of Historic Places.

During a 1965 restoration project an exciting discovery was made: Early wall murals were uncovered beneath layers of old wallpaper. The paintings, dating from between 1825 and 1835, proved to be the work of well-known muralist Rufus Porter. They were painstakingly restored and are now one of the *Birchwood*'s most prized features.

The simple comforts of a village inn are reflected in the furnishings and amenities in the common rooms: There's an 1878 Steinway square grand piano in the living room, wide-plank floorboards (some in the tavern are stenciled), antique pieces, plush easy chairs, soft classical background music, and a gameroom with jigsaw puzzles, backgammon, and chess. The front porch with rockers overlooks the village green.

The seven guestrooms have period furnishings and are decorated in various themes. The *Music Room,* for example, has an organ, a lamp fashioned from a violin, and an old music rack. The *Train Room* has a railroad theme, with an old railroad lantern and pictures of trains on the wall.

Breakfast here might include bacon and eggs or Belgian waffles. The evening meal attracts neighbors as well as inn guests. Bill does the cooking, while Judy bakes the breads and prepares the desserts. Entrées include fresh New England seafood, chicken, or veal, with a special Saturday-night dinner featuring she-crab soup and roast duckling. Judy likes to make desserts from local fruit and berries, so a blueberry cobbler or fruit pie might end the meal. All jams, jellies, and relishes are made at the inn, and the homemade marmalade, spicy crab-apple jelly, and elderberry jam also are for sale.

The inn's southern New Hampshire location makes it ideal for hiking, skiing, ice skating, and attending summer theater.

BIRCHWOOD INN Rte. 45, Temple, NH 03084 (phone: 603-878-3285). This inn has seven guestrooms with private baths, twin, double, or queen-size beds, and TV sets. Closed two weeks in April and one week in November; dining room also closed Sunday and Monday dinner. Rate for a double room (including full breakfast): $59 to $70. Three-day minimum stay on *Columbus Day* weekend. No credit cards accepted. Not appropriate for children under 10. No pets. One basset hound in residence. Smoking permitted in one common room only. Judy and Bill Wolfe, innkeepers.

DIRECTIONS: From Boston take Route 3 north to Nashua. Take Exit 8 and follow Route 101A west beyond Milford to Route 45. Turn left onto Route 45 and travel 1½ miles to Temple. The inn is in the center of town on the left.

TWIN FARMS

BARNARD, VERMONT

When Nobel Prize–winning novelist Sinclair Lewis and his wife, writer Dorothy Thompson, purchased a farm with two farmhouses in this bucolic valley, they treasured the peaceful setting. Today, guests can experience that same sense of serenity on their former farm.

Twin Farms is no ordinary inn. Painstaking attention to detail has created an exclusive retreat that spoils guests for future experiences. The staff members are so helpful and friendly, yet so professional, that they seem to anticipate every need.

The architecture of the inn is stunning, the ambience highly personal. There is no lobby, cashier, or reception area, but a multitude of common rooms. The *Barn Room,* highlighted by the massive picture window Lewis installed to view Mt. Ascutney, has raftered ceilings and an enormous fireplace, making it snug in winter and bright and airy in summer. The walls of the foyer are decorated with charming hand-painted murals depicting Barnard and other Vermont scenes. An eclectic array of original paintings and art objects from the private collection of the owners, the Twigg-Smith family, lends a whimsical air. A garden terrace, a covered bridge to the pub and gameroom, a fully equipped fitness center, and a forest building containing a *furo* (a Japanese-style soaking tub) are just a few of the features. The pub contains a pool table and a complimentary bar.

Each of the guestrooms is unique and spacious, with amenity-laden baths, featherbeds, interesting fabrics, fine woodwork, and abundant fireplaces. Guests can stay in *Red's Room* (a nickname Sinclair earned for his red hair), *Dorothy's Room,* or two suites in the main house. The *Guest Room* is a dream, with an oak sleigh bed facing a green marble fireplace. Its bathroom, reached through a dressing room, has a claw-foot tub and a separate shower. The walls and windows are hung with green French toile. A former artist's studio next to the main house contains two more guestrooms. In addition, seven new stone-and-timber cottages have been built in wooded settings near the main house, though they look as if they've been there for a hundred years. The *Orchard Cottage,* for example, is set amid apple trees in the old orchard, where it surveys, through its wall of windows, the terraced beaver ponds and ski slopes beyond. It has two carved granite fireplaces and a split-ash herringbone ceiling, and is decorated in neutral tones accented by cranberry and teal. The *Treehouse* has a lofty ceiling and an ebony four-poster bed. Its screened porch looks across the fields at treetop level.

Before dinner, guests (unless they have chosen to eat privately in their room) gather in the barn for drinks and hors d'oeuvres. Dinner is served on antique English china, with crystal and silver gracing the tables. Guests may dine at a private table or share a larger table with other guests, heightening the sense of visiting with friends at their country estate. A fine wine selection complements the superb cuisine of Neil Wigglesworth, who is justifiably proud of the kitchen garden, where he grows herbs, edible flowers, and vegetables. An evening's four-course meal may include a shrimp timbale with three-grain *blinis,* char-grilled black sea bass with a compote of fiddleheads and fennel, and a dessert of apple chrysalis—a blown-sugar apple filled with Granny Smith mousse, accompanied by a warm caramel sauce.

The full breakfast might include berry-filled crêpes or blueberry pancakes with homemade sausage. A variety of fresh-baked croissants and other breads arrives in a basket. A full lunch also is served and, in the afternoon, delicate sandwiches, cakes, cookies, and tea tempt even folks who have spent the morning in the fitness center.

Bicycle and walking trails lace the 255-acre property. Tennis courts, a private ski slope and tow, croquet lawns, canoeing, swimming, and fishing in the seven-acre trout-stocked lake all are available. The inn will pack a picnic of lobster and champagne for an excursion on a mountain bike. Nearby is Woodstock, with its quaint shops and museums (including *Billings Farm Museum*), as well as facilities for golf and additional downhill and cross-country skiing.

TWIN FARMS Barnard, VT 05031 (phone: 802-234-9999; 800-TWIN-FARMS; fax: 802-234-9990). This country retreat in a very rural, wooded setting in central Vermont has six suites and seven cottages with private baths, queen- or king-size beds, telephones, TV sets, and air conditioning. Wheelchair accessible. Closed April. Rate for a double room (including breakfast, lunch, afternoon tea, dinner, all alcoholic beverages, all activities, and use of sports equipment): $700 to $1,500, plus a 15% gratuity. Two-night minimum stay on weekends; three nights on holidays. Major credit cards accepted. Not appropriate for children. No pets. One dog, Maple, in

residence. No smoking. Laila and Thurston Twigg-Smith, innkeepers; Shaun and Beverley Matthews, managers.

DIRECTIONS: From New York take I-91 north to the White River Junction/Lebanon exit. Get on Route 89 north and turn off at Exit 1. Turn left onto Route 4 and head to Woodstock. In Woodstock take Route 12 north to Barnard. Turn right at the general store and drive for 1½ miles, bearing left at the fork. Two stone pillars mark the entrance to *Twin Farms* on the right.

LILAC INN

BRANDON, VERMONT

Painted the same pale yellow as the rare lilacs that bloom in the courtyard in spring, the *Lilac Inn* exudes a charm and gentility that's as special as its namesake blossoms. A mix of Greek Revival and Southern Plantation architectural styles, this eight-room hostelry is the pride and joy of innkeepers Michael and Melanie Shane, who have put their own distinctive stamp on its decor and gracious ambience.

Prior to opening in 1993, the inn underwent a two-year restoration overseen by Melanie, an architect, and Michael, a contractor. Today, it boasts polished oak floors, a curving staircase, and an elegant ballroom and cozy library, both adorned with carved fireplace mantles and fine antiques. The owner's museum-quality collections give the inn a distinctive character; there are enameled Russian box lids in the library, and Melanie's antique dolls are displayed in every guestroom.

Each spacious guestroom has a private tiled bath, many with a pedestal sink or claw-foot tub. In some cases, sinks have been placed in antique dressers or tables in the bedroom to allow more room in the baths. All the rooms are special, but two of our favorites are room No. 5 and the *Bridal Suite.* The former, with pink walls and yellow trim, features an antique bed with Ralph Lauren floral linen, and a deep green marble-topped dresser that contains the sink. The *Bridal Suite,* decorated in shades of pink and plum, has a massive iron canopy bed, a large oak table with twisted legs and claw feet, a wood-burning fireplace, a built-in vanity, and a bath with a two-person Jacuzzi. Impressive bride and groom dolls, accompanied by their bridal party, sit atop the armoire.

A full breakfast (included in the room rate) is served to overnight guests; the pastries are a house specialty. On Sundays the inn offers a huge brunch that's also open to non-guests; be sure to try the cream-filled carmelized French toast.

The inviting restaurant, which features a tavern and a more formal dining room, draws food lovers from far and wide. Lunch and dinner are served to overnight guests and others on Wednesdays through Saturdays. The dining room, romantically lit at night by candlelight, offers views of the garden, where the trees are adorned with hundreds of tiny white lights. Entrées may include rosemary lamb tenderloin or Brandon haddock, a local fish prepared with seasoned bread crumbs. The chocolate coffee *crème brûlée,* a house specialty, is a masterpiece. Lighter fare is offered in the tavern, which features a cozy seating area in front of a carved oak fireplace.

Another pleasant common area is the broad marble-tiled verandah, a secluded oasis lined with antique wicker chairs and sofas. The gazebo in the garden has become a favorite backdrop for weddings, while the putting green is a pleasant place to fritter away an afternoon.

Special inn events—from lawn concerts to wine tastings—take place throughout the year. Brandon lies in the Otter Valley between the Adirondack and the Green Mountains; the Battenkill River meanders through town. Downhill and cross-country skiing, golf, fishing, and hiking are nearby.

LILAC INN 53 Park Street, Brandon, VT 05733 (phone: 802-247-5463; fax: 802-247-5499). An eight-guestroom Victorian mansion with private baths, twin, queen-, or king-size beds, and TV sets. Open year-round; dining room closed January. Rate for a double room (including full breakfast): $100 to $250. Two-night minimum preferred during fall foliage season and for special events. Major credit cards accepted. Children welcome. No pets. Three cats and two dogs in residence. No smoking. Michael and Melanie Shane, innkeepers.

DIRECTIONS: From I-87, take Exit 20 in Glens Falls, New York, and follow NY 149 east to US 4 in Fort Ann, New York. Follow US 4 north and east to Rutland, Vermont. In Rutland, take US 7 north to Brandon. At the monument on the village green, follow signs for Route 73 north. The inn is in the first block on the right.

TULIP TREE INN

CHITTENDEN, VERMONT

Like the old town crier, innkeeper Ed McDowell announces breakfast and dinner, here, by ringing a bell and, in his resonant baritone, recites the menu. And that's only one of the dramatic roles Ed plays. With a theatrical background, he is also a storyteller, eagerly spinning yarns for guests' enjoyment.

Nestled in *Green Mountain National Forest* beside East Creek, the *Tulip Tree* is exactly what we hope an inn will be. It was built as a farmhouse in 1842 and purchased by William Barstow, a collaborator of Thomas Edison, in the early 1900s. With its white shutters, impressive columned entry, and airy porch, the forest green house looks as if it belongs on a Vermont postcard. Since 1984 it has been owned by Ed and his wife, Rosemary.

The common rooms include a den with a massive stone fireplace, braided rugs, Victorian antiques, overstuffed couches, and windows on three sides that bring the outdoors in. The living room contains another fireplace, original oil paintings, including one of Andrew Carnegie (Rosemary once worked for a Carnegie foundation). The vest-pocket library/pub has floor-to-ceiling bookcases and offers a wide selection of imported beers, spirits, and wines.

The eight guestrooms vary in size, but all are warm and inviting. They boast oak dressers, oak beds covered with floral spreads that match the wallpaper, braided rugs, and stenciled doors and doorjambs. Room No. 4 has a four-poster pineapple-post bed. All have private baths, and five have Jacuzzis.

Rosemary prepares both a full breakfast and dinner. The evening meal is served in the dining room at common tables, creating a dinner-party atmosphere. Candles are lit, and soft classical music plays. The menu may include curried carrot soup swirled with yogurt, a green salad, veal rolls in a cognac sauce, and pumpkin cheesecake with warm Vermont maple syrup or an English trifle. Excellent wines, for which the inn consistently has won awards, complement the meal. Popular breakfast selections include blueberry pancakes or raisin-bread French toast.

Thanks to the inn's location in *Green Mountain National Forest,* guests can find plenty of skiing, fishing, golf, and tennis nearby.

TULIP TREE INN Chittenden Dam Rd., Chittenden, VT 05737 (phone: 802-483-6213; 800-707-0017). This inn has eight guestrooms with private baths and queen-size beds. Closed April through mid-May and the first two weeks in November. Rate for a double room (including full breakfast and dinner): $120 to $265. Two-night minimum stay on weekends and during fall foliage season. MasterCard and Visa accepted. Not appropriate for children under 12. No pets. A cat, Hoover, and a Bernese mountain dog, Juni, in residence. No smoking. Ed and Rosemary McDowell, innkeepers.

DIRECTIONS: Traveling north on Route 7, pass through Rutland and look for the red brick power station on the left about 2 miles outside of town. Just beyond the station is a Y in the road with a red country store in the middle. Stay to the right of the store and travel approximately 6 miles. The inn is on the left, a half mile beyond the fire station.

INN ON THE COMMON

CRAFTSBURY COMMON, VERMONT

Tucked away on a rural hilltop in Vermont's Northeast Kingdom, in a village that's hardly changed a street sign or a clapboard in its more than 200-year history, the *Inn on the Common* is a decidedly uncommon inn.

But, in truth, the name is something of a misnomer. The inn, which comprises three historic white clapboard houses, is located not on Craftsbury Common's village green but on its broad Main Street. Not that it matters. Romantic and serene, the 15-acre property includes lush perennial and rose gardens and walking trails that lead past quaint birdhouses to a garden with Leutens benches, a formal English croquet lawn, a red-clay tennis court, and a belvedere where Adirondack chairs provide front-row seats for watching the sun set behind the Green Mountains. In winter, when the fields are covered with snow, cross-country ski trails lace the grounds. There's also a free-form swimming pool.

Penny and Michael Schmitt, owners of the inn since 1973, have anticipated every guest need. The common rooms, decorated with fine English antiques, are gracious and warm. Oriental rugs cover wide-plank pine floors, and wood-burning fireplaces glow in winter. An honor bar is discreetly placed within a cabinet in the library of the *Main Inn,* where guests can read old cookbooks, chat, and nibble hors d'oeuvres before dinner. In the *South Annex,* selections from the large collection of classic movies can be viewed on a large-screen TV set.

The 16 guestrooms reflect the same careful attention to detail as the rest of the inn. The antique furnishings include four-poster and canopy beds and elegant dressers; some rooms have fireplaces or wood-burning stoves. Distinctive decorative touches include a huge butter churn in one room, a pine bed with fishnet canopy in another, and English furnishings in another.

A full breakfast and dinner (also open to non-guests) are served either in the formal dining room decorated with elegant oil portraits and antiques, or on the outside deck in warm weather. Fine sterling silver, elegant china and crystal, tall tapered candles, and an extensive wine list create the backdrop for romantic and intimate dinners. The menu changes nightly, but game and fish are often featured; there might be venison cutlets with brandied peaches and plums, or sea bass accompanied by pineapple and jalapeño salsa. A delicate chocolate-raspberry torte is a tasty dessert selection. Coffee, chocolates, and cordials are available in the library following dinner.

The *Craftsbury Nordic Ski Center* is nearby, as are opportunities for golf, mountain biking, canoeing, and horseback riding.

INN ON THE COMMON Main Street, Craftsbury Common, VT 05827 (phone: 802-586-9619; 800-521-2233; fax: 802-586-2249). A genteel, sophisticated country inn in Vermont's remote Northeast Kingdom with 16 guestrooms with private baths, and twin, double, queen-, and king-size beds. Open year-round. Rate for a double room (including full breakfast, afternoon hors d'oeuvres, and dinner): $200 to $270. Two-night minimum stay during fall foliage season and *Christmastime.* MasterCard and Visa accepted. Children welcome. Pets welcome with prior permission (additional charge of $15 per pet per visit). Smoking permitted in some guestrooms. Michael and Penny Schmitt, innkeepers.

DIRECTIONS From I-91 take Exit 21 in St. Johnsbury and follow US 2 west to Danville. In Danville take Route 15 west to Hardwick and from there follow Route 14 north for eight more miles. Take a sharp right at the sign for Craftsbury Common and follow this road for three more miles. The inn office will be on the right before the village green.

CORNUCOPIA OF DORSET

DORSET, VERMONT

Located on the main street of a quaint Vermont town that retains its white, steepled church and old-fashioned country store, the *Cornucopia of Dorset* is a special find. Bill and Linda Ley, both with backgrounds in the travel business, have owned the white clapboard, 1880s inn since 1986 and they bring to it a friendliness and a commitment to guest comfort that are exceptional. Coffee is delivered to guests' rooms every morning, and a selection of fine wines may be enjoyed in front of either the living room or the library fireplace in the evening. Throughout the day, refreshments such as cookies, cake, or fresh berries are laid out.

The living room is furnished with priceless antiques and family heirlooms. An abundance of books is available in the library, where a friendly game of backgammon may be in progress. A large sunroom contains videos for viewing on the VCR and, in the warmer months, guests enjoy relaxing on the patio, the side porch, and in the gardens.

The inn has four rooms and a suite, each richly decorated in warm paisleys, with four-poster or canopy beds covered with colorful Vermont quilts in the summer and European down comforters in cooler weather. Some of the rooms have wood-burning fireplaces, and each has a private bath stocked with fluffy terry robes. The charming cottage suite in back has a full kitchen and a living room with a fireplace.

Breakfasts are served in the formal dining room. The table is set with one of Linda's many antique china services—maybe the Wedgwood or the Lenox "Monroe" pattern. Sterling silver is used, and linen napkins are folded into stemmed glasses. A typical breakfast might include a melon boat filled with fresh local berries topped with *crème fraîche,* followed by cinnamon puff pancakes with Vermont maple syrup or cheese blintzes with warm cranberry and raspberry toppings.

The inn is within walking distance of the famed *Dorset Playhouse,* and guests will find art galleries, skiing, tennis, swimming, golf, and horseback riding nearby.

CORNUCOPIA OF DORSET PO Box 307, Rte. 30, Dorset, VT 05251 (phone: 802-867-5751; fax: 802-867-5753). This country inn has four guestrooms and one cottage suite with private baths, twin, queen-, or king-size beds, and air conditioning. Open year-round. Rate for a double room (including full breakfast): $100 to $135; rate for cottage suite: $179 to $195. Major credit cards accepted. Not appropriate for children under 12. No pets. A dog, Kitt, in residence; Rutland, a rabbit, makes his summer home outside in a hutch. No smoking. Bill and Linda Ley, innkeepers.

DIRECTIONS: From Manchester Center take Route 30 north approximately 6 miles to Dorset. The inn is on the right, just south of the Dorset village green.

BLUEBERRY HILL

GOSHEN, VERMONT

Tony Clark is an avid cross-country skier, so it's no surprise that *Blueberry Hill,* the inn he has owned since 1968, is noted for the 40 miles of groomed cross-country ski trails that wind through its 120 acres.

Nestled at the foot of Romance Mountain in the *Green Mountain National Forest,* the blue clapboard inn was built in 1813 as a farmhouse and later expanded to provide overnight lodging for loggers. Its guestrooms remain simple and functional, but all have private baths and several have lofts with twin beds. Access to most of the rooms is through an exotic greenhouse/solarium, abloom with foliage and flowering plants year-round, reflecting co-owner Shari Brown's background in garden design.

The inn is reminiscent of grandmother's farm, with a hot-water bottle hanging on the back of each door and handmade patchwork quilts on the beds. In fact, the quilts are so unusual and beautiful that guests often ask to buy them. That's not a problem, as the artisan is also the inn's baker, and she's happy to oblige. The inn's common rooms are cozy and welcoming as well, with fireplaces, antique furnishings (including an old spinning wheel), and braided rugs.

A full breakfast starts the day, perhaps including wild-blueberry pancakes made from berries picked on the property. Lunch and dinner (open to the public by reservation) also are served, and guests may opt to sit at common or individual tables. Dishes include sautéed duck breast with homemade apple and black currant sauces and chocolate-hazelnut torte. Diners are advised to bring their own wine or liquor.

In winter, the inn specializes in cross-country skiing, but downhill skiing is nearby. Summer activities also lure visitors. Hiking on Vermont's Long Trail can begin right at the inn. The inn provides an excellent trail map and trekking guide. Backpacking, mountain biking, fishing in tumbling mountain streams, swimming or fishing in the pond in back (it's stocked with trout), and relaxing in the sauna at day's end are other attractions.

BLUEBERRY HILL Goshen, VT 05733 (phone: 802-247-6735; fax: 802-247-3983). This country inn has 12 guestrooms with private baths and twin or double beds. Wheelchair accessible. Closed April. Rate for a double room (including full breakfast and dinner): $168 to $220; bed and breakfast: $148 to $200. MasterCard and Visa accepted. Children welcome. No pets. One dog in residence. No smoking. Tony Clark and Shari Brown, innkeepers.

DIRECTIONS: Traveling north on Route 7 to Brandon, take Route 73 east for 3 miles through Forest Dale. Follow the signs to *Blueberry Hill,* located on Forest Access Road 32.

OLD TAVERN AT GRAFTON

GRAFTON, VERMONT

Little has changed in the sleepy village of Grafton since the 1800s, or at least it seems that way. A horse-drawn wagon still deposits travelers at the doorstep of the *Old Tavern at Grafton,* just as the Boston-to-Montreal stagecoach once did.

The illusion that the 19th century lives on here is by design. The Windham Foundation, a not-for-profit organization established in 1963, has restored and operates many of the local businesses, including the inn and the Grafton Village Cheese Company, which began production in 1890.

A fine white brick and clapboard structure, the *Old Tavern at Grafton* was built in 1801. Daniel Webster, Oliver Wendell Holmes, Ulysses S. Grant, Nathaniel Hawthorne, Ralph Waldo Emerson, Rudyard Kipling, and Henry David Thoreau are but a few of the American notables who have rocked gently on the wraparound porch. It remains a popular spot for an afternoon libation to this day.

Thanks to meticulous restoration, the exterior and interior of this historic inn fairly gleam. Colonial-era antiques furnish the common rooms as well as the guestrooms. Fireplaces grace the *Kipling Library,* with its floor-to-ceiling bookcases, and the lobby.

The inn offers 66 guestrooms, 14 of them in the main inn, 22 in *Homestead* and *Windham Cottages* across the street, 29 in six guesthouses located in the village, and one in a honeymoon cottage. All the rooms are charming, with colonial-style fabrics and antique furnishings; all but four have private baths. Nearly half the rooms have four-poster or canopy beds so high that step stools are set by them, and ten have private porches. The room rate includes a breakfast buffet of fresh fruit, muffins, bagels, cold and hot cereal, and yogurt.

The dining room, here, is noted for its fine fare. Among the traditions are Grafton garlic cheddar and ale soup and New England lobster pie, but the chef also has added lighter options to the menu such as grilled sesame chicken and halibut filet. For light meals—or a sampling of more than a dozen Vermont ales–there's also the *Phelps Barn Pub,* the restored original barn. Sofas are positioned near the pub's downstairs fireplace, and a loft contains a game and TV lounge with another fireplace. Entertainment—perhaps jazz, country music, or Old English ballads—takes place here nightly.

Guests may enjoy such local pleasures as a stroll of museum-like Grafton, with its stately old homes; blacksmith shop; exhibits of old tools, carriages, and photos at the *Windham Foundation Center;* the *Grafton Historical Society Museum* and the *Grafton Museum of Natural History;* and numerous craft, art, and antique shops. Visitors may watch cheese being made (and purchase it, too) at the Grafton Village Cheese Company. Other activities include swimming in the inn's pond, cross-country skiing, tennis, fly-fishing, and downhill skiing nearby.

OLD TAVERN AT GRAFTON Grafton, VT 05146 (phone: 802-843-2231; 800-843-1801; fax: 802-843-2245). This Georgian-era inn has 66 guestrooms (62 with private baths) with twin and queen-size beds. Wheelchair accessible. Closed April and *Christmas Day.* Rate for a double room (including continental buffet breakfast) weekends: $79 to $220; midweek: $95. Rate for entire guesthouses (with four to seven rooms each): $460 to $510. Two-night minimum stay holiday weekends. MasterCard and Visa accepted. Children welcome. No pets. Smoking permitted in the *Phelps Barn Pub* only. Tom List II, innkeeper.

DIRECTIONS: From I-91 traveling north, take Exit 52 in Bellows Falls. Bear right off the exit ramp; at the end of the access road turn left onto Route 5. Travel 5 miles to a traffic light. Turn left onto Route 121 west and continue 12 miles to Grafton. The inn is in the center of town.

RABBIT HILL INN

LOWER WATERFORD, VERMONT

Just above the meandering Connecticut River in the hamlet of Lower Waterford, with the White Mountains as its backdrop, the *Rabbit Hill Inn* sits on a village green that has changed little in 150 years. With its steepled Congregational church, tiny post office, honor-system library, and cluster of restored homes, the village is so perfectly preserved it feels as if time has stood still. Consequently, it is one of the most photographed towns in Vermont.

The inn is composed of two restored buildings—the Jonathan Cummings home, dating from 1825, and Samuel Hodby's 1795 tavern. Polished wide-plank pine floors and fireplaces are found in the common rooms. Outside are spacious porches and decks furnished with antique wicker. Across the manicured lawns and past the flower garden is a charming gazebo.

It's obvious that innkeepers John and Maureen Magee love the history of their inn and the surrounding countryside. The 21 guestrooms are named for people who had a connection with the place, and they're furnished accordingly. For example, a Victorian dressing-room suite on the top floor of the old tavern is furnished with hatboxes, bonnets, and letters of the period, and Victorian clothing hangs in the wardrobe. The guestrooms' priceless antiques, canopied and four-poster beds, fireplaces, and balconies are enhanced by such modern creature comforts as individual stereo systems, in-room coffee makers, and terry robes. The "Fantasy Suites" are outfitted with Jacuzzis, glassed-in showers, fireplaces, separate dressing areas, and numerous extras.

To complete guests' immersion in the Federal era, candles light the common and dining rooms at night. The Federal-period parlor in the main inn is decorated with period antiques and original oil paintings, as is the sitting room, where guests also will find a collection of 8,000 hand-cut mahogany puzzles and unusual gameboards. The video den, with the inn's only television, contains an extensive videocassette library (bowls of freshly popped popcorn are available on request). The *Snooty Fox Pub* is a convivial spot to enjoy an aperitif.

A stay at the *Rabbit Hill Inn* includes a four-course breakfast, afternoon tea, and dinner (also open to non-guests), and the food is certainly one of the highlights. Dinner, by the expert hand of chef Russell Stannard, may include an appetizer of smoked chicken and sweet potato pie with pecans and dried apples; an entrée of beef tenderloin with blue goat cheese, oregano sauce, and rosemary-garlic noodles; and the inn's specialty dessert, chocolate bourbon pecan pie. Heart-healthy menu items are provided as well. Live chamber music accompanies the meal, frequently with Maureen, a music teacher, performer, and arranger, playing the flute.

In summer, guests enjoy croquet, horseshoes, shuffleboard, a pond for swimming, fishing and canoeing on the river, and hiking trails that lead over bridges spanning a stream and past meadows of grazing cows. There are snowshoes and toboggans for winter entertainment. Nearby are golf courses, *Franconia Notch State Park,* and downhill and cross-country skiing.

RABBIT HILL INN Rte. 18 and Pucker St., Lower Waterford, VT 05848 (phone: 802-748-5168; 800-76-BUNNY; fax: 802-748-8342). This luxurious country inn has 21 guestrooms with private baths and twin, queen-, or king-size beds; 17 of the rooms have air conditioning. Wheelchair accessible. Closed April and the first two weeks in November. Rate for a double room (including full breakfast, afternoon tea, and dinner): $179 to $269; bed and breakfast: $139 to $229. Two-night minimum stay

on weekends. Major credit cards accepted. Not appropriate for children under 12. No pets. One cat, Zeke, in residence. No smoking. John and Maureen Magee, innkeepers.

DIRECTIONS: Traveling north on I-89, take Exit 44 to Route 18. Follow Route 18 north for 2 miles. The inn is on the left. From I-91 north take Exit 19 to I-93 south. Then take Exit 1 to Route 18 south and follow this for 7 miles. The inn is on the right.

GOVERNOR'S INN

LUDLOW, VERMONT

Built as a summer home by Vermont governor William Wallace Stickney in the 1890s, the Victorian mansion known as the *Governor's Inn* retains much of its former elegance. Exquisite examples of stained glass grace the tea alcove, the parlor, and the second- and third-floor stair landings. Unusual marbleized slate fireplaces warm the parlor and the front hall.

Charlie and Deedy Marble, who have owned the inn since 1982, have decorated the rooms with family heirlooms and original art. All of the eight guestrooms have antique beds—burled walnut in one, a brass four-poster in another. Private baths with a variety of amenities reflect the innkeepers' thoughtful attention to guest comfort. There's also a "welcome to the inn" gift, a cordial and chocolates at turndown time, and a box of maple-sugar candy at departure. A stay, here, is not just a night in the country. It's an unforgettable and romantic experience.

As lovely as the common rooms and guestrooms are, the inn also is renowned for its food. Both Charlie and Deedy are accomplished cooks:

Charlie is the breakfast chef, and Deedy prepares dinner. She's won too many awards to list, but it would be wise to fast for several days prior to a visit in order to savor all the culinary pleasures here.

Plan to arrive no later than 3 PM for afternoon tea, an array of perfect little sandwiches and delectable pastries served on silver trays and antique china. Deedy has several interesting collections she loves to share with her guests. At dinner, she pours coffee from one of her Limoges chocolate pots, and some of her 110 knife rests also are used.

Dinner guests gather in the den for hors d'oeuvres and cocktails at 6 PM. At 7 they are escorted to their tables by waitresses clad in Victorian dresses. The candlelit tables are set with antique bone china and silver. Deedy describes the menu as soon as the guests are seated, then fully describes each dish again as the six courses are presented. An appetizer might consist of mushrooms in puff pastry or sherried apricot soup; perhaps the nightly entrée will be potato-wrapped salmon or lobster in brandy-cream sauce. Desserts are equally innovative. Dinner is also open to non-guests.

The next morning Charlie's five-course breakfast starts with coffee and a mimosa delivered to the room. You may have apple pie for breakfast, just as our colonial ancestors did, or a three-cheese soufflé served in puff pastry. If you've saved room—or run 20 miles after breakfast—order one of Deedy's picnic baskets to take on a hike through the forest. Even if you don't picnic, you'll get one of the unique baskets when you leave. Made with handles that fold down, they become a table after the food has been removed.

Throughout the year the Marbles sponsor "Culinary Magic Cooking Seminars," during which Deedy shares her secrets. A box of recipe cards is for sale at all times. Other special events include an antiques extravaganza, a weekend in September when guests are taken to a farm to select their *Christmas* tree (it will later be cut and shipped to them), and an apple-picking weekend. Downhill and cross-country skiing, hiking, summer theater, and antiquing are all available in the area.

GOVERNOR'S INN 86 Main St., Ludlow, VT 05149 (phone: 802-228-8830; 800-GOVERNOR). This inn has eight guestrooms with private baths, twin, double, or queen-size beds, and air conditioning. Open year-round. Rate for a double room (including full breakfast, afternoon tea, and dinner): $170 to $325; with full breakfast and afternoon tea only: $95 to $265. Two-night minimum stay on weekends during fall foliage season and at *Christmas.* MasterCard and Visa accepted. Not appropriate for children under nine. No pets. No smoking. Charlie and Deedy Marble, innkeepers.

DIRECTIONS: Traveling north on I-89, take Exit 6 to Route 103 north. Ludlow is located at the junction of Route 103 and Route 100. The inn is just off the village green on Route 103.

1811 HOUSE

MANCHESTER VILLAGE, VERMONT

Except for the brief period when Mary Lincoln Isham, President Lincoln's granddaughter, used it as a residence, this house has been a wayside inn since it was built in the 1770s. Purchased by Marnie and Bruce Duff in 1990, it has been meticulously restored to its Federal-period style: Twelve-over-twelve windows and clapboard siding characterize the structure. Located in a charming historic village with broad, tree-lined streets, marble sidewalks, and magnificent vintage houses, the *1811 House,* listed on the National Register of Historic Places, sits on seven and one-half acres with views of the surrounding mountains. Its landscaped gardens—including a pond, colorful flower beds, and a rose garden–are all carefully tended by Bruce.

The inn's rooms are filled with authentic English and American antiques and Oriental rugs, giving guests the opportunity to stay in a living museum, yet one that encourages relaxation and comfort. Chinese porcelain lamps and sterling and china objets d'art grace polished mahogany tables. Original oils and drawings line the walls.

A roaring fire in the library/gameroom attracts guests for a game of chess, but the hub of the inn is the dark-beamed pub. The windows are draped with the MacDuff family tartan, and a pewter collection, gleaming brass horns, pub tables, and a regulation dart board add to the thoroughly British atmosphere. You know this is the real thing when you see the choice of 46 single-malt whiskies and the Scottish ale on tap. A downstairs recreation room houses pool and Ping-Pong tables.

There are 14 guestrooms, some with fireplaces, each with a private bath. Lace-canopied four-poster beds, exquisite Persian rugs, stenciling, and fine fabrics decorate the rooms.

Marnie used to be a cooking teacher, and not surprisingly, breakfast is one of the highlights of a stay here. Vermont products such as Harrington ham and Cabot cheddar cheese are featured, as are herbs and edible flowers from the Duffs' own gardens. The meal is served on fine china with Georgian sterling silver and fine old linen. A typical breakfast might include fresh-squeezed juice, fruit, home-baked breads, and an entrée such as French toast or a casserole served with homemade chicken-sausage patties.

Several excellent golf courses are in the area, as are tennis, fly fishing, and skiing. Also nearby are a tony factory-outlet village and a number of historic attractions, including *Hildene,* the former home of Robert Todd Lincoln.

1811 HOUSE Rte. 7A, PO Box 39, Manchester Village, VT 05254 (phone: 802-362-1811; 800-432-1811; fax: 802-362-2443). This historic inn has 14 guestrooms with private baths, double, queen-, or king-size beds, and air conditioning. Closed one week prior to *Christmas.* Rate for a double room (including full breakfast): $110 to $200. Two-night minimum stay on weekends; three nights on holidays and during fall foliage season. Major credit cards accepted. Not appropriate for children under 16. No pets. Heath and Heather, two cats "who love guests," in residence. No smoking. Bruce and Marnie Duff, innkeepers.

DIRECTIONS: Traveling north on Route 7 in Vermont, exit at Manchester Center. Turn left at the bottom of the ramp and travel through town to Route 7A. Turn left onto 7A south. The inn is 1.2 miles away, at the monument in Manchester Village.

INN AT ORMSBY HILL

MANCHESTER VILLAGE, VERMONT

During the early 1900s, Manchester Village was the hub of a glittering social scene. Here, Robert Todd Lincoln, President Lincoln's only child to survive to adulthood, built his glorious estate, *Hildene,* overlooking the Battenkill River. One of Lincoln's law partners, Edward Swift Isham, adapted a 1790s farmhouse into his own grand estate in 1890, creating the manor house now known as the *Inn at Ormsby Hill.* It is believed that Isham was the first to call the house "Ormsby Hill," after Captain Gideon Ormsby of the Green Mountain Boys. The inn supposedly offered refuge to Ethan Allen when he was fleeing the British. A "secret" room is still here, so be sure to ask to see it. Sometime during Isham's stewardship, President Taft was a visitor.

Since 1991 the inn has taken on a new look: New siding, new paint, new porches, a sunny conservatory overlooking newly landscaped gardens, polished floors, beautiful antiques, fireplaces, and whirlpool tubs. Yet the core of this magnificent home is still the original 1790 keeping room with its huge kitchen fireplace. Today, this room and two others are comfortable sitting rooms.

The 10 guestrooms are enormous. Nine have working fireplaces and antique queen- or king-size (they've been enlarged) four-poster or canopy beds with step stools to reach them. The rooms are decorated with tasteful chintz bed drapes, down comforters, bouquets of fresh flowers, upholstered chairs or love seats, and antique desks; all have views of the surrounding mountains. Isham's former library (now one of the guestrooms) retains the rich, clubby look of a man's den: It has a fireplace, bookcases line three sides of the room, and all the wood is painted a creamy white. The *Taft Room* has a fireplace, a canopy bed, and a private breakfast room. Its bath contains a whirlpool, a bidet, and an ample stall shower. All the bathrooms have heat lamps, hair dryers, and terry robes. At press time, the new owners were in the process of redecorating the entire inn.

A four-course breakfast is served in the conservatory with bow-shaped windows at the end of the room, wainscoted ceilings, and a spectacular carved walnut fireplace. In the past, the menu has featured such crowd pleasers as fresh strawberries and blueberries with almond cream sauce, homemade breads, and herbed eggs with Vermont ham and browned new potatoes.

Don't miss the clever gift shop on the second floor, where local crafts are displayed.

Guests who enjoy golf, fishing, or skiing will find facilities nearby. Others may prefer a visit to *Hildene* (Robert Todd Lincoln's home is now a historic house museum), the *Dorset Playhouse,* or some of the area's many art galleries and discount outlets (Christian Dior and Giorgio Armani, among others).

INN AT ORMSBY HILL Historic Rte. 7A, RR2, PO Box 3264, Manchester Village, VT 05255 (phone: 802-362-1163). This Federal-style inn just outside historic Manchester Village has 10 guestrooms with private baths, double, queen-, or king-size beds, and air conditioning. Closed April. Rate for a double room (including full breakfast): $95 to $205. Two-night minimum stay on weekends and during fall foliage season. Major credit cards accepted. Not appropriate for children under 10. No pets. Keeley, a keeshond, and Maxi, a cat, in residence. Smoking permitted outside only. Ted and Chris Sprague, innkeepers.

DIRECTIONS: Traveling north on Route 7 in Vermont, take Exit 3 (Arlington/Manchester Village) onto Route 7A toward Manchester. Follow Route 7A north. The inn is on the right, 2.3 miles north of the *Basket Barn* store and before Manchester Village.

SWIFT HOUSE INN

MIDDLEBURY, VERMONT

When Andrea and John Nelson purchased this inn in 1985, they embarked on an extensive renovation project—not the first that this sophisticated spot has seen in its lifetime. The main house was built by Samuel Swift in 1815 and later became the home of Vermont governor John W. Stewart, who moved to the house when his daughter Jessica was five years old. Jessica became a Swift when she married the builder's grandson, and she lived in the house until she died at the age of 110 in 1981. Over the years a carriage house and a Victorian gatehouse were added to the three-and-a-half-acre property. Today each of these buildings, set amid formal gardens that contain more than 200 rosebushes and are terraced by low stone walls, contains guestrooms or suites.

The main house has five common rooms, including a formal dining room with cherry paneling and a marble fireplace. The elegant parlors, in shades of peach and buttercup, are furnished with Queen Anne antiques and reproductions, architectural renderings and paintings of the house, and English chintz. Oriental rugs cover the oak and maple floors.

The 21 guestrooms are equally elegant, especially in the main house, where the lavishly draped rooms have antique four-poster or canopy beds, fine armoires, exquisite antique desks and chests, fireplaces, and private balconies. The *Swift Room,* for example, has a cherry canopy bed with an eyelet spread, a fireplace, and a private terrace; the *Governor's Room* also has a fireplace, an antique armoire, and is decorated in a handsome marine blue. The *Addison Room* contains a quilt handed down through Andrea's family. Baths in the main house maintain their old-fashioned quality with claw-foot tubs and pedestal sinks. The *Carriage House,* which was renovated in 1990, offers spacious rooms with new baths that include Jacuzzis, plus a sauna and steamroom that are especially popular after a day on the ski slopes. The *Gatehouse,* a splendid turreted Victorian that overlooks busy Route 7, has a porch furnished with antique wicker, Tennessee rockers, and an old buckboard. The Victorian atmosphere carries inside with fretwork and period chandeliers and furniture. Here, the guestrooms are more whimsically decorated: No. 32 is pretty in shades of pink, for example, and No. 35 has purple walls.

Candlelit dinners (also open to the public) are served nightly in the dining rooms and on a pretty side porch. The menu features Vermont products. Appetizers might include smoked Maine salmon with an endive-and-radicchio salad dressed with watercress aiole and croustades; the entrée might be pan-seared pork tenderloins with a sauce of Vermont cheddar and ale, served with fruit compote. For dessert, try Andy's famous coffee toffee pecan torte. A continental breakfast is included in the room rate, but a full breakfast is available for an additional charge.

Guests enjoy visiting Middlebury, a delightful college town with exceptional craft and art galleries. Don't miss the *Frog Hollow Vermont State Craft Center,* where Vermont's finest artisans sell their wares. Skiing, hiking, and golf also are nearby, as are the *Morgan Horse Farm* and the *Sheldon Museum.*

SWIFT HOUSE INN 25 Stewart La., Middlebury, VT 05753 (phone: 802-388-9925; fax: 802-388-9927). In historic Middlebury, this inn has 21 guestrooms with private baths, twin, double, queen-, or king-size beds, telephones, and air conditioning. Wheelchair accessible. Open year-round; dining room closed Tuesdays and Wednesdays. Rate for a double room (including continental breakfast): $85 to $155. Children welcome. No pets. Smoking permitted except in the dining room and some guestrooms. Andrea and John Nelson, innkeepers.

DIRECTIONS: Via Route 7, Middlebury is 30 miles north of Rutland and 35 miles south of Burlington. The inn is two blocks north of the village green, on the corner of Stewart Lane and Route 7.

FOUR COLUMNS INN

NEWFANE, VERMONT

This place calls to mind the era when people took leisurely vacations in the country to enjoy the fresh air, stroll in the woods, and spend long quiet afternoons reading beside a picturesque stream. The *Four Columns Inn* aims to appeal to those who appreciate the beauty of the outdoors and are searching for what innkeepers Jacques and Pam Allembert call "a relaxing interlude in a less complicated world."

The inn's stately white Greek Revival facade, with the four Ionic columns that give it its name, are visible from the common of the sleepy New England village of Newfane. Originally a private home, the main building was built in the 1930s by General Pardon Kimball, who selected the architectural style to remind his wife of her childhood home in the South.

Today, the main house is the site of 10 guestrooms and there are another six in the adjacent converted barn. Both the guestrooms and the public rooms are decorated with an eclectic collection of Colonial and Victorian antiques, but the overall effect is one of easy elegance and comfort. One large suite in the main house features original wood plank floors and pocket doors, a large four-poster bed, a Jacuzzi, and French and Victorian antiques, including a "swooning chair." All the rooms are spacious, and the suites would be comfortable for a week-long stay—one has 1½ baths, and the largest has a separate dressing room that may be used as a child's room. Two guestrooms have fireplaces. The common rooms include a charming sitting room with a fireplace, and the small *Tavern Room,* which features a pewter-topped bar.

The dining room is open to non-guests and is know for its fine gourmet dinners. The menu changes regularly, but always emphasizes local food products. A meal might begin with fennel, spinach, and acorn squash soup or country pâté made with pistachios, apricots, and cognac. Among the excellent main courses that have been offered in the past are grilled pheasant with ginger raspberry sauce and currants, grilled sirloin steak with a cream, cognac, and peppercorn sauce, and venison chops with a juniper demiglace. Pear tart and chocolate pâté might be among the dessert offerings, all of which are made on the premises. The cozy, candlelit dining room has a large fireplace and is decorated with copper pots, old farm implements, and other country antiques. Continental breakfast features fresh fruit, cereal, and homemade muffins and pastry.

Although this is not the spot for folks seeking lots of excitement or lively nightlife, nature lovers and those who enjoy the quiet pleasures of strolling, cycling, swimming, or simply sitting in a garden beneath a shady tree can while away many pleasant hours here. The inn property consists of 150 acres of wooded land—especially beautiful in the fall—that guests may hike through. Also on the grounds are a pool, a brook, a pond, and gardens bursting with color.

Activities available nearby include downhill and cross-country skiing in winter. Another popular attraction is the *Marlboro Music Festival,* held in July or August in the town of Marlboro, about a half-hour's drive from the inn. For visitors looking for some help with their itineraries, Jacques is always available at breakfast time to offer some suggestions.

FOUR COLUMNS INN 230 West St., PO Box 278, Newfane VT 05154 (phone: 802-365-7713). In the quiet village of Newfane, this inn has 11 guestrooms and five suites with private baths and queen- or king-size beds and telephones. Closed April; dining room closed Tuesdays except during fall foliage season. Rate for a double room during fall foliage season (including breakfast and dinner): $200 to $275. Rate for a double room the rest of the year (including continental breakfast): $100 to $175. Additional guest in a double room: $25 per night. American Express, MasterCard, and Visa accepted. Children welcome. Pets welcome (additional charge of $10 per night). One dog in residence. No smoking. Jacques and Pam Allembert, innkeepers.

DIRECTIONS: From Boston, take the Mass Pike to I-91 north. Get off at Brattleboro (Exit 2) and take a left onto Route 9 east (Western Ave.). Drive 6 miles and take a left on Cedar Street and then a right onto Route 30 at the stop sign. Continue 11 miles to Newfane and take a right on West Street. The inn is just off the town common, behind the courthouse.

From New York and New Jersey, take the New York Thruway to Albany (Exit 23). After the toll, take the 1-787 bypass to Route 7. In Bennington get on Route 9 east and continue to Wilmington. Go left on Route 100 north and after 4 miles take a right on Dover Road and proceed to South Newfane. Take a left at the stop sign for Route 30 and a left to Newfane, then follow the directions above.

INN AT SHELBURNE FARMS

SHELBURNE, VERMONT

This inn, set on 1,400 hilltop acres overlooking Lake Champlain, was for many years a Vanderbilt family retreat. The imposing brick turn-of-the-century Queen Anne mansion was built in 1886 by railroad baron Dr. William Seward Webb and his wife, Lila Vanderbilt Webb. It sits high on the hill amid lawns and gardens designed by Frederick Law Olmsted, who was assisted in the selection of trees by Gifford Pinchot, founder of the *US Forest Service.*

The manor house shares the property with *Shelburne Farms,* a nonprofit educational and working farm where Brown Swiss cows produce the milk from which the farm makes its renowned creamy Vermont cheddar. Even the livestock was beautifully housed in the Vanderbilts' day: The massive *Farm Barn,* where 80 teams of carriage horses once were quartered, resembles a French château, with an interior courtyard and turreted brick walls.

Past the barn, some two miles farther up the driveway, is the inn itself. The mansion counts among its treasures elaborate oak paneling, arched doorways, common rooms with six massive fireplaces, and family portraits. Lila Vanderbilt's gardening books are still in the library. The Vanderbilt era lives on in such details as the original chandeliers, sconces, and bathroom fixtures, even as the inn is updated with modern creature comforts.

The 24 guestrooms (most with private baths) retain exquisite Vanderbilt and Webb antiques—including canopy beds, armoires, and elaborate dressers—in their original settings. *Frederica's Room* (the Webbs' daughter's bedroom) still holds her bookcases filled with books, her carved canopy bed with its horsehair mattress, a pink satin striped chaise, and an ornate bureau; a wall of windows overlooks the terraced gardens with Lake Champlain and the mountains beyond. The bath includes its original claw-foot tub and double pedestal sink. The *Brown Room* contains a stunning 10-piece suite of marquetry furniture. Even the rooms on the third floor, once the children's quarters, are large and very special (some share baths). The light and pretty *White Room* has a coffered ceiling, a half-canopied bed with a pink satin bedskirt, wicker furniture, and a long hallway to an enormous private bath with a claw-foot tub.

Guests enjoy afternoon tea in the sunny parlor in the north wing, just as the Webbs did. Breakfast and dinner (open to the public) are served in the dining room, which retains its marble floor, spectacular carved ceiling, and a massive white marble, claw-footed serving buffet. The 13 tables are laid with heirloom silver, pretty china, and crystal—a fitting setting for the impressive meals. Appetizers might include puff pastry with a sauté of wild mushrooms, marjoram, and lemon or a salad of Miskell tomatoes grown at the farm. Entrées include roasted rack of Vermont lamb with fennel purée and grilled filet of beef tenderloin with a Tennessee bourbon and rosemary sauce. An extensive selection of wines is available. Picnic lunches are prepared for guests by request. No meals are included in the room rate.

Guests may enjoy a 90-minute tour in an open wagon to the *Farm Barn* to watch cheese being made; children delight in collecting eggs and petting farm animals there. The tour also passes the *Dairy Barn,* the *Coach Barn,* and the inn's spectacular gardens. Just beyond the front gates is a gift shop purveying cheeses, jams, and maple syrup.

A tennis court, a beach, rowboat, kayak, and canoes also are on site, and summer concerts frequently are held on the grounds. Among the nearby attractions is the *Shelburne Museum,* which occupies 37 buildings on 45 acres and contains one of the country's finest collections of Americana—everything from hats and quilts to a grand private railroad car. Also in the area are the *Morgan Horse Farm* and *Ben and Jerry's Ice Cream Factory* (where tours and samples are offered).

INN AT SHELBURNE FARMS c/o Shelburne Farms, Shelburne, VT 05402 (phone: 802-985-8498; fax: 802-985-8123). This manor house and farm on Lake Champlain has 24 guestrooms (17 with private baths) with twin, double, or queen-size beds, and telephones. Closed mid-October to mid-May. Rate for a double room: $90 to $275. Two-night minimum stay on weekends. Major credit cards accepted. Children welcome. No pets. Farm animals on property. No smoking. Kevin G. O'Donnell, director.

DIRECTIONS: From I-89, take Exit 13 in Burlington and drive south on Route 7 for approximately 5 miles. Turn right at the stop light in the center of Shelburne. Drive 1⅗ miles to the entrance of *Shelburne Farms.* Turn left through the stone gate beside the *Visitors' Center* and follow signs for 2 miles up the driveway to the inn.

ROWELL'S INN

SIMONSVILLE, VERMONT

Established in 1820 as a stagecoach stop, this venerable inn presides over a bend in Route 11 between Londonderry and Chester beside Lyman Brook. Restored by innkeepers Lee and Beth Davis, its five guestrooms and five common rooms are brimming with antiques and oddities that always offer small surprises, even for its many repeat visitors.

The inn, on the National Register of Historic Places, boasts broad brick walls and expansive porches lined with rockers. The lobby/parlor, which formerly served as Simonsville's stagecoach stop, general store, and post office, contains photographs of the inn and of visitors who stayed here in the 1920s.

Overlooking the Green Mountains, the library features a fireplace, built-in bookcases, wing chairs, and custom-woven English carpets. The inviting *Tavern Room,* in a 1790s farmhouse, offers a selection of English ales, porters, and stouts, as well as an old-fashioned soda fountain; a toasty wood stove and a moose head complete the picture. In the afternoon an array of cheeses, hors d'oeuvres, cookies, and teas is served in the sunroom. Guests often spill out onto the slate patio with its Adirondack chairs to watch the goings-on at the bird feeder.

Guestrooms (some with fireplaces) feature brass beds and Oriental rugs. Pedestal basins, claw-foot tubs, and heated towel bars enhance the baths. Two suites have been carved out of the top-floor ballroom. Room No. 1, on the second floor, has a wood-burning fireplace and a bath with a deep tub.

Dinners at *Rowell's Inn* (open to the public by reservation) are five-course meals featuring Yankee fare. Selections include roast chicken, a New England boiled dinner, and such traditional desserts as chocolate cake, bread pudding, and apple pie. A full breakfast is served to guests.

Hiking, biking, downhill and cross-country skiing, golf, tennis, fishing, and theaters are all nearby.

ROWELL'S INN RR1, Box 267-D, Simonsville, VT 05143 (phone: 802-875-3658; fax: 802-875-3680). In the mountains of central Vermont, this inn has five guestrooms with private baths and twin, double, queen-, or king-size beds; most have air conditioning. Closed April through mid-May and the first two weeks of November. Rate for a double room (including full breakfast, afternoon tea, and dinner): $140 to $160; bed and breakfast (available Sundays through Thursdays mid-November through March): $90 to $110. Two-night minimum stay on weekends. MasterCard and Visa accepted. Not appropriate for children under 12. No pets. Smoking in designated areas only. Beth and Lee Davis, innkeepers.

DIRECTIONS: From I-91 take Exit 6 at Bellows Falls and drive north on Route 103 to Chester. Turn west onto Route 11 and travel 7 miles to Simonsville.

EDSON HILL MANOR

STOWE, VERMONT

Serenely situated on a hilltop surrounded by 225 acres of forest laced with hiking, horseback-riding, and groomed cross-country ski trails, *Edson Hill Manor* is truly an inn for all seasons.

As guests wind up the driveway past the inn's private riding stables and pond, views of the spacious lawns, abundant flower beds, and secluded pool come into view. The handsome wood-and-brick manor house sits on the hillside, surveying its domain.

Inside, the gracious pine-paneled living room has tapestry-covered chairs and sofas, pine floors covered with Persian rugs, a massive fireplace, elegant oil paintings (including one of the owner's ancestor Sophie Bronfman), and a multitude of books and games. The beams here were originally hewn for Ira and Ethan Allen's barn, a structure that once stood in North Burlington.

The manor house contains nine antiques-filled guestrooms, most with canopy beds and fireplaces. Dormer windows, fabric wall coverings, fireplaces with imported Dutch tile, and goose-down comforters in pretty duvets are typical embellishments. Yet the bathrooms are what leave the most lasting impression. Each has been hand-painted by artist Gail Kiesler with exuberant scenes of flower gardens and playful birds, cats, dogs, and fish. Four carriage houses just up the hill from the manor house contain 16 additional pine-paneled guestrooms, each with a fireplace and hand-crafted Shaker-style furniture.

More whimsical murals adorn the dining room. Painted stone arches frame sponge-painted walls, and the ceiling is painted with beams and ivy to create the illusion of a secluded arbor in Provence. Elegant French provincial furniture and leaded casement windows add to the ambience. A large covered flagstone terrace serves as an additional dining room in summer. Another mural, a pastel garden scene, greets guests in the dining room foyer, and the bar downstairs, which has its own patio, is painted with hunt scenes and stenciled designs. Even more lovely than the painted panoramas are the real views, down to lake and beyond, that can be glimpsed from this hilltop aerie.

A full breakfast and dinner (both open to non-guests) are served on marvelous oversized china hand-painted especially for the inn. The bill of fare at dinner might include fresh salmon wrapped in bacon or a spectacular Cornish game hen.

In addition to horseback riding and cross-country skiing, the inn offers hayrides and carriage rides in summer, and sleigh rides in winter. Nearby, guests will find downhill skiing, mountain biking, golf, and tennis. Stowe's six-mile recreation path is one of the finest in the nation, offering a broad, paved, dedicated roadway that meanders across covered bridges, alongside rushing streams, and through wooded forests.

EDSON HILL MANOR 1500 Edson Hill Road, Stowe, VT 05672 (phone: 802-253-7371; 800-621-0284). A refined 25-guestroom country inn on 225 acres near Vermont's finest ski resorts with private baths, twin, double, queen-, and king-size beds, and telephones. Open year-round. Rate for a double room (including full breakfast and dinner): $190 to $250. Two-night minimum stay during fall foliage season; five-night stay at *Christmastime.* Major credit cards accepted. Children welcome. No pets. Two dogs in residence. No smoking except in bar and on terrace. Eric and Jane Lande, innkeepers.

DIRECTIONS From I-89 take Exit 10 in Waterbury. Travel north on Route 100 for 10 miles to Stowe. In the village, take Route 108 north for 3 miles to Edson Hill Road. Follow Edson Hill Road north for 1½ miles to the entrance to the inn, which will be on the left.

INN AT THE ROUND BARN FARM

WAITSFIELD, VERMONT

The Shakers were masters at finding ingenious solutions to everyday problems, and round barns were one of their most clever inventions. Hay was stored on the top level and pitchforked down into a center manger every day. Cows were then brought into the middle level of the barn, where they were placed in a circle to feed while they were milked. The waste was shoveled through holes down to the lowest level, where waiting carts would carry it out to fertilize the fields.

This particular round barn, built in 1910, is actually a 12-sided structure. Now listed on the National Register of Historic Places, it is one of only 12 round barns still standing in Vermont. Staying at the *Inn at the Round Barn Farm* presents a rare opportunity to appreciate Shaker craftsmanship up close.

We can thank the Simko family, the innkeepers, for the pleasure. When they purchased the 85-acre property in 1987, the barn, as well as the rest of the farm, was almost beyond repair. Now, after their meticulous research and restoration, the 1810 farmhouse contains beautifully decorated guestrooms; the barn is a special setting for weddings, concerts, and meetings, and also serves as gallery space for local artists.

The common rooms are in the farmhouse. To preserve the polished pine floors, guests are asked to remove their shoes upon entering; in winter they are provided with slippers. Guests congregate in the living room/library for coffee in the morning and hors d'oeuvres and sherry in the evening. The gameroom lures guests with a billiards table, board games, and television. Throughout the inn an abundance of fresh flowers suggests the innkeepers' former occupation: florists.

Guestrooms feature wide-plank pine floors, hand-carved moldings, antique chairs and desks, Oriental rugs, fireplaces, and bookcases. The baths are thoroughly modern, with steam showers (several with Jacuzzis), thick towels, terry robes, special soaps and lotions, and lighted makeup mirrors. Turndown service includes warm chocolate-chip cookies.

A full breakfast, prepared by daughter AnneMarie, is served in the solarium overlooking the meadows. It might be Belgian waffles with maple cream or cottage-cheese pancakes with raspberry sauce. Fresh fruit is served in antique cut-glass goblets.

A stone terrace lined with hibiscus and a formal garden make relaxing summer havens. For the energetic, a 60-foot lap pool is located in the lower level of the barn, and the nearby pond is warm enough for summer swimming; it freezes over in winter for ice skating. There are 19 miles of groomed cross-country ski trails on the property, as well as a ski-touring center. Guests can rent skis here, but ski at no additional charge. The *Round Barn* is the site of the *Green Mountain Cultural Center,* where a lively schedule of performing arts, art workshops, and community cultural events take place year-round. There's also plenty of hiking, bicycling, canoeing, golf, tennis, horseback riding, and antiquing in the area.

INN AT THE ROUND BARN FARM **E. Warren Rd., RR1 Box 247, Waitsfield, VT 05673 (phone: 802-496-2276; fax: 802-496-8832). In the Mad River Valley of central Vermont, this inn has 11 guestrooms with private baths and twin, double, queen-, or king-size beds. Closed two weeks in April. Rate for a double room (including full breakfast and evening sherry): $100 to $185. Major credit cards accepted. Not appropriate for children under 14. No pets. A calico cat and two dogs in residence. No smoking. Jack and Doreen Simko, innkeepers; AnneMarie DeFreest, manager.**

DIRECTIONS: From I-89 north take Exit 9 (Moretown/Middlesex) to Route 100 south to Waitsfield. In Waitsfield drive east on Bridge Street, passing through the covered bridge, and travel 1½ miles up East Warren Road to the inn, which is on the left.

INN AT WEATHERSFIELD

WEATHERSFIELD, VERMONT

Situated on 21 acres along a quiet country road, the picturesque *Inn at Weathersfield* is an escape to the past. A private pond for summer dipping and winter ice skating; hiking trails; blackberries, raspberries, and apples to pick; horseback-riding trails; and stalls and pastures for guest horses are among the inn's old-fashioned attractions. Another unique feature is an amphitheater in the forest, often the site of weddings and parties.

Built in 1792 as a four-room farmhouse, the inn building has been expanded and substantially changed over the years, serving at times as a stagecoach stop and a home for elderly women. It has been operating as a hostelry since 1961. When innkeepers Mary Louise and Ron Thorburn purchased the inn in 1979, they utilized their extensive knowledge of history, their 4,000 volume library, and their strong sense of hospitality in creating a special retreat, far removed from the pressures of big-city living. From the moment guests enter the gracious foyer, they are immersed in an authentic colonial ambiance.

Freshly-baked cookies and iced or hot drinks are laid out every afternoon in the foyer, which boasts well-trodden board pine floors, a massive fireplace with a beehive oven, and original paneling and cupboards. Other common rooms are adorned with museum-quality antiques, among them an inlaid chest, an ornately carved secretary, original oil paintings, and elegant silver candlesticks. Massive bouquets of flowers grace all the rooms.

The 12 guestrooms contain equally fine antiques that include four-poster and canopy beds, a Sheraton desk, elegant chests, and armoires. Among the interesting details that lend character to the rooms are stenciled decorations, an unusual needlepoint picture, and ceramic bowls and wastebaskets made by the Thorburn's daughter, a potter.

There are two concert grand pianos in the dining room; Ron is a pianist and singer, and he and another musician perform nightly during dinner. The room, which is lined with floor-to-ceiling bookcases, is lit by soft tapers.

Mary Louise is a noted chef who has won considerable recognition for her cuisine. Dinner might include beef tenderloin filet with walnut and mushroom sauce or baked Vermont trout with mustard-yogurt-dill sauce. Her specialty, *solyanka,* a baked vegetarian dish, receives rave reviews. The comprehensive wine list is also award-winning and an extensive beer list is offered as well. Desserts include a mouth-watering chocolate terrine that combines white and dark chocolate and hazelnuts.

Breakfast (open to non-guests), is served in the *Willow Wood* room off the dining room. The bountiful buffet includes waffles and French toast with locally made syrup, eggs, and breakfast cakes.

On *Thanksgiving* and *Christmas,* the inn hosts memorable celebrations reserved for overnight guests. Everyone dresses in authentic colonial attire, and food is selected and prepared as it would have been in colonial times. The beehive oven is pressed into service, and a groaning board is laid with an array of dishes. *Christmas* festivities include tree decorating, a yule log ceremony, and a *Christmas Eve* service under the stars in the amphitheater.

There are numerous activities at the inn and its vicinity year-round. On property, guests can go on sleigh or carriage rides, picnic beside a babbling brook, bicycle, and play volleyball, croquet, badminton, or horseshoes. In winter, there's ice skating on the pond. A fitness center, numerous board games, a pool table, and a TV lounge offer indoor diversions. Guests also can enjoy golf, boating, and fishing nearby, and the local *Grange Hall* occasionally offers such activities as square dancing accompanied by old-time fiddlers.

INN AT WEATHERSFIELD Rte. 106, Weathersfield, VT 05151 (phone: 802-263-9217; 800-447-4828; fax: 802-263-9219). A historic 12-guestroom country house inn on 21 acres in the Vermont countryside with private baths, twin, queen-, and

king-size beds, and telephones. Open year-round. Rate for a double room (including full breakfast, afternoon tea, and dinner): $175 to $220. Two-night minimum stay weekends year-round; three-night minimum stay holidays. Major credit cards accepted. Children over eight welcome. Pets allowed with prior permission. One dog, Oreo, in residence. No smoking. Ron and Mary Louise Thorburn, Innkeepers.

DIRECTIONS From I-91 take Exit 7 in Springfield. Travel west on Route 11 through Springfield to Route 106 at the shopping center. Continue on Route 106 for five miles. The inn will be on the left, a half mile before Perkinsville.

INN AT SAW MILL FARM

WEST DOVER, VERMONT

Rod and Ione Williams have owned the *Inn at Sawmill Farm* since 1968. From the beginning, Rod's background in architecture, Ione's decorating wizardry, and their combined love of fine food and wine have made the place a model for other innkeepers. Ione has even traveled to other inns to act as an interior design consultant.

Their casual yet sophisticated inn consists of a collection of restored buildings, once a dilapidated barn (now the main inn), a millhouse, a woodshed, a farmhouse, and a cider house. The rooms in the main inn are connected by quaint little hallways and staircases. The public rooms all have beamed ceilings. The bar, which is filled with copper tables and upholstered wing chairs, boasts a cheerful fireplace and walls finished with barn siding. The living room also has a fireplace large enough for an adult to stand in.

The 20 large guestrooms and suites contain four-poster and canopy beds, fireplaces, and antique desks, chests, and chairs. The decor includes quilted spreads, English chintz adorning the windows and chairs, numerous plants, and bookcases filled with books. All have private baths and several have Jacuzzis.

Dinner at the *Inn at Saw Mill Farm* (also open to non-guests) is a very special experience. Brill Williams, who was a teenager when his parents purchased the inn, is now chef and part owner. Try his appetizer of shrimp in beer batter with pungent fruit sauce or his entrée of veal marsala with an eggplant-cheese crêpe. The 36,000-bottle, award-winning wine cellar will satisfy the most sophisticated oenophile.

The 21-acre property includes gardens with a gazebo, a patio, porches, a swimming pool, tennis courts, trout ponds, and groomed cross-country ski trails. It is near the *Mt. Snow, Stratton, Bromley,* and *Magic Mountain* ski areas. There's golf, fishing, and boating in the area. Another popular attraction is the *Marlboro Music Festival,* held in July or August in the town of Marlboro (about an hour's drive from the inn).

INN AT SAW MILL FARM Crosstown Rd., Box 367, West Dover, VT 05356 (phone: 802-464-8131; fax: 802-464-1130). This delightful country inn has 20 guestrooms with private baths, double, queen-, or king-size beds, and air conditioning. Closed mid-April to mid-May. Rate for a double room (including full breakfast, afternoon tea, and dinner): $330 to $400. Major credit cards accepted. Not appropriate for children under 10. No pets. Smoking permitted in common rooms (except the dining room) only. Rodney, Ione, Brill, and Bobbie Dee Williams, innkeepers.

DIRECTIONS: From I-91 traveling north, take Exit 2 in Brattleboro and travel west on Route 9 to Route 100 in Wilmington. Travel 6 miles north on Route 100 to the village of West Dover. Take the first left past the village church; the inn is on the left.

TRAIL'S END—A COUNTRY INN

WILMINGTON, VERMONT

As its brochure states, *Trail's End* is not an old sea captain's house, an authentic Victorian, or a Federal-style mansion; it is a much newer property, decidedly different from other country-style inns. Built in 1956 as a lodge for the nearby *Mt. Snow* ski area, the building was purchased in 1985 by Bill and Mary Kilburn, who transformed it into a 10-acre country haven.

The common rooms are comfortably furnished with family antiques. In the living room, a fieldstone fireplace rises some 15 feet to the cathedral ceiling. Hot cider, cookies, pastries, and fruit are served here, in winter, and, in summer, there's chilled lemonade. The soaring picture windows overlook the property's landscaped grounds and meadows.

Six of the 15 guestrooms feature stone fireplaces, and all have brass, wicker, iron, four-poster, or canopy beds, country antiques, and fluffy comforters. Two romantic suites have stone fireplaces, canopy beds, kitchens, skylights, decks, and whirlpools. All the rooms have private baths, and several have Jacuzzis.

Breakfast is served in the dining room and includes home-baked muffins, eggs, pancakes or waffles with Vermont maple syrup, bacon or sausage, and a choice of coffees. In the afternoon, Mary bakes a cake or cookies to tide her guests over until dinner. During the *Marlboro Music Festival,* held in July or August, she has another batch of goodies waiting for returning guests who, she knows from experience, will be eager to discuss the evening's performance.

A heated pool, a clay tennis court, and a trout pond are all on the property. Skiing, golf, and hiking are nearby.

TRAIL'S END—A COUNTRY INN Smith Rd., Wilmington, VT 05363 (phone: 802-464-2727; 800-859-2585) This inn has 15 guestrooms with private baths and twin or queen-size beds. Closed *Easter Monday* to *Memorial Day.* Rate for a double room (including full breakfast and afternoon refreshments): $90 to $170. Two-night minimum stay on weekends; three nights on holidays. Children welcome. No pets. Madison, a black labrador, in residence. Smoking permitted. Bill and Mary Kilburn, innkeepers.

DIRECTIONS: From I-91 traveling north, take Exit 2 in Brattleboro to Route 9 west. Wilmington is 17 miles from Brattleboro. At the traffic light in Wilmington, take Route 100 north for 4 miles, then turn right and follow the signs to the inn.

JACKSON HOUSE

WOODSTOCK, VERMONT

If the charming town of Woodstock is a reflection of the Rockefellers' commitment to historic preservation, then this inn is certainly a reflection of the similar sensibilities of its owners, Bruce McIlveen and Jack Foster. A gingerbread Victorian painted yellow with white trim, surrounded by exquisite flower gardens, and furnished with equally exquisite antiques, *Jackson House* is a jewel.

Built in 1890 by Wales Johnson, a local sawmill operator, the house exhibits examples of the finest woods milled in Woodstock: polished floors of the high-quality cherry and maple generally reserved for fine furniture, wainscoting of alternating cherry and maple, decorative exterior woodwork hand-crafted for the house. In 1940, the Jackson family purchased the house and began taking in guests. In 1983, it was purchased by Bruce and Jack, who embarked on a massive renovation project.

The 12 guestrooms are decorated with imagination and wit—each in a different style, with the finest antiques, furnishings, and Scalamandre silks. *Francesca,* for example, is an opulent suite in muted champagne and mauve with a queen-size cherry sleigh bed, burgundy sofa, Italian marble bath, and French doors opening to a deck that overlooks the landscaped grounds. *Miss Gloria Swanson,* named after the star who stayed here in 1948, is done in peach and green and contains a bed, bureau, chairs, mirrors, and even a floor of curly and bird's-eye maple.

Stroll the formal gardens, sit on the bench by the pond to read a book, or take a cup of tea to the wicker-furnished front porch. Downstairs in the main house is a spa that contains an exercise room and a steamroom. A wine and champagne bar and a buffet of hors d'oeuvres are offered in the parlor, each evening, and turndown service includes a Godiva chocolate on each pillow.

Bountiful breakfasts are served at an antique Queen Anne mahogany table. Jack is the chef, and he's likely to start the meal with a selection of buttermilk scones, banana bread, and apple–wheat germ muffins as well as fruit—perhaps bananas and cream with toasted almonds. A main course of Santa Fe omelettes with rosemary potatoes, broccoli with lemon butter, and sausage may follow, accompanied by mimosas. The round table facilitates convivial conversation.

Located just outside the quaint village of Woodstock, the inn is near downhill and cross-country skiing, antiquing, horseback riding, and the *Billings Farm Museum.*

JACKSON HOUSE 37 Rte. 4 W., Woodstock, VT 05091 (phone: 802-457-2065; 800-448-1890). This Victorian inn has 12 guestrooms with private baths and twin, double, or queen-size beds and air conditioning. Open year-round. Rate for a double room (including full breakfast and evening wine and hors d'oeuvres): $135 to $250. Two-night minimum stay on weekends and holidays. No credit cards accepted. Not appropriate for children under 14. No pets. One cat and ducks on the property. No smoking. Bruce McIlveen and Jack Foster, innkeepers.

DIRECTIONS: From I-91 traveling north, take Exit 9 to Route 12 north. When Route 12 crosses Route 4, travel west on Route 4 through Woodstock. The inn is located 1½ miles west of the village on the right.

Quebec

MANOIR DES ERABLES

MONTMAGNY, QUEBEC

Serenely situated on four acres, the *Manoir des Erables* stands back from the road, almost obscured from passing travelers. When you arrive, a game of croquet may in be progress on the lawn.

Accommodations are in a variety of buildings, all of which surround a central courtyard with a flower garden and a pool. *Le Manoir* itself, a stately mansion dating from 1812, contains guestrooms with polished hardwood floors and antique furnishings. The common room and dining room are located here, as are three conference rooms. The rooms in *Le Pavillon Collin* also are furnished with antiques, and *Le Motel* is a collection of nine motel rooms, some with whirlpools or saunas. A massive suite has a fireplace and a Jacuzzi.

Owned since 1993 by Jean Cyr, the inn is acclaimed for its fine French fare. Cyr's father, a chef, purchased the inn in 1975 and dedicated himself to promoting Quebecois cuisine. Jean, himself a chef, carries on the tradition. Dinner (also open to non-guests) is a relaxing seven-stage repast that begins with soup, progresses through salad, entrée, and cheese courses, and ends with dessert and coffee. Entrées might include pork medallions with apples or lamb in a port sauce. Following the meal, guests may enjoy a glass of port in the cozy pub. Breakfasts are all-American feasts of bacon, eggs, and toast.

Montmagny is located on the St. Lawrence Seaway, and only a short walk from the inn is an excursion ferry that threads its way through the estuary's 21 islands. Also nearby is the interesting *Centre Educatis des Migrations* (Center of Migration Education), which documents the arrival of millions of Irish immigrants to Quebec in the 19th century. The center also features exhibits on the annual migration of thousands of snow geese to the bird sanctuary on nearby Grosse-Ile. Golf, boating, and downhill skiing also are nearby.

MANOIR DES ERABLES 220 Bd. Taché E. (Rte. 132), Montmagny, QUE G5V 1G5, Canada (phone: 418-248-0100; 800-563-0200; fax: 418-248-9507). On the St. Lawrence Seaway, this inn has 23 guestrooms with private baths, double, queen-, or king-size beds, telephones, and TV sets. Open year-round. Rate for a double room (including full breakfast, dinner, and all gratuities): CN $158 to $283 (US $125 to $224 at press time). Major credit cards accepted. Children welcome. Pets allowed by prior arrangement only. Smoking permitted. Jean Cyr, innkeeper.

DIRECTIONS: From Quebec City cross the seaway and follow Highway 20 east for 36 miles (58 km). Take Exit 376 (Des Poiriers and Montmagny). Follow Route 132 for 1⅓ miles (2 km). The inn is on the right.

AUBERGE HATLEY

NORTH HATLEY, QUEBEC

A retreat in the Quebec countryside may seem as remote to many Americans as a château on the Loire River in France, but North Hatley is only 24 miles from the Vermont border.

Owned by Robert and Liliane Gagnon since 1980, *Auberge Hatley* is a sprawling, gray-shingled, three-story, 30-plus-room house on the shores of Lake Massawippi. Built in 1903 by the Holt family, Canadians with their roots in Scotland, it was then, and is now, an impressive haven. The country French theme of the decor includes antique pine furniture, braided rugs on polished hardwood floors, and bright floral wallpaper. Many of the rooms have Jacuzzis, saunas, fireplaces, and French doors leading to balconies overlooking the lake. Several have four-poster or canopy beds.

Liliane, who once owned an art gallery, has created an octagonal pavilion with a 32-foot ceiling, where the works of Quebec artists are displayed. The living room contains English antiques and leather sofas and chairs, a comfortable spot for reading before the massive brick fireplace or just enjoying the ambience.

As lovely as the rooms are, it's the food that attracts people from miles around. Exotic lettuces, herbs, and edible flowers are grown hydroponically in a spectacular 8,500-square-foot greenhouse. Because of the short local growing season, extensive research went into the construction and maintenance of the greenhouse, which now yields crops in such abundance that the produce itself inspires new recipes.

In a candlelit dining room overlooking Lake Massawippi, dinner (also open to non-guests) is presented with exceptional flair. A meal might start with a *mille-feuille* of salmon and scallops with lime dressing and seaweed, followed by a sliver of Barbary duck leg with fresh foie gras. The extensive wine list, featuring current and collector vintages, will satisfy the most serious oenophile. Desserts are equally impressive. In the morning, a full buffet breakfast is served.

Auberge Hatley is an inn for all seasons. In the spring, there is horseback riding, fishing, and bird watching on the 10-acre grounds. Summer means swimming in the heated pool or a concert on the lawn. The fall foliage season is ideal for hiking and photography, while ice fishing and skiing occupy guests during the winter months.

AUBERGE HATLEY 325 Chemin Virgin, PO Box 330, North Hatley, QUE J0B 2C0, Canada (phone: 819-842-2451; fax: 819-842-2907). On the shores of Lake Massawippi, this inn has 25 guestrooms with private baths, double, queen-, or king-size beds, telephones, and air conditioning. Wheelchair accessible. Closed two weeks in November; lunch served in summer only. Rate for a double room (including full breakfast and dinner): CN $180 to $340 (US $142 to $269 at press time). Major credit cards accepted. Not appropriate for children under 12. No pets. Smoking permitted. Robert and Liliane Gagnon, innkeepers.

DIRECTIONS: Take I-91 from Vermont north to the Canadian border, then continue on Route 55 north for 18 miles (29 km) to Exit 29 (North Hatley). Follow Route 108 east for 6 miles (10 km) to North Hatley, then follow the signs to the inn, which is 1 mile (1.6 km) from the center of the village.

HOVEY MANOR

NORTH HATLEY, QUEBEC

The village of North Hatley was settled by Loyalists who fled America after the Revolutionary War. *Hovey Manor* was named for one of them, Colonel Ebenezer Hovey, who was granted a plot of land by the crown in 1785. After the Civil War, the village became a popular summer retreat for American Southerners, who had formerly summered in New England. Many of the spectacular homes here are remnants of that era. Today, the area is a haven for artists, writers, theater lovers, and sportsmen.

Inspired by *Mt. Vernon,* Henry Atkinson of Atlanta built *Hovey Manor* in 1899. It's a large house with broad verandahs and white columns overlooking Lake Massawippi. Atkinson needed a sizable house: He would arrive for his summer stay with an entourage of 18 servants, 10 horses, and a full housekeeping staff, all packed into two private railway cars and several carriages.

Today *Hovey Manor* is a year-round retreat owned since 1979 by Stephen and Kathy Stafford. The resort is decorated with priceless antiques, many from Atkinson's original collection; spectacular bouquets of fresh flowers abound. Most of the guestrooms have fireplaces, Jacuzzis, antique canopy beds, and balconies with views of the lake, and all have coffee makers. In addition to the 32 guestrooms in the mansion, 10 other rooms are tucked away in the caretaker's residence, the pump house, the icehouse, and the electric house (a former electric plant that has been renovated).

A complimentary full breakfast is served every morning to guests, and an English cream tea is served every afternoon (at additional charge). Dinner (also open to non-guests) is an event, with a menu of French dishes prepared with Asian and Middle Eastern influences (such as duckling with rhubarb galette and caramelized ginger, or lobster and fish with champagne and green papaya salsa). The food is enhanced by herbs and edible flowers from the inn's gardens. Tasting dinners with five or six courses of regional fare (including game in season) also are offered. Classical music often is played on the grand piano for the enjoyment of dinner patrons.

In summer, guests can roam the resort's 25 acres, where they'll find English gardens, lighted tennis courts, a heated pool, a lake with two beaches, and a private dock with canoes, paddleboats, windsurfers, and sailboats, or they might take a jaunt on one of the inn's touring bikes. Cruises to North Hatley and water skiing also are possible (for an additional charge). Also nearby is *The Piggery,* a summer stock theater that mounts productions in English. Wintertime attractions are a skating rink, an ice fishing cabin, and 31 miles of groomed cross-country ski trails. Board games, Ping-Pong, and billiards are available in the *Tap Room,* which occupies the old stables and has a fireplace so large that it took 10,000 bricks to build it. Golf and downhill skiing are nearby.

HOVEY MANOR 575 Hovey Rd. (Rte. 108 E.), Box 60, North Hatley, QUE J0B 2C0, Canada (phone: 819-842-2421; 800-661-2421; fax: 819-842-2248). This manor house resort has 42 guestrooms with private baths, twin, double, queen-, or king-size beds, and telephones. Wheelchair accessible. Open year-round. Rate for a double room (including full breakfast, dinner, and service charges): CN $186 to $396 (US $137 to $289 at press time). Major credit cards accepted. Not appropriate for children under 10. No pets. Smoking permitted, but some guestrooms are designated nonsmoking. Stephen and Kathryn Stafford, innkeepers; Steven G. Beyrouty, manager.

DIRECTIONS: Take I-91 from Vermont north to the Canadian border, then continue on Route 55 north for 18 miles (29 km) to Exit 29 (North Hatley). Follow Route 108 east for 6 miles (10 km) to North Hatley, then follow *Manoir Hovey* signs to the private driveway, which is on the left.

Southern New England

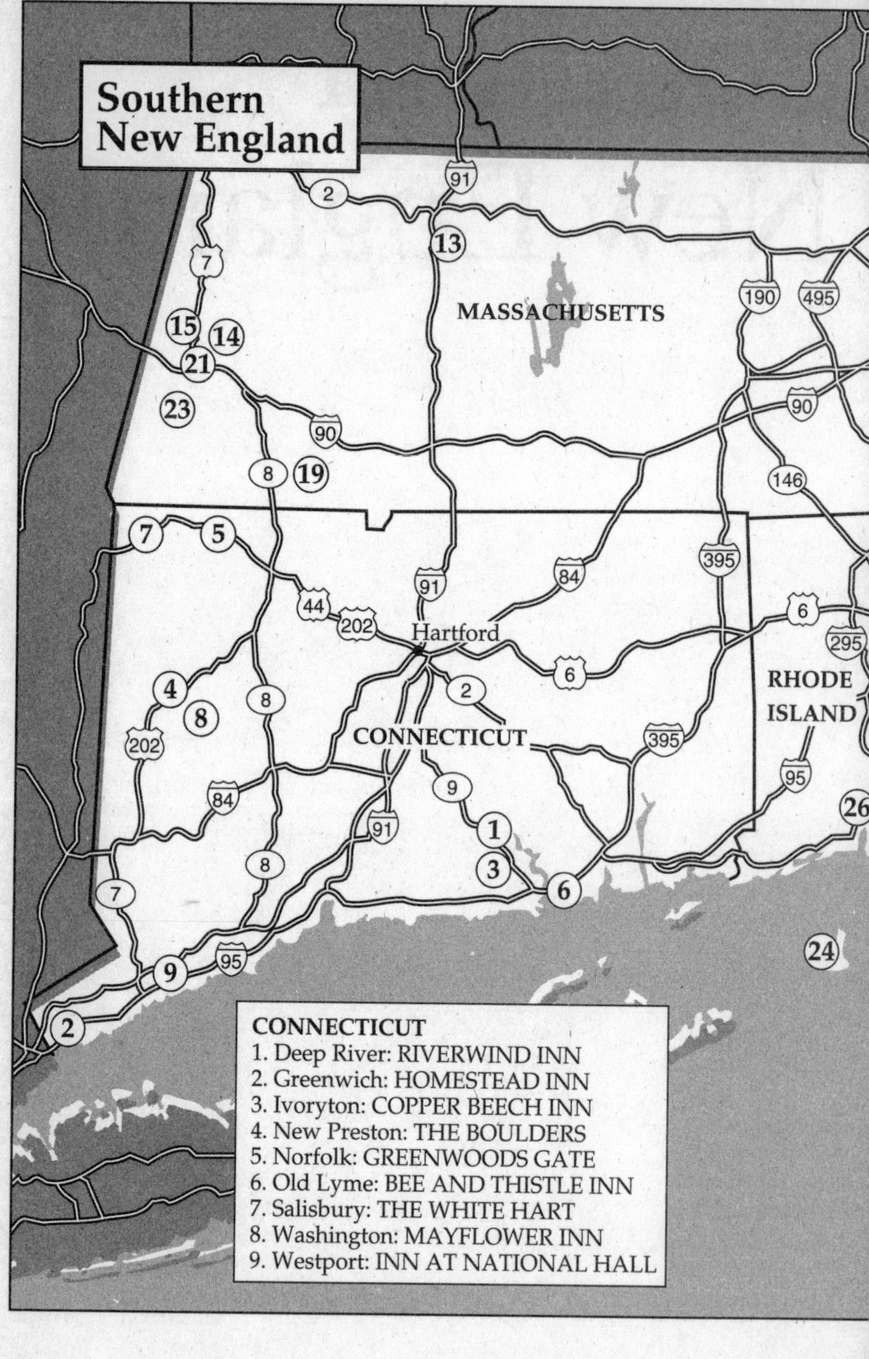
Southern New England
MASSACHUSETTS
CONNECTICUT
RHODE ISLAND
Hartford
CONNECTICUT
1. Deep River: RIVERWIND INN
2. Greenwich: HOMESTEAD INN
3. Ivoryton: COPPER BEECH INN
4. New Preston: THE BOULDERS
5. Norfolk: GREENWOODS GATE
6. Old Lyme: BEE AND THISTLE INN
7. Salisbury: THE WHITE HART
8. Washington: MAYFLOWER INN
9. Westport: INN AT NATIONAL HALL

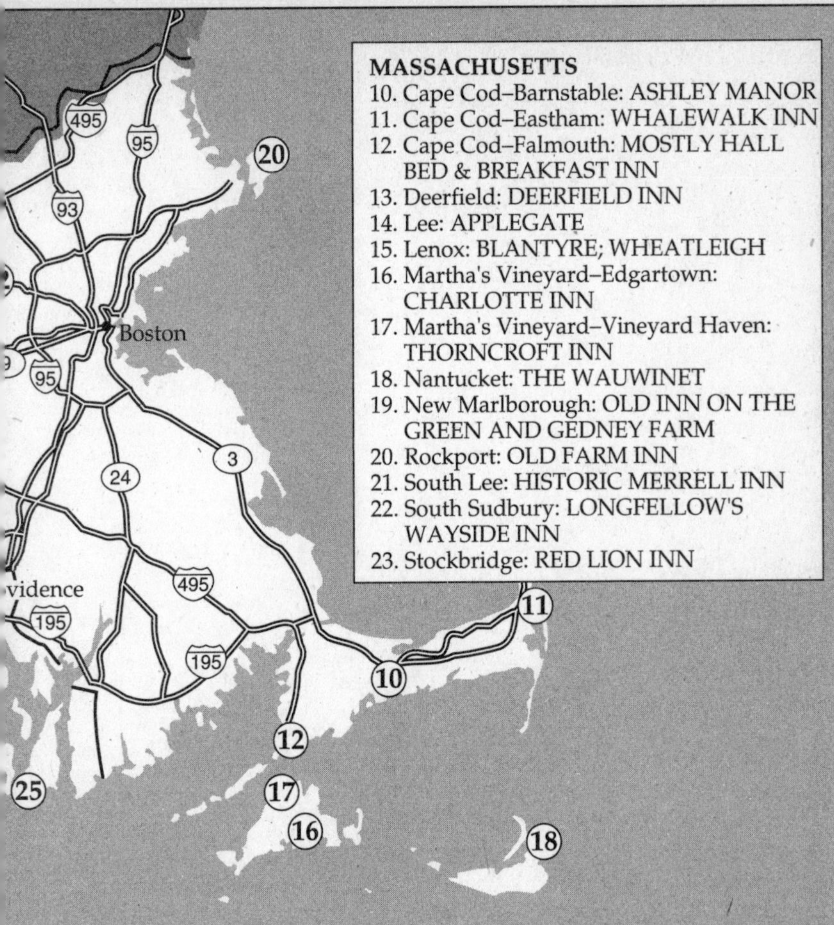

RHODE ISLAND
24. Block Island: 1661 INN & HOTEL MANISSES
25. Newport: ELM TREE COTTAGE; FRANCIS MALBONE HOUSE; IVY LODGE
26. Wakefield: LARCHWOOD INN

tlantic Ocean

0 —— 10 Miles
0 —— 10 Kilometers

Southern New England

Connecticut

RIVERWIND INN

DEEP RIVER, CONNECTICUT

A pink-beige Victorian inn in a hamlet near the Connecticut River, *Riverwind* might best be described as a collection of collections. Strewn among the eight common rooms is enough eclectic folk art to fill a museum. There are flags, quilts, whirligigs, moose heads, baskets, stuffed birds, jugs, doorstops, and pigs—pigs in copper, pigs in tin, pigs on patchwork pillows, pigs on cookie jars—you get the picture. Collections are innkeeper Barbara Barlow's passion, as are pigs.

Barbara discovered the 1850s house in 1983 after moving to the area from Smithfield, Virginia. The building was an abandoned derelict, but she bought it and embarked on a year-long restoration that included installing a kitchen. With its brick walls, open shelves, and hemlock counters, the 20th-century kitchen looks for all the world as if it were plucked from an authentic colonial house. In 1988 Barbara married her contractor, Bob Bucknall, and together they added a new wing. As with the kitchen, "new" is misleading here. The addition is so skillfully integrated into the old house that it looks older than the original. It has wide floorboards, hand-hewn beams, and a massive 12-foot fireplace with Shaker benches positioned close by. In all, there are four fireplaces throughout the inn, and all are lit on chilly days, permeating the house with a heady aroma.

The folk-art theme continues in the eight guestrooms. The *Barn Rose Room* has a canopy bed, sheet music decorating the walls, and a footed tub. The *Willow Room* has an antique maple canopy bed, a bird's-eye and curly maple chest-on-chest, oak chairs, and a private deck. Elegant old laces, fabrics, and a christening dress add to the charm. The *Quilt Room* is a harmonious blend of old and new, with quilts and a blue tile floor. Be aware that the *Havlow Room*'s bath is down the hall.

A full buffet breakfast is served in the dining room on fine china, with an ornate silver coffee service. Selections always include Smithfield ham and hot biscuits in the shape of—what else?—pigs; other dishes might include an egg casserole, fresh fruit, coffee cake, and French toast.

Activities in the area include hiking on marked trails in a nearby 400-acre nature preserve, tennis, golf, and antiquing.

RIVERWIND INN 209 Main St., Deep River, CT 06417 (phone: 203-526-2014). This informal inn in the Connecticut River Valley has eight guestrooms with private baths, double or queen-size beds, and air conditioning. Limited wheelchair accessibility. Open year-round. Rate for a double room (including full buffet breakfast): $95 to $165. Major credit cards accepted. Not appropriate for children under 12. No pets. One cat, Miss Hickory, in residence. Smoking permitted. Barbara Barlow and Bob Bucknall, innkeepers.

DIRECTIONS: From I-95 traveling north, take Exit 69 just before crossing the Connecticut River to Route 9. Follow Route 9 to Exit 4. Turn left onto Route 154. The inn is 1½ miles farther on the right.

HOMESTEAD INN

GREENWICH, CONNECTICUT

Located in a residential neighborhood of elegant estates in one of Connecticut's most exclusive communities, the *Homestead Inn* was built in 1799. It began welcoming guests in 1859, but not until Nancy Smith and Lessie Davison purchased it in 1978, did it acquire an upscale reputation.

It's hard to believe that portions of the Victorian Gothic structure are nearly 200 years old, but if you look closely, remnants of the original square Federal farmhouse are still visible in front. Today, the High Victorian gingerbread is admired most. The large wraparound porch, with its pretty antique furniture, is the kind that invites guests to "sit a spell," and the patio has a murmuring fountain.

Set on a knoll on three acres, surveying orchards, sloping lawns, and gardens, the inn is superbly furnished with period antiques. The seven-drawer Philadelphia cherry chest and 1816 tallboy clock in the front hall are prized treasures.

Guestrooms in the main house retain their historic ambience, right down to the polished pine floors. Those in the outbuildings, such as the cottage and barn, have private porches. Each room is individually decorated with Schumacher and Waverly fabrics, as well as antiques, and includes a queen-size bed or two twins and a thoroughly modern bathroom.

The dining room, known as *La Grange,* is renowned in the area for its French menu and romantic decor, complete with candlelight and flowers. Dinner entrées include duck with black currant sauce and roast Florida red snapper with an asparagus-and-mushroom ragout. For dessert, the triple chocolate cake puts all diets on hold. A continental breakfast of juice, muffins, and coffee is served in the morning.

There is plenty for guests to do in this suburban Connecticut town and the surrounding region—from playing golf or tennis to exploring local beaches and nature preserves, or visiting the many shops and museums.

HOMESTEAD INN 420 Field Point Rd., Greenwich, CT 06830 (phone/fax: 203-869-7500). This sophisticated suburban inn, 45 minutes from New York City, has 23 guestrooms with private baths, twin or queen-size beds, telephones, TV sets, and air conditioning. The dining room is wheelchair accessible. Open year-round. Rate for a double room (including continental breakfast): $137 to $185. Major credit cards accepted. Older children welcome. No pets. Smoking permitted. Lessie Davison and Nancy Smith, innkeepers; Donna Oldford, manager.

DIRECTIONS: From I-95, take Exit 3 in Greenwich. At the traffic light just before the railroad overpass, turn left onto Horseneck Lane. At the next traffic light turn left onto Field Point Road and continue for a quarter mile. The inn is on the right.

COPPER BEECH INN

IVORYTON, CONNECTICUT

Ivoryton put itself on the map in the 19th century by importing elephant tusks from Africa and transforming them into piano keys and combs. Long before the prohibition of the ivory trade, the town's number one industry was wiped out with the depression in the 1920s. Since then, the sleepy hamlet, off the traveled tourist routes, has been best known for its topnotch summer theater, the *Ivoryton Playhouse.*

The *Copper Beech Inn* was built as a private home in the 1880s by the foremost ivory importer, A. W. Comstock. It sits beneath the giant spreading arms of a 200-year-old copper beech tree that shelters it from the sun and rain and inspired the inn's name. The seven acres include both formal and informal gardens, and nearly half the acreage has been carefully retained as natural woodland. There's a sunken side garden, a profusion of plants at the entrance, and a broad variety of evergreen and ornamental trees.

The main floor of the inn houses its acclaimed restaurant as well as a delightful Victorian conservatory with a tile floor, wicker furniture, and an extensive collection of 19th-century botanical and Audubon prints—a lovely spot to sip after-dinner coffee and admire the gardens, which are illuminated at night. The main floor also boasts a notable display of the fine antique Chinese export porcelain collected by the innkeepers, Eldon and Sally Senner; some pieces are offered for sale.

Upstairs are four spacious antiques-furnished guestrooms, authentically restored to colonial charm, with canopy or brass beds and old-fashioned baths with pedestal sinks. In the serenely private carriage house out back, nine more rooms are beautifully furnished with high-quality reproduction four-poster and canopy beds. These rooms have decks overlooking the woodlands, TV sets, and Jacuzzis. Those on the top floor have raftered cathedral ceilings.

Each of the four elegant dining rooms has its own ambience: The *Comstock Room,* originally the billiard room, contains its original dark oak paneling and has Oriental rugs on the floor; the *Ivoryton Room* is decorated in peachy-toned floral fabric; the *Copper Beech Room,* overlooking the gardens, is more informal; and the intimate *Garden Porch* has dramatic red-sponged walls and a profusion of plants. Each table is set with tall tapered candles and a bud vase containing a single rose. The French-inspired cuisine is equally refined. Dinner entrées may include such French classics as bouillabaisse and *ris de veau* (sweetbreads), as well as such new preparations as saddle of lamb roasted in puff pastry and garnished with goat cheese. Desserts include a fine selection of cheese and fresh fruit, a trio of sorbets, and a decadent chocolate mousse served with fans of pastry and dark chocolate and topped with a bourbon cream sauce.

Nearby activities include tennis, hiking, boating, swimming, and antiquing. For music and theater, there's the picturesque *Goodspeed Opera House* (where *Man of La Mancha, Annie,* and *Shenandoah* premiered) in nearby East Haddam, as well as the summer productions at the *Ivoryton Playhouse.* Guests also may visit *Gillette Castle,* a crenelated extravaganza built by an eccentric actor, high above the river in Hadlyme. The property offers numerous hiking trails and picnic spots.

COPPER BEECH INN 46 Main St., Ivoryton, CT 06442 (phone: 203-767-0330). This inn has 13 guestrooms with private baths, twin, double, queen-, or king-size beds, telephones, and air conditioning. Wheelchair accessible. Open year-round; dining room closed Monday year-round and Tuesday January through March. Rate for a double room (including continental breakfast): $105 to $165. Major credit cards accepted. Not appropriate for children under eight. No pets. No smoking. Eldon and Sally Senner, innkeepers.

DIRECTIONS: From I-95, take Exit 69 in Old Saybrook to Route 9 north. Follow it to Exit 3 west. The inn is 1¾ miles farther on the right.

THE BOULDERS

NEW PRESTON, CONNECTICUT

Snugly situated at the base of the Pinnacle Mountains overlooking quiet Lake Waramaug, *The Boulders* offers a warm and inviting atmosphere. Built of massive granite boulders in 1895, it boldly surveys its 27-acre domain. Manicured lawns lead to perennial beds filled with daylilies, phlox, peonies, irises, dahlias, and delphiniums, which, along with a nearby rose garden, supply the inn with cut flowers.

Ulla and Kees Adema, who have owned *The Boulders* since 1988, have infused it with their own special charm. Ulla is a talented artist who made all of the "cut-and-pierced" lamp shades—there are more than 80—that grace the inn. In this unusual form of American folk art, paper is cut in intricate designs that allow light to filter through.

The inn's welcoming living room is furnished with overstuffed sofas and wing chairs, arranged to capture the view across the lake—and to receive the warmth of the fireplace. A gameroom downstairs is equipped with a pool table, darts, an antique pinball machine, and a piano.

The guestrooms are distributed among the main house, a carriage house, and several guesthouses. Rooms in the main house are furnished with elegant antiques, including canopy and brass beds, and embellished with pretty fabrics. Rooms in the carriage house have a Shaker-style simplicity with pine furnishings and pencil-post beds. The guesthouses, high on a hill with unobstructed views of the lake, contain hand-crafted four-poster or canopy beds, quilts, fireplaces, and spacious decks.

Excellent food is part of the appeal here. Meals are served in three dining rooms or on the terrace in summer. A full breakfast starts with a buffet table of fresh fruits, breads, and cereals and concludes with a hot dish such as Dutch babies (a cross between popovers and pancakes, served with butter and syrup) or an omelette. Dinner (which is open to the public) garners rave reviews for its sophisticated American fare. The menu might include rosemary seared red snapper with tomato and cucumber salad. For dessert, try the Italian ricotta cheesecake with golden raisins and marsala. There's an excellent wine list, and at least 25 wines are available by the glass.

There's something for everyone here. The tennis court is in frequent use in summer, as is the private dock with sailboats, canoes, and paddleboats. Winter brings ice skating on the lake. The surrounding area offers golf, hiking, summer theater, antiquing, and winery visits.

THE BOULDERS **Rte. 45 (E. Shore Rd.), New Preston, CT 06777 (phone: 203-868-0541; 800-55-BOULDERS; fax: 203-868-1925). This granite inn on the shore of Lake Waramaug has 17 guestrooms with private baths, double, queen-, or king-size beds, telephones, and air conditioning. Wheelchair accessible. Open year-round; restaurant closed Mondays through Wednesdays January through April. Rate for a double room (including full breakfast and dinner): $200 to $300; bed and breakfast: $150 to $200. Two-night minimum stay on weekends. Major credit cards accepted. Not appropriate for children under 12. No pets. Two cats in residence. Smoking permitted in the carriage house, the guesthouses, the living room, and the library. Kees and Ulla Adema, innkeepers.**

DIRECTIONS: From I-684 north take I-84 east to Exit 7. Turn onto Route 7 north to New Milford. In New Milford take Route 202 north to New Preston. In New Preston turn onto Route 45 (East Shore Road) and follow the signs to Lake Waramaug. The inn is on the right.

GREENWOODS GATE

NORFOLK, CONNECTICUT

Slip away to *Greenwoods Gate* for a weekend steeped in romance. The 1797 Federal Colonial inn sits on an acre and a half of land in a residential area of Norfolk, a half mile from the east village green. From the moment you enter the cheerful yellow living room set for afternoon tea, you know this is a special place. This is often touted as the most romantic inn in the United States, so, not surprisingly, it's hard to choose a favorite suite here—each has its own irresistible charm. In the *Captain Phelps,* where sunlight shimmers on the peach-and-green headboard and comforter, are an antique Victorian sofa with down cushions and an antique turned-and-carved maple dresser and dressing table. The *Trescott Suite* is a feminine confection with an elaborate cast-iron bed, numerous dolls, and collections of seashells and doorstops. The *Levi Thompson Suite,* on the other hand, is a medley of masculinity on three levels: The parlor is all polished dark woods and antique chests; the bath, with a Jacuzzi for two, is downstairs; and the bedroom is tucked away in an upstairs loft. The *Lillian Rose,* an upstairs suite named for the innkeeper's grandmothers, has an unusual oak Larkin desk with a leaf that folds down to reveal a series of cubbyholes and a pretty shelf with a beveled mirror.

Innkeeper George Schumaker worked for Hilton Hotels for many years, so he knows the ins and outs of inns. In fact, he's a consultant on the subject, conducting off-season internships at the inn for prospective innkeepers. With a local caterer and cookbook author, he also stages "Romantic Cooking Weekends."

There's an exceptionally high standard of comfort at *Greenwoods Gate.* In every room guests find cookies and candies, liqueurs, books, robes, fresh flowers, bath salts, bubble bath, lotions, a rubber duck to float in the oversize tub, and "Romantic Liaisons," a couples-only game to play before retiring. Special services include in-room massages, delivery of roses, or perhaps a limousine to whisk you to a local restaurant.

Breakfast may be taken communally or in bed (the latter is continental fare only). The group breakfast is a two-part repast with coffee and fresh-baked pastries served in the living room, followed by a formal meal in the dining room with Waterford crystal, fine china and silver, and pretty linen. The entrée might be a cranberry-apple oven puff with raspberry sauce and sausage. Afternoon tea, light refreshments, and wine are served in the living room.

Guests can enjoy theater, shops, and hiking in the area, as well as car racing at *Lime Rock Park,* riding stables, tennis, and golf. Summertime brings a wealth of concerts, including *Music Mountain* (held June through August)—one of the country's oldest music festivals—and the *Yale Chamber Music Festival* (late June through August).

GREENWOODS GATE 105 Greenwoods Rd. E., PO Box 491, Norfolk, CT 06058 (phone: 203-542-5439). This inn has four suites with private baths, twin, double, or queen-size beds, and air conditioning. Open year-round. Rate for a double room (including full breakfast, afternoon tea, and wine): $160 to $225. Two-night minimum stay on weekends and holidays. No credit cards accepted. Not appropriate for children under 12. No pets. No smoking. George Schumaker, innkeeper.

DIRECTIONS: Traveling north on I-84, take Exit 21 in Waterbury to Route 8 north. In Winsted take Route 44 west for 9 miles to Norfolk. In Norfolk Route 44 makes a sharp right just before the blinking light. Continue on Route 44 for about half a mile; the inn is on the left.

BEE AND THISTLE INN

OLD LYME, CONNECTICUT

In the late 19th century, the historic hamlet of Old Lyme attracted a distinguished array of American Impressionist painters. They lived in the home of art patron Florence Griswold and painted in the nearby fields. Today, their work hangs in the galleries of Old Lyme's *Florence Griswold Museum,* and their legacy is apparent at the adjacent *Lyme Academy of Fine Arts,* where contemporary artists' work is displayed.

Next door to the museum is the *Bee and Thistle Inn,* a fine home that long predates the arrival of the Impressionists. Built in 1756 on five and a half acres bordering the Lieutenant River, this gracious, yellow clapboard house with green shutters recalls its colonial ancestry in its stone garden walls, paneled parlors, grand center hall staircase, and multitude of fireplaces.

The house was transformed into an inn in the 1930s at the suggestion of actress Elsie Ferguson, who was starring in a play at the nearby *Goodspeed Opera House* at the time. It was Ferguson's idea that her friend, who owned the house, should take in boarders, and it is from her Scottish clan emblem of a bee and thistle that the inn's name derives. Today, the inn is run with experienced care and friendliness by the Nelson family.

The *Bee and Thistle Inn* is infused with romance. On the main floor, two parlors are filled with antique tables, comfortable sofas, and wing chairs placed before the fireplaces. It's a convivial setting for the weekend entertainment, which ranges from a harpist to a duet singing hits from the 1950s and 1960s.

The seven guestrooms in the main house are furnished with handsome chintzes and antiques, including four-poster and fishnet canopy beds, elegant nightstands and chests, and baths with the original pedestal sinks and porcelain faucet handles. A cottage in back holds four more guestrooms, which are decorated in a more contemporary style with colonial touches, and have individual decks, fireplaces, and kitchens.

Meals are served in four dining rooms, two with fireplaces and two on glassed-in porches with views of the gardens. The decor—tables laid with flowered fabric topped by white cloths, ladderback chairs, and baskets hanging from the ceiling—might suggest old-fashioned country fare, but the kitchen turns out sophisticated, contemporary American cuisine. Breakfast (which is not included in the room rate) offers such choices as popovers filled with eggs, bacon, and cheese; homemade sausages made with meat, pistachios, and raisins; crêpes; and waffles. Dinner begins with melt-in-your-mouth scones that accompany soup or salad. Entrées include a knot of salmon—a filet that's tied in a knot, roasted, and served on green onion sauce—and roasted rack of lamb coated with Dijon mustard, honey, and rosemary breadcrumbs. For dessert, there might be a light bread pudding or an apple-strawberry-rhubarb crisp. Afternoon tea is served Monday, Wednesday, and Thursday from November through April (at an additional charge). Lunch, tea, and dinner are open to non-guests.

Adirondack chairs are strategically placed near the riverbank to capture views of the sunset. In addition to the local museums and the *Goodspeed Opera House,* area attractions include *Mystic Seaport, Gillette Castle, the Essex Steam Train,* and *Rocky Neck State Park.* Bicycling is a popular pastime.

BEE AND THISTLE INN 100 Lyme St., Old Lyme, CT 06371 (phone: 203-434-1667; 800-622-4946; fax: 203-434-3402). This colonial mansion and cottage has 11 rooms (nine with private bath) with twin, double, queen-, or king-size beds, air conditioning, and telephones. Closed *Christmas Eve, Christmas Day,* and two weeks in January. Rate for a double room: $69 to $195. Major credit cards accepted. Not appropriate for children under 12. No pets. Smoking permitted in parlors only. The Nelson family, innkeepers.

DIRECTIONS: Traveling on I-95, take Exit 70 in Old Lyme. At the end of the ramp, turn left. Make the first right onto Halls Road (Route 1 north). Go to the end and turn left. The inn is the third house on the left.

THE WHITE HART

SALISBURY, CONNECTICUT

The White Hart was built as a tavern in 1810 at the junction of two stagecoach routes—one heading north into Massachusetts and the other continuing east through Connecticut. Its *Tap Room,* which looks today much as it did originally, with dark walls and a cheery fireplace, has always been the heart of the inn. Additional floors and rooms were added in front and in back as the inn's popularity increased.

The inn has had its good days and its bad. At one time, it was owned and restored by Edsel Ford, and assured him of a proper place to stay when visiting his son at *Hotchkiss,* one of three exclusive prep schools nearby. When Terry and Juliet Moore purchased the stately dowager at auction in 1989, however, it was definitely in a down mode. Today, after another massive renovation, the inn is basking in its restored glory.

The broad front lawn serves as the village green, and the pillared front porch, with clusters of white wicker chairs and sofas, is the ideal viewing venue for local activities. The town of Salisbury lights a massive evergreen tree on the green every *Christmas,* and in summer antiques and craft shows, as well as musical events, take place here.

Juliet has decorated the guestrooms, many of which have such charming idiosyncracies as slanted ceilings and angled doorways, with spritely floral chintzes, antiques, and high-quality period reproductions. The *Ford Room,* for example, has a canopy bed; room No. 15 has a four-poster bed and lace curtains; No. 18 has a bath with an enormous cast-iron tub and a pedestal sink, and is lavishly decorated with Waverly's First Lady fabric pattern; No. 21 is a stunning rooftop suite with slanted ceilings and a boudoir chair and makeup table in the bathroom.

The inn offers three distinctly different dining rooms (which are open to non-guests). The *Tap Room,* with its wide-plank floors, low ceilings, and brick fireplace, is flanked by the inn's bar. The mood here is decidedly British (a reflection of Terry's roots), and much of the food is hearty pub-style fare, such as liver and onions, Welsh rarebit, and juicy hamburgers. The bright and sunny *Garden Room,* with its cathedral ceiling, floor-to-ceiling windows, abundant plants, and flagstone floor, is a delightful place for breakfast and lunch. *Julie's New American Sea Grill,* on the other hand, is one of the prettiest formal dining rooms in Connecticut. Mirrors and gilt-framed oil paintings hang on the salmon-pink walls, and the serious food here emphasizes fresh fish. Filet of salmon is roasted with an almond crust and served with chive butter, while red snapper comes with a nectarine, rosemary, and Vidalia onion *confit.*

Nearby are downhill and cross-country skiing, numerous hiking trails (including the Appalachian Trail, which meanders merely 500 yards beyond *The White Hart's* boundaries), *Lime Rock Raceway,* and summer theaters.

THE WHITE HART The Village Green, PO Box 385, Salisbury, CT 06068 (phone: 203-435-0030; 800-832-0041; fax: 203-435-0040). In northwestern Connecticut, this historic inn has 26 guestrooms with private baths, double or queen-size beds, telephones, TV sets, and air conditioning. Wheelchair accessible. Open year-round. Rate for a double room: $75 to $190. Two-night minimum stay on weekends May through October; three-night stay holiday weekends. Major credit cards accepted. Children welcome. Pets allowed in designated rooms for a $10 fee per day. Smoking permitted except in two dining rooms. Terry and Juliet Moore, innkeepers.

DIRECTIONS: From New York City, take the Henry Hudson Parkway north to the Saw Mill River Parkway to I-684. Follow I-684 north until it becomes Route 22. Continue on Route 22 north to Millerton, New York. In Millerton take Route 44 east for 6 miles to Salisbury. The inn is in the center of town at the junction of Route 44 and Route 41.

MAYFLOWER INN

Washington, Connecticut

The charming village of Washington, in the Connecticut hills, is said to be the first town named for the nation's first president. Although the *Mayflower Inn* wasn't built until 1894, it has seen a considerable amount of history itself. Eleanor Roosevelt unexpectedly drove up the inn's circular driveway in her blue Buick Roadster on a May night in 1933 to spend a quiet night alone.

Originally the main building of the *Ridge School,* it was converted to an inn in 1920, but fell into a sad state of disrepair when the school eventually closed. Today, the *Mayflower* is reminiscent of a fine English manor house, thanks to Adriana and Robert Mnuchin, who bought it in 1992 and spared no expense on renovation. The entire place glows with the patina of polished antiques, crystal chandeliers, and friendly spirits. As its owners say, the inn is "stylishly informal, full of sensibility, and lavish enough to spoil the soul."

Common rooms include the parlor, sitting room, dining room, gameroom, and library—which has leather sofas and bookcases filled with leather-bound books, including more than 200 first-edition mysteries. A separate building, styled like an Adirondack hunting lodge, is dedicated to corporate meetings. Outside, the sun porch, with its elegant wicker furniture, is a pleasant place from which to survey the gardens: 28 acres of stately maples, stone walls, a gazebo, boxwood hedges, ancient rhododendrons, and formal perennial and rose gardens. For the more active, there's a heated pool, a tennis court, and a fitness center, where a battery of exercise machines complements the sauna, steamrooms, and yoga classes. Massages include Swedish, aromatherapy, shiatsu, and reflexology.

Guestrooms are furnished with exquisite antiques, and many have fireplaces as well as balconies. Oriental rugs muffle footsteps; Frette linen cover the beds. The baths are done in marble with mahogany wainscoting; there are brass and Limoges fittings on the sinks and handwoven tapestries on the floors. Decanters of sherry and crystal glasses stand on sideboards.

Breakfast is available each morning, although it's not included in the room rate. The house specialty is salmon—smoked and cured on the premises—with bagels and cream cheese.

Dinner at the *Mayflower Inn* (also open to non-guests) is as impressive as its decor. Entrées such as Muscovy duck breast with a mushroom-thyme sauce and *gaufrette* potatoes (similar to au gratin) are complemented by an excellent wine selection. Spa-inspired fare is offered to those watching their diets. The outstanding gift shop features local and imported items made especially for the inn, including rugs like those found in the bathrooms.

Located in the Litchfield Hills, the inn is near golf courses, *Steep Rock Nature Preserve,* concerts, theater, and a multitude of antiques shops.

MAYFLOWER INN **118 Woodbury Rd., Rte. 47, Washington, CT 06793 (phone: 203-868-9466; fax: 203-868-1497). This inn has 25 guestrooms with private baths, twin, queen-, or king-size beds, telephones, TV sets, and air conditioning. Wheelchair accessible. Open year-round. Rate for a double room: $225 to $350; for suites: $395 to $495. Two-night minimum stay on weekends; three nights on holidays. Major credit cards accepted. Not appropriate for children under 12. No pets. Smoking permitted in the bar and parlor and on guestroom balconies. Robert and Adriana Mnuchin, innkeepers; John Trevenen, manager.**

DIRECTIONS: Take I-684 north to the Danbury exit onto I-84 east. Travel on I-84 to Route 7/202 north. Remain on Route 202 past New Preston to the junction with Route 47. Follow Route 47 south to the village of Washington. Travel through the small village, past *The Gunnery* (a private school), to the bottom of the hill. The inn's driveway is on the left.

INN AT NATIONAL HALL

WESTPORT, CONNECTICUT

A historic 1873 brick Italianate building overlooking the Saugatuck River (and the heart of Westport's National Hall Historic District) today is one of the finest inns in America. Built as a bank, it subsequently served as a newspaper office, as Westport's first high school, and as headquarters for the Connecticut State Police. The capacious first floor was the quintessential town meeting hall and also provided space for village concerts, dances, graduations, election-night revelries, and Friday-night basketball games. Through painstaking care, the building has been faithfully restored by owner Arthur Tauck.

Reminiscent of a fine English manor house, the inn exudes elegance—but spiced with wit. An elevator, whimsically painted in trompe l'oeil to resemble a library, brings guests to the third-floor reception area, where a host or hostess provides an introduction to the inn. The drawing room features a carved wood mantle, English antiques, and a mural that pays homage to all the artisans who worked on the restoration. Tables are laid with newspapers, magazines, and games. In the vestibule is a full bar with elegant glassware, and there's a boardroom with a spectacular crystal chandelier and a complete audiovisual system for small meetings.

The seven suites and eight guestrooms are equally extravagant, decorated by San Francisco interior designer Joszi Meskan with canopy beds, armoires, and decor by local artists that includes fanciful wall stencils. The ceilings reach to 20 feet. Every accommodation includes a wet bar, VCR, and fax, as well as such charming touches as a book of bedtime stories placed on the nightstand. The *Turkistan Suite* (No. 304) has taffeta drapes striped in pink and seafoam green covering the massive windows, a floor-to-ceiling library, and puffy loveseats with needlepoint pillows; the loft bedroom has a bowed balcony (with river views) and a king-size canopy bed. The *Willow Suite* (No. 305), which is decorated in shades of pink and yellow, features a canopy bed draped in fringed polished cotton; the walls of the bedroom are painted with dogwood branches, and gardenias are splashed across the walls of the bath. The *Sheriff Room* (No. 207), in peach and black, has stars painted on the ceiling and bookcases that line three walls of the bath. The baths are so luxurious they are like private spas, with marble showers, floors, and walls, Jacuzzis, scales, and fluffy robes.

On the main floor, *Restaurant Zanghi,* which is not managed by the inn, is chef-owned and earns high praise for its French-influenced American cuisine. An entrée of pepper-crusted beef tenderloin with port and mashed foie gras is one possibility, as is a dessert of *pithiviers* (almond cream baked in puff pastry). The restaurant will provide room service. A full breakfast is offered to guests.

The inn provides guest passes to the fitness facilities at the nearby *YMCA,* and the village of Westport boasts numerous exclusive boutiques, antique shops, and gourmet food emporiums. Local recreation includes bicycling, sailing, boating, and golf.

INN AT NATIONAL HALL 2 Post Rd. W., Westport, CT 06889 (phone: 203-221-1351; 800-NAT-HALL; fax: 203-221-0276). This inn on Connecticut's south shore has 15 guestrooms and suites with private baths, twin, queen-, or king-size beds, telephones, TV sets, and air conditioning. Closed *Christmas.* Rate for a double room (including full breakfast): $195 to $450. Two-night minimum stay weekends June through November. Major credit cards accepted. Children welcome. No pets. No smoking. Arthur Tauck, owner; Nick Carter, general manager.

DIRECTIONS: From I-95 take Exit 17 (Westport/Saugatuck). At the bottom of the ramp turn left onto Saugatuck Avenue. At the next traffic light Saugatuck Avenue becomes Riverside Avenue. Continue on Riverside, which becomes Wilton Road at the next traffic light. The entrance to the inn will be on the right immediately after crossing Post Road West.

Massachusetts

ASHLEY MANOR

BARNSTABLE, CAPE COD, MASSACHUSETTS

A graceful gabled inn whose cedar shingles have weathered to a soft dove gray, *Ashley Manor* is located at the end of a curving driveway, hidden behind privet hedges on two lush acres of manicured lawns.

Steeped in history and exhibiting a variety of architectural styles, the house was built by the Delap family, avid Tories who fled to Nova Scotia following the American Revolution. The original part of the building was built in 1699; the massive front gable was added in 1750 (the fireplace with its beehive oven in the keeping room also dates from this era). Throughout the inn's common rooms are reminders of the estate's long history: hand-blown six-over-six windows, open-hearth fireplaces, and hand-glazed wainscoting. Enhancing the sense of history and romance is a "secret" passageway connecting the upstairs and downstairs suites, thought to have been a hiding place for Tories during the Revolution.

Donald and Fay Bain, owners of the inn since 1987, have infused the house with their own warmth and style. Oriental rugs, a baby grand piano, original oil paintings, antiques, and plush sofas characterize the common rooms. The corner cupboards in the exquisitely appointed dining room are filled with a fine collection of antique Oriental porcelain. The suites have canopy beds, most guestrooms have working fireplaces, and all have luxurious bathrooms. Fresh flowers, bedside chocolates, and fragrant soaps and lotions are special touches. Outside, among the flower gardens, are a secluded gazebo, fountain garden, brick terrace, and tennis court.

Breakfasts at *Ashley Manor* are bountiful. Guests gather around the pine dining room table, where four courses are served by candlelight on Meissen, Lowestoft, and Spode china; when the weather is cool, a fire blazes in the fireplace. In summer, breakfast is served on the brick terrace. In addition to being "chief putterer," Donald is the chef. Expect to start with fresh-squeezed orange juice, followed by a fruit course of poached pears or strawberries and cream, Donald's renowned granola, homemade muffins and breads, and perhaps a main course of stuffed crêpe with strawberry sauce or French toast.

The inn is near beaches, bicycle trails, bird sanctuaries, antiquing, golf, whale watching, boating, and summer theaters. Bicycles are available for guests' use, and there just might be a lively game of croquet being played on the lawn.

ASHLEY MANOR 3660 Old Kings Hwy. (Rte. 6A), PO Box 856, Barnstable, MA 02630 (phone: 508-362-8044). This country estate on the north shore of Cape Cod has six suites and guestrooms with private baths, double, queen-, or king-size beds, and air conditioning. Open year-round. Rate for a double room (including full breakfast): $115 to $175. Two-night minimum stay on summer weekends; three nights on some holiday weekends. Major credit cards accepted. Not appropriate for children under 14. No pets. Smoking permitted in guestrooms only. Donald and Fay Bain, innkeepers.

DIRECTIONS: From I-495, I-95, or Route 3, take Route 6 across the Sagamore Bridge onto Cape Cod. Continue on Route 6 to Exit 6. At Exit 6 turn left onto Route 132 north. Take this road for a half mile to its end and turn right onto Route 6A east. Travel 3 miles through the village of Barnstable and about a half mile past the traffic light. The inn is on the left.

WHALEWALK INN

EASTHAM, CAPE COD, MASSACHUSETTS

Innkeepers Dick and Carolyn Smith love what they do, and it shows in their gracious hospitality. Their inn is an 1830s whaling master's home with shingles mellowed to a driftwood gray, now artfully restored. Salt-tinged sea breezes, a seashell knocker on the door, and lots of tastefully arranged flowers inside are just a few of the details adding to the *Whalewalk's* appeal.

Guestrooms have a warm, comfortable feeling, thanks to the wood-burning fireplaces, massive bouquets in wicker baskets, and brass beds piled high with pillows, shams, quilts, and comforters. Other touches: an English pine wardrobe complemented by an artistically painted chest; a pink-and-green wool blanket draped over a white rattan chair; watercolor seascapes on the walls. Small kitchens and private patios complete the facilities found in the suites.

Guests begin their day with fresh fruit, juice, and hot-from-the-oven bread, muffins, or apple–sour cream coffee cake. For an entrée, Dick may prepare cranberry-blueberry pancakes or vegetable *strata* (a dish of French bread and vegetables soaked in eggs overnight, sprinkled with cheese, and baked). Every evening, hors d'oeuvres (guests may bring their own wine) are served in the living room, where the fireplace glows in cool weather. It's a chance for guests to become acquainted and discuss local activities with the owners. In summer, the get-together takes place on the patio.

The inn is near the *Cape Cod National Seashore,* the Cape Cod Rail Trail Bike Path, whale watching, sailing, and fishing.

WHALEWALK INN 220 Bridge Rd., Eastham, MA 02642 (phone: 508-255-0617; fax: 508-240-0017). This whaling master's home has 12 guestrooms with private baths and twin, queen-, or king-size beds. Closed December through March. Rate for a double room (including full breakfast and evening hors d'oeuvres): $100 to $185. Two-night minimum stay June through September and on weekends throughout the year; three nights on holiday weekends. MasterCard and Visa accepted. Not appropriate for children under 12. No pets. No smoking. Carolyn and Dick Smith, innkeepers.

DIRECTIONS: Cross the Sagamore Bridge to Cape Cod. Traveling east on Route 6, go to the Orleans traffic circle. Three-fourths of the way around, exit onto Rock Harbor Road. Take the first right onto Bridge Road. The inn is on the right.

MOSTLY HALL BED & BREAKFAST INN

FALMOUTH, CAPE COD, MASSACHUSETTS

Although *Mostly Hall* was built in 1849 by a Yankee ship captain, it is distinctly Southern in style: A wide verandah encircles the main floor, and there are 13-foot ceilings, a front-to-back central hallway, and massive windows on the upper floors. Like a typical plantation house, it is set back from the road amid rolling lawns and landscaped gardens, yet its location on the historic village green of Falmouth is strictly New England. This seeming contradiction is easily explained: Captain Albert Nye built the house as a wedding present for his New Orleans bride. It received its odd name about a hundred years ago when a child walked through the front doors and exclaimed, "Why, Mama, it's mostly hall!"

Caroline and Jim Lloyd purchased the house in 1986; they have created a refined village inn furnished with Victorian antiques, including Lincoln rockers and a variety of chiming clocks. Among them is a navy clock that strikes bells, a Viennese regulator, a banjo clock, and a French marble mantel clock. The warm peach walls in the living room are accented by Oriental rugs, while the interior wooden shutters are charming reminders of an earlier era.

Each of the spacious corner guestrooms, which overlook clipped lawns and flower beds, has a private bath, a queen-size canopied bed, and Oriental rugs. Converted to a sitting room, the enclosed widow's walk cupola with multiple windows is a favorite hideaway. The gazebo in the garden entices guests outside on balmy days, as does the verandah, where tea and sherry are enjoyed on summer afternoons.

Breakfast is a delight whatever the season. In winter, a gas-log fire burns in the fireplace in the dining room and guests sit at the spacious table; in summer tables are set up on the verandah. The meal has become such a popular tradition that the inn has published a collection of its most popular recipes—treats such as stuffed French toast with apricot sauce, eggs Benedict soufflé, and cheese blintz muffins with warm blueberry sauce. The entrées are accompanied by fresh fruit and a variety of fresh-baked breads. In the afternoon, tea, coffee, hot chocolate, cider, and iced tea (in summer) are offered on a self-serve basis in the living room.

Bicycles are available for guests' use; the Shining Sea Bikeway to Woods Hole is a short pedal from the inn. Also nearby are beaches, boating, golf, tennis, and cultural events.

MOSTLY HALL BED & BREAKFAST INN 27 Main St., Falmouth, MA 02540 (phone: 508-548-3786; 800-682-0565). This plantation-style inn on the south shore of Cape Code has six guestrooms with private baths, queen-size beds, and air conditioning. Closed January through mid-February. Rate for a double room (including full breakfast): $85 to $125. Two-night minimum stay May through October and all weekends. Major credit cards accepted. Not appropriate for children under 16. No pets. No smoking. Caroline and Jim Lloyd, innkeepers.

DIRECTIONS: Traveling north, take I-95 to I-195 and the Cape Cod and Islands exit onto Route 25. Follow Route 25 (a one-way road) 4 miles to Route 28 south. Take Route 28 across the Bourne Bridge into Falmouth. The inn is located on the village green behind a wrought-iron fence and massive rhododendrons.

DEERFIELD INN

DEERFIELD, MASSACHUSETTS

Historic Deerfield Village is the Williamsburg of New England—a perfectly preserved town steeped in authentic colonial history and listed as a National Historic Landmark. Thirteen of the 18th- and 19th-century houses on the mile-long, tree-lined way known as The Street are museums that tell the story of Indian attacks, of the valor of 300 people who were captured by Indians after the Deerfield Massacre in 1704 and forced to march to Canada, and of the town's rebirth and the rural life of its residents. The museum houses sit side by side with privately owned homes of the same vintage, as well as *Deerfield Academy,* one of the oldest boarding schools in the country.

In the midst of all this history is the *Deerfield Inn,* built in 1884 to replace a 1730s inn that had been on the busy Hartford–New York stage route. When Mr. and Mrs. Henry Flynt bought it in 1936, their collection of antiques that now graces the inn found a home. The Flynts also were responsible for purchasing the fine old homes that comprise the museums of Historic Deerfield Village (a visitors' center with museum information is across the street from the inn). Today, the inn is owned by Historic Deerfield, Inc.; it has been managed by Karl and Jane Sabo since 1987.

The overall look is Early American, in both the public areas and the guestrooms. The spacious bedrooms are furnished with a combination of antiques and high-quality reproductions and decorated with Greeff and Waverly fabrics; most have four-posters. Old prints of Deerfield line the walls. The rooms are named for historic local luminaries, and some guests claim to have seen the amiable spirits wandering the hallways.

A full country-style breakfast of fruit, juice, cereal, bacon, eggs, and pancakes is served in the formal dining room, a gracious room with brass chandeliers, a bay window, and candles flickering within hurricane lamps on the tables. Dinner is served here as well. Highly acclaimed entrées include the venison and the beef tenderloin wrapped in bacon and served with sautéed mushrooms; for dessert, there is chocolate cake or Indian pudding. Afternoon tea, cookies, and other pastries are offered in the parlor. All meals are open to non-guests.

In addition to visits of the historic houses, the area offers several other activities, including hiking and shopping.

DEERFIELD INN The Street, Deerfield, MA 01342 (phone: 413-774-5587; fax: 413-773-8712). This historic inn has 23 guestrooms with private baths, twin or queen-size beds, telephones, TV sets, and air conditioning. Wheelchair accessible. Closed three days at *Christmas.* Rate for a double room (including full breakfast and afternoon tea): $122 to $141. Two-night minimum stay on holiday weekends. Major credit cards accepted. Children welcome. No pets. No smoking. Karl and Jane Sabo, managers.

DIRECTIONS: From I-91 north take Exit 24 at Deerfield to Route 5 north. Travel 6 miles on Route 5, and turn left onto The Street at the "Historic Deerfield" sign. The inn is in the center of town.

APPLEGATE

LEE, MASSACHUSETTS

Driving through the iron gates and up the road to the porte cochère, you'll find a little piece of tranquillity tucked away on six acres in the Berkshires called *Applegate.*

Rick and Nancy Cannata, who were married nearby, have always loved the Berkshires, and they never gave up their desire to live here full-time. Although both are airline employees (Rick is a pilot, Nancy a flight attendant, and they juggle their schedules so one is on premise at all times) they took the plunge in 1990, buying and restoring this stately columned colonial, built in the 1920s for a New York surgeon.

It's hard to imagine a detail that hasn't been attended to by these thoughtful innkeepers. On arrival, guests find a crystal decanter of brandy with two snifters in their rooms; in the evening, Godiva chocolates are left on the nightstand. The six spacious guestrooms are done in a variety of styles: No. 1 has a king-size four-poster bed, a fireplace, and a shower built for two (with two shower heads); No. 2 is furnished with a pine four-poster bed and an antique carved oak dressing table; No. 3 has a sleigh bed, a Chinese hooked rug, and French prints on the wall; No. 4 has a pretty brass-and-iron bed plus wicker accent pieces.

With a baby grand piano, plush loveseats, a fireplace, and a lovely Oriental rug, the formal living room is as refined as the main room in a stately manor house should be, yet it has whimsical touches as well. Martha, Heather, and Claudia, three of Nancy's favorite dolls, observe the daily activity from their antique wicker chairs. (Similar dolls are available for adoption.) Testimony to the Cannatas' love for their adopted business are the framed photographs of inn guests scattered on the mantel, in the bookcases, and on tables. Beyond the living room is a sun porch with a TV/VCR, a collection of video classics, and games. On the covered verandah, cushioned wicker chairs provide vantage points for viewing the gardens. Just beyond is an inviting swimming pool. Throughout the formal gardens (Rick's passion) and the orchard are pretty benches, perfect for relaxing and watching butterflies flit among the dahlias, delphiniums, and phlox.

Breakfast is served on Nancy's antique bone china in the formal dining room, where the mantelpiece displays a collection of apples, many contributed by former guests. It's an elegant setting, with flickering candles in silver candelabra. A selection of fruit and juices, yogurt, granola, and fresh-baked muffins and breads are offered.

There's skiing, golf, tennis, hiking, and biking in the area, and guests can visit *Tanglewood,* the *Norman Rockwell Museum, Jacob's Pillow Dance Festival,* and the *Berkshire Theatre Festival* nearby.

APPLEGATE 279 W. Park St., RR1 Box 576, Lee, MA 01238 (phone: 413-243-4451; 800-691-9012). This stately inn has six guestrooms with private baths, double, queen-, or king-size beds, and air conditioning. Open year-round. Rate for a double room (including continental breakfast): $85 to $225. Two-night minimum stay on weekends in June, September, and October; three nights on weekends in July and August and on all holidays. MasterCard and Visa accepted. Not appropriate for children under 13. No pets. Six cats on the property. No smoking. Nancy and Rick Cannata, innkeepers.

DIRECTIONS: Coming from Albany or Boston on the Massachusetts Turnpike, take Exit 2 at Lee. At the bottom of the ramp turn right onto Route 20 and follow it through town to the first stop sign. Route 20 turns right here, but you should continue straight ahead. Cross the railroad tracks and ascend the hill. You are now on West Park Street; *Applegate* is approximately one-quarter mile farther on the left.

BLANTYRE

LENOX, MASSACHUSETTS

As imposing as this massive stone manor may appear, the warm greeting guests receive from managing director Roderick Anderson dispels all apprehensions. At *Blantyre,* the tone is unpretentious and friendly.

A 23-room summer "cottage" on 85 acres in the heart of the Berkshires, *Blantyre* was built by a wealthy New Yorker in 1902. To help his wife feel at home, he built the house in a style prevalent in her native Scotland. The exterior is embellished with gargoyles, carved friezes, turrets, and balconies. A glass-enclosed conservatory (where continental breakfast is served) and several terraces, surrounded by flower beds, overlook clipped lawns and a tournament-size croquet lawn.

Upon entering the ornately carved oak doors of the *Great Hall,* guests find themselves in a room resplendent with stained glass, Oriental rugs, exquisite Victorian antiques, and a massive stone fireplace. The adjacent music room leads to a covered side terrace, where parties often are held. The wood-paneled dining room, refined and dignified, contains another fireplace, lighted on chilly evenings.

The eight guestrooms in the *Manor House* are as elegantly decorated as the common rooms, furnished with museum-quality chests, dressers, armoires, and beds (some are four-posters). Each has interesting features; one, for example, has a "fainting" couch, another a gilded French chandelier. Twelve more rooms are located in the *Carriage House,* about a quarter mile away. Although the decor here is more contemporary, the same attention to detail is evident. Several rooms feature loft bedrooms; others have downstairs sitting rooms with frescoed walls; all have handsome baths with limestone or marble floors and separate dressing areas. Three whimsically decorated cottages complete the picture: *Cottage by the Path,* with a fireplace and a kitchen; *Winter Palace* with a kitchen; and *Cottage Queen.* Fresh flowers, a fruit basket, bottled water, and a cheese tray are among the amenities.

Dining at *Blantyre* (also open to non-guests) is a memorable experience. Guests gather in the *Great Hall,* now bathed in the soft glow of candlelight. As they relax on the plush sofas, listening to a harpist and sipping an aperitif from the honor bar, they make their appetizer and entrée selections. They are escorted to the dining room when the table has been laid with the appetizers. Chef Michael Roller, who trained in some of America's finest kitchens, prepares such inventive dishes as seared Muscovy duck with mustard, junipers, and wild mushrooms, and pepper-charred yellowfin tuna on grilled onions with a young leek and blood orange salad. Dessert might be a bittersweet chocolate *daquoise* or a raspberry *genoise* tart.

Tennis courts, a pool, two regulation croquet lawns, and a spa with a hot tub and sauna are right on the property. Nearby attractions include hiking, bicycling, golf, horseback riding, *Tanglewood,* the *Norman Rockwell Museum,* the *Berkshire Theatre Festival,* and Edith Wharton's home *The Mount,* where plays are presented by *Shakespeare and Company.*

BLANTYRE 16 Blantyre Rd., PO Box 995, Lenox, MA 01240 (phone: 413-637-3556, May through October; 413-298-3806, November through April; fax: 413-637-4282). This elegant country estate has 23 guestrooms with private baths, double, queen-, or king-size beds, telephones, TV sets, and air conditioning. Wheelchair accessible. Closed November through mid-May; restuarant closed for lunch September through June and for dinner Mondays. Rate for a double room (including continental breakfast): $245 to $600. Two-night minimum stay on weekends; three nights on holidays. Major credit cards accepted. Not appropriate for children under 13. No pets. Smoking permitted. Jack and Jane Fitzpatrick, owners; Roderick Anderson, managing director.

DIRECTIONS: From the Massachusetts Turnpike, take Exit 2 at Lee. Follow signs for Route 20 toward Pittsfield. Traveling north on Route 20, pass through the town of Lee and continue for 2 miles. Look for the sign to the inn. Blantyre Road is on the right.

WHEATLEIGH

LENOX, MASSACHUSETTS

When Henry H. Cook, a New York banker, railroad director, and real estate tycoon, learned that his daughter, Georgie, was marrying Spanish count Carlos de Heredia, he commissioned a grand estate for their summer use. It was designed in 1893 in the style of a 16th-century Florentine palazzo; more than 150 artisans were imported from Italy to execute the intricate carvings found both inside and outside. Frederick Law Olmsted was responsible for the 380-acre "Wheatleigh Park," 22 acres of which remain in landscaped gardens with spectacular vistas.

Wheatleigh has been an inn since the 1960s, and many of its exquisite original features remain intact: an unusual wrought-iron and glass canopy over the double entry doors, Tiffany lanterns at the gates, a massive and ornate mantelpiece in the *Great Hall,* 20-foot ceilings, fluted columns that flank grand archways, a spectacular Tiffany window over the stairway. A loggia with a carved oak ceiling runs the length of one side, and a broad terrace extends across the back.

Following a complete refurbishment in 1993, *Wheatleigh*'s furnishings now match the quality of the building itself. The *Great Hall* has Oriental rugs on the parquet floors, and its Queen Anne–style furniture is upholstered in urbane damasks and velvets. There's a grand piano in a parlor, and an antique marquetry table.

Guestrooms range in size from baronial to tiny, but all are decorated with subdued elegance. Those on the second floor, which include the *Count's Room* and the *Countess's Room,* are the grandest, and they have views of the Stockbridge Bowl with the Berkshire Mountains beyond. Room No. 21, one of largest, features heavy ivory brocade drapes and a blue brocade spread on a bed with a tailored half canopy; an antique lady's writing desk of inlaid woods; ornate ceiling moldings; and a private loggia. Leonard Bernstein often stayed in a two-level suite in the former aviary.

The dining room is considered to be the finest in the Berkshires. Chef Peter Platt creates original and bold fare, which is served on antique china with heavy silver and lovely crystal. Every evening he presents three prix fixe menus (a low-fat, vegetarian, and regular meals), each including four courses. Guests may mix and match courses from the three menus, perhaps beginning with a vegetarian appetizer like the napoleon of wild mushrooms with leek compote and red wine sauce, then choosing between the low-fat roasted free-range chicken with slivers of black truffles and tiny vegetables and an entrée from the regular menu, such as roast rack of lamb with ratatouille, polenta, and olive sauce. An irresistible finish is the sinful warm liquid-center chocolate cake with three ice creams (a fitting reward for those who otherwise adhered to the low-fat menu). Breakfast is also available daily, but is not included in the room rate.

Guests enjoy the heated pool and tennis court on premise. The inn also provides passes to a local fitness center. *Tanglewood* is so close that guests can walk to concerts; so is a small red house that replicates one used by Nathaniel Hawthorne when he lived and wrote in the Berkshires. Other nearby attractions include skiing, hiking, and numerous historic museum houses.

WHEATLEIGH Hawthorne Rd., Lenox, MA 01240 (phone: 413-637-0610; fax: 413-637-4507). This mansion has 17 guestrooms with private baths and double, queen-, or king-size beds, telephones, and air conditioning. Wheelchair accessible. Open year-round. Rate for a double room: $155 to $525. Two-night minimum stay weekends; three nights on weekends in July, August, and October. Major credit cards accepted. Not appropriate for children under 12. No pets. Smoking permitted except in dining room. Linfield and Susan Simon, innkeepers; François Thomas, general manager.

DIRECTIONS: From the Massachusetts Turnpike take Exit 2 in Lee. At the bottom of the ramp turn right onto Route 20, traveling through the town of Lee. Follow signs to Lenox by turning left onto Route 7 at its junction with Route 20. At the monument in Lenox, take Route 183 south past the entrance to *Tanglewood.* At the next intersection, turn left onto Hawthorne Road. The entrance to *Wheatleigh* is 1 mile farther on the left.

CHARLOTTE INN

EDGARTOWN, MARTHA'S VINEYARD, MASSACHUSETTS

The village of Edgartown on Martha's Vineyard, with its narrow streets and shingled cottages, was settled in the 1670s. Ever since, its inhabitants have made their livelihood from the sea, and Samuel Osborne, owner of a whaling company and the builder of the 19th-century *Charlotte Inn,* was no exception. The main house is a grand, three-story, white Italianate structure with an impressive widow's walk on top, where Osborne's wife watched for the return of his ships.

Gery Conover and his wife, Paula, have been the innkeepers here for more than 20 years. Their goal has been to offer a quiet and romantic retreat on this very special island—and they do so in grand style. Moreover, their interest in art led them to create a gallery on the main floor of the inn, where fine oils and watercolors, by both 19th-century European and contemporary American painters, are for sale.

Accommodations are scattered among the main house and four adjacent buildings: the *Carriage House,* the *Garden House,* the *Summer House,* and the *Coach House.* The separate buildings are unified into a kind of private compound by the grounds, with brick walkways, sculpted English boxwood hedges, and even an old water pump and a gardener's toolshed. All the guestrooms are furnished with fine antiques: four-poster, brass, or pineapple-post beds, polished English chests, and gilt-framed 19th-century English oil paintings, often of sporting scenes. A number of the rooms have fireplaces; floral or paisley wallpapers and an abundance of fresh flowers add romance.

Despite those similarities, each room has its own personality. Consider the huge *Coach House* suite, for example. It is entered through a garage resembling a British stable that houses a collection of restored antique vehicles, including a surrey with a fringe on top, a 1939 Ford Woody, and a 1933 Ford sedan. The light-filled upstairs room has a Palladian window and is outfitted with antique sports equipment—a croquet mallet, a golf club, and tennis racquets—as well as old hatboxes. A four-poster bed with a lace spread and an 1860s mahogany dressing table displaying antique silver mirrors, hairbrushes, and jars complete the decor.

With large windows, glass accents, and hanging plants, the inn's restaurant, *L'Etoile,* is known for its fine fare. A prix fixe dinner (also open to non-guests) featuring local seafood is served nightly and might include such specialties as chilled lobster terrine, scallops and smoked salmon with *wasabi* mayonnaise sauce, or pan-roasted sirloin with green peppercorns. A continental breakfast of juice, fruit, muffins, cereal, coffee, and tea is served here as well. On summer afternoons tea, lemonade, sandwiches, and cookies are offered on the porch.

The ferry ride to Martha's Vineyard is half the fun of getting to the *Charlotte Inn.* The other half is driving along the winding road past bluff-top vistas and rose-covered cottages. On arrival, guests can enjoy all the activities the island has to offer—from beaches and boating to bicycling and shopping.

CHARLOTTE INN 27 South Summer St., Edgartown, MA 02539 (phone: 508-627-4751 or 508-627-4151; fax: 508-627-4652). This jewel of an inn has 25 guestrooms and suites with private baths and double or queen-size beds, most with telephones, TV sets, and air conditioning. Wheelchair accessible. Open year-round. Rate for a double room (including continental breakfast and afternoon tea) June through mid-October: $250 to $650; mid-October through May: $125 to $550. Two-night minimum stay on weekends; three nights on holidays. Major credit cards accepted. Not appropriate for children under 12. No pets. Two dogs and two cats in residence. Smoking permitted except in dining room. Gery and Paula Conover, innkeepers; Carol Read, manager.

DIRECTIONS: The Woods Hole/Vineyard Haven ferry runs year-round; automobiles may be taken aboard or left in the parking lot at Woods Hole. Taxis are available in Vineyard Haven for the 8-mile trip to Edgartown. Those driving should exit the ferry and follow the signs to Edgartown. In Edgartown proceed down Main Street to the large whaling church on the left. South Summer Street is the second on the right after the church. The inn is the third building on the left.

THORNCROFT INN

VINEYARD HAVEN, MARTHA'S VINEYARD, MASSACHUSETTS

In 1918, when it was the guesthouse on the estate of John Herbert Ware, a Chicago grain merchant who summered on Martha's Vineyard, the *Thorncroft Inn* was filled with visitors enjoying their host's hospitality. It's hard to imagine they would have been more pampered or had lovelier surroundings than do guests today. Innkeepers Lynn and Karl Buder, who have owned *Thorncroft* since 1981, make a visit here seem like staying with friends at their country estate. Every need has been anticipated—perhaps that's one reason they have received several prestigious hospitality awards.

A romantic retreat for couples, the inn has accommodations in both the main house and a new *Carriage House.* The spacious rooms and suites have wood-burning fireplaces, private balconies, and palatial baths, the latter with claw-foot tubs, two-person Jacuzzis, or hot tubs. All are furnished with antique four-posters with hand-tied fishnet canopies or turn-of-the-century carved mahogany beds, polished highboys and, perhaps, a Victorian doll or two.

For quiet relaxation there is a living room with fireplace. Be sure to note the Seth Thomas mantel clock that fits neatly into a niche, painted by Ware's mother more than a century ago. Outdoors enjoy the three and a half acres of gardens from one of the many Adirondack chairs.

A stay at the *Thorncroft Inn* includes a full breakfast—perhaps almond French toast or cheese *strata* (a casserole of bread, eggs, and cheese) and sausage. On summer days the meal may be served in the sunroom. There's afternoon tea with pastries as well. It's no wonder that patrons return again and again to this quiet retreat by the sea.

Guests may enjoy all the recreational advantages of Martha's Vineyard, including beaches, sailing, and summer theater.

THORNCROFT INN **278 Main St., PO Box 1022, Vineyard Haven, MA 02568 (phone: 508-693-3333; 800-332-1236; fax: 508-693-5419). This exclusive inn on Martha's Vineyard has 13 guestrooms with private baths, double or queen-size beds, telephones, TV sets, and air conditioning. Open year-round. Rate for a double room (including full breakfast and afternoon tea): $149 to $349. Three-night minimum stay on summer weekends and holidays. Major credit cards accepted. Not appropriate for children under 12. No pets. No smoking. Karl and Lynn Buder, innkeepers.**

DIRECTIONS: From the Vineyard Haven ferry dock (see the *Charlotte Inn,* above), turn right at the first stop sign, then right again onto Main Street. The inn is located 1 mile up Main Street on the left. Taxi service from the ferry also is available.

THE WAUWINET

NANTUCKET, MASSACHUSETTS

The old *Wauwinet* is no more, but a new one with the same wild, windswept-seacoast ambience has taken its place in a spectacular spot on a remote neck of land between the Atlantic Ocean and Nantucket Bay.

Stephen and Jill Karp, who had summered on Nantucket for a number of years, watched with dismay as the old *Wauwinet* resort, which had operated continuously since 1876, sank into disrepair. In 1986, they purchased the derelict inn and embarked on a $3-million renovation project that restored the weathered exterior but created an entirely new interior.

Rooms were enlarged, and opulent tile bathrooms with wainscoted walls and brass fixtures were installed in each room and suite. The huge suites on the third floor, each with two bedrooms, a kitchenette, and a parlor, are great for families. The style—casual beach resort with luxurious overtones—translates to light, airy colors, antique pine armoires, iron and brass headboards, and light wool Berber carpeting. Fresh flowers abound, and lovely chintz fabrics decorate the windows and beds. The common areas are decorated in similar fashion, with lots of wicker furniture, rag rugs, flowers, and fireplaces.

The inn's fine restaurant, *Toppers* (named for the owners' terrier), specializes in new American cuisine (and also is open to non-guests). Breakfasts are hearty affairs, with muffins, eggs, French toast, cereal, wild turkey hash, and the inn's version of eggs Benedict (made with turkey instead of ham). Dinner entrées are equally interesting, including grilled arctic crab with matchstick potatoes and lemon beurre blanc sauce, and veal chops served with polenta and crisp leeks.

An hourly shuttle bus takes guests the 8 miles from the inn to the cobblestone streets of Nantucket village and back again; a 28-passenger launch makes the journey by water. More unusual outings include naturalist-led tours to Sconset, a quaint old fishing village; visits to the natural cranberry bogs; or bird watching jaunts along the beach to view oyster catchers, ospreys, and least terns. The inn will pack a picnic lunch for a perfect afternoon of sun, sand, water, and wine on a hideaway sand spit. There also are two beaches (one on the Atlantic, the other on Nantucket Bay), 26 miles of Nature Conservancy trails, a private sailboat, rowboats, bicycles, two Har-tru tennis courts, a croquet court, and a whimsical outdoor chess set (with waist-high pawns). Golf, sailing, antiquing, shopping, museums, and other cultural attractions are nearby.

THE WAUWINET 120 Wauwinet Rd., PO Box 2580, Nantucket, MA 02584 (phone: 508-228-0145; 800-426-8718; fax: 508-228-6712). This seafront inn has 25 guestrooms and suites in the main inn and 10 more in five cottages, all with private baths, twin, queen-, or king-size beds, telephones, TV sets, and air conditioning. Wheelchair accessible. Closed November through mid-May. Rate for a double room (including full breakfast): $190 to $690. Rate for a two- to four-bedroom cottage: $390 to $1,400. Four-night minimum stay on summer and holiday weekends. Major credit cards accepted. Children welcome in cottages. No pets. One dog, Paco, in residence. No smoking. Stephen and Jill Karp, innkeepers; Russ Cleveland, manager.

DIRECTIONS: The inn provides complimentary pick-up and drop-off service at the ferry landing. If you decide to drive, take Orange Street from the ferry to the traffic circle in Nantucket village, then take Milestone Road. Bear left onto Polpis Road, follow it to Wauwinet Road, and take a left. The inn is at the end of Wauwinet Road.

OLD INN ON THE GREEN AND GEDNEY FARM

New Marlborough, Massachusetts

Time seems to stand still in New Marlborough, a village that has remained unchanged for more than 200 years. Sitting back from the road on the pretty village green, the *Old Inn on the Green* shows the same resistance to change. The first building on the property was built in 1760 as a frontier trading post and store, where local farmers could trade grain and produce for packaged goods. In the late 18th century, the current structure was built to serve as a post office, general store, and inn for travelers on the passing stagecoach route. The two-level porch that spans the front of the building dates to that time, as do the guestrooms upstairs.

Bradford Wagstaff and Leslie Miller have owned the inn since 1973. Respecting its colonial roots, they have made few changes, except for the addition of several private bathrooms. The wide-plank red pine floors in the five bedrooms still slant and tilt, showing their years, and the furnishings are as close as possible to those that graced the original.

Gedney Farm, a short distance down the lane from the inn, is another matter. The six suites (some with two levels) and four deluxe guestrooms fill a massive old barn that once housed prize-winning horses. The architecture is stunning: In the lobby, for example, ceilings soar 28 feet to the rafters above. The four-poster beds are authentic colonial gems with crocheted or fishnet canopies; Turkish kilims, Early American woven rugs, or Orientals cover the burnished floors. Many of the rooms and suites feature fireplaces and boldly tiled Jacuzzis for two (the master suite also has an eating area and a sitting room).

A continental breakfast—juice, fruit, granola, and fresh-baked breads—is served to guests either in the terraced *Tap Room* of the old inn or in the barn of *Gedney Farm.* The *Gallery at Gedney Farm,* where fine and decorative art is displayed, also is the setting for summer weekend lunches.

Dining is one of the joys of a stay at the *Old Inn on the Green.* The intimate dining rooms are lighted only by candles glowing from wrought-iron colonial chandeliers, wall sconces, and pewter, brass, or silver holders. (The inn takes pride in eschewing electric lights in the dining rooms to create the ambience of colonial times; however, for guests' comfort, the rooms are air conditioned.) Four of the six dining rooms have impressive fireplaces, and on the wall in the *Gallery* dining room is a hand-painted mural depicting colonial New Marlborough. Spectacular floral displays abound. In summer and fall, dinner also is served on a canopied garden terrace overlooking a colonial flower and herb garden.

The food matches the setting for drama and excellence. Dinner (which is open to non-guests) is served on a prix fixe basis Saturday nights and à la carte the rest of the week. Frequent wine tastings and special culinary events are held as well. A typical summer Saturday menu might include an appetizer of foie gras–stuffed yellow tomato with sweet corn sauce and an entrée of seared breast of cured moulard duck with lentil-pistachio pancakes. Leslie makes the desserts, and choosing between riesling *crème* in chocolate shells and sour cherry–buttermilk pie isn't easy.

Located in a hamlet in the Berkshires, the inn is near the Appalachian Trail, skiing, art galleries, and music festivals.

OLD INN ON THE GREEN AND GEDNEY FARM **Star Rte. 70, New Marlborough, MA 01230 (phone: 413-229-3131; fax: 413-229-3132). This rural inn has 20 guestrooms (17 with private baths) with double or queen-size beds and telephones. Wheelchair accessible. Open year-round; restaurant closed Mondays through Wednesdays November through June. Rate for a double room (including continental breakfast): $90 to $245. Two-night minimum stay on weekends from July through October. Major credit cards accepted. Children welcome. No pets. No smoking. Bradford Wagstaff and Leslie Miller, innkeepers.**

DIRECTIONS: From New York take the Taconic State Parkway north to the Hillsdale exit and follow Route 23 to Great Barrington, Massachusetts. Continue on Route 23 (it will be joined by Route 7 through town). When Route 23 turns right at the traffic light, follow it about 3½ miles east to Route 57. Bear right onto Route 57 and continue for 5¾ miles. The inn is on the left, on the village green.

OLD FARM INN

ROCKPORT, MASSACHUSETTS

Bill and Susan Balzarini are the second generation in their family to operate the aptly named *Old Farm Inn.* Documents date the farmhouse to 1799 (though many locals believe it's much older). Bill's grandfather purchased the land and began operating a dairy farm on the property in the early 1900s. In 1964, Bill and his parents renovated the original farmhouse and created a popular inn and restaurant that operated until the 1980s. Now Bill and his wife, Susan, run this charming inn.

Painted in traditional red with white trim, the *Old Farm Inn* is an unpretentious bed and breakfast establishment with overstuffed chairs, rustic wood tables, creaky floors, braided rugs, and Adirondack chairs on the lawns. A red-and-white-striped awning shades the screened porch that serves as the breakfast room, where a continental buffet of juice, fresh fruit, muffins, bagels, cereal, and yogurt is laid atop an old wood-burning stove. Guests, who are encouraged to select a book from the library, find that a chair by the sitting room fireplace makes a comfortable spot for afternoon reading on cool days.

There are four double rooms and a suite with a deck in the *Main Inn,* another four doubles in the *Barn,* and a cottage with two bedrooms, a bath, a kitchen, and a living room. Patchwork quilts give the rooms a rustic charm; three have decorative fireplaces.

The inn occupies a five-acre patch of fields and woodlands, and *Halibut Point State Park* is nearby. A walk to the abandoned granite quarry may yield a basket of fresh blueberries. Continue along the path to the craggy coastline and explore the crab- and mollusk-rich tidal pools. From the overlook on the coast, the view stretches all the way to Maine—the perfect spot to watch the sunset. Other area attractions include art galleries, local festivals of chamber music, and summer theater.

OLD FARM INN 291 Granite St., Rte. 127, Rockport, MA 01966 (phone: 508-546-3237; 800-233-6828). This country inn on Cape Ann, near Rockport, has 10 guestrooms with private baths, twin, queen-, or king-size beds (cribs available for $10), telephones, TV sets, and air conditioning. Closed November through March. Rate for a double room (including continental breakfast): $73 to $125. Two-night minimum stay on weekends; three nights on holidays. Major credit cards accepted. Children welcome. No pets. Smoking permitted in public areas only. Bill and Susan Balzarini, innkeepers.

DIRECTIONS: Traveling from Boston, take Route 128 north to its end at a traffic light. At this point turn left onto Route 127 and travel 4½ miles toward Pigeon Cove and Rockport. From Rockport continue on Route 127 approximately 2½ miles to the inn, which is straight ahead.

HISTORIC MERRELL INN

South Lee, Massachusetts

When Charles and Faith Reynolds purchased the *Historic Merrell Inn* on two and a half acres bordering the Housatonic River in 1981, it was already almost 200 years old, but it had been vacant and neglected for the last hundred. The new innkeepers' task was monumental. With the help of the *Society for the Preservation of New England Antiquities,* former owners of the property, they installed electricity, heating, and plumbing—always careful to remain faithful to the building's original Federal style. Charles is a retired history teacher, and he wouldn't have it any other way.

Because of this dedication to historic preservation (the building is on the National Register of Historic Places), guests walk into the inn and into 1794 (when the place was a stop on the Boston–Albany stagecoach run). The red brick exterior with its first- and second-floor porches was unchanged over the passing years, and inside, numerous remarkable features remain. There are eight original 18th-century Count Rumford fireplaces (three of them in guestrooms), and the *Tavern Room*'s original circular colonial "birdcage" bar, complete with till drawer, is thought to be the only one remaining in America.

The guestrooms are furnished with equal attention to historical detail, except that all have thoroughly modern baths. Four rooms were carved from the third-floor ballroom, which was added in 1837. There are antique canopy beds—one with cornflower posts, another with pencil posts—antique chests, lace curtains, fluffy pillows, and colonial-motif wallcoverings and spreads.

An artist as well as a historian, Charles's most recent contribution to the inn is a mural, in the style of the Hudson River School, that wraps around the entry wall and parades up the staircase. Faith is a gardener (as well as a weaver) and is carefully restoring the gardens, which are bordered by neat stone walls. Down by the river is a pretty gazebo.

Breakfast is served in the *Tavern Room,* where a fire may glow in the fireplace. Candles illuminating the paneled walls and polished wide-plank pine floors, original oil paintings, and period tables and chairs make this room seem a charming throwback to a bygone age. The meal includes juice, fruit, and perhaps an omelette or blueberry-walnut buttermilk pancakes with sausage and pure maple syrup, all served on Bennington pottery, which is made in nearby Bennington, Vermont. Afternoon refreshments are served in the original *Keeping Room,* with its grand cooking fireplace, overstuffed sofas, and Hepplewhite breakfront.

The inn is in the heart of the Berkshires, near *Tanglewood,* the *Norman Rockwell Museum,* summer theater, skiing, and hiking.

HISTORIC MERRELL INN 1565 Pleasant St., South Lee, MA 01260 (phone: 413-243-1794; 800-243-1794; fax: 413-243-2669). This historic inn has nine guestrooms with private baths, double or queen-size beds, telephones, and air conditioning. Open year-round. Rate for a double room (including full breakfast and afternoon refreshments): $55 to $135. Two-night minimum stay on weekends; three nights July and August weekends. MasterCard and Visa accepted. Not appropriate for children under 12. No pets. Brandy, a golden retriever, and cats Callie and Patches in owners' residence. No smoking. Charles and Faith Reynolds, innkeepers; Pamela Hurst, manager.

DIRECTIONS: From the Massachusetts Turnpike, take Exit 2 at Lee. Follow signs for Route 102 to Stockbridge. Travel 3 miles east on Route 102; the inn is on the left.

LONGFELLOW'S WAYSIDE INN

SOUTH SUDBURY, MASSACHUSETTS

As ancient as this Hostelry
As any in the land may be,
Built in the old colonial day,
When men lived in a grander way,
With ampler hospitality.

Henry Wadsworth Longfellow, "Tales of a Wayside Inn," 1864

When the *Wayside Inn* was built in 1702, it was called *Howe's Tavern.* Located on the busy stagecoach route between Boston and Albany, the red clapboard inn with white trim witnessed many historic events. In 1775, the

Sudbury farmers, led by innkeeper Ezekiel Howe, were among the men who fought at nearby Concord, and many a battle's strategy must have been discussed hotly over a flip or toddy at the inn's tables. Today, the Sudbury Minutemen muster at the inn on April 19 in preparation for the annual reenactment of the march from Sudbury to Concord.

Ever since Longfellow immortalized the inn with his poem, it's been known as *Longfellow's Wayside Inn.* Thanks to a grant from the Ford Foundation, the buildings and priceless antiques have been preserved as a historic museum—but one that provides food and "lodging for man, woman, and beast" much as it did in colonial days.

The authentic character has been preserved down to the spare but functional rooms. There are Oriental rugs on the maple floors and reproduction period beds and dressers. All guestrooms have private tiled baths. Guests often congregate in the *Old Bar,* a pub decorated in Early American style.

In keeping with the colonial atmosphere, a waterwheel-powered gristmill on the property stone-grinds the wheat and corn the inn uses for its breads. Replicas of the *Martha-Mary Chapel* (which Henry Ford built and named after his mother and wife) and of the *Redstone School* (which inspired "Mary Had a Little Lamb") are located here.

Meals (also open to non-guests) are served in the six old dining rooms, which are warmed by fires in winter, by waiters and waitresses in colonial garb. The menu features such traditional fare as New England clam chowder, roast beef, baked Cape Cod scallops, and Indian pudding.

On the grounds are several lovely gardens and 100 acres of fields for hiking; golf, cross-country skiing, and antiquing are all available nearby.

LONGFELLOW'S WAYSIDE INN **Wayside Inn Rd., South Sudbury, MA 01776 (phone: 508-443-1776; fax: 508-443-2312). This historic inn near Lexington and Concord has 10 guestrooms with private baths, twin or double beds, telephones, and air conditioning. The dining rooms are wheelchair accessible. Closed *July 4* and *Christmas.* Rate for a double room (including full breakfast): $100. Major credit cards accepted. Children welcome. Pets allowed. Smoking permitted in guestrooms only. Robert Purrington, innkeeper.**

DIRECTIONS: From the Massachusetts Turnpike take I-495 north to Route 20 east. Follow Route 20 east for 7 miles to Wayside Inn Road. Watch for signs to the inn.

RED LION INN

STOCKBRIDGE, MASSACHUSETTS

From its strategic position at the crossroads in Stockbridge (once on the Albany–Boston Post Road), the *Red Lion Inn* has witnessed more than 200 years of history, and its walls literally tell the story. Photographs, historical documents, old paintings, and prints line the walls from floor to ceiling, and innumerable antiques, many rescued from a disastrous inn fire in 1895, fill the lobby and other public rooms. An old painted *Red Lion Inn* tavern sign can be found in a booth in the *Widow Bingham's Tavern.*

Today, the inn is considerably larger than it was in 1773. The main building contains 86 rooms, while an additional 22 are in a variety of historic outbuildings behind the inn and across the street. Jack and Jane Fitzpatrick have owned the inn since 1968; their daughter, Nancy, is president.

"Mrs. Fitz," as Jane is known, furnished all the rooms in colonial style. There are antique four-poster beds with crocheted canopies, pencil-post four-posters, mahogany chests, polished pine mirrors, and bed coverings and drapes in colonial-style fabrics. The hallways are lined with curio cabinets displaying collections ranging from teapots to silver, and also with original Norman Rockwell drawings and prints. The famed illustrator spent the last 25 years of his life in Stockbridge, and his classic 1968 painting

Stockbridge Main Street at Christmas features the *Red Lion Inn.* Every room at the inn contains at least one Rockwell print.

The formal dining room, a popular and festive place for family dinners and special occasions, features traditional New England fare (and is open to non-guests). New England clam chowder, roast turkey, and salmon cakes are on the menu. For dessert, there's Indian pudding, apple crisp, bread pudding with warm whiskey sauce, or chocolate-chip pie—sinfully delicious, especially when warmed and served with a scoop of ice cream and hot fudge sauce. Meals also can be taken in the *Widow Bingham's Tavern,* in the *Lion's Den* (which has live jazz or folk music in the evenings), or in summer in the courtyard under the trees.

Guests can take advantage of the inn's proximity to *Tanglewood,* the *Norman Rockwell Museum,* and summer theaters; it also is near golf, tennis, bicycling, hiking, and skiing.

RED LION INN Main St., Stockbridge, MA 01262 (phone: 413-298-5545; fax: 413-298-5130). This historic inn has 108 guestrooms (92 with private baths) with twin, double, queen-, or king-size beds, telephones, and air conditioning; most have TV sets. Wheelchair accessible. Open year-round. Rate for a double room (including continental breakfast): $70 to $250. Two-night minimum stay on weekends in July and August. Major credit cards accepted. Children welcome. No pets. No smoking except in *Lion's Den.* Jack and Jane Fitzpatrick, owners; Nancy Fitzpatrick, president; Brooks Bradbury, general manager.

DIRECTIONS: From the Massachusetts Turnpike, take Exit 2 at Lee. Follow signs for Route 102 to Stockbridge. Go 5 miles east on Route 102; the inn is on the left in the center of Stockbridge.

Rhode Island

1661 INN & HOTEL MANISSES

Block Island, Rhode Island

Block Island is a little oasis—a sheltered retreat with salt marshes, sea-cleft bluffs, and sunny beaches, where herons feed and ospreys build their nests. The island was first charted by Italian explorer Giovanni da Verrazano in 1524, then sighted by Dutch adventurer Adrian Block in 1614. In the early 1960s, the Abrams family—Justin, Joan, and their three children, Rita, Mark, and Rick—made a discovery of their own.

Sailing the waters of Block Island Sound, the Abramses became enchanted with the island and found themselves returning again and again. Eventually, in 1969, they purchased their first property, a little inn in need of a major overhaul. They all pitched in, and soon the *1661 Inn* was pretty and proud. (It originally had 18 rooms with shared baths but now has nine rooms with private baths, some even boasting Jacuzzis.) The inn is decorated with Early American art and antiques, and its decks afford spectacular views of the ocean.

For the energetic Abramses, the odyssey had just begun. In 1972, they bought the *Hotel Manisses;* an 1870 relic across the street from the inn, it had been boarded up for years and was scheduled for demolition. Despite its run-down condition, the hotel, with its mansard roof and square turret, was a reminder of the late 1800s, when Block Island was a fashionable seaside resort. Today, its 17 rooms, all named for local shipwrecks and all with private baths (some with Jacuzzis), are decorated in lively fabrics and

Victorian furniture; instead of suffering the wrecker's ball, the hotel now is listed on the National Register of Historic Places.

The Abrams historic preservation team still wasn't finished. In succession they tackled the *Nicholas Ball Cottage,* next door to the inn on the former site of *St. Anne's-by-the-Sea Episcopal Church* (it has three luxurious rooms with fireplaces, Jacuzzis, and lovely antiques), and the nine-room *Guest House* (five rooms have private baths and four share). Today, daughter Rita and her husband, Steven Draper, manage the properties.

A bountiful New England buffet breakfast is served to all guests at the *1661 Inn.* The extravaganza includes such specialties as baked bluefish, hash, and baked beans, as well as eggs, pancakes, muffins, fruit, and juices. In the afternoon a complimentary wine and "nibbles" hour offers guests a chance to mingle with their hosts and other visitors. Dinner, which is served at the *Hotel Manisses* (and is open to non-guests), is a food lover's fantasy, featuring seafood and the provender of the Abramses' gardens. Oysters, mussels, bluefish, and tuna are matched with spinach, peppers, tomatoes, zucchini, string beans, kale, rhubarb, and herbs for a distinctive Block Island taste.

During the nibbles hour, guests can sign up for one of the inn's free excursions around the island—perhaps a sunset tour, a picnic and walk along the Clayhead Nature Trail, or a tour of the owners' farm, where they raise llamas, pygmy and fainting goats, Scottish Highland steer, and black swans. On their own guests can enjoy nearby ocean beaches and nature walks, whale watching, bicycling, sailing, shopping, and fishing.

1661 INN & HOTEL MANISSES 1 Spring St., Block Island, RI 02807 (phone: 401-466-2421, 401-466-2063, or 800-MANISSES, inn and hotel; 401-466-2836, restaurant; fax: 401-466-2858). The hotel, inn, and cottages on pastoral Block Island have 38 guestrooms (34 with private baths) with twin, double, queen-, or king-size beds. Open year-round; restaurant closed weekdays mid-December through mid-April. Rate for a double room (including full breakfast, afternoon wine, and gratuity): $59 to $325. Three-night minimum stay on weekends in July and August; two nights the rest of year. Major credit cards accepted. *Hotel Manisses* not appropriate for children under 10; all children welcome in the other guestrooms. No pets. Smoking permitted in designated rooms. Justin and Joan Abrams, innkeepers; Steve and Rita Draper, managers.

DIRECTIONS: Block Island is located 13 miles off the Rhode Island coast; car-service ferries make daily runs from Point Judith, Rhode Island. Seasonal service and non-car ferries also go to Block Island from Newport, Rhode Island; New London, Connecticut; and Montauk, New York. From the Point Judith ferry turn left up Main Street, then turn right onto Spring Street (just past the theater) and drive one block; the *1661 Inn* is on the left.

ELM TREE COTTAGE

NEWPORT, RHODE ISLAND

Innkeepers Priscilla and Thomas Malone—and their three daughters, Keely, Briana, and Erin—purchased this lovely 1882 house, with its views of Easton's Pond and First Beach, in 1990. They have breathed new life into a home that once had a questionable future. Today, the inn and its landscaped gardens look much as they did when Mrs. Crawford-Hill, the first owner, used to entertain her friend Wallis Simpson to tea.

The gracious entryway with its Oriental rug opens onto a formal parlor overlooking the bay. In the parlor are overstuffed sofas upholstered in white jacquard and a magnificent mirror with garlands of carved roses, purchased at auction. Priscilla, who is a fine artist, painstakingly re-created missing pieces of the mirror's frame and then painted it its original pale blue and ivory.

Such restorations are the Malones' business. In addition to innkeeping, Tom and Priscilla restore stained glass windows and religious interiors for museums and corporate and residential clients. Not surprisingly, you'll see some exceptional examples of stained glass here, and you'll understand why the Malones have won numerous awards for their inn.

Adjacent to the parlor is the sun-drenched, wicker-filled *Morning Room.* It overlooks the perennial gardens, where an abundance of tulips and daffodils heralds the coming of spring, followed by a procession of peonies, roses, and lilies. A tiny, clubby bar, where guests can mix drinks with their own liquor (the inn does not have a liquor license), has an unusual reverse-painted mirror, featuring the Pekinese dogs Mrs. Crawford-Hill loved so much, and a bar embedded with 1921 silver dollars.

Each guestroom seems more impressive than the last, so it would be hard to select a favorite, but each reflects the Malones' background in interior design, woodworking, and fine arts. Each is decorated with polished French and English antiques, complemented by designer linen and lace. The *Library* has floor-to-ceiling bookshelves, a wood-burning fireplace, and a spectacular carved walnut bed and matching armoire. The *Harriman Room,* also with a wood-burning fireplace and carved walnut bed, was once a gentleman's dressing room. All baths in the house are elegant, but the one in the *Harriman Room* contains a porcelain sink with Austrian crystal legs, a huge porcelain soaking tub, and the original shower stall.

Breakfast is served in the sunny formal dining room, painted blush pink and accented by arrangements of flowers and potted plants. A buffet is set out every morning on the antique Hepplewhite-style sideboard, where guests can help themselves to an appetizer (perhaps a berry cobbler), fruit, and yogurt. That's followed by an entrée such as puffed pear pancakes. Individual tables are set with floral chintz cloths, and Priscilla selects the daily china to complement the day's entrée.

Newport offers a wealth of extravagant mansions, a cliff walk, sailing, boating, tennis, golf, concerts, antiquing, and shopping.

ELM TREE COTTAGE 336 Gibbs Ave., Newport, RI 02840 (phone: 401-849-1610; 800-882-3ELM; fax: 401-849-2084). This elegant inn has six guestrooms with private baths, queen- or king-size beds, and air conditioning. Closed December 24 through 26. Rate for a double room (including full breakfast): $125 to $325. Two-night minimum stay on weekends; three nights on weekends June through *Columbus Day,* holiday weekends, and during special events. Major credit cards accepted. Not appropriate for children under 14. No pets. Rabbit in hutch in back. No smoking. Priscilla and Thomas Malone, innkeepers.

DIRECTIONS: From New York take I-95 north to Exit 3 in Rhode Island. Follow 138 east for approximately 30 miles, always following the blue signs to the Newport Bridge. After crossing the bridge, exit at "Scenic Newport" and turn right off the exit ramp. At the second traffic light turn right onto America's Cup Avenue. Follow this road to the seventh traffic light, stay to the left, and proceed up the hill onto Memorial Boulevard toward First Beach. Cross Bellevue Avenue and make a left onto Gibbs Avenue (if you pass *Cliff Walk Manor,* you've gone too far). Proceed to the first stop sign. *Elm Tree Cottage* is the third house after the stop sign on the right. From Boston follow Route 128 south to Route 24 south via the Sakonner River Bridge to Route 138 south (exit at the *Ramada Inn* and bear left). Continue on Route 138 south until you reach the Fleet National Bank on the right. Take a left onto Route 138A south toward Newport Beaches. At the second traffic light bear left and continue past the beaches and up the hill. Make a right onto Gibbs Avenue, then follow directions above.

FRANCIS MALBONE HOUSE

NEWPORT, RHODE ISLAND

When guests walk from busy Thames Street through the front doors of the *Francis Malbone House,* they step back to 1760, when ship merchant Francis Malbone built the stately brick home on Newport's waterfront, a perfect vantage point from which to survey his private fleet. The architect he hired was Peter Harrison, who had designed other Newport gems, including the *Tuoro Synagogue* and *Redwood Library.* Although he seldom admitted it, Malbone traded principally in slaves and rum, and a secret tunnel ran under the street from his house directly to the docks.

In this century, the house was used for many years as a nursing home, but in 1989 it was purchased by a group of Newporters, restored, and converted into an inn. Today, with its graceful colonial woodwork and doors, its 10 fireplaces, 15-foot ceilings, and elegant proportions, it looks much as it did in Malbone's day. Three formal parlors contain lovely Federal-era antiques, and fires glow in the fireplaces on chilly nights.

Guestrooms are decorated with taste and charm. The *Counting House,* on the main floor, was added during the British occupation of Newport in the 1770s. This suite features 18-foot ceilings, shell corner cabinets, a king-size four-poster bed, and a magnificent bathroom with a whirlpool tub. Many of the upstairs guestrooms have wood-burning fireplaces and views of either the gardens or the harbor; all are furnished with antiques, including four-poster beds. Pretty floral fabrics adorn the windows, beds, and chairs.

Guests are served a full breakfast at the Queen Anne mahogany table in the formal dining room, where there is yet another fireplace. The meal might include eggs Benedict, peach pancakes, pumpkin waffles, or raspberry crêpes.

The inn is within walking distance of antiques shops, boutiques, and the historic houses along Bellevue Avenue. Bicycling, boating, golf, and tennis can be found nearby. For anyone who would rather stay put, there's a spectacular raised and enclosed garden in back of the inn with benches and Adirondack chairs for reading.

FRANCIS MALBONE HOUSE 392 Thames St., Newport, RI 02840 (phone: 401-846-0392; 800-846-0392; fax: 401-848-5956). This Federal house in the heart of historic Newport has nine guestrooms with private baths, queen- or king-size beds, and air conditioning. Open year-round. Rate for a double room (including full breakfast): $125 to $295. Major credit cards accepted. Not appropriate for children under 13. No pets. No smoking. Will Dewey, innkeeper.

DIRECTIONS: From New York follow the directions to *Elm Tree Cottage* (see page 137) as far as America's Cup Avenue. Follow this road to the sixth light, turn right onto lower Thames Street at the *Perry Mill Market,* and drive three blocks. The inn is on the left. (To reach the private parking lot in back, turn left onto Brewer Street and into the first driveway on the right.) From Boston follow the *Elm Tree Cottage* directions to Route 138A south. At the second traffic light bear left and continue past the beaches and up the hill. At the fourth light (bottom of hill) turn left onto Thames Street, then follow directions above.

IVY LODGE

NEWPORT, RHODE ISLAND

Hidden behind a privet hedge, *Ivy Lodge*'s rather unassuming, gray-shingled exterior belies its elegant interior. Built in 1886, the house is much more conservative in style than the nearby summer "cottages" of the Vanderbilts and Astors, but it is nevertheless a stunner. The entry hall, with its carved solid-oak walls and elaborate 33-foot Gothic staircase with 365 spindles, sets the scene. There are fireplaces everywhere: in the entry hall, in the elegant pink reception room with its wicker and chintz, in the formal living room. Done in hunter green and cream, the latter has a grand piano (sometimes used for chamber music concerts) and bay windows overlooking the formal gardens. Open the French doors and step onto the wraparound verandah, outfitted with vintage wicker chairs.

Innkeepers Maggie and Terry Moy have furnished the bedrooms just as they have the common rooms—with museum-quality antiques. Maggie also has added decorative stenciling to the walls of some of the guestrooms. The *Library Room* has lace curtains on its shuttered bay windows and a sleigh bed piled high with pillows. Its wood-burning fireplace of blue Delft tiles sits below a mantel with built-in bookshelves. The marble-and-tile bath has a Jacuzzi. The *Turret Room* (where Arnold Schwarzenegger and Maria Shriver once stayed) is done up with antique oak furniture, including a king-size bed, and has a private rooftop deck; its bath features a claw-foot tub and an original pull-chain toilet. The *Ivy Room* is bright and fresh with a four-poster bed, a whitewashed antique pine vanity and mirror, and sea green carpeting.

The dining room is so large that the 21-foot cherry table, seating up to 18, fits comfortably. It's set with silver, bone china, and crystal for breakfast. Entrées may include Scotch eggs or Grand Marnier French toast stuffed with cream cheese.

Ivy Lodge is located in Newport's mansion area, near museums, beaches, tennis, golf, and the cliff walk.

IVY LODGE 12 Clay St., Newport, RI 02840 (phone: 401-849-6865). This lavish shingled inn has eight guestrooms with private baths (Room No. 1's is off the hallway), twin, double, queen-, or king-size beds, and air conditioning. Closed Monday through Thursday from January through March. Rate for a double room (including full breakfast): $100 to $175. Two-night minimum stay on weekends. MasterCard and Visa accepted. Children welcome. No pets. Kelly, a German shepherd, and White Cat in residence. Smoking permitted outdoors only. Maggie and Terry Moy, innkeepers.

DIRECTIONS: From New York follow the directions to *Elm Tree Cottage* (see page 137) onto Memorial Boulevard toward First Beach. At the next traffic light turn right onto Bellevue Avenue. Follow Bellevue to the first light, then turn left onto Narragansett Avenue. Clay is the first street on the left, and the inn is located two houses up on the right. From Boston take the *Elm Tree Cottage* directions "past the beaches and up the hill." Turn left onto Bellevue Avenue and follow the directions above.

LARCHWOOD INN

WAKEFIELD, RHODE ISLAND

Francis Browning started doing yard work at the *Larchwood Inn* in 1946 and just never left. He and his wife, Diann, purchased it with a group of investors, in 1971, and have been sole owners since 1978.

The building dates to 1831, but it wasn't until 1925 that the grand old house and its adjacent property were opened as an inn. In 1947 its then owner, who hailed from Nova Scotia, began the ritual of celebrating Robert Burns's birthday here on January 25 every year. Although the event no longer is commemorated, many Scottish touches remain. Throughout the inn, the walls are hung with quotations by Burns and Sir Walter Scott and photographs and prints of Scottish historical and literary figures.

With a columned front porch, tall windows, a sloping roof, and two chimneys, the three-story mansion sits on three and a half acres of lush green lawns and wonderful old trees, including copper beech, ginkgo, pin oak, spruce, mountain ash, maple, Japanese cherry, fir, dogwood, and an 1830s mulberry. At the entrance to the circular driveway, stone gates are flanked by flowering dogwoods and rhododendrons.

The first floor of the gentle old main house is divided into four dining rooms, each of which has a fireplace. There's another hearth in the *Tam o' Shanter Pub,* and yet another in the living room, which also has comfortable overstuffed sofas, several antique pieces, plush carpeting, and plants. Twelve guestrooms are in the main inn and seven more are in *Holly House,* a house of the same vintage across the street. All are decorated with Waverly wallpaper, lace curtains, and period antiques, including several four-poster beds.

The *Larchwood Inn* boasts a fine restaurant, which is open (also to nonguests) for breakfast, lunch, and dinner; no meals are included in the room rate. The French toast with strawberries, made from inn-baked bread and served with either sour or whipped cream, is a crowd pleaser. Whole lobsters are on the menu every night except Mondays, when twin lobster tails are offered at a special price.

The inn is located near ocean beaches, fishing, the *Gilbert Stuart Birthplace,* shopping, and art galleries.

LARCHWOOD INN 521 Main St., Wakefield, RI 02879 (phone: 401-783-5454; 800-275-5450; fax: 401-783-1800). This country inn has 19 guestrooms (13 with private baths) with twin, double, or queen-size beds. Open year-round. Rate for a double room: $50 to $100. Major credit cards accepted. Children welcome. Pets allowed for an additional $5 per night. A cat in residence. Smoking permitted except in some dining rooms. Francis and Diann Browning, innkeepers.

DIRECTIONS: Traveling from New York, take I-95 north to Exit 3. Follow Route 138 east to Kingston. In Kingston take Route 108 to Wakefield. Turn right onto Main Street; the inn is on the right. Traveling from Boston, take I-95 south to Exit 9 and follow Route 4 until it merges with Route 1. Continue on Route 1 to the first exit for Wakefield. From this exit pick up Main Street, and the inn is on the right.

Mid-Atlantic and Ontario

NEW JERSEY
1. Cape May: MAINSTAY INN
2. Milford: CHESTNUT HILL ON THE DELAWARE

NEW YORK
3. Amagansett: BLUFF COTTAGE
4. Blue Mountain Lake: THE HEDGES
5. Bridgehampton: BRIDGEHAMPTON INN
6. Brooklyn: BED & BREAKFAST ON THE PARK
7. Cazenovia: LINCKLAEN HOUSE
8. Clarence: ASA RANSOM HOUSE
9. Dover Plains: OLD DROVERS INN
10. East Hampton: CENTENNIAL HOUSE; MAIDSTONE ARMS
11. Garrison: BIRD AND BOTTLE INN
12. Ithaca: ROSE INN
13. Lake Placid: LAKE PLACID LODGE
14. Mumford: GENESEE COUNTRY INN
15. New York City: INN NEW YORK CITY
16. Pittsford: OLIVER LOUD'S INN
17. Sag Harbor: AMERICAN HOTEL
18. Saranac Lake: THE POINT
19. Saratoga Springs: ADELPHI HOTEL

PENNSYLVANIA
20. Beach Lake: BEACH LAKE HOTEL
21. Churchtown: INN AT TWIN LINDEN
22. Doylestown: HIGHLAND FARMS
23. Ephrata: SMITHTON INN
24. Fogelsville: GLASBERN
25. Lititz: SWISS WOODS B & B
26. Mercersburg: MERCERSBURG INN
27. New Hope: WHITEHALL INN
28. Upper Black Eddy: BRIDGETON HOUSE ON THE DELAWARE

ONTARIO, CANADA
29. Cambridge: LANGDON HALL COUNTRY HOUSE
30. Elora: ELORA MILL COUNTRY INN
31. Fenelon Falls: EGANRIDGE INN AND COUNTRY CLUB
32. Grafton: STE. ANNE'S COUNTRY INN AND SPA
33. Jackson's Point: THE BRIARS

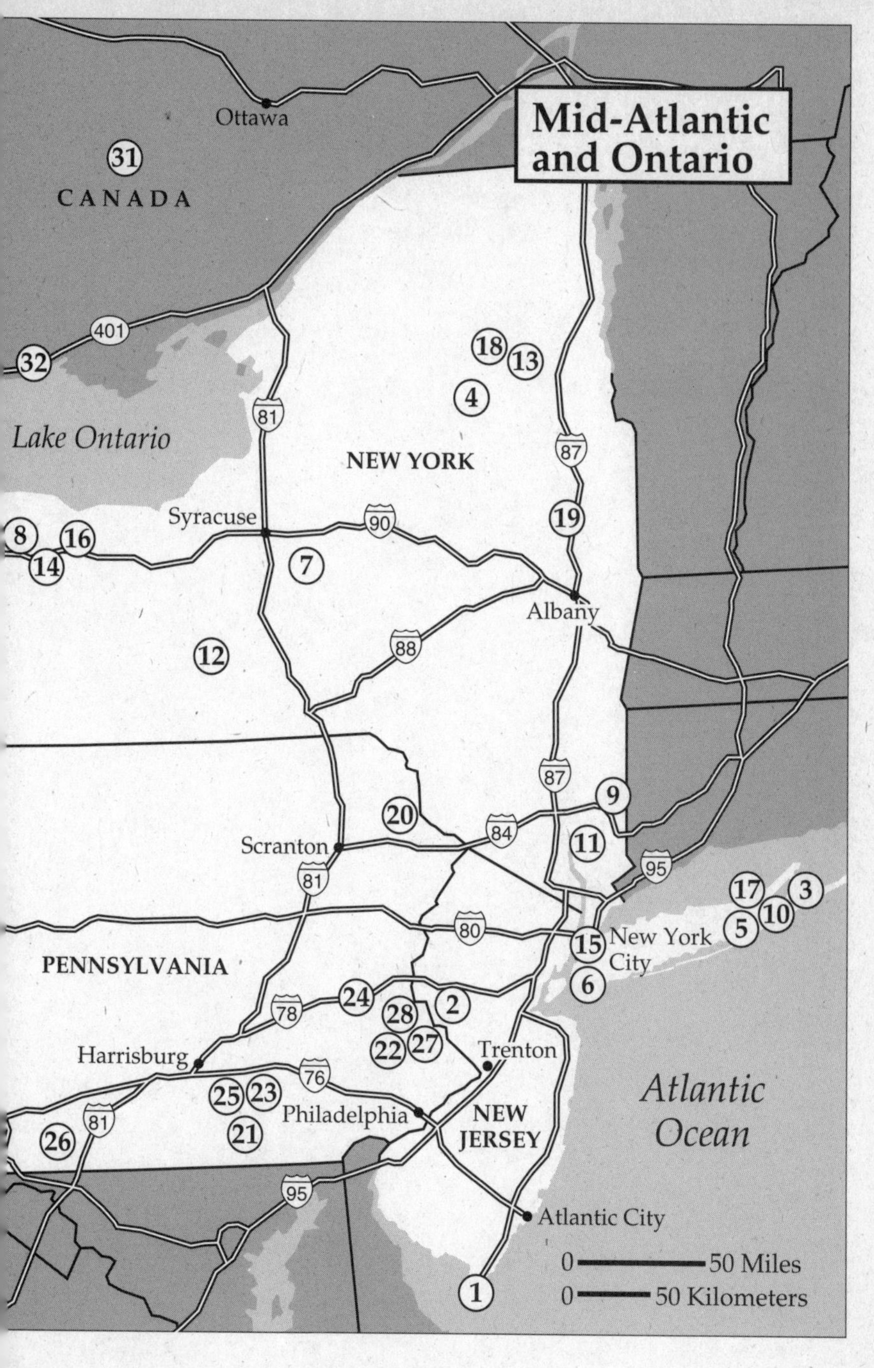
Mid-Atlantic and Ontario
Ottawa
31
CANADA
401
32
Lake Ontario
81
18
13
4
87
NEW YORK
Syracuse
90
19
8
16
14
7
Albany
88
12
87
9
20
84
11
Scranton
81
95
17
3
10
5
80
15
New York City
PENNSYLVANIA
6
24
2
78
28
22
27
Trenton
Harrisburg
76
25
23
Philadelphia
NEW JERSEY
Atlantic Ocean
81
26
21
95
Atlantic City
0 50 Miles
0 50 Kilometers
1

Mid-Atlantic and Ontario

New Jersey

MAINSTAY INN

CAPE MAY, NEW JERSEY

Located at the southernmost tip of New Jersey and surrounded by broad sandy beaches on the Atlantic Ocean, the Victorian town of Cape May was founded in 1848 and settled by people who came to enjoy the cool, salty air. Fortunately for today's visitors, the village eluded the trend toward urbanization and modernization that was so prevalent during the early 20th century. More than 600 Victorian structures still stand in Cape May, and the entire town has been designated a National Historic District.

When Tom and Sue Carroll bought the *Mainstay Inn*, in 1976, they were in the forefront of the innkeeping industry in the US. Recognizing the uniqueness of their great Victorian home, the Carrolls sought to preserve the ambience of the mid-19th century. The broad front verandah provides the ideal spot to sip afternoon tea and listen to the clip-clop of the horse-drawn carriages passing by and the whisper of sea breezes rustling through the giant sycamore trees that line the street—all echoes of a more gracious age. The grounds are beautifully landscaped and lined with flower beds containing tulips, hydrangeas, lilies, and roses. The intimate belvedere, high on the roof, is a romantic place from which to watch the sun set.

This elegant Italianate villa, built in 1872 as a gentlemen's gaming club, still has many of its original features, including 14-foot ceilings, a huge chandelier in the dining room, and such furnishings as a 12-foot pier mirror in the entrance hall. Museum-quality antiques (in the dark, polished walnut so popular in the 19th century) and silk-screened wallpapers by Bradbury & Bradbury, enhance the Old World charm of the common rooms.

The guestrooms are distributed among the main house, an adjacent summer cottage, and the *Officers' Quarters,* a former World War I navy officer's home across the street. Those in the main house and the summer cottage are furnished in a lavish style the Carrolls call "Renaissance Revival," featuring tall, carved walnut headboards, dressers, and armoires. The four suites in the *Officers' Quarters* are a bit more contemporary, boasting fireplaces and whirlpool tubs.

On summer mornings guests enjoy breakfast on the verandah—juice, fruit, fresh-baked breads and muffins, cereal, and yogurt. Throughout the rest of the year, a full breakfast is served in the formal dining room of the main house. The hearty entrées might include strawberry French toast, cheese-blintz soufflé, or an English muffin with a poached egg, tomato slice, and cheese sauce. Afternoon tea is accompanied by homemade sweets, cheese and crackers, or finger sandwiches.

Historic tours, bicycling, beaches, and bird watching are available nearby, and the village sponsors several special events, including a music festival in May and June, *Victorian Week* in October, and *Christmas in Cape May* throughout December.

MAINSTAY INN 635 Columbia Ave., Cape May, NJ 08204 (phone: 609-884-8690). This historic inn has 16 guestrooms and suites with private baths and twin, double, queen-, or king-size beds. Four of the rooms have telephones, TV sets, and air conditioning. Wheelchair accessible. Suites in the *Officers' Quarters* open year-round; other rooms closed early January through mid-March. Rate for a double room (including breakfast and afternoon tea): $95 to $250. Three-night minimum stay requested June through September. No credit cards accepted. *Officers' Quarters* not appropriate for children under six; other rooms not appropriate for children under 14. No pets. A family of cats lives on the grounds. No smoking. Tom and Sue Carroll, innkeepers.

DIRECTIONS: From Philadelphia take the Walt Whitman Bridge to the Atlantic City Expressway. After approximately 50 miles, take the Garden State Parkway south another 40 miles to Cape May. In Cape May, turn left at the first light onto Madison Street. Proceed three blocks and turn right onto Columbia Avenue. The inn is three blocks down the street on the right.

CHESTNUT HILL ON THE DELAWARE

MILFORD, NEW JERSEY

For those who enjoy the exuberance of Victorian architecture, a visit to this historic inn is a must. Built in 1860 as a wedding present for a bride by her husband, the house, as well as an adjacent cottage, has been meticulously restored by innkeepers Linda and Rob Castagna.

The mansion and its little sister are painted to highlight individual architectural elements. The main house is pale green with accents of forest green and cranberry; the fanciful wrought-iron grapevine that dances across the front of its wraparound porch and down the pillars is dark green with gold-leaf trim. The *Country Cottage* is painted a rich cream with taupe and teal trim. Both houses are merely steps away from the Delaware River and have magnificent views.

In the main house, the spacious entry hall with its cherry-and-oak parquet floor opens into the *Fireplace Room* on one side, decorated with an ornate painted mantel, and the spacious *Drawing Room* on the other, with a richly carved walnut fireplace. Spanning a wall in the *Drawing Room* is a black-walnut apothecary unit that serves as a lending library and gift shop. For the musically inclined, both a pump organ and an upright piano are located here as well, although these instruments are no match for the clear, sweet trill of Keats the canary, in his antique brass cage. Mannequins dressed in lacy Victorian garb that once belonged to the house's original owner greet modern-day guests.

The decor of the guestrooms continues the whimsical Victorian theme. *Peaches and Cream* has a spindle spool bed with a key quilt and a black-walnut armoire; *Teddy's Place,* a third-floor suite with a splendid view of the Delaware, is home to more than 150 stuffed bears. The *Country Cottage* boasts a bedroom with a fireplace, a fully stocked kitchen, a private porch (on which a permanent resident is an authentic hand-painted carousel horse), and views of the river from the queen-size bed. It's furnished in country French style.

Breakfast, including juice, fruit, fresh-baked bread and pastries, and perhaps a puffy apple pancake or a soufflé, is served in the formal dining room on a black-walnut table.

For sheer relaxation, spend an afternoon in one of the large antique rockers on the verandah—drinking iced tea, listening to the birds and the splash of the inn's fountain, enjoying the perennial gardens, and watching the Delaware River roll past. Nearby are river rafting, country fairs, antiques shops, a hiking trail along the old Delaware Canal towpath, bicycling, summer theaters, and musical events.

CHESTNUT HILL ON THE DELAWARE **63 Church St., PO Box N, Milford, NJ 08848 (phone: 908-995-9761). This Victorian mansion and cottage on the Delaware River offers five guestrooms (three with private baths) with double or queen-size beds and air conditioning. Open year-round. Rate for a double room (including full breakfast) in the main house: $80 to $105; in the *Country Cottage:* $135 per night or $750 per week. Two-night minimum stay on weekends and holidays. No credit cards accepted. Not appropriate for children under 12. No pets. A canary, Keats, in residence. Smoking permitted on outside porches only. Rob and Linda Castagna, innkeepers.**

DIRECTIONS: From New York take I-78 west to Exit 11 (Pattenburg). Follow Route 614 for 8 miles south to Spring Hill. Turn left onto Route 519, and travel 3 miles south to Milford. In Milford turn right onto Bridge Street and then right onto Church Street. At the end of Church Street turn left; the inn's parking lot is straight ahead.

BLUFF COTTAGE

AMAGANSETT, NEW YORK

Just down the hill and across the street from *Bluff Cottage,* the rolling surf crashes onto the white sand of Atlantic Beach. The inn's small second-floor balcony, with its comfortable wicker chairs, provides a popular viewing platform. From the broad front porch, furnished with more wicker and decorated with ferns and red and pink impatiens, guests enjoy a view of the lawns and colorful gardens, hidden from the street behind a clipped privet hedge.

With weathered shingles and white trim, this Dutch colonial house was built in 1892 by Dr. Rossiter Johnson, an editor at the New York publishing firm of Funk & Wagnalls. John Pakulek and Clem Thompson purchased it in 1971 and 21 years later opened their home as a bed and breakfast inn.

After many years of travel, Pakulek and Thompson had acquired some rare museum-quality antiques and, today, they happily share these treasures with their guests. The common rooms contain several interesting pieces. There's an ornately carved mahogany partners' desk in the den. In the living room, an eight-foot country French fruitwood confessional dominates one corner; and a magnificent primitive painting hangs over the fireplace.

The four guestrooms are furnished in a style that combines elegance and comfort. The *Green Room,* for example, has forest green carpeting and walls; a plaid silk spread covers the Charleston rice four-poster bed. In the *Blue Room* is another four-poster, while the *Peach Bisque Room* has a canopy bed, an antique marble-topped Bombay chest, and an English fruitwood armoire.

A continental breakfast of juice, fruit, and fresh-baked muffins, croissants, and scones is served in the dining room. Here, the decor is highlighted by a lovely collection of rose medallion Chinese export china.

Bluff Road, with its vistas of grassy dunes and beaches, is a popular place for bicycling, jogging, walking, and in-line skating, especially on sunny afternoons. The inn also is near the *Amagansett Farmers' Market,* sailing, fishing, and nature preserves.

BLUFF COTTAGE 266 Bluff Rd. (mailing address: PO Box 428), Amagansett, NY 11930 (phone: 516-267-6172). This gray-shingled bed and breakfast establishment has four guestrooms with private baths, queen-size beds, and air conditioning. Closed November through April. Rate for a double room (including continental breakfast): $195 to $225. Two-night minimum stay May and October; three nights June through September; four nights on major holidays. Major credit cards accepted. Not appropriate for children under 12. No pets. No smoking. John J. Pakulek III and Clement M. Thompson, innkeepers.

DIRECTIONS: Traveling east on Montauk Highway, continue through the village of Amagansett, turn right onto Atlantic Avenue (just before the fire station), and proceed two blocks. The inn is on the right, on the corner of Atlantic Avenue and Bluff Road.

THE HEDGES

BLUE MOUNTAIN LAKE, NEW YORK

An uncommon Adirondack resort located on twelve and a half mountain acres, *The Hedges* has spurned the "standard" inn accoutrements: There are no whirlpools or four-poster beds here, just the simple comforts and clean mountain air that have been attracting guests since 1921.

Built with a textured-bark exterior in 1880, this house was originally the summer retreat of Col. Hiram B. Duryea, a Civil War veteran. The colonel loved the wild beauty of Blue Mountain Lake and especially appreciated its insulation from the hustle and bustle of his winter home and business in New York. He was adamant that there be no indoor toilets or electric lights. Over the years, however, he did add a cottage of massive hand-cut stones with cypress shingles imported from California, a caretaker's cottage, a horse barn, and a carriage house. Eventually plumbing and electricity were installed, and four additional cottages followed in the 1930s. The current owner, Richard J. Van Yperen, purchased the property in 1972 and has maintained the rustic flavor.

The stunning beauty of the lodge and stone house, with lawns that slope to the edge of the lake, reminds us of Duryea's foresight. Dotting the property are Adirondack chairs that invite relaxation and contemplation. Inside is a library with a collection of old western novels, excellent children's books, and games such as backgammon, chess, and Ping-Pong, as well as a piano for sing-alongs.

Each guestroom has wood-beamed ceilings and is simply furnished with such elements as country-style rockers, dressers, and beds. At night, the smell of the forest's pine and the sound of loons calling to each other soothe the senses.

The Hedges serves two meals daily in a dining room that has changed little since the 1920s. Guests are assigned a table for the duration of their stay. Breakfasts are hearty and plentiful, with juice, fruit, eggs, pancakes, and muffins. A single entrée, such as roast pork or barbecued meat, is served nightly except Saturdays, when a buffet with two main courses is offered. No alcohol is allowed in the dining room. After dinner, guests gather around the dining room's stone fireplace to socialize and enjoy coffee, tea, hot chocolate, cookies, cakes, and popcorn.

All the activities of a typical Adirondack family resort are available, including swimming, water skiing, fishing, boating, tennis, horseshoes, volleyball, and hiking.

THE HEDGES Rte. 28W, Blue Mountain Lake, NY 12812 (phone: 518-352-7325; fax: 518-352-7672). The property has 28 guestrooms with private baths and twin or double beds. Three cottages are wheelchair accessible. Closed mid-October through mid-June. Rate for a double room (including full breakfast, dinner, and an evening snack): $128 to $152. No credit cards accepted. Children welcome. No pets. Smoking permitted in guestrooms only. Richard J. Van Yperen, innkeeper.

DIRECTIONS: Traveling from the west, take the New York State Thruway to Exit 31 in Utica, then Route 12 to Alder Creek. Turn onto Route 28 and proceed to Blue Mountain Lake; the inn is on the left. From the south take the New York State Thruway to Exit 24 in Albany, then I-87 to Exit 23. Follow Route 9 north for 3 miles beyond Warrensburg, then turn onto Route 28 to Blue Mountain Lake. Continue on Route 28 through the village toward Old Forge; *The Hedges* is a mile along on the right.

BRIDGEHAMPTON INN

BRIDGEHAMPTON, NEW YORK

The Hamptons, on Long Island's eastern end, were first settled in 1640. Although the area remained largely agricultural, by the mid-1700s it had become a well-traveled pass-through to Connecticut; George Washington came this way when he traveled to Boston to receive his commission to lead the colonies' army in the Revolutionary War. Travelers needed places to stay, and many of the large homes took in boarders. The fine home that was built in 1795 and is now the *Bridgehampton Inn* was undoubtedly one of them.

A stately white clapboard with mullioned windows and a columned entrance, it was known as the *Boxwood Inn* during the 1980s. It fell on hard times, however, and had long stopped taking in travelers when it was purchased by Anna and Detlef Pump in 1993. After a massive renovation, the rechristened inn reopened in 1994.

This is not a fussy inn. The decor has a sophisticated elegance that's accented with clever artwork and extravagant floral displays in the common rooms. In the living room, filled with burnished antique chests, Victorian tables, and a pretty Victorian settee covered in forest green velvet, a fire glows in the hearth on cool days. Beyond the French doors, brick terraces with tables and chairs overlooking refined gardens offer quiet places to relax.

The room decor is crisp and serene, with beige wall-to-wall carpeting, hand-crafted four-poster beds, and antique dressers and tables. Room No. 7 has a Victorian settee in a spritely red-striped twill and a polished antique chest with brass pulls. Room No. 6 is furnished with a spectacular eight-piece antique Biedermeier suite. All the baths are outstanding. European in style, they are custom-designed in gray marble, with square sinks surrounded by broad gray counters, enormous marble showers, and European fixtures.

Breakfast is served on the terrace or in a sunny breakfast room decorated with antique blue-and-white china from Denmark, where Anna grew up. The continental breakfast, which is included in the room rate, features freshly baked muffins, scones, and croissants from *Loaves and Fishes,* the local catering firm also owned by the Pumps. A full breakfast is available for an additional charge.

In the heart of the hamlet of Bridgehampton, the inn is within walking distance of shops and fine restaurants. Recreational possibilities include bicycling, horseback riding, canoeing, fishing, antiquing, and sunning on the magnificent ocean beaches. Other activities include visits to local wineries and the *Corwith House* (a museum house), theater, concerts, and book readings.

BRIDGEHAMPTON INN 2266 Main St., Bridgehampton, NY 11932 (phone: 516-537-3660). This historic inn has four guestrooms and two suites with private baths, queen- or king-size beds, telephones, TV sets, and air conditioning. Closed January and February. Rate for a double room (including continental breakfast): $180 to $250. Two-night minimum stay *Memorial Day* through *Labor Day;* three nights on holiday weekends. MasterCard and Visa accepted. Children welcome. No pets. No smoking. Anna and Detlef Pump, innkeepers; Barbara Cavagnaro, manager.

DIRECTIONS: From New York City take I-495 (the Long Island Expressway) to Exit 70 (Manorville) and follow Route 111 south to Highway 27 (Sunrise Highway). Take Highway 27 (which becomes the Montauk Highway) east for 25 miles to Bridgehampton. The Montauk Highway becomes Main Street as it reaches Bridgehampton. The inn is on the left, a half mile beyond the traffic light at the entrance to *Bridgehampton Common* shopping center.

BED & BREAKFAST ON THE PARK

BROOKLYN, NEW YORK

Prospect Park is one of the glories of New York City. Designed between 1866 and 1874 by Frederick Law Olmsted and Calvert Vaux (who also collaborated on *Central Park*), it contains 526 acres of lakes, meadows, sculptures, paths, quaint buildings, roads, and gardens. By the 1880s, sumptuous mansions had been built on the neighboring streets, and the area soon acquired such cachet that it was known as New York's Gold Coast.

Bed & Breakfast on the Park is in one of those mansions. A wide, gray limestone townhouse with tall windows and a traditional stoop, it was built in 1892 by George Brickelmeier, a liquor merchant. It was restored to a Victorian confection by innkeeper Liana Paolella (a former antiques dealer and real estate agent) and her daughter Jonna in 1985.

Oil paintings line the walls of the parlor-floor rooms and continue above the oak-banistered stairway. The front parlor, where guests are greeted today much as they were a hundred years ago, boasts exquisite African mahogany woodwork, a massive oil painting by Liana's step-father, William Earl Singer, tall windows softened with frothy lace curtains, and a Pairpoint lamp (whose blown glass is reverse-painted with poppies) on an antique table in the center of the room. An elegant powder room is hidden behind the foyer's carved oak walls. There's a second parlor with fringed sofas and chairs and elaborate, bead-fringed lamps, plus a dramatic, paneled dining room with Victorian fretwork, stained glass bay windows overlooking the back garden, and china cabinets filled silver and china.

The guestrooms are also authentic Victorian re-creations. All but two have elaborate mantelpieces (over nonworking fireplaces). The *Park Suite,* overlooking *Prospect Park,* has an antique lace crown canopy and bedspread and a stunning stained glass window. A paneled dressing area with bird's-eye maple closets and mirrored doors includes a built-in vanity. The *Lady Liberty* room has a canopy bed, handsome marble-topped Victorian dressers, and a stairway to the stars–literally: French doors lead to a deck, where another staircase rises to a roof deck with sensational views of New York's skyline, stretching from the Empire State Building, past the World Trade Center, to Lady Liberty herself.

Breakfast is served on gold-rimmed china with the finest Victorian silver and cut crystal. The meal includes fresh fruit, homemade breads, and such entrées as baked French toast with pecans and currants in a caramel sauce and sweet-potato frittata. The resident parakeet, Nonni-Nonni, entertains breakfasters.

Nearby attractions include the *Brooklyn Museum*, the *Brooklyn Botanic Garden*, the *Brooklyn Library*, and the *Brooklyn Academy of Music*, where dance performances, theater, and concerts are held. Other possibilities include riding the magnificent restored Victorian carousel in *Prospect Park*, bicycling, and antiquing in the numerous shops nearby. Manhattan is 15 minutes away by subway.

BED & BREAKFAST ON THE PARK 113 Prospect Park W., Brooklyn, NY 11215 (phone: 718-499-6115; fax: 718-499-1385). This Victorian townhouse has seven guestrooms (five with private baths) with twin, double, or king-size beds, TV sets, and air conditioning. Open year-round. Rate for a double room (including full breakfast): $100 to $250. Two-night minimum stay weekends; three nights on holiday weekends. Major credit cards accepted. Children welcome in two rooms. No pets. Shiva, a German shepherd and Nonni-Nonni, a parakeet, in residence. No smoking permitted indoors. Liana Paolella and Jonna Paolella, innkeepers.

DIRECTIONS: Driving from Manhattan, take the Brooklyn Bridge to Brooklyn. After crossing the bridge continue straight ahead to Atlantic Avenue. Turn right at the intersection with Fourth Avenue. Continue for 1 mile, then turn left onto Fifth Street. At the end of the street, turn right onto Prospect Park West. Continue two blocks to the inn, which will be on the right.

LINCKLAEN HOUSE

CAZENOVIA, NEW YORK

Lincklaen House has welcomed Grover Cleveland, John D. Rockefeller, stage celebrities, and plenty of just plain folks since it opened in 1835. Twenty or more stagecoaches passed through Cazenovia daily when *Lincklaen House* stood on the road then known as the Third Great Western Turnpike (now called Albany Street). These stages carried the mail and as many as 14 passengers, who must have found the inn a welcome respite from the hours spent in those lumbering, horse-drawn conveyances.

Fashioned of locally made bricks, this fine structure with numerous chimneys, broad front steps, and a columned entry has been called one of the best examples of early 19th-century architecture in central New York State. The formal dining room is dominated by a massive fireplace, while the quaint *Seven Stone Steps Tavern* downstairs retains its low-beamed ceilings, worn floorboards, wooden shutters, and original paintings of Cazenovia in the 1940s.

The dining room serves such delicacies as chilled salmon mousse on grilled apples and roast veal chops with cinnamon-and-port sauce, crispy forest mushrooms, and whipped garlic potatoes. Informal meals may be taken in the tavern, where a jazz combo performs Friday nights. The *Delft Room*, named for its ceramic chandelier, is where continental breakfast is served to inn guests every morning. Other meals are open to non-guests.

The guestrooms are individually decorated in period style, with stenciled walls and a mixture of antiques and reproductions; modern baths have been added.

Available activities include swimming, tennis, and boating on nearby Cazenovia Lake, visiting the *Erie Canal Museum,* and shopping on the town's well-preserved streets.

LINCKLAEN HOUSE 79 Albany St., PO Box 36, Cazenovia, NY 13035 (phone: 315-655-3461; fax: 315-655-5443). This hotel, 20 miles east of Syracuse, has 21 guestrooms with private baths, twin, double, queen-, or king-size beds, telephones, TV sets, and air conditioning. Open year-round; dining room closed Mondays and Tuesdays. Rate for a double room (including continental breakfast and afternoon tea): $99 to $140. Two-night minimum stay on weekends during events at the many nearby colleges. MasterCard and Visa accepted. Children welcome. Pets allowed. Smoking permitted except in the dining room. Tobin family, owners; Elizabeth Whiting, innkeeper.

DIRECTIONS: Traveling from the west on the New York State Thruway, take Exit 34A (Fayetteville). Follow Route 481 south, and take Exit 3E to Route 92 east to Cazenovia. The inn is on the main street. From the east on the New York State Thruway, take Exit 34 and follow Route 13 south to Cazenovia.

ASA RANSOM HOUSE

CLARENCE, NEW YORK

In 1799, Asa Ransom, a young silversmith, saw an ad offering land in a wilderness area now known as Clarence to "any proper man who would build and operate a tavern upon it." Not one to let opportunity pass him by, Ransom bought the land and soon constructed a log home and tavern. In 1801, he added a sawmill and, two years later, a gristmill—the first in Erie County. These buildings did not survive, but the library, gift shop, and taproom of the present building date to 1853, and remnants of the gristmill are visible.

Current innkeepers Bob and Judy Lenz purchased the white frame and brick farmhouse in 1975. They filled it with period antiques and Oriental rugs and added two dining rooms, in keeping with its architectural style. The property is on eight acres with flower gardens, a gazebo, and a pond.

Waverly fabrics in subtle colors accent the guestrooms and suites, all of which feature four-poster, canopy, iron-and-brass, oak, or carved mahogany beds and well-stocked, built-in bookshelves. Several also have fireplaces and balconies or porches overlooking the grounds.

Here, dinner, which consists of sophisticated country fare and chop-house-style dishes, includes such entrées as shepherd's pie, Ransom mixed grill (lamb chops, chicken, mushrooms, bacon, and grilled tomatoes), and apple-cheddar chicken. Herbs from the inn's gardens flavor sauces and salads. In winter, a wood-burning fireplace warms the dining rooms, while, in summer, diners can enjoy a lovely view of the gardens along with their meal. On Wednesdays, lunch also is available; a delightful afternoon tea, complete with scones and clotted cream, finger sandwiches, and pastries, is served on Thursdays. A full breakfast of juice, muffins, French toast, soufflés, and crêpes is offered to guests each morning. The other meals attract locals as well as guests.

Golf, swimming, tennis, and fishing are available nearby, and there's a large antiques market in Clarence. The *Clarence Historical Society* maintains a museum nearby.

ASA RANSOM HOUSE **10529 Main St. (Rte. 5), Clarence, NY 14031 (phone: 716-759-2315; fax: 716-759-2791). Located 15 miles from Buffalo and 28 miles from Niagara Falls, this country inn has nine guestrooms with private baths, twin, double, queen-, or king-size beds, telephones, TV sets, and air conditioning. Wheelchair accessible. Closed Fridays and January; the dining room, which is closed Friday dinner, also serves lunch on Wednesdays and afternoon tea on Thursdays. Rate for a double room (including full breakfast and dinner): $150 to $195; bed and breakfast: $90 to $150. Discover, MasterCard, and Visa accepted. Not appropriate for children under 12. No pets. No smoking. Robert and Judy Lenz, innkeepers.**

DIRECTIONS: From the New York State Thruway traveling west, take Exit 48A (Pembroke). Turn right onto Route 77 and right again onto Route 5. Travel 11 miles to Clarence, where Route 5 becomes Main Street. The inn is on the left. When traveling on the thruway east, take Exit 49, turn left onto Route 78, turn right onto Route 5, and continue 5½ miles to Clarence.

OLD DROVERS INN

Dover Plains, New York

Enter the low-slung doorway and duck under the ancient beamed ceiling. Pull a stool up to the old oak bar, close to the mammoth stone fireplace, and listen carefully. History is preserved so thoroughly at the *Old Drovers Inn* that you can almost hear the rough-tongued banter of the 18th-century drovers (cowboys who drove cattle along the old Post Road from upstate New York to the markets in New York City) who warmed up with hot buttered rum and gambled the night away here. In later years the inn welcomed the likes of the Marquis de Lafayette, Elizabeth Taylor, and Richard Burton.

Nestled on 12 acres in the Berkshire foothills, this charming 1750 white clapboard colonial—frequently called the most romantic inn on the East Coast, and a member of the prestigious Relais & Châteaux group—is surrounded by majestic maples and landscaped flower gardens. Alice Pitcher and Kemper Peacock have owned the inn since 1989.

A romantic dining room (also open to non-guests) takes over the entire first floor. With the dark paneling, intimate seating, and the glow from the fireplace and from candles in massive, etched hurricane globes, it's possible to sink into a corner and pretend you are alone in the room. The menu features such regional American favorites as hearty cheddar cheese soup, turkey hash with mustard sauce, and double-cut lamb chops with tomato chutney. There are also dishes with a French twist, such as breast of duckling with roasted pears in a claret sauce, and escalopes of veal with sautéed apples and calvados. Beware of the mixed drinks! They're served in double portions.

Narrow stairs from the dining room lead to the rest of the inn, all of which is decorated in elegant country-house style. The gracious library, featuring chintz fabrics and another fireplace, is reminiscent of the drawing room in an English manor. A shell curio cabinet that stands in the corner originally had a mate in the opposite corner, but it now can be seen in the American Wing of New York City's *Metropolitan Museum of Art.*

Equally elegant are the four antiques-filled guestrooms, three of which have fireplaces. One of our favorites is the *Meeting Room,* with a barrel-vaulted ceiling. Before it became a bedroom, this space served as a ballroom and as the town meeting hall.

Breakfast is served in the *Federal Room,* lined with historical murals of the area, painted in the style of the Hudson River School by Edward Paine in 1942. The meal is continental style on weekdays; a full breakfast is served on weekends.

Concerts are held on Sundays, in summer, in the inn's pasture, and there is much of interest in the surrounding area, including several wineries (one in the very handsome adjacent town of Millbrook), golf, hiking on the Appalachian Trail, and a riverside craft village nearby.

OLD DROVERS INN Old Rte. 22, Dover Plains, NY 12522 (phone: 914-832-9311; fax: 914-832-6356). This historic inn in the Berkshire foothills has four guestrooms with private baths, double and queen-size beds, telephones, and air conditioning. The restaurant is wheelchair accessible. Closed the first two weeks of January. Rate for a double room Sundays through Thursdays (including continental breakfast, taxes, and gratuities): $150 to $250; weekends and holidays (including full breakfast, dinner, taxes, and gratuities): $325 to $425. Two-night minimum stay on weekends. Diners Club, MasterCard, and Visa accepted. Not appropriate for children under 12. Pets welcome for a $10 additional charge and with prior permission. Three Yorkshire terriers in residence. Smoking permitted. Alice Pitcher and Kemper Peacock, innkeepers.

DIRECTIONS: From New York City take the Hudson River Parkway north to the Saw Mill River Parkway (which eventually merges into I-684). Continue north on I-684 to Route 22 north and travel another 23 miles, watching for the sign on the right to the *Old Drovers Inn.* Turn right at the sign and travel a half mile. The inn is on the right.

CENTENNIAL HOUSE

East Hampton, New York

When David Oxford and Harry Chancey Jr. bought this property in 1988, they found a board the builder had signed in 1876. The serendipity of the house's having been built in America's centennial year inspired the new inn's name.

The house sits at the entrance to tony East Hampton on a slight knoll, well back from the road. It is a classic Hamptons beach cottage of gray shingles and white trim with a porch across the front. Guests especially enjoy the seclusion of the side and back gardens with their beds of roses, dahlias, and climbing clematis. The gardens, as well as the inn's pool, are the perfect places to spend a lazy summer afternoon. To obtain a svelte beach physique, a fitness center is located in the barn. From the inn it's an easy 10-minute walk to the beach in one direction and the village in the other.

Inside, the atmosphere is suffused with English country-home gentility. The parlor has polished pine floors topped with Oriental rugs, floral chintz–covered sofas, a baby grand piano, a fireplace, and original oil paintings. The walls of the dining room are covered in a green floral Schumacher fabric; floor-to-ceiling bookshelves dominate one corner. Breakfast, including juice, fruit, home-baked breads, and an entrée such as sourdough French toast or eggs, is served on gilt-edged china at a mahogany table lighted by a Czechoslovakian crystal chandelier.

The guestrooms are as elegant as the public rooms. The *Rose Room* has a canopy bed, Oriental rugs, and a claw-foot bathtub in a curtained alcove. The *Bay Room* has a Charleston rice four-poster bed, wide-plank pine floors, and a church pulpit imported from England that has been turned into a sink. The green-and-burgundy *Lincoln Room* contains an ornate Victorian walnut bed, similar to the one in which that president died, and an armoire; there's a marble sink with brass legs in the bathroom. Tucked into the gardens, the three-bedroom *Guest House* has two baths, a full kitchen, and its own dining room, making it an ideal choice for families.

Nearby attractions include swimming, bicycling, hiking, bird watching, ice skating in winter, museums, art galleries, theater, and shopping.

CENTENNIAL HOUSE 13 Woods La., East Hampton, NY 11937 (phone: 516-324-9414; fax: 516-324-2681). A country inn in the heart of the Hamptons, it has four guestrooms and one cottage with private baths, double, queen-, or king-size beds, telephones, and air conditioning. Open year-round. Rate for a double room (including full breakfast): $125 to $325; rate for guest house (including full breakfast): $325 to $475. Two-night minimum stay weekends on April through June and in September and October; three nights in July and August. MasterCard and Visa accepted. Not appropriate for children under 12. No pets. Two small dogs, Earl and Edwinna, and two cats, in residence. No smoking. David A. Oxford and Harry Chancey Jr., innkeepers; Bernadette Meade, manager.

DIRECTIONS: From New York City take I-495 (the Long Island Expressway) to Exit 70 (Manorville) and follow Route 111 south to Highway 27 (Sunrise Highway). Follow Highway 27 east, which becomes the Montauk Highway. Continue another 32 miles to East Hampton. The inn is on the right, just before the light at the intersection of Main Street and the Montauk Highway. (If you pass Town Pond, you have gone too far.)

MAIDSTONE ARMS

EAST HAMPTON, NEW YORK

Steeped in history and tradition, the *Maidstone Arms* has been the heart of East Hampton village for more than 150 years. It is still the place where the entire village assembles every December for the lighting of the *Christmas* tree and the singing of carols, warmed by hot cider and freshly baked cookies, and where the first signs of spring emerge in clusters of yellow daffodils on the front lawn. This grand dowager (parts of whose foundation date to 1740) received a new lease on life in 1992, when it was purchased and restored by architect Coke Anne Saunders.

Located across from Town Pond, where swans regally float by, this is a classic country inn of white clapboard, blue shutters, flower-filled window boxes, a canopied porch, and a Greek Revival doorway. Inside, one of the most popular spots is the clubby *Water Room,* warmed in winter by a wood stove. Deep green walls, plaid cushions on chairs, and such hunting and fishing gear as antique decoys and fishing poles give the room the look of a hunt club.

The guestrooms are uniquely decorated in a crisp but elegant style. Room No. 14 features an iron bed and French doors leading to a private porch overlooking the Town Pond. A dazzling red "Hunting Toile" print by Brunschwig & Fils drapes the windows and bedskirt. Behind the main house are three cottages, all with fireplaces, VCRs, stereo systems, and private patios. The *Duplex Cottage* has whimsical "bookcase" wallpaper climbing the stairs to a mahogany sleigh bed; the *Studio Cottage* has a cathedral ceiling and a four-poster bed.

There are two dining rooms (open to non-guests), each with its own atmosphere. The intimate front room, with wide-plank wood floors, a paneled fireplace, and a bar in one corner, is reminiscent of a colonial tavern. The other is refined, with plaid carpeting, a classical fireplace, and pale yellow walls. In both, the service and food are exceptional. The contemporary American fare includes such offerings as lacquered duck with Chinese five spices and marinated *soba* noodles, and grilled *ahi* tuna with portobello mushrooms and a white peach and truffle vinaigrette. The menu is complemented by an award-winning wine list.

The area offers many recreational activities, including swimming, beachcombing, golf, tennis, bicycling, hiking, and ice skating in winter. Cultural facilities include the *John Drew Theatre,* art galleries, boutiques, museums, and winery tours.

MAIDSTONE ARMS 207 Main St., East Hampton, NY 11937 (phone: 516-324-5006; fax: 516-324-5037). This village inn has 16 guestrooms and three cottages with private baths, twin, double, queen-, or king-size beds, telephones, TV sets, and air conditioning. Wheelchair accessible. Open year-round. Rate for a double room (including continental breakfast): $165 to $325. Two-night minimum stay on weekends; three nights on summer weekends. Major credit cards accepted. Children welcome. No pets. No smoking. Coke Anne Saunders, innkeeper; Christophe Bergen, managing director.

DIRECTIONS: Follow the directions to *Centennial House* (above) as far as East Hampton. At the entrance to the village is a traffic light, and Route 27 bears sharply left. Follow Route 27 for about 200 yards. The inn is on the left.

BIRD AND BOTTLE INN

GARRISON, NEW YORK

The history of this inn stretches back to 1761, when it opened as *Warren's Tavern,* a popular watering station on the New York–to–Albany stage route. Historians believe it was the site of the September 1780 meeting at which treacherous *West Point* commander Benedict Arnold agreed with British spy Major John André to reveal the secrets of *West Point*'s fortifications for a handsome sum.

The handsome white clapboard building, with double porches and a steeply pitched roof, welcomed travelers with food and drink until 1832, when steamboats on the Hudson River eclipsed the stagecoach business. For many years after, the property was the centerpiece of a prosperous farm owned by the Nelson family, who added a sawmill and gristmill (some of which still remains) and dubbed the site Nelson Corners. The old tavern was fully restored to its 18th-century ambience in 1940, when it reopened as the *Bird and Bottle Inn.* Ira Boyar has been the owner since 1982, now ably assisted by his daughter Jodi.

The inn is located on eight serene acres that include manicured lawns, magnificent maple, oak, and birch trees, pristine flower beds, and a babbling brook crossed by a romantic bridge, the site of many weddings. The main floor of the inn retains its colonial atmosphere with the smell of wood fires smoldering in the fireplaces; the play of candlelight across the low-beamed ceilings and paneled walls; the slanted wide-plank pine floors; and the wavy-paned windows. The *Drinking Room,* the inn's cozy bar, is a snug retreat with another fireplace.

There are four guestrooms, three upstairs in the original tavern and one in a cottage nearby. All boast colonial-style antiques, paneled walls, and fireplaces. The *Beverly Robinson Suite* has a canopy bed swagged in peach-and-beige damask, Oriental rugs, original oil paintings, and a deck. The *Nelson Cottage,* decorated in shades of pink and cream with blue accents, has a carved four-poster.

The inn's noteworthy restaurant is dispersed among three rooms on the main floor, where dinner (also open to non-guests) is a four-course event.

It may start with the inn's justifiably famous gorgonzola-and-mascarpone fritters with honey mustard sauce, followed by a salad, and such entrées as baked Norwegian salmon in a potato crust or roast pheasant (for two) served with pâté and a truffle sauce. For dessert, the choices may include chocolate ganache tart—a bitter chocolate and cream confection with a macadamia-nut crust and caramel sauce—or a sugar cone filled with fresh berries and served with *crème anglaise.* The outstanding wine list includes excellent local wines as well as rare vintages, and is remarkably well priced.

Golf, horseback riding, hiking in the adjacent *Fahnestock State Park,* and antiquing are popular pastimes, as are visits to *West Point, Cold Spring, Boscobel Restoration, Van Cortland Manor, Kykuit, Sunnyside, Lindhurst,* and *Hyde Park.*

BIRD AND BOTTLE INN Nelson Corners, Rte. 9, Old Albany Post Rd., Box 129, Garrison, NY 10524 (phone: 914-424-3000; fax: 914-424-3283). This inn in the Hudson River Valley offers three guestrooms and one cottage with private baths, double or queen-size beds, and air conditioning. Open year-round; dining room closed Mondays and Tuesdays. Rate for a double room (including full breakfast and a $75 credit per couple toward dinner) Wednesday through Sunday: $210 to $240; rate for a double room (with full breakfast) Monday and Tuesday: $135 to $165. Two-night minimum stay on weekends. Major credit cards accepted. Not appropriate for children under 12. No pets. No smoking except in *Drinking Room.* Ira Boyar, owner; Jodi Boyar, innkeeper.

DIRECTIONS: From New York City take the George Washington Bridge to New Jersey. Take the first exit off the bridge for the Palisades Parkway north. Continue on the Palisades Parkway to the exit for the Bear Mountain Bridge. Cross the Hudson River via the Bear Mountain Bridge. At the end of the bridge turn left onto Route 9D north. Continue for 4½ miles to Route 403 and turn right. Traveling east on Route 403, continue for 1 mile. Turn left on Route 9 and travel north for 4 miles to the inn.

ROSE INN

Ithaca, New York

The story of the completion of this inn is fairly incredible. Millwright Abram Osmun built it between 1848 and 1851; the house features heavy timbers, hand-carved doors of chestnut and butternut, and parquet floors of quarter-sawn oak. The centerpiece was to be a circular staircase of Honduras mahogany, but none of the craftsmen working on the original project was capable of executing the delicate design. Hundreds of feet of the priceless wood were put in storage—and remained there for more than 70 years. Then, in 1922, an itinerant tinker came to Ithaca looking for employment. Hearing of the unfinished staircase, he drove up to the house in his battered truck and went to work. Over the next two years he erected a magnificent circular staircase that extended from the main hall up through two stories to a cupola on the roof. The rail, constructed in a flowing triple curve, was so exquisitely fashioned that it seemed to be made of one solid piece of wood. When the job was done, the man left as mysteriously as he had arrived, leaving behind a legend and a lasting legacy.

Today, guests of the *Rose Inn* are treated not only to its lovely architecture but to the thoughtfulness of its owners, Sherry and Charles Rosemann. Friendly but thoroughly professional, Charles is a career hotelier with experience in Germany and the United States. Before opening the inn, Sherry was an interior designer, and her skill can be seen in the inspired decor and faithful re-creation of the period rooms. High ceilings, marble fireplaces, and antiques provide an elegant yet comfortable atmosphere in the guest- and common rooms. Several suites have Jacuzzis.

The 17½-acre grounds include patios, a fish pond, a rose garden, abundant perennial flower beds, a vegetable garden, a huge raspberry patch, and a variety of fruit trees. An 1850s carriage house now contains a spectacular conference room.

A full breakfast is served to guests, including juice, a crystal bowl of fresh fruit and berries, and one of Charles's breakfast entrées. A particular favorite is the puffy apple pancake served with homemade apple butter or fresh raspberry sauce. Be sure to sample his jams, all made from fruit grown on the property; they also are sold in the gift shop.

A prix fixe dinner is served in the inn's four dining rooms Tuesdays through Saturdays; guests are asked to select their entrées when they make their reservations. Choices might be chateaubriand with béarnaise sauce, rack of lamb, grilled salmon, or honey-almond duck.

Several lakes in the area are ideal for boating or swimming; guests also can visit the nearby *Corning Glass Museum.*

ROSE INN **Rte. 34 N., Box 6576, Ithaca, NY 14851-6576 (phone: 607-533-7905; fax: 607-533-7908). A luxurious inn near *Cornell University,* it has 10 guestrooms and five suites with private baths, twin, double, queen-, or king-size beds, and telephones; most have air conditioning. Open year-round; dining rooms closed Sundays and Mondays. Rate for a double room (including full breakfast): $100 to $160; rate for suites (including full breakfast): $185 to $250. Two-night minimum stay on weekends; three nights during holidays and university events. MasterCard and Visa accepted. Not appropriate for children under 10. No pets. One dog, Brandy, in residence. No smoking. Sherry and Charles Rosemann, innkeepers; Patricia Cain, manager.**

DIRECTIONS: The inn is 10 miles north of Ithaca. From the New York State Thruway take Exit 40 to Route 34 south and continue for approximately 39 miles. The inn is on the left before entering Ithaca. From Ithaca, head north on Route 34 and travel 6 miles to the intersection with a red flashing light. Turn right and continue for a half mile. At the fork in the road go left (onto Route 34, not Route 34B). The inn is 3½ miles farther on the right.

LAKE PLACID LODGE

LAKE PLACID, NEW YORK

As you awaken at *Lake Placid Lodge* to the lonesome cry of a loon and the smell of fresh pine in the air, you'll find it easy to understand why early industrialists were attracted to the haunting majesty and beauty of the Adirondack Mountains. Few places on earth can match the pristine clarity of the 2,300 lakes, the pounding water of the 31,500 miles of rivers and streams, or the grandeur of the 46 mountains in the 6½ million acre wilderness known as *Adirondack State Park.*

This lodge, overlooking Lake Placid and facing Whiteface Mountain, is the perfect place to enjoy the mountain scenery without sacrificing anything in the way of creature comforts. Composed of 22 rooms, suites, and cottages in six buildings built of rough-hewn cedar and spruce, the lodge has twig-framed porches offering glorious lake and mountain views. Inside, the decor continues the rustic Adirondack theme, but with more than just a touch of elegance and sophistication. Rooms with bark or bead-board paneled walls are furnished with overstuffed chairs covered in bright plaids and paisleys, painted wooden dressers, and coffee tables made of bark-covered logs. Most guestrooms have massive stone fireplaces with log mantles; the charming *St. Regis, Hawkeye,* and *Cascade Suites* each offer two fireplaces and two baths.

Every guest need has been anticipated. In every guestroom there are featherbeds and down pillows, monkeywood bowls of fragrant pine cones, and clever, fat pincushions made of bark and containing buttons, needles, pins, snaps, and spools of thread attached with hat pins.

Breakfast, lunch, and dinner are served in the dining room (also open to non-guests), which has an outside porch overlooking the lake, and the fare is equal in sophistication to the decor: A chicken breast is stuffed with a mousse of wild mushrooms and herbs and served over braised pearl barley; a *confit* of duck leg comes with sautéed potatoes and foie gras; and the dessert menu, which changes frequently, might include a summer pudding with raspberries or a classic lemon tart with *crème anglaise.* The extensive wine list is supplemented by brandies, ports, and liqueurs, which may be enjoyed in the cozy bar, the *Moose Room* (a lounge with a moose head over the fireplace), or in the guestrooms.

Among the multitude of facilities on premise, guests enjoy an 18-hole championship golf course; four tennis courts; hiking trails; a sandy beach for lakeside swimming; a marina with canoes, fishing boats, paddleboats, and Sunfish; an open-decked sightseeing barge that offers a lake cruise every morning and a cocktail cruise every evening at sunset; mountain bicycles; and a cross-country-ski-touring center. Downhill skiing, ice skating, and hunting are available nearby.

LAKE PLACID LODGE Whiteface Inn Road, Lake Placid, New York 12940 (phone: 518-523-2700; fax: 518-523-1124). This romantic 22-guestroom Adirondack Mountain retreat on the shores of Lake Placid offers private baths, twin, double, queen-, and king-sized beds, and telephones. Open year-round; dining room closed Tuesdays from *Labor Day* through *Memorial Day.* Rate for a double room (including full breakfast): $175 to $425. Two-night minimum stay on weekends; three-night minimum stay on holidays. Major credit cards accepted. Children welcome. Pets permitted in two units at $50 per day. No smoking permitted indoors. Christie and David Garrett, owners; Kathryn Kincannon, managing director.

DIRECTIONS From I-87 take Exit 30 and travel northwest on Rte. 73 for 30 miles to Lake Placid. In the village take Rte. 86 for 1½ miles toward Saranac Lake. At the top of the hill, turn right onto Whiteface Inn Road. Follow the road for 1½ miles and turn right at the *Lake Placid Lodge* sign. Proceed through the golf course to the lodge.

GENESEE COUNTRY INN

MUMFORD, NEW YORK

The Seneca Indians who settled this area called it the Genesee (Pleasant Valley), and with good reason. Today, although the city of Rochester is only 20 minutes away, the valley remains remarkably peaceful. The building that is now the *Genesee Country Inn* was erected, in 1833, as a plaster mill and was enlarged twice—first, in the year it was built, to accommodate a sawmill and then, in 1917, to serve as the residence of the company manager. The original section has two-foot-thick limestone walls.

The common areas and guestrooms are decorated with fine stenciling and quilts. The furnishings, including several four-poster beds with crocheted canopies, are a mix of antiques and reproductions. Some rooms have fireplaces, balconies, or views of a splashing brook that attracts ducks, herons, and even mink.

Breakfast, served in an airy, cheery room overlooking the millpond and forest, always features juice, fresh fruit, fresh-baked muffins, and a tasty entrée such as cheddar-cheese egg-bake or pancakes with cinnamon-vanilla sauce. In cold weather, a fire crackles in the hearth.

There's plenty to do right on the inn's eight-acre grounds, including fly fishing for rainbow and brown trout (the stream, here, has been rated one of the best in the state), picnicking beside a rock fountain or in the gazebo, and birding. The inn even has its own gift shop, and there are plenty of antiques and crafts shops nearby. Another local attraction is the *Genesee Country Village,* a restored "living museum" on 200 acres that re-creates the lifestyle of the 19th century. Also nearby is *Letchworth State Park,* known as the "Grand Canyon of the East."

GENESEE COUNTRY INN 948 George St., Mumford, NY 14511-0340 (phone: 716-538-2500; 800-NY-STAYS; fax: 716-538-4665). This country inn has nine guestrooms with private baths, double or queen-size beds, telephones, TV sets, and air conditioning. Open year-round. Rate for a double room (including full breakfast and afternoon tea): $85 to $135. Two-night minimum stay on some weekends. Major credit cards accepted. Older children welcome. No pets. Three cats in residence. No smoking. Glenda Barcklow, innkeeper.

DIRECTIONS: From the New York State Thruway (I-90), take Exit 47 to Route 19 south to Le Roy. In Le Roy turn east onto Route 5 to Caledonia. In Caledonia take Route 36 north to Mumford, turning left onto George Street. The inn is one and a half blocks farther on the right.

INN NEW YORK CITY

NEW YORK, NEW YORK

In 1989, Ruth Mensch and her daughter Elyn found themselves with a townhouse on Manhattan's residential Upper West Side, spare cash from selling their popular restaurant *Ruelles,* and no real plans for the future. They decided to turn to innkeeping—and succeeded beyond their wildest dreams, creating a homey place in the heart of the Big Apple where guests can snuggle in for weeks at a time (and many do just that).

A quintessential New York atmosphere pervades this four-story brownstone with ornate balustrades and a wrought-iron front door flanked by sandstone pillars. In the charming vestibule and front parlor are high ceilings, elaborate moldings, carved fireplaces, fine cabinetwork, inlaid hardwood floors, and crystal chandeliers.

Each suite is decorated with individual flair. The *Parlor Suite,* for example, boasts 12-foot carved ceilings, an 18-foot living/dining room with a Baldwin piano, and an entryway with a spectacular stained glass ceiling. Its bedroom has a balcony, a fireplace, and a queen-size bed in which the headboard is outfitted with stained glass cabinets; the bath features a pedestal sink and a Jacuzzi. The *Spa Suite,* which takes up an entire floor, is highlighted by a king-size bed with a headboard set into antique chestnut armoires. The pièce de résistance, however, is the spa-like bathroom, with a double Jacuzzi set on a platform, a fireplace with a carved mantel, an old barber's chair, a cast-iron footed bath, a Victorian dresser with a sink, a sauna for two, and a shower enclosed in glass blocks. All four suites feature such personal touches as private libraries, fresh flowers, and fluffy robes.

In the morning, fresh-baked muffins and scones, cereal, fruit, juice, coffee, and tea are delivered to the guestrooms.

The inn is convenient to many of Manhattan's prime attractions, including *Lincoln Center,* the *American Museum of Natural History,* the *New-York Historical Society, Central Park,* and *Riverside Park,* as well as numerous restaurants and fine shopping.

INN NEW YORK CITY 266 W. 71st St., New York, NY 10023 (phone: 212-580-1900; fax: 212-580-4437). This brownstone has four suites with private baths, queen- or king-size beds, telephones, TV sets, and air conditioning. Open year-round. Rate for a double room (including continental breakfast): $195 to $295. Two-night minimum stay. Major credit cards accepted. Not appropriate for children under 12. No pets. No smoking. Elyn Mensch and Ruth Mensch, innkeepers.

DIRECTIONS: The inn is located on the south side of West 71st Street, between Broadway and West End Avenue.

OLIVER LOUD'S INN

PITTSFORD, NEW YORK

In 1979, Vivienne Tellier acquired and extensively refurbished *Richardson's Canal House,* the oldest surviving tavern on the Erie Canal, and opened it as a superb restaurant. Then, in 1985, she learned that the *Oliver Loud Tavern,* an old stagecoach inn in the nearby hamlet of Egypt, was scheduled for demolition. Tellier rescued the structure from the wrecker's ball, moved it to its present site near *Richardson's,* fully restored its 1812 appearance, and began taking in overnight guests.

When refurbishing the inn, Vivienne painstakingly re-created many of the original refinements, including the buttercup yellow exterior, Federal moldings, French and English wallpapers, and wallpaper borders. She also used Loud's own "recipe for making any wood look like mahogany" to fashion the hand-grained pseudo-mahogany doors. Guestrooms, several with views across the canal, are appointed with antique and Stickley reproduction furniture, including either four-poster or canopy beds.

The original inn's warm hospitality has been faithfully reproduced as well. On arrival, guests receive a basket filled with fresh fruit, bread sticks, homemade cookies, and a bottle of mineral water. Continental breakfast comes in another charmingly outfitted basket, complete with the morning paper. On balmy summer mornings, guests may enjoy the repast in rocking chairs on the porch, watching the canal waters.

Dinner awaits at *Richardson's Canal House,* a few steps away. Built in 1818, it retains virtually all of its architectural details (it is listed on the National Register of Historic Places). There are two-story porches in the front and rear, a cooking fireplace in the kitchen, and Federal trim in the public rooms, which are stenciled and painted in the original colors of ocher and green. Oil paintings of stern-faced gentlemen and ladies and other period artifacts appear in all 10 dining rooms. (The *Porter Room*—painted with whimsical scenes of marching soldiers and playful bears by Ruth Flowers in the style of famed muralist Rufus Porter—is particularly interesting.) The multi-course, prix fixe menu features American fare prepared in innovative ways; dishes include terrine of rabbit and pistachio nuts on wild-berry *coulis* and orange-and-rosemary-glazed pork tenderloin.

The towpath on the grounds is great for running, biking, walking, and even cross-country skiing in winter. Nearby attractions include the *International Museum of Photography* at *George Eastman House* in Rochester and the scenic Finger Lakes.

OLIVER LOUD'S INN **1474 Marsh Rd., Pittsford, New York, 14534 (phone: 716-248-5200, inn; 716-248-5000, restaurant; fax: 716-248-9970). A historic inn on the banks of the Erie Canal, it has eight guestrooms with private baths, double or king-size beds, telephones, TV sets, and air conditioning. Wheelchair accessible. Open year-round; restaurant closed *Memorial Day, Independence Day, Labor Day, Christmas,* and Sundays except *Easter* and *Mother's Day.* Rate for a double room (including continental breakfast): $125 to $155. Major credit cards accepted. Not appropriate for children under 13. No pets. Smoking permitted in some rooms. Vivienne Tellier, innkeeper.**

DIRECTIONS: The inn is 3½ miles from the New York State Thruway. Traveling west, take Exit 45 to I-490 west. Then take Exit 27 (Bushnell's Basin), turning right at the Marsh Road traffic signal and then immediately right again into Richardson's Canal Village.

AMERICAN HOTEL

SAG HARBOR, NEW YORK

A classic stagecoach poem ends:

Soft may they slumber and trouble no more,
For their dusty journey, its jolt and roar,
Has come to an end at Fordham's door.

In 1772, the above-mentioned *Fordham's* was the last stop on a three-day stagecoach journey that began at the Fulton Ferry dock in New York and deposited passengers in Sag Harbor for an overnight stay before they continued their travels to Connecticut or Boston by steamer. *Fordham's* no longer exists, but the *American Hotel* is a worthy offspring.

Built in 1836 as an office and apartment building, the brick early Victorian structure has been operated as an inn since 1877. When the hotel received its first guests, it was touted as the most elegant and modern hotel on Long Island, as it was equipped with all the latest amenities, including indoor baths, steam heat, and electric lights. Purchased in 1972 by Ted Conklin, it remains a sophisticated jewel among American inns. With a colonnaded entrance, a small porch, and a balcony, the inn has the atmosphere of an exclusive club.

The eight spacious guestrooms retain their distinctive Victorian ambience, but with some classy modern-day amenities. All have 10-foot ceilings and tall windows and are furnished with posh pieces: oak tables, alabaster lamps, overstuffed chairs, massive dressers with ornate mirrors, carved walnut armoires, and Oriental rugs worn to faded gentility. Some of the rooms have mahogany sleigh beds, others have carved walnut or brass beds.

Yet, for all its Victoriana, the *American Hotel* has none of the fussiness associated with the era. It has a masculine, turn-of-the-century appeal. The *Apartment,* a two-level suite, has a Victorian velvet sofa and a massive Victorian desk outfitted with bookshelves; atop it sits a vintage Underwood typewriter that seems to be waiting for Scott Fitzgerald to peck out a new novel. This suite's bath has a wonderful old French porcelain and brass sink. The garret bedroom is a charming hideaway, reached by a bookshelf-lined stairway. The room has one brick wall painted white, another wall of rough-sawn cypress, a beamed ceiling, Victorian dressers, and a rooftop window with distant views of the harbor.

The unique bathrooms are the hotel's tour-de-force. Each has a tile floor, a Jacuzzi for two, and such amenities as shampoos and body lotions; some are entered through old etched glass or carved doors. In addition, each bathroom holds an elegant Victorian table stocked with an array of high-quality liquors and crystal glasses.

The *American Hotel* serves classical French food in four intimate dining rooms (also open to non-guests), accompanied by wine selected from a 45-page, award-winning list. Dinner entrées might include tournedos Rossini with foie gras and truffle sauce Perigordine or seared tuna coated with sesame seeds. During dinner on weekends a pianist entertains on the baby grand. A continental breakfast of juice, fruit, and freshly baked muffins and scones is set out on a sideboard in the atrium each morning.

Set in the historic town of Sag Harbor, this inn is convenient to beaches, golf, sailing, tennis, boating excursions, and several local attractions, including the *Bay Street Theatre Festival, the Old Custom House,* and the *Sag Harbor Whaling Museum.*

AMERICAN HOTEL Main St., PO Box 1349, Sag Harbor, NY 11963 (phone: 516-725-3535; fax: 516-725-3573). This inn has eight guestrooms with private baths, queen- or king-size beds, telephones, and air conditioning. Open year-round. Rate for a double room (including continental breakfast): $165 to $250. Two-night minimum stay on weekends; three nights on holiday weekends. Major credit cards accepted. Not appropriate for children under 18. No pets. Smoking permitted in designated areas. Ted Conklin, innkeeper.

DIRECTIONS: From New York City take I-495 (the Long Island Expressway) to Exit 70 (Manorville) and follow Route 111 south to Highway 27 (Sunrise Highway). Take Highway 27 (which becomes the Montauk Highway) for 25 miles to Bridgehampton. At the monument in Bridgehampton turn north onto the Sag Harbor Turnpike. After about 5 miles this road becomes Main Street in Sag Harbor. The inn is on the right in the center of town.

THE POINT

SARANAC LAKE, NEW YORK

Between the Civil War and the Great Depression, wealthy families built retreats in the wild Adirondacks as blessed escapes from big-city life. Careful to intrude on nature no more than was absolutely necessary, they built camps from logs and stones, twigs, branches, and slate on vast tracts of forested land; often, these massive complexes encompassed entire lakes.

When William Avery Rockefeller (great-nephew of John D.) built *Camp Wonundra* in 1933, he captured the character of the Adirondack camps with architecture that was considered to be the finest of its genre. Located on a 10-acre peninsula that pierces Upper Saranac Lake, it consisted of a main house and eight outbuildings. Unlike many of his friends, Rockefeller intended to use the resort year-round, so it was geared for winter as well. This complex was converted to *The Point* to provide housing for visitors to the 1980 *Winter Olympics* at nearby Lake Placid.

The property (a member of the prestigious Relais & Châteaux group) comprises 11 guestrooms distributed among four log cottages. The buildings commune so completely with nature that it often seems there are no walls, making it that much easier to appreciate a lovely mist shrouding the lake at dawn, deer grazing in a nearby meadow, or a red fox darting through the trees. The rooms contain massive stone fireplaces, sturdy antique furnishings, sofas upholstered in rustic wool checks, moose and deer heads on the walls, and Oriental rugs on the rich hardwood floors; bay windows overlook the lake and the Adirondack wilderness.

The atmosphere is casual and welcoming, as though you're staying with friends. The day begins with a thermos of fresh-brewed coffee delivered to each room, followed by a tray laden with fresh fruit, juice, and hot or cold cereal; a heartier breakfast of eggs or pancakes may be eaten in the *Great Hall.* Lunch, dinner, and drinks also are included in the daily rate. Executive Chef Bill McNamee, who co-manages the inn, is classically trained. (His experience includes a year as apprentice to Albert Roux at London's *Le Gavroche.*) Meals are formal affairs (jacket and tie required; black tie suggested Wednesday and Saturday nights) featuring such French dishes as roast sea bass *antiboise* (served on a bed of julienned vegetables with a tomato-herb sauce), roast rack of lamb with ratatouille, and baby chicken on a corn fritter. Be sure to leave room for the sinfully rich desserts, like white and dark chocolate mousse.

As the morning fog lifts, guests may choose to take out a small outboard for some lake fishing or water-ski behind the inn's Mastercraft speedboat. Other activities include hiking, tennis, sunset cruises, swimming, volleyball, badminton, bicycling, cross-country skiing, and ice skating. There are several museums in the area.

THE POINT HCR 1, Box 65, Saranac Lake, NY 12983 (phone: 518-891-5674; 800-255-3530; fax: 518-891-1152). An Adirondack retreat on the shore of Saranac Lake, it has 11 guestrooms with private baths and twin, queen-, or king-size beds. Wheelchair accessible. Closed mid-March to mid-April. Rate for a double room (including breakfast, lunch, dinner, drinks, and sports equipment): $775 to $1,025. Two-night minimum stay on weekends; three nights on holidays. American Express accepted. Not appropriate for children under 18. Pets allowed by prior permission only. Two dogs and one cat in residence. Smoking permitted in designated areas, but not in dining room. Christie and David Garrett, owners; Bill and Claudia McNamee, general managers.

DIRECTIONS: From New York City take the New York State Thruway to Exit 30. Follow Route 73 north for 34 miles to Upper Saranac Lake. Detailed directions are given when reservations are confirmed.

ADELPHI HOTEL

SARATOGA SPRINGS, NEW YORK

Gregg Siefker and Sheila Parkert purchased this establishment in 1979, just as it was about to be demolished—a fate that had already befallen other hotels in this fabled spa town. Rolling up their sleeves, they plunged into the long, arduous task of restoring the largely run-down building, doing most of the work themselves. Gradually, they refurbished and reopened the lobby and the bar, then the 37 guestrooms, one by one.

The structure is a spectacular example of High Victorian architecture. A façade of Lombard brickwork is fronted by three-story wooden columns adorned with elaborate masses of fretwork. There's a tile-floored loggia and a brick garden courtyard surrounded by flower beds. A brick stairway leads to the flagstone-terraced sculpted pool, its covered colonnade backed by trellises and ferns.

The hotel's opulent lobby is a tribute to the Gilded Age: Gilt peeks out from pediments, mirror frames, and molded ceilings, and it accents painted swags and columns. Elaborately hand-stenciled walls set off the rich, damask-covered Victorian chairs and sofas. The inn is furnished throughout with antiques, and the walls are lined with period prints and engravings—some of old Saratoga, some of stern-looking Victorian personages, still others by Maxfield Parrish. A piazza on the second floor is furnished with wicker and Adirondack-style chairs and tables—an ideal place to sit and watch the bustling activity along the shop-filled street that runs past the inn.

Most of the guestrooms have a uniformly Victorian decor, but each boasts some playful touches. The *Riviera Room* has a sitting room with a mural of stone battlements and views of the Riviera. The bedroom, here, has pink walls, a pink armoire, and yellow and green accents. Another guestroom, No. 19, has striped wallpaper, a Victorian ottoman, and a needlepoint rug.

A continental breakfast is delivered to guestrooms every morning, but many guests prefer to take their coffee in one of the public rooms, such as the *Rose Room,* with pink wicker chairs and green accents, or on a porch with white rattan chairs. Wednesdays through Sundays, during July and August, dinner is served in *Café Adelphi,* the inn's dining room (also open to non-guests); at other times, coffee and dessert are available here. The menu features grilled seafood, pork, and other meat, as well as salads, fresh fruit, and pâtés.

In the 1800s, Saratoga Springs was called the Queen of Spas. The baths, concerts, horse races, and gala balls, here, attracted America's aristocrats in droves. You can still take "the cure" at Saratoga, and the August races are still *the* social event of the season, but today the town also is known for the *Saratoga Performing Arts Center,* the summer headquarters of the *Philadelphia Orchestra* and the *New York City Ballet.*

ADELPHI HOTEL 365 Broadway, Saratoga Springs, NY 12866 (phone: 518-587-4688; fax: 518-587-0851). This hotel has 37 guestrooms with private baths, double or queen-size beds, telephones, TV sets, and air conditioning. Closed November through mid-May; restaurant also closed Mondays and Tuesdays from mid-May through June and all of September and October. Rate for a double room (including continental breakfast): $90 to $295. Two-night minimum stay on July weekends; three nights on August racing weekends. Major credit cards accepted. Children welcome. Small pets allowed by prior arrangement only. Smoking permitted except in dining room. Gregg Siefker and Sheila Parkert, innkeepers.

DIRECTIONS: From New York City take I-87 north to Exit 13N in Saratoga Springs, which leads to Route 9 north. Route 9 becomes Broadway in town. The hotel is on the left.

Pennsylvania

BEACH LAKE HOTEL

BEACH LAKE, PENNSYLVANIA

Located in the Pocono Mountains of rural Pennsylvania, this hotel snuggles comfortably into the countryside. Built in 1830, the little Victorian served many functions (including post office, tavern, boardinghouse, and general store) until 1986, when Erika and Roy Miller bought it and turned it into a hotel.

The Millers masterminded a complete overhaul of the property, including restoration of the yellow-pine woodwork and the wainscoted walls and ceilings. Erika is an expert in Victorian antiques, and her quest for the perfect pieces for each nook and cranny has resulted in some lovely acquisitions. For example, *Plymouth* has a great high-headboarded canopy bed accented with colorful quilts. Another room, *Caldefore,* features a massive old bed and wardrobe, a Victorian sofa and dressing table, and a huge bath with a claw-foot tub. A lace tablecloth serves as the canopy over the bed in *Tester,* which also is furnished with a fanciful Chinese end table. Each room has beautifully upholstered overstuffed chairs and plenty of bookshelves filled with old volumes. Reproduction Victorian wallpapers, imported lace curtains, and oil paintings complete the period effect. If you can't live without the curlicued wicker nightstand, ask about its price; everything is for sale.

An inviting Victorian parlor inspires reading and quiet conversation with its plush burgundy velvet sofa, tapestry-covered easy chairs, and imposing grandfather clock. After-dinner desserts are laid on the sideboard here. The tiny pub, set in the space once occupied by the general store, is accented with lovely examples of faceted and stained glass and whimsical paintings. Two porches with antique wicker chairs are ideal spots to enjoy early-morning coffee or afternoon contemplation of the outdoors.

The dining rooms have the same Victorian ambience as the rest of the house; one has a wainscoted ceiling and a glass-fronted oak cabinet. The excellent dinners (also open to non-guests) are served on antique china; dishes might include duckling Grand Marnier, veal Rockefeller, or quail in cognac sauce. For dessert, the decadent chocolate cake with caramel sauce is everything it's advertised to be—decadent. A full breakfast with a broad selection of entrées, including Erika's fresh-baked surprise, is served to inn guests.

Planters of nasturtiums (which are used in salads served at dinner) and a cutting garden of zinnias, lilies, black-eyed Susans, cosmos, and snapdragons decorate the side yard. Behind the hotel, blackberry bushes and a tiny orchard of apple and pear trees remind us what truly fresh fruit tastes like.

The beach is only a short walk from the hotel; fishing, hiking, swimming, cross-country skiing, tennis, and golf are available nearby.

BEACH LAKE HOTEL PO Box 144, Beach Lake, PA 18405 (phone: 717-729-8239; 800-382-3897). A small hotel in the Poconos near the Delaware River, it has six guestrooms with private baths, twin or double beds, and air conditioning. Open year-round. Rate for a double room (including full breakfast): $95. Two-night minimum stay on weekends May through August. MasterCard and Visa accepted. Not appropriate for children under 18. No pets. One small dog, a shih tzu, in residence. Smoking permitted in pub, parlor, and one dining room only. Erika and Roy Miller, innkeepers.

DIRECTIONS: From New York City take the New York State Thruway to Exit 15 (Harriman), then Route 17 west to I-84. Take I-84 to Exit 1 in Port Jervis, then Route 6 through Port Jervis to Route 97 north. Follow Route 97 for 30 miles to Narrowsburg and bear left at the blinking traffic light, going down the hill and across the bridge into Pennsylvania. In Pennsylvania pick up Route 652 west and continue to the Mobil station. Turn right, travel one block, then take another right. The inn is a quarter mile farther along on the left, at the corner of Church and Main Streets.

INN AT TWIN LINDEN

CHURCHTOWN, PENNSYLVANIA

When you enter Churchtown, you may feel as if you've stepped into the 19th century. Cars share the road with horse-drawn carts driven by men and women in traditional Amish dress. But even though this is the heart of Amish and Mennonite country, which is characterized by simple living, the *Inn at Twin Linden* has a sophisticated ambience.

In the center of this little town, guarded by 100-foot linden trees, stands the three-story white clapboard house, which was built in the 1840s by a local forge owner as a home for his daughter and her new husband. By the time current owners Donna and Bob Leahy came across it in 1987, however, the house had degenerated into a rather seedy apartment building. The Leahys had a hard task ahead of them, and despite Bob's other life (he's a nationally recognized underwater photographer and teacher at *Temple University*), they completed the task in three years and opened the inn with six rooms and one suite. It's set on two acres of lush gardens, complete with winding pathways and benches tucked into secluded corners, three porches, a brick courtyard, and an outdoor Jacuzzi.

The living room is decorated with comfortable chairs and sofas, plenty of books, and a fireplace; complimentary sherry and brandy are here for the sipping. A wicker-filled porch is a pleasant place to sit on hot days. The decor in the guestrooms is 19th-century traditional—oak beds with hand-crocheted canopies, stenciled walls, antique furnishings, and fresh flowers—but the bathrooms are completely modern.

Guests awaken to the aroma of hot-from-the-oven croissant cinnamon buns and coffee made from freshly ground beans. The full breakfast includes Donna's creative entrées. (Her raspberry croissant French toast with sausage and her dill crêpes filled with smoked salmon and eggs have even been featured on the "Today" show.) Afternoon tea is served, and on Friday and Saturday nights Donna prepares sumptuous dinners (also open to non-guests by reservation) that take advantage of the abundant local produce. Rack of lamb is a menu staple, but crab cakes with almonds also are popular. Be sure to save room for the fresh pear-lemon mousse. The inn has no liquor license, but guests may bring their own wine.

Activities in the area include antiquing and shopping at country auctions and farmhouse crafts stores (handmade Amish quilts are a particularly good find).

INN AT TWIN LINDEN **2092 Main St., Rte. 23, Churchtown, PA 17555 (phone: 717-445-7619; fax: 717-445-4656). This inn has seven guestrooms with private baths, twin, double, or queen-size beds, TV sets, and air conditioning. Closed January 2 through 31; dining room also closed for dinner Sundays through Thursdays. Rate for a double room (including full breakfast, afternoon tea, sherry, and brandy): $85 to $200. Two-night minimum stay on weekends. Major credit cards accepted. Children welcome on weekdays. No pets. A dog and a cat on the property. No smoking. Bob and Donna Leahy, innkeepers.**

DIRECTIONS: From the Pennsylvania Turnpike take Exit 22 (Morgantown) to Route 10 south. Turn west onto Route 23 and travel for 4 miles into Churchtown. Route 23 becomes Main Street; the inn is in the center of town on the left.

HIGHLAND FARMS

DOYLESTOWN, PENNSYLVANIA

At *Highland Farms,* the longtime home of lyricist Oscar Hammerstein, it's easy to understand the inspiration for such classics as *Oklahoma, Carousel, The Sound of Music,* and *The King and I.* Gazing in summer from a window across the nearby planted fields, you too will see "the corn is as high as an elephant's eye," and you'll understand when you awake in his former bedroom why Hammerstein rejoiced, "Oh, what a beautiful morning." (In his youth, composer/lyricist Stephen Sondheim gained inspiration here as well.)

Innkeeper Mary Schnitzer has faithfully maintained the graciousness of this building, which is listed on the National Register of Historic Places. Upon entering the 1740 stone-and-stucco house, guests find themselves in a grand foyer with oak floors and a massive mirror. The living room features a pastel Savonnerie rug and a 1700s lime-wood cabinet Hammerstein's wife, Dorothy, had built into the room. The lovely garden room has curlicued wicker furniture cushioned with Italian tapestry pillows; the breakfast-room table is draped with a white, hand-crocheted linen bedspread dating from the 1800s. A massive brass chandelier illuminates the majestic dining room, with its Chippendale-style table, plum walls, saddle tan and cream woodwork, and an Oriental rug on a deep-hued oak floor. Upstairs, the walls of the huge library are covered with sheet music from the master's musicals; a videotape collection of the shows is available for guests to view.

Each guestroom has been named for one of Hammerstein's musicals and features unique touches. *The King and I,* Oscar and Dorothy's bedroom, contains a hand-painted fireplace mantel and a bed with a frothy white canopy. In the *Carousel* room, with another canopy bed, a fanciful carousel has been painted on the floor and carousel horses prance across the walls of both the bedroom and bath. The *Oklahoma* room is furnished with antique oak furniture, including a bed draped with a canopy crocheted by Mary's grandmother. Hand-painted magnolias border the ceiling and embellish the corner cupboard. The *Show Boat* room is decorated with 18th-century mahogany furniture (and shares a bath with *Oklahoma*).

Mary goes to great lengths to ensure guests' comfort. Her four-course breakfasts are painstakingly planned, with such treats as grapefruit marinated in blackberry brandy, homemade granola, fresh-baked popovers, mushroom tarts with chive cream, and freshly brewed coffee. In the afternoon she prepares canapés or finger sandwiches to enjoy with wine, lemonade, or iced tea. At night, when guests return to their rooms, they find a silver tray bearing sherry or blackberry brandy and a personal note from their hostess.

The 10-acre grounds contain a tennis court, a large pool, grazing sheep, and a grape arbor where Henry Fonda got married. A baby elephant's bath is left over from an owner prior to Hammerstein who had a circus. Flower gardens, terraces, and a wraparound porch complete the picture.

Area attractions include the *Moravian Tileworks, Mercer Museum, James Michener Art Gallery,* and *Pearl Buck Home,* as well as golf, cross-country skiing, bicycling, art galleries, and antiques shops.

HIGHLAND FARMS 70 East Rd., Doylestown, PA 18901 (phone: 215-340-1354). A country estate, it has four guestrooms (two with private baths) with double or queen-size beds and air conditioning. Open year-round. Rate for a double room (including full breakfast, afternoon refreshments, sherry, and brandy): $125 to $175. Two-night minimum stay on weekends; three nights on holidays. MasterCard and Visa accepted. Not appropriate for children under 13. No pets. A dog, a cat, and sheep in residence. Smoking permitted in designated areas only. Mary Schnitzer, innkeeper.

DIRECTIONS: From New York take the New Jersey Turnpike south to I-78 west. Take Exit 29 to I-287 south, then Exit 13 to Route 202 south. Follow Route 202 across the Delaware River about 10 miles to Doylestown. In Doylestown cross Route 313, then take the second left onto East Road. The inn is the fourth house on the right. From Philadelphia take I-95 north to Route 332 west (Newtown). Follow this road for about 3½ miles, then take Route 413 north for about 10½ miles. At this point take Route 202 south to Doylestown and follow the directions above.

SMITHTON INN

EPHRATA, PENNSYLVANIA

The town of Ephrata is in the heart of Pennsylvania Dutch country—Lancaster County—where the residents live much as their 18th-century ancestors did. Their customs remain remarkably unchanged with the passage of time, and a visit here affords a greater appreciation of America's past.

The *Smithton Inn* exemplifies the local dedication to hand-crafted construction. An inn and stagecoach stop in prerevolutionary days, this sandstone house was built in 1763. The handsome *Great Room,* decorated with handmade furniture and braided rugs, has a fireplace. There's also a library. The gardens contain an extensive collection of lilies and award-winning dahlias, a fish pond, and a family of flop-eared rabbits.

Each guestroom has a fireplace, as well as an antique four-poster, canopied bed covered with a hand-sewn quilt. In the evening, when candlelight flickers on the walls and a fire crackles in the hearth, it's easy to imagine that you've traveled back in time. (The inn even provides red flannel nightshirts to enhance the old-fashioned flavor.)

Each morning a full country breakfast is offered, including juice, fruit, and an entrée such as blueberry waffles. In the afternoon, freshly baked cookies, tea, and lemonade are available.

This area of Pennsylvania abounds with activities. There are museums, crafts shops, antiques malls, theater, concerts, winery tours, and art exhibits. Auctions of antiques and furniture take place daily, and local farmers sell their produce on Tuesdays and Fridays. A nearby antiques market with some 3,000 dealers is held every Sunday, and the *Renaissance Fair* extends all summer long.

SMITHTON INN 900 W. Main St., Ephrata, PA 17522 (phone: 717-733-6094). This country inn has seven guestrooms and one suite with private baths, double, queen-,

or king-size beds, and air conditioning. Wheelchair accessible. Open year-round. Rate for a double room (including full breakfast and afternoon snacks): $75 to $175. Two-night minimum stay on weekends and holidays. Major credit cards accepted. Children welcome. Dogs allowed by prior arrangement only. No smoking. Dorothy Graybill and Allan Smith, owners; Dorothy Graybill, innkeeper.

DIRECTIONS: Take the Pennsylvania Turnpike to Exit 21, then follow Route 222 south for 5 miles to the Ephrata exit. Turn right onto Route 322 west, continue for 2½ miles, then make a left onto South Academy Drive. Immediately turn right off Academy Drive into the inn's driveway.

GLASBERN

FOGELSVILLE, PENNSYLVANIA

Glasbern sits on a 100-acre plot in a suburban setting where the atmosphere straddles both country and city. Built as a farm more than 150 years ago, the inn combines the feel of rural living with the contemporary amenities modern travelers expect. The oldest part of the farm is the Pennsylvania German bank barn, built into the bank of the hillside, with a ceiling that rises 26 feet to hand-hewn beams punctuated by skylights. In this *Great Room* rough shale walls contrast with the smooth, clean lines of the plaster fireplace and chimney. The corn crib remains from the days when this was a working barn, as do the ladders that lead to where the hayloft used to be. One wall consists almost entirely of windows and gave the inn its name (*glasbern* is a Middle English word meaning "glass barn").

Purchased in 1985 by Beth and Al Granger, the inn offers numerous creature comforts. The guestrooms, distributed among the barn, the original farmhouse, the carriage house, the gatehouse, and the garden cottage, are all equipped with modern amenities, including VCRs for use with the extensive video library. Some contain whirlpools and fireplaces; many are duplex suites with skylights and views of the countryside. Green plants, patchwork quilts, and Oriental rugs create an elegant yet country-style ambience.

At breakfast, served in the *Great Room* and the *Granary* (a small adjoining room), guests may choose to eat family-style at a large mahogany table or at individual tables. The hearty entrées might include French toast made with raisin bread, ham-cheese-and-egg strudel, or "egg blossoms in a silo" (eggs and phyllo dough baked in a muffin tin).

In the evening, the *Great Room,* the *Granary,* and the *Harvest Room* (in a wing off the *Great Room*) serve as dining rooms (open to non-guests). The menu features herbs and vegetables organically grown on the farm. Breast of duck with "four p's" (stuffed with pheasant-pistachio forcemeat and sauced with port wine and green peppercorns) is one example of the inventive fare. Sunday brunch (also open to non-guests) is served here as well.

Tucked into a fold of rolling meadows and woods, the spacious grounds invite outdoor activities. There are trails for nature walks in mild weather and cross-country skiing in winter, flower beds filled to overflowing, and a pool surrounded by a flagstone patio. If you like, take apples from the orchard to feed Megan and Charlie, the inn's horses. Not far away, golf, hot-air balloon rides, and rafting are available.

GLASBERN 2141 Pack House Rd., Fogelsville, PA 18051-9743 (phone: 610-285-4723; fax: 610-285-2862). This inn has 24 guestrooms with private baths, double, queen-, or king-size beds, telephones, TV sets, and air conditioning. Wheelchair accessible. Open year-round. Rate for a double room (including full breakfast, but not Sunday brunch): $90 to $300. Two-night minimum stay on some weekends. MasterCard and Visa accepted. Not appropriate for children under 10. No pets. Several farm animals and one dog on the premises. Smoking permitted (though there are nonsmoking guestrooms). Beth and Al Granger, innkeepers.

DIRECTIONS: Traveling from New York on I-78 west, take Exit 14B north onto Highway 100, turning left at the first light onto Old Route 22. Turn right onto North Church Street and continue about a half mile. Turn right onto Pack House Road; the inn is on the right an eighth of a mile down.

SWISS WOODS B & B

LITITZ, PENNSYLVANIA

You might well ask, what's a Swiss chalet doing in Pennsylvania Dutch country? This one reflects the heritage of its owners: Lancaster native Debrah Mosimann and her Swiss husband, Werner. The Mosimanns have combined their talents and cultures to offer American hospitality in a Swiss-German environment.

The chalet looks modern, and in fact it is: The Mosimanns built it in 1984. Construction was a family project. In the common room, called *Anker Stube* after the Swiss artist, is a massive sandstone fireplace; the mantel was hand-hewn by Debrah's father. Natural pine and cypress furniture, comfortable Biedermeier camelback sofas, and a profusion of cascading ferns create an inviting atmosphere. The seven guestrooms are decorated in the spare style that is very popular in Switzerland, with pine-framed beds (two are canopied) and fluffy European goose-down comforters. All have private patios or balconies; two have Jacuzzis.

Debrah makes good use of her degree in home economics when she prepares the inn's sumptuous breakfasts. Her raisin-bread French toast stuffed with strawberry cream cheese has become a local legend; another tasty entrée is eggs Florentine.

The inn is located on 30 acres overlooking Speedwell Forge Lake. Take a stroll through the extensive gardens, nurtured by agriculturalist Werner. Canoes are available for guests to use on the lake, and an extensive network of hiking trails laces the property. The area is also popular for bird watching. *Hershey's Chocolate World,* the *Hand-Twisted Pretzel Factory,* and a farmers' market are nearby.

SWISS WOODS B & B 500 Blantz Rd., Lititz, PA 17543 (phone: 717-627-3358; 800-594-8018; fax: 717-627-3483). A chalet-style inn, it has seven guestrooms with private baths, queen-size beds, and air conditioning. Closed several days at *Christmas.* Rate for a double room (including full breakfast): $80 to $130. Two-night minimum stay on weekends; three nights on holidays. Discover, MasterCard, and Visa accepted. Children welcome. No pets. Dogs, cats, and rabbits on property. No smoking. Werner and Debrah Mosimann, innkeepers.

DIRECTIONS: From Lancaster travel north on Route 501 through Lititz for 3 miles. Turn left on Brubaker Valley Road and travel 1 mile, then turn right onto Blantz Road. The inn is down the first lane on the left.

MERCERSBURG INN

MERCERSBURG, PENNSYLVANIA

The colonial village of Mercersburg, located in the beautiful Cumberland Valley at the foot of the Tuscarora Mountains, has maintained its historic architecture and small-town character since its founding in 1750. Later, it became a frontier trading post. Although dusty, rutted Main Street was paved long ago, it still is lined with buildings made of limestone, brick, or logs, many of which date to the 18th century.

Built in 1909, this estate was the creation of local businessman Harry Byron and his wife, Ione, who spared no expense in the construction of their dream home. The impressive three-story Georgian brick mansion has six massive columns at the entrance. Large double porches at either end overlook six acres of lawns, and bowed stone bridges grace the gardens. Transformed into an inn in the 1950s, the property gradually became rundown and was eventually abandoned.

In 1986, Fran Wolfe, an artist with more than 18 years of experience renovating buildings, purchased the dilapidated mansion and began an extensive restoration. Today her son, Chuck Guy, owns the inn. The grand entrance hall features a parquet floor, a fanlight over the broad doors, and polished chestnut paneling. The house's most unusual features are twin curving staircases wending their way to the second floor between two rose-colored faux marble columns. Serpentine banisters and elaborate wrought-iron balustrades add to the dramatic impact. On the landing above, sunlight filters in through stained glass windows.

The public rooms are as elegant as the entrance. The grand hall has four sets of French doors leading to various rooms. One of the most luxurious settings is the bright, airy sunroom, featuring a wallpaper pattern also used at *Monticello,* Thomas Jefferson's home. White wicker furniture and floral cushions on the window seats provide a comfortable spot in which to enjoy an iced tea laced with mint. The large windows afford a lovely view of grassy lawns in summer and pristine snow in winter. In the formal dining room a fireplace glows in chilly weather. The downstairs gameroom has an antique pool table, board games, a TV set, and a VCR.

The 15 guestrooms are furnished with canopied four-poster beds, cherry antiques, and floral fabrics. Several have fireplaces or balconies with views of Mercersburg, the Cumberland Valley, and the mountains in the distance. Original oil paintings and photographs by local artists grace the walls.

Continental breakfast is offered to inn guests. Dinner (open to the public) is served on weekends. Such tempting continental fare as rack of lamb with dried cherry sauce and chocolate pâté with raspberry sauce are among the choices.

Attractions in the region include the birthplace of President James Buchanan, *Gettysburg National Military Park, Antietam,* Harpers Ferry, golf, and skiing at *Whitetail Ski Resort.*

MERCERSBURG INN 405 Main St., Mercersburg, PA 17236 (phone: 717-328-5231; fax: 717-328-3403). This mansion has 15 guestrooms with private baths, twin, double, queen-, or king-size beds, telephones, and air conditioning. Open year-round. Rate for a double room (including continental breakfast): $110 to $180. Two-night minimum stay in October and during ski season. Discover, MasterCard, and Visa accepted. Children welcome. No pets. Maggie, a Labrador retriever, in residence. No smoking. Chuck Guy, owner; John Mohr and Sally Brick, innkeepers.

DIRECTIONS: Traveling on I-81 west, take Exit 3, then go west on Pennsylvania Route 16 to Mercersburg, where it becomes Main Street. The inn is on the left.

WHITEHALL INN

NEW HOPE, PENNSYLVANIA

This stately inn, in a white clapboard plantation house built in 1794, is a very classy establishment. The setting is as bucolic as anyone could want—13 acres, complete with an old barn, grazing horses, and a swimming pool. And if that weren't enough, there are the thoughtful innkeepers, Mike and Suella Wass, who go to great lengths to ensure their guests' comfort. From the number of repeat visitors they get, it seems the Wasses are succeeding admirably.

The Wasses' pampering is evident in the many small luxuries in each guestroom: fresh roses in a cut-glass vase, bottled water and glasses on a silver tray, burgundy velour bathrobes, Crabtree & Evelyn toiletries and specially milled soaps in the bathroom, and the nightly turndown service (complete with chocolate-raspberry truffles). Each guestroom is named for a former owner of the house and decorated with priceless colonial antiques. The *Gerald McGimsey Room* features a canopy bed with a white spread; the *Albert Hibbs Room* has a fishnet canopy bed and a fireplace; the *Phineas Kelly Room* has an antique brass-and-iron bed and a fireplace.

The public rooms are filled with family treasures. In the living room portraits of Mike's ancestors hang over the mantel. The Shaker cradle in this room was purchased by the Wasses, just before their daughter was born, and Suella's exquisite needlework hangs on the walls. Other family relics include the upright piano on which Suella learned to play as a child and a side table that was handmade by Mike's father.

Breakfast is a major event here. Beckoned by the heady aroma of fresh-brewed coffee, guests congregate in the breakfast room/art gallery, and the multi-course feast begins. Freshly blended juice and bread or muffins hot from the oven comprise the first course, followed by an inventive fruit dish (perhaps a baked nectarine stuffed with almonds and served on a pool of vanilla custard). An appetizer comes next—maybe chilled strawberry-orange-champagne soup. The entrée could be a vegetable tart or Suella's special crêpes with apples, tangerines, dates, almonds, and cream cheese. If you aren't already bursting, you can finish the meal with a sweet. Then there's the formal afternoon tea, which might include poppyseed-orange scones with clotted cream and strawberry jam, finger sandwiches, fresh cherries, and butter cookies crusted with cinnamon.

With all this sumptuous food, you may want to work off some calories by hiking, bicycling, or playing golf (there are plenty of facilities in the area). Other activities include visiting the nearby *James Michener Art Center, Washington Crossing National Park, Pennsbury Manor,* and the region's many antiques shops.

WHITEHALL INN **1370 Pineville Rd., New Hope, PA 18938 (phone: 215-598-7945).** **Set in the countryside, this manor house has six guestrooms (four with private baths) with double or queen-size beds and air conditioning. Open year-round. Rate for a double room (including full breakfast and afternoon tea): $130 to $190. Two-night minimum stay on weekends; three nights on holiday weekends. Major credit cards accepted. Not appropriate for children under 13. No pets. No smoking. Mike and Suella Wass, innkeepers.**

DIRECTIONS: From New York take the New Jersey Turnpike south to Exit 10, then take I-287 north to Exit 13. Follow Route 202 south to Lahaska. Turn left onto Street Road in Lahaska and continue to the second intersection (a short distance beyond the railroad tracks). Bear right onto Pineville Road. The inn is 1½ miles farther along on the right.

BRIDGETON HOUSE ON THE DELAWARE

UPPER BLACK EDDY, PENNSYLVANIA

Take one run-down 1836 terra cotta apartment house overlooking the Delaware River, combine it with the creativity and entrepreneurial daring of an enthusiastic couple, and what do you get? In the case of *Bridgeton House on the Delaware,* a unique inn characterized by youthful energy and style, and a bold, innovative decor.

Innkeepers Bea and Charles Briggs, working with Bea's cousin, artist Cheryl Raywood, have blended comfort and practicality with whimsy and artistry. After purchasing the building in 1981, Charles, who is a master craftsman, added windows and French doors along the back walls, to bring more light into the rooms and built balconies that overlook the river. Cheryl's life-size oil paintings of nudes hang in several rooms. Each guestroom is painted in bold colors and decorated with imagination and flair. In one suite, for example, red plaid pillows accent the king-size bed and walls painted half yellow, half checkerboard, with a molding dividing the two. Other features include a corner fireplace and a screened porch. The walls of another guestroom are fuchsia and gold; the bath is stenciled. Another room has a cobalt blue ceiling painted with gold stars. Several baths boast polished mahogany cabinets hand-crafted by Charles, and eight of the rooms have balconies or porches.

The penthouse suite, by contrast, is positively restrained. Spanning most of the top floor, it features white walls, a 12-foot cathedral ceiling, and a fireplace of black-and-white marble. The king-size bed faces a wall of windows that affords unobstructed views of the river. There are black leather Barcelona-style chairs, an Art Nouveau hanging bar with stained glass doors that was crafted by Charles, and a huge bath with a marble floor, a pedestal sink, a deep tub surrounded by a marble border, and a separate shower.

The dining room is furnished rather simply and embellished with wall stencils. A full breakfast is served, here, each morning. The first course is a fruit dish, perhaps a baked apple with walnuts and raisins accompanied by fresh-baked bread; the entrée that follows might be orange-pecan waffles with cranberry-orange sauce, or an asparagus-cheddar omelette. An afternoon snack—featuring tea, sherry, and such sweets as lemon bars or chocolate chip cookies—also is offered.

This fanciful retreat is some 18 miles from the tourist traffic of busy New Hope, yet close enough so that guests can take advantage of the area's many fine restaurants and cultural attractions. The inn has a dock on the Delaware River that's convenient for boating, swimming, fishing, or canoeing; hiking and bicycling are available nearby.

BRIDGETON HOUSE ON THE DELAWARE **1525 River Rd., Upper Black Eddy, PA 18972 (phone: 610-982-5856). On the banks of the Delaware River, this inn has 10 guestrooms with private baths, double or king-size beds, and air conditioning. Open year-round. Rate for a double room (including full breakfast and afternoon tea): $69 to $225. Two-night minimum stay weekends from April through December. MasterCard and Visa accepted. Children under eight welcome mid-week only. No pets. No smoking. Bea and Charles Briggs, innkeepers.**

DIRECTIONS: Traveling on the I-78 west, take Exit 15 (Clinton/Pittstown) onto Route 513 south. After 4 miles you'll see the *Hoff Mill Inn* on the right; make a right after the inn and stay on Route 513 south to Frenchtown. In Frenchtown cross the bridge into Pennsylvania and turn right onto Route 32 north. The inn is another 3½ miles farther on the right. From Philadelphia take I-95 north for 23 miles to Exit 31 (New Hope). Make a left at the stop sign at the end of the exit ramp and follow Route 32 (River Road) through New Hope. The inn is 18 miles beyond New Hope, on the right-hand side of Route 32.

Ontario

LANGDON HALL COUNTRY HOUSE

CAMBRIDGE, ONTARIO

Elegance and grandeur characterize *Langdon Hall Country House* as much today as they did almost a century ago. Built in 1898 by Eugene Langdon Wilks, a direct descendant of John Jacob Astor, this Federal Revival brick mansion with a columned portico was a summer house in its early years, the site of numerous balls and theatrical presentations. Eventually Wilks's daughter and her family made it their full-time residence, remaining until 1982. In 1987 restoration architect William Bennett bought the magnificent house and began the long process of refurbishing it and turning it into an inn. Two years later, he opened *Langdon Hall* with his partner, Mary Beaton.

Today, it is the quintessential fine historic home. In the style of an English country-house hotel, it boasts eight formal common rooms, including the *Conservatory;* the *Map Room* (named for the old map of *Langdon Hall* and the surrounding area that hangs on one wall), with a full-size pool table; the *Card Room,* with board games and decks of cards; and the *Red Room,* a sitting room with dark burgundy walls.

There are 41 guestrooms and suites distributed between *Langdon Hall* itself and *The Cloisters,* a newer house (featuring similar Federal Revival architecture) connected to the main building by an underground passage. All the rooms are decorated in subdued colors and furnished with lovely antiques (some of which belonged to the Astor family) and Oriental rugs on burnished wood floors. Many of the beds were hand-crafted by local artisans in the sleigh style that was a favorite of Wilks's daughter. The large baths boast luxurious appointments, including mahogany trim and separate dressing areas with makeup tables. Seven of the guestrooms have fireplaces, and twelve feature either a deck, a patio, or a balcony.

In the much-acclaimed restaurant (also open to non-guests), which overlooks the water garden filled with lilies, continental fare is prepared using fresh vegetables and herbs grown in the large kitchen garden. In the afternoons, watercress sandwiches, fresh-baked scones with clotted cream, and cakes are served on Limoges china, either in the glass-enclosed *Conservatory* or on the verandah overlooking the *Cloister Gardens.* Vinegars, condiments, jams, honey, and herbed oils made on the premises are sold in the gift shop.

The inn is located in an area of Ontario known as Carolinian Canada, which enjoys an exceptionally mild climate. Bennett hired one of the province's foremost gardeners to re-create the estate's formal gardens, and tulip trees, sassafras, crab apple, bittersweet, and other trees and plants normally found much farther south all flourish here. The 40-acre grounds also offer a tennis court, a croquet lawn, a heated pool, a volleyball court, a fitness center, and a spa where guests can indulge in a variety of massages, facials, and beauty treatments.

Walking, jogging, and cross-country ski trails lace the adjacent 200 acres. Nearby attractions include several country markets (the inn lies at the heart of Ontario's Mennonite country), the *Seagram Museum* in Waterloo, and the *Stratford Shakespeare Festival* in summer.

LANGDON HALL COUNTRY HOUSE RR 33, Cambridge, ONT N3H 4R8, Canada (phone: 519-740-2100; 800-268-1898; fax: 519-740-8161). This country-house hotel has 41 guestrooms with private baths, queen-, or king-size beds, telephones, TV sets, and air conditioning. Wheelchair accessible. Open year-round. Rate for a double room (including continental breakfast): CN $175 to $290 (US $138 to $229 at press time). Two-night minimum stay on weekends from late May through early September. Major credit cards accepted. Children welcome. No pets. Two dogs in residence. Smoking permitted in guestrooms, but not in the dining room. William Bennett and Mary Beaton, innkeepers.

DIRECTIONS: From Toronto take Highway 401 west beyond Cambridge to Exit 275 (Homer Watson Boulevard and Fountain Street). Drive south on Fountain Street to Blair Road (the second road on the right) and follow the signs to Blair. Drive through the hamlet of Blair, pass the town tavern, and turn right onto Langdon Drive. After about 100 feet (30 meters), turn into the first driveway on the left, and follow the lane a quarter mile (0.4 km) to *Langdon Hall.*

ELORA MILL COUNTRY INN

ELORA, ONTARIO

Long before the British settled this area, the Native Americans thought Elora Gorge was a sacred place. Perhaps it is. Here, the waterfall cascading from 60-foot stone walls onto the rocks below, is a spectacular sight.

In 1832, Captain William Gilkison purchased the land, naming it Elora after his brother's ship (which, in turn, had been named after the Ellora Caves near Bombay). Other Scotsmen followed, and Elora quickly became a prosperous village of houses built from local stone. Perched on the edge of the limestone precipice, the five-story *Elora Mill* was erected in 1843 as the community's gristmill; several other buildings were constructed later. Its solid stone foundation and heavy wood beams are a testament to the expert work of the Scottish stonemasons. The complex of buildings was converted to an inn in 1976, and the current owners, Toronto natives Kathy and Tim Taylor, bought the place 10 years later.

The guestrooms are furnished with simple Shaker-style pine furniture, including four-poster beds, chests, and tables made for the inn by local craftspeople. Local Elora pottery was used for the bathroom sinks, while handmade quilts decorate the beds and wooden quilts (pieces of inlaid wood depicting scenes) grace the walls. Several of the rooms have fireplaces and balconies, and most overlook the gorge or the Grand River.

The balconied *Penstock Lounge,* in an old stable on a rocky outcrop, seems to be suspended over the falls. A jazz pianist entertains here on weekends; this is also the site of winter jazz weekends. The country-style dining room has stone walls and lofty beams. Breakfast, lunch, and dinner are served (also open to non-guests); entrées might include tweed of salmon Elora (a fresh salmon filet wrapped in spinach, encased in brie, and baked in puff pastry) or pork Wellesley (a stuffed tenderloin baked and glazed with apple-cider honey). Both Taylors are well-known oenophiles. The restaurant's award-winning wine list, 30 pages long, includes the area's largest selection of Ontario wines as well as some very rare vintages. The inn also has a small brewery that turns out Elora pale ale, and Kathy prepares the tasty jams featured at breakfast.

The inn sponsors several activities during the year, including *Octoberfest* and *Christmas* feasts. Nearby attractions include the *Elora Music Festival,* the *Guelph Spring Festival,* the *Theatre on the Grand,* and the *Wellington County Museum.* Boutiques and antiques shops are also on site. Bicycling and hiking in the *Elora Gorge Conservation Area* are other popular pastimes.

ELORA MILL COUNTRY INN 77 Mill St. W., Box 218, Elora, ONT N0B 1S0, Canada (phone: 519-846-5356; fax: 519-836-9180). This historic inn has 32 guestrooms with private baths, twin, double, queen-, or king-size beds, telephones, TV sets, and air conditioning. Closed *Christmas* and the week following *New Year's Day.* Rate for a double room (including full breakfast): CN $125 to $200 (US $99 to $158 at press time). Two-night minimum stay on weekends. Major credit cards accepted. Children welcome. No pets. Restricted smoking. Kathy and Tim Taylor, innkeepers.

DIRECTIONS: Elora is 50 miles (80 km) west of Toronto and 180 miles (288 km) east of Detroit. From Toronto take Highway 401 west for 26 miles (42 km) to Highway 6 (Guelph). Travel north on Highway 6 for 10 miles (16 km) to Elora Road. Proceed 10 miles (16 km) to Elora and turn right into the business district. The inn is at the end of Mill Street. From Detroit cross the bridge to Windsor, Ontario, then take Highway 401 for 170 miles (272 km) to Highway 6. From there follow the above directions.

EGANRIDGE INN AND COUNTRY CLUB

FENELON FALLS, ONTARIO

Nestled in the hills of Ontario overlooking Sturgeon Lake, this bucolic retreat is part country club, part resort, and part inn. The young Victoria had just become Queen of England when the main house, here, a 3,000-square-foot log building called *Dunsford House,* was built in 1838.

Dunsford House now contains six luxurious suites with spacious bedrooms and bathrooms featuring Jacuzzis. Two of these rooms have fireplaces; all have reproduction period furniture and are decorated with floral chintz fabrics. In addition, there are five newer cottages, each with a whirlpool and private deck. Common areas include a broad deck and a sunroom.

The dining room is in the original barn overlooking the lake; in warm weather many guests choose to eat on the screened porch. A continental breakfast of juice, fruit, coffee, tea, and muffins is served. Lunch and dinner are served here as well (also open to non-guests). Typical dinner entrées include roast rack of lamb with a glaze of mustard and fresh rosemary, and oven-baked chicken breast with calvados.

Set on 105 acres in the Kawartha Lakes region of Ontario, the inn has its own nine-hole golf course, tennis courts, a marina with 25 slips, and a lake beach with natural sand (a rarity in this part of Ontario). The *Eganridge Inn* also is popular with boating enthusiasts, thanks to the Treat Seven Waterway, a 240-mile (384-km) course that passes through a series of lakes, canals, and locks between Lakes Ontario and Huron. Sturgeon Lake is part of this system, and the world's largest lift locks are minutes from the inn. Many guests also enjoy strolling through the inn's landscaped gardens. Other attractions in the area include summer theater and fishing.

EGANRIDGE INN AND COUNTRY CLUB RR 3, Fenelon Falls, ONT KOM 1NO, Canada (phone and fax: 705-738-5111). A log manor house with adjacent cottages, it has 11 guestrooms with private baths, queen- or king-size beds, telephones, TV sets, and air conditioning. Wheelchair accessible. Closed November through April. Rate for a double room (including continental breakfast): CN $140 to $175 (US $111 to $138 at press time). Major credit cards accepted. Not appropriate for children under 18. No pets. Smoking permitted in cottages only. Patty and John Egan, innkeepers.

DIRECTIONS: From Toronto travel east on Highway 401 to Exit 436 in Newcastle. Pick up Highway 35/115 north, then take Highway 35 to Lindsay. At the light turn right onto Highway 36 and continue 26 miles (42 km) via Bobcaygeon to County Road 8. Turn left onto County Road 8 and watch for the *Eganridge* sign.

STE. ANNE'S COUNTRY INN AND SPA

GRAFTON, ONTARIO

The solid fieldstone buildings on this delightfully serene place are reminiscent of a monastery or cloister. Built in 1857 by a farmer named Samuel Massey, the estate was bought in 1939 by the Blaffer family of Texas. Adding turrets, archways, and walled gardens to the estate, the Blaffers used it as a summer home until 1975. The estate sat neglected and forlorn until 1981, when the Corcoran family purchased it with the idea of turning it into an inn. Four years later, after an extensive renovation, *Ste. Anne's* opened its doors.

The 11 spacious guestrooms and suites have fireplaces and private baths; five also feature Jacuzzis. The decor, with antiques and newer country-style furniture, is comfortable and unpretentious.

The dining room serves well-prepared continental fare that manages to be both tempting and healthful. Entrées may include poached Atlantic salmon and teriyaki chicken, accompanied in summer by fresh vegetables and herbs grown in the inn's garden. No liquor is served, but guests may bring their own. Every morning a full breakfast is offered; the menu changes daily but always includes juice, fruit, muffins, and an entrée such as pancakes or eggs.

Nestled on 560 acres of wooded hills, the estate overlooks shimmering Lake Ontario and meadows where herds of fallow deer graze. For the active, there are three clay tennis courts and a spring-fed swimming pool. More sedentary entertainment is available in the living room, with its stock of jigsaw puzzles, games, and books. There's also a spa that provides rejuvenating paraffin baths, reflexology, body polishing (scrubbing with a granular cream), flower-essence scalp treatments, and massage; there's a hot tub and sauna as well. Golf courses, fishing, *Presqu'île Provincial Park,* and antique shops are nearby.

STE. ANNE'S COUNTRY INN AND SPA RR 1, Grafton, ONT K0K 2G0, Canada (phone: 905-349-2493; 800-263-2663; fax: 905-349-3531). Set in the Northumberland Hills of Ontario, this property has 11 guestrooms with private baths, twin, double, queen-, or king-size beds, and air conditioning. Limited wheelchair accessibility. Open year-round. Rate for a double room (including breakfast, lunch, and dinner, plus a $50 credit toward spa treatments): CN $325 to $410 (US $257 to $324 at press time). Two-night minimum stay on weekends. Major credit cards accepted. Not appropriate for children under 16. No pets. One dog in residence. No smoking. The Corcoran family, owners; Jim Corcoran and Anne Harris, innkeepers.

DIRECTIONS: From Toronto take Highway 401 east to Exit 487 (Grafton/Centreton). Travel north on Aird Street for 1 mile (1.6 km), then turn left at the top of the hill onto Massey Road. Watch for the inn's entrance on the left.

THE BRIARS

JACKSON'S POINT, ONTARIO

John Sibbald, the current "squire" of *The Briars,* is justifiably proud of this estate, now home to the fifth generation of Sibbalds. The 200-acre grounds contain a wide variety of buildings, including the 1840 *Manor House* with a 65-foot observation tower, the *Coach House,* stables, the brick *Peacock House,* with its bell roof and arched windows that once housed peacocks, and several much newer cottages. The *Manor House* is furnished with family antiques, John's personal art collection, and pictures and china from the days when Frank Sibbald, the owner in the late 19th century, was a physician in Shanghai.

Despite its large size (92 guestrooms), the estate retains a private, secluded feeling that makes it popular with celebrities (Jaclyn Smith and Brian Dennehy have stayed here). The guestrooms in the *Manor House* boast Regency-style antiques, including canopy and four-poster beds, and Georgian chests and tables of gleaming wood. Rooms in the 12 cottages are decorated with floral chintz fabrics and have an English country ambience. Most of the rooms have either balconies or patios, and 24 have working fireplaces. Several of the cottages have views of the beautiful golf course, while others look beyond Jackson's Point to the far shores of Lake Simcoe.

The dining rooms provide a fine setting for meals (also open to nonguests): One has bay windows and 14-foot ceilings topped by elaborate cornices and moldings; another, the *Garden Court,* has exposed brick walls and columns and overlooks the gardens and lake. The tasty Canadian regional cuisine includes Cornish game hen glazed with maple syrup and a luscious black-and-white mousse torte.

Nestled into the mature forests and gently rolling land, the estate's 18-hole *Scottish Woodlands* golf course captures the resort's relaxing character. Each hole is framed by majestic pine, birch, and maple trees. Other facilities include an exercise center, a whirlpool and sauna, a gameroom, tennis courts, fishing, swimming in indoor and outdoor pools as well as in the lake, boating, and fishing. In winter, when the property is blanketed with snow, guests can cross-country ski, ice skate, and snowshoe. The *Red Barn Theatre,* in the estate's former barn, presents various productions in July and August. Be sure to request a copy of the map of the property that also traces its ownership through its 170-year history. Besides being fascinating reading, the map highlights recreational opportunities that might otherwise be missed.

If you should want to venture off the grounds, the inn is near several points of interest, including *Canada's Wonderland,* the *McMichael Canadian Art Collection,* the *Sharon Temple and Museum,* the famous lift locks in Kirkfield, and all the attractions of metropolitan Toronto.

THE BRIARS 55 Hedge Rd., RR 1, Jackson's Point, ONT L0E 1L0, Canada (phone: 905-722-3271; 800-465-2376; fax: 905-722-9698). This resort has 92 guestrooms with private baths, twin, double, queen-, or king-size beds, telephones, TV sets, and air conditioning. Wheelchair accessible. Open year-round. Rate for a double room (including breakfast, lunch, and dinner): $163 to $258 (US). Major credit cards accepted. Children welcome. No pets. Smoking permitted in designated areas. The Sibbald family, innkeepers.

DIRECTIONS: From Toronto take Highway 404 north to Davis. Turn east onto Woodbine Avenue, then travel north 20 miles (32 km) to Sutton. In Sutton turn north onto Dalton Road to Jackson's Point, then east onto Lake Drive. Proceed about half a mile (0.8 km), then turn onto Hedge Road and continue to the inn.

Upper South

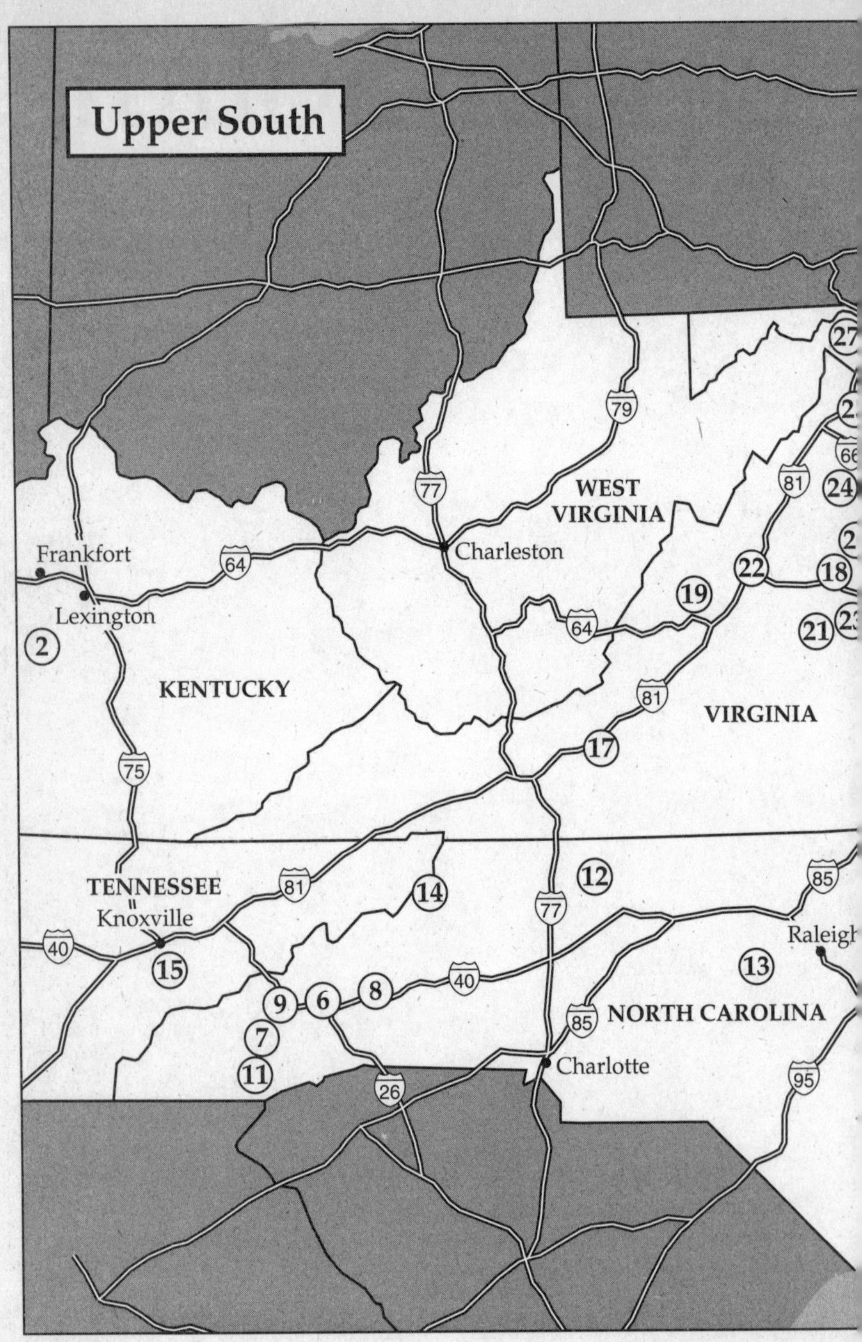
Upper South
WEST VIRGINIA
Charleston
Frankfort
Lexington
KENTUCKY
VIRGINIA
TENNESSEE
Knoxville
NORTH CAROLINA
Raleigh
Charlotte
2
6
7
8
9
11
12
13
14
15
17
18
19
21
22
24
64
77
79
81
75
40
26
85
95
66

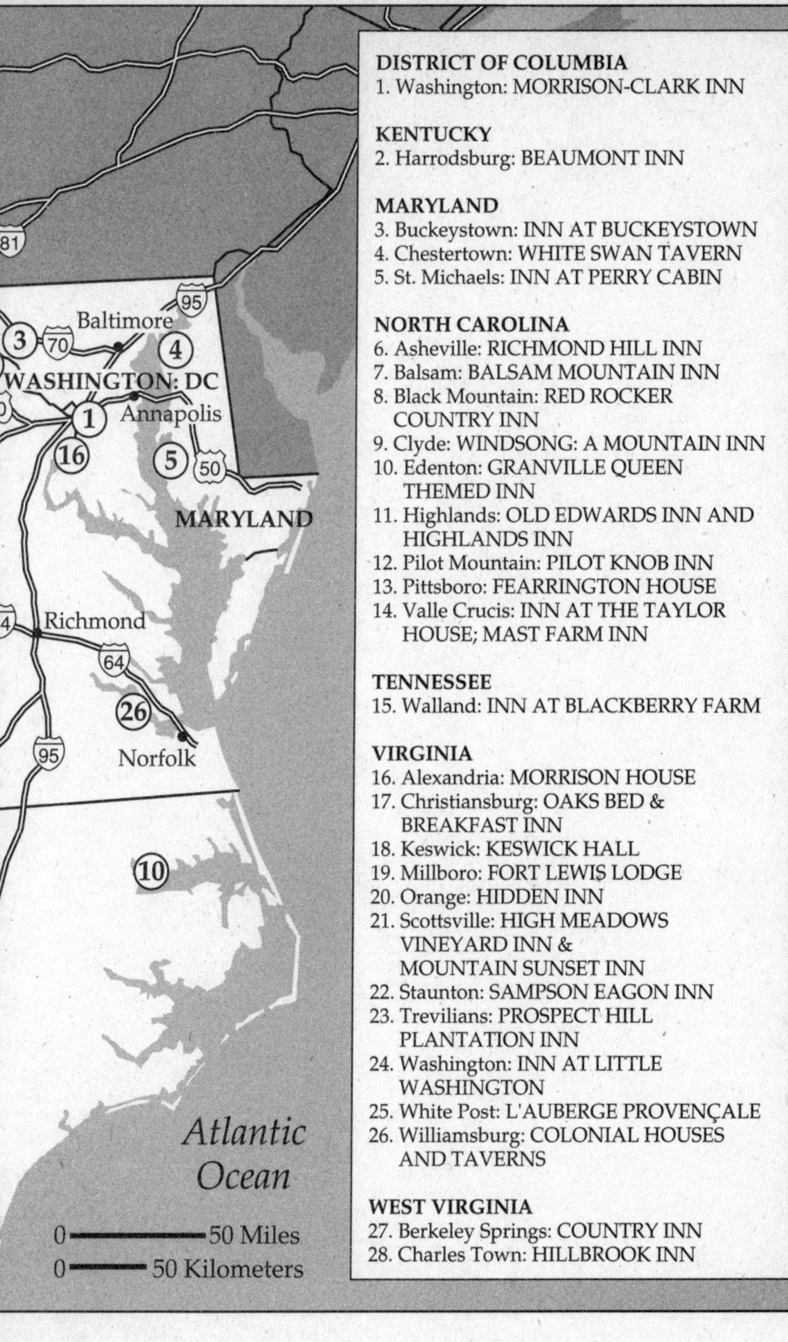
81
95
Baltimore
3
70
4
WASHINGTON: DC
1
Annapolis
16
5
50
MARYLAND
64
Richmond
64
26
95
Norfolk
10
Atlantic Ocean
0 50 Miles
0 50 Kilometers
DISTRICT OF COLUMBIA
1. Washington: MORRISON-CLARK INN
KENTUCKY
2. Harrodsburg: BEAUMONT INN
MARYLAND
3. Buckeystown: INN AT BUCKEYSTOWN
4. Chestertown: WHITE SWAN TAVERN
5. St. Michaels: INN AT PERRY CABIN
NORTH CAROLINA
6. Asheville: RICHMOND HILL INN
7. Balsam: BALSAM MOUNTAIN INN
8. Black Mountain: RED ROCKER COUNTRY INN
9. Clyde: WINDSONG: A MOUNTAIN INN
10. Edenton: GRANVILLE QUEEN THEMED INN
11. Highlands: OLD EDWARDS INN AND HIGHLANDS INN
12. Pilot Mountain: PILOT KNOB INN
13. Pittsboro: FEARRINGTON HOUSE
14. Valle Crucis: INN AT THE TAYLOR HOUSE; MAST FARM INN
TENNESSEE
15. Walland: INN AT BLACKBERRY FARM
VIRGINIA
16. Alexandria: MORRISON HOUSE
17. Christiansburg: OAKS BED & BREAKFAST INN
18. Keswick: KESWICK HALL
19. Millboro: FORT LEWIS LODGE
20. Orange: HIDDEN INN
21. Scottsville: HIGH MEADOWS VINEYARD INN & MOUNTAIN SUNSET INN
22. Staunton: SAMPSON EAGON INN
23. Trevilians: PROSPECT HILL PLANTATION INN
24. Washington: INN AT LITTLE WASHINGTON
25. White Post: L'AUBERGE PROVENÇALE
26. Williamsburg: COLONIAL HOUSES AND TAVERNS
WEST VIRGINIA
27. Berkeley Springs: COUNTRY INN
28. Charles Town: HILLBROOK INN

Upper South

District of Columbia

MORRISON-CLARK INN

WASHINGTON, DC

Built in 1864 as two separate townhouses for businessmen David Morrison and Reuben Clark, the *Morrison-Clark* has undergone many changes over the years. Along the way, one of the houses even took on several distinctive Asian touches, including a Chinese Chippendale porch and a Shanghai roof. The two eventually were joined into one large house.

In 1923, the complex became the *Soldiers, Sailors, Marines and Airmen's Club,* and for 60 years it functioned as an inexpensive hostel for servicemen traveling to Washington, DC. During its peak, in 1943, some 45,000 servicemen, many fresh from the front, slept here. Traditionally, the club was under the wing of the First Lady, who held teas and benefits to raise operating funds. Mamie Eisenhower and Jacqueline Kennedy, in particular, expended considerable effort on its behalf.

Eventually it was sold and, some say, scheduled for the wrecking ball. In 1987, however, it was purchased by a group of local developers and, after a thorough restoration and a new addition, opened its doors the following year as the *Morrison-Clark Inn.* The restoration efforts have earned it a place on the National Register of Historic Places.

In the common rooms are original fireplaces with elaborately carved marble mantelpieces and mirrors that almost reach the 13-foot ceilings. The individually appointed guestrooms have elaborate moldings, marble vanities in the baths, and ornately carved armoires. The decor ranges from antique in the original Victorian houses to country French and neoclassical in the newer wing. Flowers adorn the inn, from the vibrant arrangement in the entranceway to the bouquets perched on the vanities in the bathrooms.

The pastel-colored dining room is a peaceful setting for the delicious American menu, which features regional specialties. Sample dishes include roasted monkfish with Swiss chard and sweet red pepper, and roasted chicken with rosemary sauce.

The inn is near Washington's *Convention Center,* midway between the *Capitol* and the *White House.* A fitness center is on site.

MORRISON-CLARK INN Massachusetts Ave. and 11th St. NW, Washington, DC 20001 (phone: 202-898-1200; 800-332-7898; fax: 202-289-8576). This Victorian inn has 54 guestrooms with private baths, twin, double, queen-, or king-size beds, telephones, TV sets, and air conditioning. Open year-round. Rate for a double room (including continental breakfast): $125 to $185; corporate and weekend rates available. Major credit cards accepted. Children welcome. No pets. Smoking permitted in designated areas only. Wayne B. Neyens, general manager.

DIRECTIONS: The inn is in downtown Washington, at the junction of Massachusetts Avenue and 11th and L Streets, just off Mt. Vernon Place. An underground garage with valet parking is available (at additional charge).

Kentucky

BEAUMONT INN

HARRODSBURG, KENTUCKY

There's a gentleness to the landscape of Kentucky. In the heart of bluegrass country, where some of the world's most pampered horses graze, Harrodsburg—and the *Beaumont Inn*—exemplify this tranquillity.

The inn has had a distinguished history that predates the present structure. On the site was the boyhood home of John M. Harlan, who later became the chief justice of the *US Supreme Court.* In 1841 it was purchased by Dr. Samuel G. Mullins, who turned the old log homestead into the *Greenville Female Institute.* After a fire destroyed the building, he replaced it in 1845 with the magnificent Greek Revival brick mansion that is now the *Beaumont Inn* and listed on the National Register of Historic Places. With sturdy walls 18 inches thick and six Ionic columns at the entrance, it was built to last. Ancestors of the present innkeepers purchased the property in 1919; it's currently enjoying its fourth generation of management by the Dedman family.

Remnants of the old school are visible in many of the rooms. The current office was the school's library, and the original cherry bookcases are filled with books well-thumbed by students and teachers. The original fireplaces still grace the double parlors.

Dedman contributions to the inn are numerous. The embroidered cutwork linen curtains were custom-made for the family on the Portuguese island of Madeira in 1919. Crystal chandeliers, pier mirrors, a mahogany parlor-grand piano (given to Bessie Dedman in 1893), and the Empire and

Victorian tables, chairs, and lamps have all been passed from generation to generation. Curio cabinets display collections of saltcellars, silver, and antique china.

Guestrooms are located in the *Main Inn* and in three other buildings, all within walking distance. Those in the former are furnished with antiques, including several highly decorated Victorian headboards, and cannonball, spool, and two-poster beds. There are additional rooms across the street in *Goddard Hall,* a pretty, white 1935 clapboard building with a covered verandah. The decor here is rich with family heirlooms, including portraits, four-poster beds, and decorative touches such as vintage clothing and antique lace tablecloths. Two units ideal for families are in *Bell Cottage,* a little 1921 house with a broad front porch. *Greystone House,* an imposing 1931 stone mansion built for May Lilly, niece of Eli Lilly of pharmaceutical fame, has four more large bedrooms.

The *Main Inn*'s gift shop presents a wide assortment of Kentucky crafts and food items. The parlors are well stocked with board games and books, and the porches are lined with split-hickory wicker chairs. The 33-acre property, shaded by more than 30 varieties of trees, holds two tennis courts, a swimming pool, a shuffleboard court, and several swings and benches that are just the thing on a lazy afternoon.

Breakfast, lunch, and dinner (all open to non-guests) are served in the dining room in the *Main Inn,* where fried chicken and locally cured ham are featured. Other typically Southern specialties, such as corn pudding and General Robert E. Lee orange-lemon cake, also are popular.

Among the attractions nearby are Civil War battlefields, superb antiquing, thoroughbred and harness racing, golf, and numerous historic museums, including the *Shaker Village of Pleasant Hill.* An outdoor drama reenacting the legend of Daniel Boone takes place every summer in Harrodsburg.

BEAUMONT INN 638 Beaumont Inn Dr., Harrodsburg, KY 40330 (phone: 606-734-3381; 800-352-3992; fax: 606-734-6897). This hotel has 33 guestrooms with private baths, twin, double, queen-, or king-size beds, telephones, TV sets, and air conditioning. Closed mid-December through February. Rate for a double room: $80 to $100; additional person in double room: $20; children under 12 (in parents' room): $15. Major credit cards accepted. No pets. No smoking permitted in the dining room or in designated guestrooms. T. C. and Mary Elizabeth Dedman, owners; Chuck and Helen Dedman, innkeepers.

DIRECTIONS: Traveling east from Louisville on I-64, take Exit 48 to Kentucky Route 151 south, then take US Route 127 south for 15 miles to Harrodsburg. Beaumont Inn Drive is on the south end of town.

Maryland

INN AT BUCKEYSTOWN

BUCKEYSTOWN, MARYLAND

The entire village of Buckeystown is listed on the National Register of Historic Places. Significant buildings—from early log cabins to brick and stone Federal homes and gingerbread Victorian mansions—line the streets. The 1897 *Inn at Buckeystown* is among the most impressive Victorians, as is its sister property, a restored 1884 Gothic-style brick church two blocks away. The inn has been owned and run by Daniel Pelz and Chase Barnett since 1980.

In the common rooms Oriental rugs grace polished wood floors and crystal chandeliers cast a soft glow on oil paintings. There are three working fireplaces. The five guestrooms in the main house are furnished with museum-quality antiques, including velvet-, mohair-, and satin-covered Victorian love seats and chairs, carved walnut headboards, and marble-topped shaving stands. Carved moldings trim the ceilings, and chintz fabrics cover the windows. On arrival, guests find a Victorian decanter of port and stemmed glasses in their room. *St. John's Reformed Church,* which is part of the inn, boasts a two-level unit where the original stained glass casts multicolored light across the walls; the bedroom is in the choir loft! There's a fireplace and grand piano in the common area, and outside a private garden surrounds a hot tub. The one-story *Parson's Cottage,* near the former church, is a two-room retreat with a fireplace and its own kitchen.

Food is an important part of any stay here; both breakfast and dinner are included in the rate. Although the owners emphasize that "this is not a restaurant but an inn," the five-course dinner is offered to non-guests as well. The menu is continental and might include such entrées as prawns in lemon-garlic butter or veal with mushrooms and wine. Desserts include Key lime and banana cream pies. The dining room is decorated in High Victorian style with Oriental rugs, carved oak sideboards, and a magnificent crystal chandelier. When the dinner bell rings, guests are seated at oak tables set with antique china, crystal, and silver.

The inn is located near Civil War battlefields, the Appalachian Trail, and New Market, the antiques capital of Maryland.

INN AT BUCKEYSTOWN 3521 Buckeystown Pike (mailing address: c/o General Delivery), Buckeystown, MD 21717 (phone: 301-874-5755; 800-272-1190). This historic inn has eight guestrooms with private baths, double and queen-size beds, and air conditioning. Closed Mondays and Tuesdays. Rate for a double room (including full breakfast, dinner with wine, and gratuities): $225 to $300. Major credit cards accepted. Not appropriate for children under 16. No pets. Two dogs and outdoor cats on the property. No smoking. Daniel R. Pelz and Chase Barnett, innkeepers; Rebecca Smith, general manager.

DIRECTIONS: Traveling on I-270 north from Washington, DC, take Exit 26 (Buckeystown) to Route 80 west; continue for 5 miles. Turn right onto Route 85 north (Buckeystown Pike). The inn is a half mile farther on the right.

WHITE SWAN TAVERN

CHESTERTOWN, MARYLAND

Chestertown is a quaint little town on the Maryland shore that has retained much of its prerevolutionary flavor. The *White Swan Tavern,* a brick building with a roof projecting over its brick porch, is one of the town's oldest and most historic buildings. An archaeological dig in the back yard determined that the oldest parts of the tavern date to 1733. It appears that the owners began taking in guests as early as 1760. Through the years, it was also used as a music store and a shoe store. It remained in the ownership of the Eliason family from 1854 to 1977.

In 1978, the tavern was purchased by Horace Havemeyer Jr. (It's now owned by his son Christian.) Archaeologists, historians, and craftspeople were hired to restore it to a style that reflected its 1790–1850 past. Many interesting artifacts were unearthed, and a fascinating museum displays examples of the finds and chronicles the restoration process.

The inn now contains six guestrooms, all decorated with colonial antiques and fabrics. One of the most popular, the *John Lovegrove Kitchen,* is located in the old kitchen with its huge fireplace; it has a brick floor, a beamed ceiling, and colonial chests and tables. The *Sterling Suite* has a reproduction canopy bed, burnished antique dressers and tables, and wonderful oil paintings.

Innkeeper Mary Susan Maisel sees to the comfort of her guests. On arrival, they find a bottle of wine and a fruit basket in their rooms. In the evening, before going out to dinner, guests gather over sherry and coffee. Tea is served daily in the *Nicholson* and *Isaac Cannell Rooms* on the main floor and also in the brick courtyard, with its lush perennial border, on comfortable summer days.

A continental breakfast of juice, fruit, fresh-baked rolls, cereal, and coffee or tea is served every morning. Following breakfast, a jaunt around town and down to the waterfront, on one of the inn's bicycles, provides an excellent perspective on the area.

Located on a Chesapeake Bay inlet, Chestertown is a popular boating destination. Also popular are its many crab houses, where mallets are provided for cracking open the local specialty. Numerous houses are open to visitors, and the village walking tour is informative. Visitors also can enjoy bird watching at the nearby *Eastern Neck Island Wildlife Refuge,* antiquing, and concerts and lectures at *Washington College.*

WHITE SWAN TAVERN **231 High St., Chestertown, MD 21620 (phone: 410-778-2300; fax: 410-778-4543). This historic tavern has six guestrooms with private baths, double, queen-, or king-size beds, and air conditioning. Wheelchair accessible. Open year-round. Rate for a double room (including continental breakfast, tea, and evening refreshments): $100 to $150. No credit cards accepted. Children welcome. No pets. Smoking permitted in two guestrooms only. Christian Havemeyer, owner; Mary Susan Maisel, innkeeper.**

DIRECTIONS: From Washington, DC, take Route 50/301 west past Annapolis and across the Bay Bridge. When Route 301 splits from Route 50, stay in the left lane and take Route 301 north for 5 miles. Turn onto Route 213 north and travel 18 miles to Chestertown. Cross the Chester River Bridge and take the second left. Turn right at the next intersection onto High Street. The inn is on the left, in the middle of the block.

INN AT PERRY CABIN

St. Michaels, Maryland

The long, rich history of the *Inn at Perry Cabin* begins with one Samuel Hambleton. During the War of 1812, Hambleton distinguished himself at the Battle of Lake Erie, where he served under Commodore Oliver Hazard Perry. On his retirement to St. Michaels in 1816, he built a manor house with a wing designed to look like Perry's ship cabin. In the middle of this century, the old house and surrounding estate were converted to a riding academy, then, in 1979, the owners of *Kentucky Derby* winner Spectacular Bid turned the property into an inn and restaurant. Ten years later, in his first venture into American innkeeping, Sir Bernard Ashley, co-founder of the Laura Ashley Company, purchased the 25-acre estate and created an American version of an English country-house hotel.

The numerous common rooms provide ample opportunity for relaxation. There's a wicker- and greenery-filled conservatory and the adjoining *Snooker Room,* with a massive table and fireplace. The *Meeting Room,* beyond, has the latest audiovisual equipment, and a tiled corridor serves as the gameroom, where chess and other board games share space with a buggy full of teddy bears. The *Morning Room* and the library with a piano both have fireplaces. There's also a fitness center and an indoor swimming pool.

The inn has 41 spacious guestrooms, several with balconies or duplex sitting rooms, and many with views of the Miles River. Not surprisingly, they are lavishly decorated with Laura Ashley fabrics, wallpapers, china, and furniture–canopied four-posters with spiral posts, soft down sofas strewn with bright pillows, and pine armoires. It's the perfect blend of elegance and comfort. The turndown service includes crisp, homemade oatmeal-raisin cookies delivered to each room.

Meals at *Perry Cabin* (also open to non-guests) are noted for their spectacular presentations as well as fine food. While guests peruse the menu, a plate of hors d'oeuvres is offered for nibbling. The appetizer might be creamy duck foie gras served with crisp brioches and grapes; the entrée, lightly grilled salmon served on a bed of shoestring potatoes. For dessert, raspberry bread pudding is dusted with powdered sugar and served in a pool of *crème anglaise.* The full breakfast, which is included, is equally delicious, with eggs Benedict, grilled kippers, French toast, muffins, and fruit on the menu. In the afternoon, guests are treated to tea and scones or pastries.

Located on Maryland's eastern shore, the inn has its own dock and boats, so guests can enjoy sailing and fishing. Antiquing and golf are nearby.

INN AT PERRY CABIN 308 Watkins La., St. Michaels, MD 21663 (phone: 410-745-2200; 800-722-2949; fax: 410-745-3348). This resort has 41 guestrooms with private baths, twin, double, queen-, or king-size beds, telephones, TV sets, and air conditioning. Wheelchair accessible. Open year-round. Rate for a double room (including full breakfast and afternoon tea): $175 to $525. Major credit cards accepted. Not appropriate for children under 10. No pets. No smoking permitted in the dining room. Sir Bernard Ashley, owner; Stephen Creese, innkeeper.

DIRECTIONS: From Washington, DC, take the Capitol Beltway to Route 50 east (John Hanson Highway), traveling across the Chesapeake Bay Bridge to Easton. From Route 50 turn right onto the Route 322/Easton bypass, then turn right again onto Route 33 and continue to St. Michaels. In St. Michaels take Talbot Avenue through town. The inn is on the right just outside of town.

North Carolina

RICHMOND HILL INN

ASHEVILLE, NORTH CAROLINA

The fine Victorian mansion that is the centerpiece of the *Richmond Hill Inn* sits on 40 acres overlooking the French Broad River, with the lights of Asheville and the dusky mountains beyond. Built in 1889 for Richmond and Gabrielle Pearson—she a Southern belle and he a congressman and ambassador to Persia and Greece—the house's fine pedigree is evident upon walking into the grand entrance, *Oak Hall.* With its 12-foot paneled walls, exposed beams, and majestic stairway with twisted spindles and fluted columns, the hall embraces visitors in a warm, rich glow. Over the carved mantel hangs a portrait of Gabrielle, painted in Paris in 1888.

Dr. Albert (Jake) Michel came upon what had become a forlorn mansion while he was out hiking one day in 1989. Unperturbed by the peeling paint, broken windows, and collapsing porches, he and his wife, Margaret, bought the estate and began the arduous restoration process. Once described by North Carolina writer Thomas Wolfe as a "big, rambling, magnificent Victorian house," it is now listed on the National Register of Historic Places.

The mansion contains 10 large fireplaces with elaborate neoclassical mantels, some of them in the elegant common rooms. The front parlor is furnished with period pieces and accented with English garden prints. An ornate octagonal ballroom and a drawing room are used for meetings and receptions. This area of North Carolina has a rich literary tradition, and the pine-paneled library houses an impressive collection of books about North Carolina and by authors with an Asheville connection.

Furnishings in the guestrooms are equally attractive. Canopy and four-poster beds, Victorian chairs and tables, Oriental rugs, and bathrooms with footed tubs are found throughout. Down pillows and fresh flowers add the finishing touches. The enormous rooms on the second floor are named for

Pearson family members or close friends. The most lavish of these has a seven-sided bedroom, a sitting room, a wet bar, a whirlpool tub, and a fireplace. Rooms on the third floor are named for authors who lived or wrote in Asheville, such as Carl Sandburg, F. Scott Fitzgerald, and O. Henry, and contain a selection of their books.

Nine more rooms are in the yellow and green Victorian *Croquet Cottages.* These have individual porches, fireplaces, pencil-post beds, and spacious baths. The adjacent croquet lawn offers popular afternoon recreation. A new Victorian-style building, *Garden House,* with a cafe and 15 rooms overlooking a parterre garden and a peaceful mountain brook and waterfall, is scheduled to open later this year.

Breakfast and afternoon tea are served to guests. Dinner (also open to non-guests) is served at *Gabrielle's,* the inn's gracious and refined restaurant. It's served either in the cherry-paneled dining room with a three-tiered brass chandelier, or on the sun porch with its wicker furniture, ceiling fans, and lavish view of the surrounding mountains. Entrées might include applewood smoke-roasted black Angus filet of beef, accompanied by white asparagus and a French camembert cheese soufflé served with a Château Rothschild Bordeaux wine sauce.

The inn is near the spectacular *Biltmore House and Gardens* (the George Vanderbilt mansion), *Chimney Rock Park,* and cultural attractions, including the *Thomas Wolfe House, Connemara* (the Carl Sandburg house), and the *Folk Art Center.*

RICHMOND HILL INN 87 Richmond Hill Dr., Asheville, NC 28806 (phone: 704-252-7313; 800-545-9238; fax: 704-252-8726). This Victorian mansion has 12 guestrooms plus nine cottages with private baths, twin, double, queen-, or king-size beds, telephones, TV sets, and air conditioning. Wheelchair accessible. Open year-round. Rate for a double room (including full breakfast and afternoon tea): $160 to $440. Two-night minimum stay on weekends. Major credit cards accepted. Children welcome. No pets. Limited smoking. Dr. Albert and Margaret Michel, owners; Susan Michel, innkeeper.

DIRECTIONS: The inn is 3 miles from downtown Asheville. From Asheville take I-240 west to the Route 19/23 (Weaverville) exit, then follow Route 19/23 to Exit 251 (UNC-Asheville). Turn left at the bottom of the ramp. At the first light turn left onto Riverside Drive. Turn right onto Pearson Bridge Road, and at the sharp curve turn right onto Richmond Hill Drive.

BALSAM MOUNTAIN INN

BALSAM, NORTH CAROLINA

Located on 26 acres near the crest of the Great Balsam Mountains, the three-story *Balsam Mountain Inn* snuggles into a forested glen, surrounded by peaks that reach as high as 6,000 feet. This gracious Victorian gem first welcomed visitors back in 1908. It was the era of train travel, and the quaint Balsam depot on the *Western North Carolina Railroad* was the highest station east of the Rockies. Lured by the seven freshwater springs on the inn grounds and the bracing mountain air, city folks came to escape the heat of summer and to enjoy therapeutic walks.

When Merrily Teasley purchased the inn in 1990, she acquired a building that had seen few cosmetic changes and even retained much of the original furniture. Extensive restoration was necessary. Today, the massive building that once contained 100 tiny warrens now has 34 spacious guestrooms (all with private baths), three common rooms, and three dining rooms.

The inn's old oak rockers, with handwoven seats and backs, welcome guests to "sit a spell" on the 100-foot, double-tiered front porch. Inside, the library boasts a collection of more than 2,000 volumes, while the gameroom has puzzles and cards. In the living room, decorated with an Oriental rug and myriad plants, are two fireplaces. Antiques, including iron beds and wicker, are used throughout; many bathrooms have footed tubs.

The dining room offers hearty Southern fare: Local trout as well as an abundance of fresh produce are on the menu. A full country breakfast with fresh-baked muffins (maybe poppyseed-lemon) and an entrée (such as dilled scrambled eggs in a bread cup) is complimentary to inn guests. Breakfast, lunch, and dinner also are open to non-guests.

Mountain trails wind from the inn through acres of rhododendrons and fields of wildflowers, circling a freshwater pond, meandering along a stream, then stopping at a mountain ledge where hikers can view the brilliant sunsets. For those who want to explore the surrounding area, the Blue Ridge Parkway is a half mile away, and skiing, mountain biking, and whitewater rafting are nearby. Guests also can enjoy North Carolina's Mountains-to-Sea hiking trail, golf, horseback riding, trout fishing, and the *Biltmore House and Gardens* (the George Vanderbilt mansion) in Asheville.

BALSAM MOUNTAIN INN **PO Box 40, Balsam, NC 28707 (phone: 704-456-9498; 800-224-9498; fax: 704-456-9298). This mountain inn has 34 guestrooms with private baths and double and king-size beds. Wheelchair accessible. Open year-round; restaurant closed for lunch weekdays November through May. Rate for a double room (including full breakfast): $90 to $130. Two-night minimum stay on holiday weekends, during fall foliage season, and during local college events. Major credit cards accepted. Not appropriate for children under 10. No pets. Two dogs in residence. Smoking permitted in lobby, some guestrooms, and a section of the dining room. Merrily Teasley, innkeeper.**

DIRECTIONS: On the Blue Ridge Parkway, the inn is closest to milepost 443. From the parkway take the exit for Route 74/23 and turn south toward Sylva. About a quarter mile south of the parkway overpass, turn off Route 74/23 at a small green sign marking the village of Balsam. Make an almost immediate right up a hill, across the railroad tracks, and continue straight for another third of a mile. Drive across the tracks again, then turn into the inn's driveway.

RED ROCKER COUNTRY INN

BLACK MOUNTAIN, NORTH CAROLINA

An old-fashioned inn in every sense of the word, the *Red Rocker* feels a lot like grandmother's house, complete with dinner around the big old dining room table.

The house was built as a wedding gift from a father to his daughter in 1894. The grand two-story, beige clapboard structure has been an inn since 1927. Red impatiens line the walkways, and lofty trees shade the wrap-around verandah in summer. No telephones or televisions disturb the silence.

The inn has been owned by Pat and Fred Eshleman since 1981, and their concern for their guests' well-being is evident throughout. The living room has a fireplace flanked by bookcases, and the sunny gameroom is supplied with board games and cards. Guestrooms are homey and comfortable, with whimsical touches. In the *Music Room,* for example, sheet music papers the wall at the head of the king-size bed.

Dinner (also open to non-guests) continues the informal mood, with food–straight from a turn-of-the-century cookbook—served family style. The meal begins with soup or chowder, followed by fresh homemade breads, including zucchini muffins and buttermilk biscuits. Listed among the entrées are such Southern favorites as chicken-fried steak and roast loin of pork with corn-bread stuffing. For dessert, there's warm blackberry cobbler topped with ice cream. The inn also serves breakfast.

The *Red Rocker* is in the Blue Ridge Mountains near Asheville, with its numerous cultural and recreational options, including hiking, golf, tennis, antiquing, and the nearby *Biltmore House and Gardens* (the George Vanderbilt mansion).

RED ROCKER COUNTRY INN 136 N. Dougherty St., Black Mountain, NC 28711 (phone: 704-669-5991). This old-fashioned inn has 18 guestrooms with private baths, double, queen-, or king-size beds, and air conditioning. Wheelchair accessible. Closed November through April. Rate for a double room: $55 to $85. No credit cards accepted. Children welcome. No pets. No smoking. Pat and Fred Eshleman, innkeepers.

DIRECTIONS: From Asheville take I-40 east to Exit 64 (Black Mountain). Then take Route 9 and turn left after crossing the railroad tracks. Proceed past the traffic light to the top of the hill. Go to the second traffic light and make another left. At the next light take a right onto Dougherty Street. The inn is on the right.

WINDSONG: A MOUNTAIN INN

CLYDE, NORTH CAROLINA

It's not unusual to find a log home in the mountains, but it is unusual to find one like *Windsong.* Donna and Gale Livengood built it in 1989, and with the help of Donna's brother, an architect, they created an authentic mountain haven. To keep the inn bright and airy, the interior logs were sandblasted and treated to give them a light finish. The spacious dining and living areas with their high, beamed ceilings are unified by Mexican floor tiles.

In the *Great Room*, the Livengood's collection of Native American accessories, including colorful rugs, handwoven pillows, and a carved totem on the mantel of the mammoth stone fireplace, coexist comfortably with rich leather sofas and stripped-pine breakfast tables. Walls of windows open onto a spectacular view of the Smoky Mountains. The *Guest Lounge* has a wet bar, a pool table, games, and books. Gale's previous career as a distributor of films is apparent in the large library of videocassettes, which can be viewed in the guestrooms.

Each of the guestrooms is based on a fantasy theme. The *Safari Room* features a bed with a bamboo headboard and a canopy of mosquito netting; hand-carved animals migrate across a beam above the bed, and a ceiling fan gently stirs the air. The *Alaska Room, Santa Fe Room,* and *Country Room* likewise are decorated to suit their names. All have private baths with deeper-than-usual tubs and separate showers, fireplaces, private patios or decks, and breathtaking mountain views. And the deluxe two-bedroom guesthouse, *Pond House,* built in 1993, offers a cathedral ceiling, full kitchen, wood-burning stove, two-person tub, and a deck overlooking the pond.

The full breakfast served features such dishes as blueberry-buckwheat pancakes and sausage or vanilla Belgian waffles. In the evening, dessert and coffee are set out in the *Great Room.*

The inn is located in the Smoky Mountains on 25 acres with a swimming pool, tennis court, gazebo, and numerous bowers in the gardens for reading. For the adventurous, the inn maintains a herd of llamas to accompany hikers on treks into the mountains. Nearby Asheville offers many cultural activities as well as the *Biltmore House and Gardens* (the George Vanderbilt mansion). Golf, horseback riding, whitewater rafting, and *Great Smoky Mountain National Park* also are nearby.

WINDSONG: A MOUNTAIN INN 120 Ferguson Ridge, Clyde, NC 28721 (phone: 704-627-6111; fax: 704-627-8080). This mountaintop inn has five guestrooms plus the *Pond House,* a two-bedroom guesthouse, with private baths, twin, queen-, or king-size beds, and TV sets. Open year-round. Rate for a double room in the inn (including full breakfast and evening dessert and coffee): $99; rate for the *Pond House:* $130 to $150. Two-night minimum stay in *Pond House.* MasterCard and Visa accepted. Inn not appropriate for children under eight; all ages welcome in the *Pond*

House. **No pets. Katie, a friendly dog, in residence. No smoking indoors. Donna and Gale Livengood, innkeepers.**

DIRECTIONS: From I-40 take Exit 24 and travel north on US 209 for 2½ miles. Turn left onto Riverside Drive and go 2½ miles. Turn right onto Ferguson Cove Loop and go 1 mile. The inn is on the left (when you see the llamas, you'll know you're there).

GRANVILLE QUEEN THEMED INN

EDENTON, NORTH CAROLINA

Southern gentility is alive and well at the *Granville Queen Themed Inn,* an unusual hostelry in the historic waterfront village of Edenton, the first capital of North Carolina. Built in 1907 as a doctor's private home, the plantation-style mansion was converted to an inn in 1989. Its massive white columns, dormer windows, balconies, and broad porch filled with wrought-iron tables and wicker chairs is straight out of a novel. One expects Scarlett to step out the front door.

The fantasy continues inside. The rooms here are anything but ordinary, and each is distinctively decorated. The *Egyptian Queen,* for example, has furnishings imported from Egypt, including an enormous pair of cast-bronze sphinxes. The windows are draped with gold satin and sheer, billowing curtains. The bathroom continues the theme with Egyptian-style paintings adorning the outside of the tub. The *Captain Quarters* contains a fantastically carved Dutch bed and matching armoire, and a boat hangs from the ceiling. The *Queen Victoriana* is a froth of lace and ruffles. Most of the rooms have fireplaces and balconies.

Weekend guests are treated to an evening wine tasting in the splendid parlor. Two five-foot bronze flamingos stand in a marble fountain beneath an intricately carved, inlaid ceiling. A stay at the *Granville Queen* also includes a lavish five-course breakfast, served either in the dining room or on the wraparound porch. The extravaganza begins with warm homemade apple crunch and pumpkin-spice muffins, followed by fresh fruit cup. Entrées include grilled chicken breast with tarragon sauce and grilled filet mignon. Dessert might be a Southern pancake topped with warm lemon butter and sprinkled with powdered sugar and pecans.

Work off the meal with a walk through the historic village of Edenton. At one time the town was a hangout of the infamous pirate Blackbeard; later it was home to Revolutionary War patriots; more recently it prospered as a port. A stroll along the marina and through the village's crafts and antiques shops will yield surprising finds. Guests may enjoy golf, tennis, and boating nearby.

GRANVILLE QUEEN THEMED INN 108 S. Granville St., Edenton, NC 27932 (phone: 919-482-5296). This plantation house has nine guestrooms with private baths, double, queen-, or king-size beds, telephones, TV sets, and air conditioning. Wheelchair accessible. Open year-round. Rate for a double room (including full breakfast and weekend wine tasting): $95 to $105. No credit cards accepted. Not appropriate for children under 18. No pets. No smoking. Marge and Ken Dunne, innkeepers.

DIRECTIONS: From Washington, DC, take I-95 south to Richmond, Virginia, then take Route 64 east to Scenic Coastal Route 17 and exit at Edenton onto Business Route 7. The inn is on the corner of Business Route 7 and Granville Street.

OLD EDWARDS INN AND HIGHLANDS INN

HIGHLANDS, NORTH CAROLINA

A spectacular drive through the Nantahala Range of the Great Smoky Mountains and Cullasaja Gorge, winding along a narrow two-lane road past dramatic cascades and waterfalls, leads to the beautiful mountain town of Highlands, where the *Old Edwards Inn* and the *Highlands Inn* have been welcoming guests for more than a century.

The Benton family has created a unique complex of these historic buildings, beginning with the 1981 purchase and renovation of the ca. 1878 *Old Edwards Inn.* They bought the adjacent *Central House* in 1983, turning it into a fine restaurant. In 1989 they added the 1880s *Highlands Inn,* across the street, to their collection. The *Highlands Inn,* larger and grander than the *Old Edwards Inn,* was originally known as the *Smith Hotel,* and was especially popular in the late 1800s, when the area's fresh mountain air attracted tourists. Today both inns are listed on the National Register of Historic Places.

Guestrooms feature numerous antiques—a "fainting" couch in one, and four-poster, sleigh, and canopy beds covered with down comforters and fluffy pillows throughout. The walls are stenciled. Several rooms have fireplaces and private porches, complete with rocking chairs.

In the parlor of the *Highlands Inn,* cushioned sofas and chairs are placed before the fire, providing inviting places to read one of the many books on the shelves. Just off the parlor is an enchanting garden room furnished in white wicker. This is also the room where guests gather for games of chess, Trivial Pursuit, and bridge. Downstairs is a masculine, paneled bar (county law permits the sale of wine only), added in 1994, which features a magnificent antique pool table, a polished mahogany bar, and hand-painted murals. A large-screen TV is a popular attraction, especially with sports fans. The *Old Edwards Inn*'s parlor is called the *Moose Room* in honor of the massive head that hangs over the mantel.

A continental buffet breakfast—fresh fruit, fresh-baked breads or muffins, cereal, and juice—is served to guests every morning. Specialties of the *Central House* restaurant, a casual eatery, are local seafood and steaks, although lighter fare is available. The *Kelsey House,* a restaurant at the *Highlands Inn,* serves fine low-country fare. Entrées might include local rainbow trout, pan-seared pork tenderloins, and pan-fried Southern chicken. Both restaurants serve only wine, but guests may bring their own liquor and beer.

In addition to enjoying the breathtaking scenery and mountain air, guests may play golf, ride horses, and hike the Appalachian Trail. The inns are also near crafts outlets and boutique shopping.

OLD EDWARDS INN AND HIGHLANDS INN Main St., Box 1030, Highlands, NC 28841 (phone: 704-526-5036; fax: 704-526-5036, ext. 33). These inns have a total of 50 guestrooms with private baths, twin, double, queen-, or king-size beds, TV sets, and air conditioning. Closed late November through March. Rate for a double room (including continental breakfast): $74 to $94. Major credit cards accepted. Children welcome in the *Highlands Inn.* No pets. Smoking permitted in designated public areas only. Rip and Pat Benton, innkeepers.

DIRECTIONS: From Asheville take I-28 south to Route 280. Follow Route 280 south to Rosman and then turn onto Highway 64, traveling west for 31 miles to Highlands. The inn is on Main Street at the intersection of Highway 64 and Route 28.

PILOT KNOB INN

PILOT MOUNTAIN, NORTH CAROLINA

The *Pilot Knob Inn* is in tobacco country, where the low, broad-leafed, green plants stretch in neat rows for miles along the roads. In the late 1800s, tobacco leaves were stored and dried in log barns that have since been replaced by metal structures.

In 1987, inspired by the great old unused barns scattered throughout the countryside, Jim Rouse purchased 11 acres on a wooded hillside of Pilot Mountain, complete with a 40-by-40-foot barn, and set about creating an inn. He dismantled five additional barns, as well as a 160-year-old homesteader's cabin, and rebuilt them as cabins on the property. Stones from the barn foundations became fireplaces, and tier poles used to dry the tobacco leaves became supports and railings for front porches.

Each of the cabins is a three-room guesthouse. The living room's massive stone fireplace might be flanked by red brocade love seats, and the hardwood floors are covered with carpets Jim collected on his world travels. In the separate upstairs bedrooms the beds are particularly unusual: The headboards and footboards were crafted from the trunks of stripped juniper trees—some even include attached limbs. Two-person Jacuzzis are a sybaritic note, while fresh flowers, fluffy bathrobes, and bowls of fruit are added indulgences.

The property's original barn serves as the common meeting place. Strains of classical music flow from the library, which has a vaulted ceiling, a 300-

year-old Italian marble fireplace, rich mahogany paneling (c. 1790), and old pine floors covered with a magnificent green floral antique Persian rug. The antique furnishings range in style from William and Mary to Georgian. Games and books are available here. In the morning, guests gather in the breakfast room for homemade waffles, sausages, biscuits, muffins, coffee cake, and fresh fruit.

A swimming pool and deck are behind the large barn and there's a six-acre stocked lake where guests can fish for bass or bluegill. Hiking trails lead to *Pilot Mountain State Park,* which borders the inn. The sunrise view of the 115-foot, solid granite Pilot Knob is unforgettable, particularly in winter. Nearby attractions include hot-air balloon rides at *Jomeokee Park* and visits to Winston-Salem, with its *Old Salem Moravian Museum, Renolda House Museum of American Art* (the former home of R. J. Reynolds), and tours of the Stroh Brewery.

PILOT KNOB INN PO Box 1280, Pilot Mountain, NC 27014 (phone: 910-325-2502). This inn has six cabins with private baths, double or queen-size beds, telephones, TV sets, and air conditioning. Open year-round. Rate for a double room (including breakfast): $100 to $115. MasterCard and Visa accepted. Not appropriate for children. Smoking permitted. No pets. Five cats on the property. Jim Rouse, innkeeper.

DIRECTIONS: From Winston-Salem take Highway 52 north to the *Pilot Mountain State Park* exit. At the bottom of the exit ramp, turn left, go 20 feet, and turn right onto small gravel road. Continue on this road, always bearing left, for about half a mile to the inn, which is at the end. (There is no sign at the entrance to the road. If you reach the entrance to the park, you've gone too far.)

FEARRINGTON HOUSE

PITTSBORO, NORTH CAROLINA

Fearrington House is more than an inn, and it's more than a restaurant: It's a picture-perfect planned country village. Owners R. B. and Jenny Fitch boldly converted 65 acres of the 1,000-acre former Fearrington dairy farm into a old-fashioned rural village. The original Fearrington home, built in 1927, now houses the acclaimed *Fearrington House* restaurant; the adjacent dairy barn is available for catered functions, and the granary is a busy country store with an upstairs café. There's also a well-stocked bookstore, pharmacy, garden shop, craft shop, and bank. The dairy's silo dominates the landscape, and cows still graze in the pastures.

In the heart of the village, next to the restaurant, the inn is built around an inner courtyard, its low-slung, white clapboard punctuated by New England–style dormers. A kaleidoscope of flowers spills from planters along the slate pathways. The *Garden House* and the *Sun Room* are relaxing hideaways where guests can congregate, but *Jenny's Garden,* just beyond the *Sun Room,* is the pièce de résistance. Bounded by white Victorian trellises and gazebos, it contains nearly 80 varieties of roses as well as herbs and other flowers. Nearby are a pool, tennis courts, and croquet and *bocci* lawns.

The guestrooms offer some delightful surprises. Nooks and crannies might hold an antique desk or chair. The bed may be an English antique pine four-poster, or the headboard might have been made from a church door. Original art graces the walls, and several units have fireplaces with hand-marbleized mantels. The lightly pickled pine flooring came from an 1850s British workhouse. Marble vanities and heated towel racks are featured in the bathrooms.

The *Fearrington House* restaurant, which opened in 1980, had a lot to do with elevating the concept of Southern cooking, and the *Fearrington House Cookbook,* which Jenny produced in 1987, brought its techniques into homes nationwide. Appetizers such as shrimp and grits with apple-onion vinaigrette and entrées such as roast lamb with bourbon-molasses sauce, showed the world that the local fare goes far beyond fried chicken and catfish. The restaurant offers a fine wine list, and its desserts, including ethereal soufflés, should not be missed. It's all served up with generous hospitality in a setting of candlelit tables, fresh flowers, original art, and antiques.

The inn is located in the Chapel Hill–Raleigh-Durham area, with golf, cultural events, antiquing, and boating nearby. Also in the area are *Duke University* and the *University of North Carolina.*

FEARRINGTON HOUSE 2000 Fearrington Village Center, Pittsboro, NC 27312 (phone: 919-542-2121; fax: 919-542-4202). This country inn has 24 guestrooms with private baths, twin, queen-, or king-size beds, telephones, TV sets, and air conditioning. Wheelchair accessible. Open year-round; restaurant closed Mondays,

but dinner is available in the *Market Café.* Rate for a double room (including full breakfast and afternoon tea): $175 to $275. Two-night minimum stay on some weekends during football season; three nights during university graduations. Major credit cards accepted. Not appropriate for children under 12. No pets. No smoking. R. B. and Jenny Fitch, owners; Richard Delany, manager.

DIRECTIONS: From Chapel Hill travel south on US Route 15/501 for 8 miles to Fearrington Village. From Raleigh take I-64 west to Cary, then Route 64 west toward Pittsboro. After 8 miles turn north onto Mt. Gilead Church Road to Fearrington.

INN AT THE TAYLOR HOUSE

VALLE CRUCIS, NORTH CAROLINA

A wooden sign showing a rooster greeting the sunrise hangs at the entrance to the *Inn at the Taylor House,* offering a sunny greeting to guests. Located in the rural center of the Blue Ridge Mountains, the pristine two-story farmhouse was built in the early 1900s; with three large dormers and a broad, wraparound verandah, it is typical of the period. An old-fashioned porch swing sways gently in the breeze.

The inn was purchased in 1987 by Chip and Roland Schwab, veterans of the innkeeping and restaurant business. Roland grew up in his family's inn in Switzerland and graduated from the acclaimed *Ecole Hôtelière de Lausanne.* Chip owned a cooking school in Atlanta, and together they still own a restaurant in that city.

Polished heart-pine floors peek from beneath creamy Oriental rugs in the living room. Pale yellow walls provide a gracious backdrop for the white sofa piled with needlepoint pillows, an antique French commode, and Chip's collection of antique blue and white Chinese export china, inherited from her grandmother.

Guestrooms are decorated in an equally refined fashion. The *Luxury Suite,* reached by private staircase, has vaulted ceilings and a sitting room, lavishly adorned with Clarence House and Scalamandre botanical prints in green and rust tones. Room No. 5, a corner room, is light and breezy with white wicker furniture and balloon shades decorated with a lattice Waverly fabric. All rooms have featherbeds dressed with luxurious linen.

Breakfasts (open to non-guests) at the *Inn at the Taylor House* are renowned. Chip might prepare sour-cream pancakes topped with fresh strawberries or eggs Benedict. Seating in the cheerful yellow dining room is at glass-topped tables, enhanced by vases of bright flowers fresh from the gardens. The inn has a shop where fine-quality gifts are sold, including the vases used.

Several nearby local excursions attract inn guests. The mile-high suspension bridge at Grandfather Mountain offers panoramic views. Numerous hiking routes wind through the Blue Ridge Mountains, and the Appalachian Trail is not far away. Golfing, fishing, horseback riding, skiing, and canoeing also are nearby.

INN AT THE TAYLOR HOUSE Hwy. 194, PO Box 713, Valle Crucis, NC 28691 (phone: 704-963-5581; fax: 704-963-5818). This inn has seven guestrooms and suites with private baths and double or king-size beds. Wheelchair accessible. Closed mid-December through mid-April. Rate for a double room (including full breakfast and afternoon refreshments): $120 to $160. MasterCard and Visa accepted. Not appropriate for children under 12. No pets. Two dogs, chickens, a flop-eared rabbit, and pygmy goats on the property. No smoking. Chip and Roland Schwab, innkeepers.

DIRECTIONS: From Winston-Salem take Route 421 west to Boone, then take North Carolina Route 105 south for 5 miles to Broadstone Road. Turn right and travel 2½ miles to Highway 194 south to Valle Crucis. Turn left onto Route 194. The inn will be on the right in eight-tenths of a mile.

MAST FARM INN

VALLE CRUCIS, NORTH CAROLINA

Thanks to the efforts of innkeepers Francis and Sibyl Pressly, the 12 buildings that comprise *Mast Farm Inn* are now preserved for future generations. Listed on the National Register of Historic Places in 1972, they were described as "one of the most complete and best-presented groups of 19th-century farm buildings in western North Carolina."

The inn began as a two-room log cabin, completed by farmer David Mast in 1810. Over the years, 16 additional buildings were added to the 18-acre homestead, including a blacksmith shop, a springhouse, a smokehouse, an apple house, a washhouse, a granary, a barn, a woodworking shop, and an 18-room farmhouse. In the early 1900s, Josie Mast, a master weaver, operated three looms in the original log cabin; today her coverlets are on display at the *Smithsonian Institution.* It was during this period that Josie and her husband, Finley, opened the farm to paying guests.

The farm remained in the Mast family until 1980, but by the time the Presslys first saw it, in 1984, the buildings had deteriorated. The main house was being used as a boardinghouse, with 13 rooms sharing one bath; today there are nine guestrooms, seven with private baths. The original two-room cabin, the blacksmith shop, the woodworking shop, and a new log cabin contain guest quarters as well. Staying at *Mast Farm Inn* gives visitors the rare opportunity to experience life on a farm as it must have been in the early 20th century.

Furnishings are homespun and simple: Country furniture, mountain crafts, and fresh flowers decorate the rooms. In the main hall, quilts cover the walls, and Mast family portraits hang over Josie's old sewing machine. In keeping with the mood, there are no televisions or telephones. Four parlors, a wraparound porch, and a library offer numerous spots for quiet relaxation; outside are vegetable and flower gardens, a fish pond, and the nearby river.

Food is an important part of the farm experience; dinners (also open to non-guests) are served family style, and guests may sit around two large communal tables or at smaller individual ones. The menu varies nightly, but always offers a choice of two entrées, usually one meat and one vegetarian: pot roast or vegetable lasagna Tuesdays, chicken and dumplings or moussaka Thursdays, and country ham or fried chicken Sundays, for example. All breads are homemade and the vegetables come straight from the garden in season.

In the Blue Ridge Mountains, the inn is near fishing, hiking, skiing, golfing, and canoeing.

MAST FARM INN State Road 1112, Camp Broadstone Rd., PO Box 704, Valle Crucis, NC 28691 (phone: 704-963-5857; fax: 704-963-6404). This farmhouse inn has 13 guestrooms (11 with private baths) with twin, double, queen-, or king-size beds. Wheelchair accessible. Closed early March through mid-April and mid-December through December 26. Rate for a double room (including full breakfast and dinner): $100 to $170. Two-night minimum stay on weekends. Discover, MasterCard, and Visa accepted. Inn not appropriate for children under 12; younger children welcome in cabins. No pets. No smoking. Sibyl and Francis Pressly, innkeepers.

DIRECTIONS: From Winston-Salem take Route 421 west to Boone, then North Carolina Route 105 south to Route 1112. Watch for the sign to Valle Crucis and turn right. The inn is 3 miles farther along.

INN AT BLACKBERRY FARM

WALLAND, TENNESSEE

Located on 1,100 acres in the foothills of the Great Smoky Mountains, the *Inn at Blackberry Farm* is both park and inn. Jogging, bicycling, walking, and hiking trails lace the property. Singing Brook Trout Pond is stocked for fishermen, Pretty Place Loop has shady nooks with picnic tables for secluded afternoons, and there are tennis courts, a swimming pool, a basketball court, and shuffleboard.

The property consisted of the main house and a collection of outbuildings when Sandy and Kreis Beall purchased it in 1976. While Sandy was busy starting what became a chain of restaurants called *Ruby Tuesday's,* Kreis leased and managed a portion of the estate as an executive retreat, then expanded the use of the site for weddings and corporate functions. In 1989, the couple's passion for good food in elegant surroundings, a love of Tennessee, and a desire to share their cherished spot with others led them to open an inn. They added a *Guest House* with 11 rooms and converted *Cove Cottage* into three more rooms. There are now 29 guestrooms at *Blackberry Farm,* but the Bealls' hands-on attention makes it feel as if you're visiting friends.

Guestrooms are named after the abundant wildflowers that bloom in the fields. With names such as *May Apple, Foxglove,* and *Doll's Eyes,* they have a country ambience—from the flowered chintz draperies, quilted spreads, and English-style antiques to the four-poster and canopy beds, polished mahogany side tables, and plush sofas piled high with fringed pillows.

Oriental carpets cover oak floors in the living room of the *Main House* and the *Great Room* in the *Guest House.* There are two fireplaces in the *Great Room,* and original oils line the walls. A library is well stocked with books, but look closely before you grab one—there's also a trompe l'oeil wallpaper of books. The dining room affords panoramic views of *Great Smoky Mountains National Park.* Of all the public spaces, the favorite is the broad porch furnished with Tennessee rockers, where guests watch the pink and orange sun set behind the Smokies.

The couple's passion for food is evident in the creative fare, which blends "fancy and familiar" in a style they call "foothills cuisine." At breakfast guests choose from a set menu, which might include fruit, freshly baked muffins and scones, and Sally Lunn French toast or lemon soufflé pancakes. Dinner (also open to non-guests by reservation), served on Royal Worcester china with a blackberry motif, consists of four courses—perhaps onion soup followed by a salad of seasonal greens, cedar-planked grouper with hoppin' John and fried carrots or hickory-smoked loin of pork with buttermilk whipped potatoes, and banana pudding cheesecake with caramel sauce and homemade vanilla wafer. The inn is in a dry county, so guests are advised to bring their own wine and liquor.

The inn provides picnic lunches to complement the day's activities—perhaps a bicycle jaunt across the trails, a swim in the pool, a scramble across the rocks in Hesse Creek, or a rowboat outing on the three-acre bass and bream lake. The inn has plenty of fishing equipment, as well as a fleet of 20 mountain bikes, tennis racquets, walking sticks, binoculars, and nature reference books. If all this is not enough, head off the property: Hiking, golf, horseback riding, and *Dollywood* are nearby.

INN AT BLACKBERRY FARM 1471 W. Millers Cove Rd., Walland, TN 37886 (phone: 615-984-8166; 615-984-9850, reservations; fax: 615-681-7753). This country estate in the Smoky Mountains has 29 guestrooms with private baths, double, queen-, or king-size beds, and air conditioning. Wheelchair accessible. Open year-round. Rate for a double room (including breakfast, lunch, dinner, and use of all equipment): $375 to $495 (package rates also available). Two-night minimum stay on weekends; three nights on holidays. Major credit cards accepted. Not appropriate for children under 10; children of all ages welcome during *Thanksgiving* and *Christmas.* No pets. Smoking permitted on the verandah only. Kreis and Sandy Beall, owners; Barry Marshall, innkeeper.

DIRECTIONS: From Knoxville take I-40 to the Airport/Smoky Mountain exit. Follow Highway 129 south for 12½ miles to *McGee Tyson Airport.* Past the airport, follow Highway 321 north 16 miles to West Millers Cove Road (a quarter mile beyond the Foothills Parkway entrance). Turn right onto West Millers Cove Road and go 3½ miles to *Blackberry Farm.*

Virginia

MORRISON HOUSE

ALEXANDRIA, VIRGINIA

Looks can be deceiving. *Morrison House* looks as if it could have welcomed George Washington and Thomas Jefferson, but owners Robert and Rosemary Morrison actually built the inn in 1985.

The Federal-style brick mansion has a porticoed entrance supported by four Ionic columns. Black shutters accent the six-over-six windows, and twin staircases circle past a fountain sculpture up to the paneled front door. In the heart of old Alexandria, the inn would be equally at home in London.

A butler greets guests at the entrance, assists with bags, and acts as concierge. Unfailing attention to English service (unobtrusive but thoughtful) extends to delivering messages to guests on silver trays. Inside, all is perfection. There's a marble floor in the foyer and parquet floors covered with Oriental rugs in the parlor, library, and dining rooms. Spectacular floral arrangements and crystal chandeliers and sconces enhance the feeling of being in an elegant home rather than a hotel. The intimate parlor, where afternoon tea is served, is furnished with chairs upholstered in pale green silk brocade.

Some guestrooms have four-poster or canopy beds, as well as armoires made especially for the inn. All have high-quality Federal reproductions—furnishings that would have been at home on Virginia estates 200 years ago. Soft tones are used throughout. One bedroom has Wedgwood blue walls with creamy white trim; another has a rose carpet. The hallways are done in pale blues and yellows. Bathrooms are finished in Italian marble, with brass fixtures. Each has a basket of Gilchrist and Soames toiletries, fluffy imported terry robes, and full-length mirrors.

With soft leather chairs and a polished mahogany bar, *Elysium,* the inn's restaurant (also open to non-guests for breakfast, lunch, and dinner), features a Mediterranean menu and a weekend piano bar. At dinner wild-mushroom strudel with white madeira sauce might be followed by garlic-crusted rack of lamb with ginger *confit.* With a nod to the waistline, the restaurant also offers vegetarian and "middle-minder" entrées.

For those who overindulge, the inn provides privileges at a nearby health club. Guests also can take advantage of the inn's location in historic Alexandria, 10 minutes from Washington, DC.

MORRISON HOUSE 116 S. Alfred St., Alexandria, VA 22314 (phone: 703-838-8000; 800-367-0800; fax: 703-548-2489). This English-style hotel has 45 guestrooms with private baths, twin, queen-, or king-size beds, telephones, TV sets, and air conditioning. Wheelchair accessible. Open year-round. Rate for a double room: $185 to $295. Major credit cards accepted. Children welcome. No pets. Smoking permitted except in the dining room. Robert and Rosemary Morrison, innkeepers; Wanda McKeon, manager.

DIRECTIONS: From Washington, DC, drive south on the George Washington Parkway to King Street. Turn right, continue for two blocks, and turn left onto South Alfred Street. The hotel is on the left at mid-block.

OAKS BED & BREAKFAST INN

CHRISTIANSBURG, VIRGINIA

Shaded by seven giant white oaks (one estimated to be more than 400 years old), this grand 1889 Victorian dwelling is situated on a knoll overlooking Main Street, amid manicured lawns, flower beds, and boxwood hedges.

The house is as romantic today as it was when it was built by Major William Pierce as a present for his bride, Julia. Even so, by the time Margaret and Tom Ray first saw it, the front door had fallen off and the basement was flooded. Now, after a meticulous restoration, it offers eight pristine guestrooms and is listed on the National Register of Historic Places. Along with nearby private homes, it also is part of the East Main Street Historic District of Christiansburg.

The spacious guestrooms are furnished with stunning antiques. The *Julia Pierce* room, for example, has a carved Victorian bed, wicker chairs, and a polished cherry chest dating to 1820. Decorated in soft green and peach floral fabrics, it has a hand-painted slate fireplace plus a five-window turret. All the rooms have private baths, and this one features a Jacuzzi for two. *Lady Melodie's Turret,* on the top floor, is decorated in rich blue and white Waverly fabrics and also has a fireplace, a canopy bed, and a sitting area with a sunset view. Every room has a refrigerator stocked with juice, soft drinks, and spring water; all but one have fireplaces. A decanter of sherry awaits guests' arrival.

The common areas are as wonderful as the guestrooms. A sunroom, a study, and a parlor offer a variety of retreats. The grand entry hall, with pine woodwork stained a rich oak hue and stained glass windows, comfortably accommodates a piano, an antique English writing desk, and a chiming clock. Soft music plays in the background. This is where five *Christmas* trees of varying sizes stand during the inn's celebrated Victorian-style holiday. The wraparound porch has Kennedy rockers and wicker chairs. On the grounds are gardens with a fish pond and fountain, a terrace, and a croquet lawn. Equally inviting are a hot tub tucked into a garden gazebo and a sauna in a garden cottage.

Breakfast in the stately dining room has won acclaim. The three-course meal is served by candlelight on fine china with sterling silver. Shirred eggs in spinach nests might be followed by whole-wheat–buttermilk pancakes in praline syrup with toasted pecans and maple cream, accompanied by meat or poultry, perhaps ginger-braised chicken breasts.

The inn is near *Virginia Tech,* golf, horseback riding, tennis, winery tours, hiking on the Appalachian Trail, and biking on the Rails to Trails path. The inn arranges canoe rentals and river cruises on the *Pioneer Maid.*

OAKS BED & BREAKFAST INN 311 E. Main St., Christiansburg, VA 24073 (phone: 703-381-1500). This Victorian inn has eight guestrooms with private baths, queen- or king-size beds, telephones, TV sets, and air conditioning. Open year-round. Rate for a double room (including full breakfast and afternoon sherry, wine, or tea): $115 to $135; corporate rates for singles Sundays through Thursdays (including full breakfast): $75. Two-night minimum stay during special event weekends at *Virginia Tech* and *Radford University.* Major credit cards accepted. Not appropriate for children under 13. No pets. Two dogs—Kaile, a West Highland terrier, and Lulu, a Scottish terrier—in residence. No smoking. Margaret and Tom Ray, innkeepers.

DIRECTIONS: From I-81, take Exit 114. At the bottom of the ramp, turn right (if traveling from the north) or left (if approaching from the south) onto Main Street. Continue for 2 miles to the fork of Park and Main Streets, bear right onto Park, then turn left into the *Oaks*'s driveway. From the Blue Ridge Parkway exit onto Route 8, which becomes Main Street in Christiansburg, and follow the directions above.

KESWICK HALL

KESWICK, VIRGINIA

If you hear the cry of a bugle and an early-morning shout of "Tallyho," you're not dreaming. *Keswick Hall,* a 600-acre estate in the Virginia countryside, is adjacent to one of the oldest hunt clubs in America. (It's not open to inn guests, but it's fun to watch the riders charge by.)

Sir Bernard Ashley, co-founder of the Laura Ashley company, opened *Keswick Hall* to guests in 1994, completing his triple crown of Ashley House hotels (there's one in Wales and one in Maryland; see the *Inn at Perry Cabin,* above). The original estate, known as *Villa Crawford* and occupying the site of a pre–Civil War mansion, was built in 1912, and it's this imposing Italianate palace that Ashley expanded and converted to an impressive country-house hotel.

Elegant and sophisticated, the public areas at *Keswick Hall* combine period antiques and Laura Ashley fabrics. In the tile-floored *Great Hall*, stately columns define intimate seating areas about the fireplace. The *Crawford Lounge* is furnished with down-filled, yellow velvet sofas and needlepoint pillows. White predominates in the *Morning Room,* while the red *Snooker Room* offers a snooker table, a fireplace, Oriental rugs, and soft leather chairs. The inn also boasts an impressive collection of museum-quality oil paintings. A 30-foot-wide terrace offers treetop views of the rolling countryside and an outside fireplace. This is a popular evening retreat, when the only sound is the croaking of frogs in the nearby lake.

Guestrooms are lavishly decorated with more Laura Ashley prints, but solid colors have been used on the walls (forest green in one room; maroon in another). Wooden shutters filter the sun, upholstered window seats invite stargazing, and overstuffed chairs are accented with needlepoint pillows. The baths have tile floors, double pedestal sinks, and Jacuzzis.

Guests are served a full breakfast that includes such British entrées as a mixed grill or smoked kippers and American standbys like Virginia ham with eggs and potatoes. Afternoon tea features fresh-baked scones with lemon curd and clotted cream, fresh berries, and cookies. The inn's accomplished French-trained chef also prepares lunch and dinner (open to non-guests), which are served in the elegant dining room on the lower level.

Light meals and snacks also are available at the members-only *Keswick Club.* Overnight guests may use its facilities, including the three outdoor tennis courts and the championship 18-hole golf course designed by Arnold Palmer. The *Pavilion Clubhouse* offers an indoor/outdoor pool, a fitness facility, the *Bistro* restaurant overlooking the golf course, and the British-style *Pub,* complete with wooden floors, leather chairs, and ale on tap.

The inn is set amid the bucolic hills of Virginia hunt country near Charlottesville, about two hours from Washington, DC.

KESWICK HALL 701 Club Dr., Keswick, VA 22947 (phone: 804-979-3440; 800-ASHLEY-1; fax: 804-977-4171). This country estate has 48 guestrooms with private baths, twin, double, queen-, or king-size beds, telephones, TV sets, and air conditioning. Wheelchair accessible. Open year-round. Rate for a double room (including full breakfast and afternoon tea): $195 to $645. Two-night minimum stay during special event weekends at the *University of Virginia.* Major credit cards accepted. Not appropriate for children under eight. No pets. Smoking permitted in designated public areas only. Sir Bernard Ashley, owner; Stephen Beaumont, general manager.

DIRECTIONS: From Washington, DC, travel west on I-66 to Route 29. Follow Route 29 south to the eastbound Route 250 bypass. Turn left onto Route 22, traveling east toward the towns of Cismont and Boyd's Tavern. After approximately 2 miles, turn right onto Route 744 (Hunt Club Drive). From the stop sign the gates of *Keswick Hall* are directly ahead.

FORT LEWIS LODGE

MILLBORO, VIRGINIA

The country roads on the way to *Fort Lewis Lodge* wind past a breathtaking view of Goshen Pass and may offer glimpses of deer feeding by a mountain stream. Turning onto the gravel lane that leads to the inn, you'll pass over a cattle guard and see a silo rising ahead and, down by the pond, a perfectly restored gristmill.

Snuggled into the Allegheny Mountains, *Fort Lewis Lodge* sits amid 3,200 acres of natural forests, meadows, and farmland that are laced with streams and hiking trails. In 1754 Colonel Charles Lewis built a stockade here to protect his family from Indian raids. Lewis died in 1774 at the Battle of Point Pleasant, considered by some historians to have been the first engagement of the American Revolution. Over its long history, the estate has remained remarkably unchanged. In the 1950s, it was purchased by Robert Cowden as his retirement retreat, and he raised black Angus cattle on the land. Today, his son and daughter-in-law, John and Caryl Cowden, own and operate the property as a country inn.

Fort Lewis Lodge is anything but ordinary, and that's true of its owners as well. By anyone's standards, John is a master craftsman; the inn his masterpiece. He meticulously restored the 19th-century gristmill, with its two-foot-thick stone walls. It now serves as the dining room, where Caryl offers such hearty home-cooked meals, as a harvest roast with scalloped apples, fresh vegetables, homemade biscuits, and sinfully rich chocolate pie. Meals are served buffet-style and with complementary wines. Guests may opt to sit at individual tables or at one of the large group tables. *Buck's Bar,* a screened porch overlooking the old millpond, is the place to get acquainted before dinner. In the evening, the old piano near the wood stove gets a workout during impromptu sing-alongs.

Guestrooms are scattered among several buildings and are furnished in Shaker-style simplicity with cherry, walnut, red oak, and chestnut furniture made by a local craftsman. John himself built the two-story cedar-shake lodge, right down to the milled pine floors, as well as the adjoining silo, which is an exact replica of the original that was here; it contains three guestrooms with views across the fields. At the very top is an observation tower, reached by a spiral staircase. Two rustic log cabins (one dating from the 1860s, the other from the 1890s) were transported to the property in 1993 and now provide romantic retreats. They have stone fireplaces, front porches with rockers or a swing, patchwork quilts, and pioneer artifacts. The "Little House on the Prairie" ambience is conveyed by clothes pegs on the walls, patchwork quilts, and the simple but utilitarian bathrooms. On the other hand, few pioneers would have known what to make of the outdoor hot tub.

There's plenty of opportunity for hiking and exploring on the property. Down by the Cowpaster River a sturdy deck hangs over a swimming hole and a boat stands ready to use. For fisherfolk, the rainbow trout in the spring and smallmouth bass are legendary. The inn also caters to hunters in season—November through December. The lodge is near Warm Springs, where Thomas Jefferson designed octagonal mineral baths and where evening concerts, championship golf courses, and shopping are available.

FORT LEWIS LODGE HCR3, Box 21A, Millboro, VA 24460 (phone: 540-925-2314; fax: 540-925-2352). This lodge has 13 guestrooms with private baths and twin, queen-, or king-size beds. Closed January through March; November and December are dedicated to hunters. Rate for a double room (including full breakfast and dinner): $140 to $190. MasterCard and Visa accepted. Not appropriate for children under five. No pets. A dog, Max, and a number of cats in residence. Smoking permitted in designated areas only. John and Caryl Cowden, innkeepers.

DIRECTIONS: Take I-81 or I-64 to Staunton. In Staunton take Route 254 west (at the railroad underpass) and follow the signs to Buffalo Gap. In Buffalo Gap turn south onto Route 42 and follow it for 29 miles to Millboro Springs (in Goshen the road becomes combined Routes 42 and 39). Follow Route 39 from Millboro Springs for three-quarters of a mile and turn right onto Route 678. Follow Route 678 for 10¾ miles, then turn left onto Route 625 and look for the inn sign on the left.

HIDDEN INN

ORANGE, VIRGINIA

It's easy to see how the *Hidden Inn* got its name. Although the inn is just off a busy highway in the center of Orange, it's tucked behind trees on eight acres in a glen that seems a world apart from the village that enfolds it.

The inn is made up of a collection of buildings that includes the *Main House*–a big, blue 1880s Victorian farmhouse with red shutters and a wraparound porch that was built by a descendant of Thomas Jefferson. In back are the skylighted *Garden Cottage* and the *Carriage House,* each of which has one guestroom overlooking the garden. Between them is a brick courtyard, bordered by herbs, with a fountain in the center and a gazebo. *Caroline House,* with two guestrooms, makes the perfect family retreat.

The *Main House* is the heart of the inn. The living room, with its formal fireplace, is painted a soft salmon with ivory accents and is furnished with floral wing chairs, a leather sofa, and an Oriental rug. A bowl of fresh-baked cookies welcomes guests, and afternoon lemonade, tea, and cakes are served here.

The owners want their guests to enjoy a memorably romantic interlude, and to that end, have created guestrooms that mix old-fashioned decor with up-to-date accoutrements. Lace curtains and beds with crocheted canopies capture the Victorian style. Handmade quilts, needlepoint and cross-stitch pieces, wicker and iron furnishings, and fresh flowers continue the theme. The bathrooms, however, are fully modern; four have whirlpool tubs.

A full breakfast—perhaps rum-raisin French toast, carrot-raisin muffins, chunky apple sauce, and juice—is served in the dining room. A five-course, set-menu dinner, available by advance reservation, might include beef with tomato-garlic-brandy sauce or chicken breast stuffed with mushrooms in puff pastry with merlot sauce. Guests are seated at candlelit tables for two. Virginia is noted for its award-winning wines from a crop first planted by Jefferson, and guests gather in the living room to learn more about local wines from the host, Ray Lonick, who is quite an expert.

A short distance from Orange is James Madison's lifelong home, 2,700-acre *Montpelier;* the *James Madison Museum* is in town. *Monticello,* the home of Madison's good friend Thomas Jefferson, is just a half hour away. Also nearby are historic battlefields, wineries, and tennis.

HIDDEN INN 249 Caroline St., Orange, VA 22960 (phone: 703-672-3625; 800-841-1253; fax: 703-672-5029). This inn has 10 guestrooms with private baths, twin, double, queen-, or king-size beds, and air conditioning. Closed *Christmas.* Rate for a double room (including full breakfast and afternoon tea): $79 to $159. Two-night minimum stay on weekends. Major credit cards accepted. Not appropriate for children under 12. No pets. Outdoor cats on the property. No smoking. Barbara and Ray Lonick, innkeepers; Chrys Dermody, manager.

DIRECTIONS: From Washington, DC, take I-495 west to I-66 west to Route 29 (Gainsville). Turn south onto Route 29 and go to Culpeper. Just outside Culpeper turn south onto Route 15 to Orange. Continue through the village of Orange. The inn is on the left.

HIGH MEADOWS VINEYARD INN & MOUNTAIN SUNSET INN

SCOTTSVILLE, VIRGINIA

Set on 50 acres in the midst of Virginia wine country, *High Meadows* encompasses two separate guest properties. The *Vineyard Inn* is actually in two distinct houses—one built in Federal style in 1832, the other an 1882 Victorian—united by a *Great Hall.* This unusual combination, together with the fine original woodwork, has contributed to the inn's placement on the National Register of Historic Places. Just minutes away is the *Mountain Sunset Inn,* a 1907 Queen Anne–style manor house facing the mountains.

The restoration of *High Meadows* has been both the joy and despair of innkeepers Peter Sushka and Mary Jae Abbitt. They acquired the houses in 1985, when they lacked both electricity and indoor plumbing. Today, there are 13 guestrooms—all with private baths. A leather-bound book containing before and after photos and histories of the furnishings tells the story of the transformation.

Guests relax in the *Patrick Henry Parlor,* which contains the mirror that stood behind Henry when he gave his famous "Give me liberty, or give me death" speech. Other tranquil spots on the property include a gazebo and a tea house surrounded by an antique rose garden, and the paths that lead to two ponds with rowboats and along the meandering creek.

Guestroom furnishings include antique four-poster and draped brass beds, Victorian walnut headboards, and antique chairs and chests. Nine rooms have wood-burning fireplaces, and the bathrooms have claw-foot tubs. A small decanter of port wine and two stemmed glasses greet guests and invite a late-night toast. The *Music Room* (once a parlor where recitals were held, now a guestroom) boasts bay windows, private porches, and a two-person Jacuzzi.

Meals are served alternately in the *Federalist Dining Room,* with its brick floor and wood stove, and the *Victorian Dining Room.* Full breakfasts include juice, muffins, fruit, and a hot entrée. The inn has its own vineyard of pinot noir grapes, and dinner begins with a sampling of local wines and hors d'oeuvres. A six-course meal (also open to non-guests) by candlelight follows; it may include such specialties as grilled tenderloin with shallot and port wine sauce, accompanied by produce from the inn's garden. Desserts include such tempting creations as blueberry cobbler with vanilla ice cream and apple-walnut cake with bourbon sauce.

High Meadows is near Virginia's historic Constitution Trail (Route 20), which links such museum houses as *Monticello, Ashlawn,* and *Montpelier.* Also in the area are winery tours and tastings, as well as inner-tubing, canoeing, and fishing on the James River.

HIGH MEADOWS VINEYARD INN & MOUNTAIN SUNSET INN High Meadows La., Rte. 4, Box 6, Scottsville, VA 24590 (phone: 804-286-2218; 800-232-1832; fax: 804-286-2124). This country inn has 13 guestrooms with private baths, queen- or king-size beds, and air conditioning. Wheelchair accessible. Closed December 24 and 25. Rate for a double room (including full breakfast and evening wine with hors d'oeuvres): $95 to $155. Two-night minimum stay on holidays and on weekends April through June and September through November. MasterCard and Visa accepted. Not appropriate for children under eight. Pets allowed with prior permission only; fee is $20 per day. One outdoor dog in residence. No smoking. Peter Sushka and Mary Jae Abbitt, innkeepers.

DIRECTIONS: From Charlottesville traveling east on I-64, take Exit 121. Travel south on Route 20 for 17 miles, passing *Monticello.* After crossing James River Road (Route 726), turn left in a third of a mile onto High Meadows Lane, which leads directly to the inn.

SAMPSON EAGON INN

STAUNTON, VIRGINIA

With a passion for collecting antiques and an equal devotion to history and historic preservation, Frank and Laura Mattingly have converted the 1840 *Sampson Eagon* house into a jewel of an inn. The cream-colored Greek Revival mansion sits on Staunton's Gospel Hill, across the street from Woodrow Wilson's birthplace.

Despite its classy decor, this is not a stuffy house. Comfort is the key, along with the innkeepers' Southern hospitality. In the peach-colored parlor are 12-foot ceilings, American antiques (including an 1840s butler's desk), oil paintings, and an Oriental rug on the pine floor. Guests enjoy walking through the flower-filled side garden and sitting on the side porch to read or sip a drink before going out to dinner.

The spacious guestrooms, each named for a figure who contributed to the history of the house, have either 12- or 10½-foot ceilings. The lovely antique furnishings span the house's long history, as each room matches the period of its namesake. The *Kayser Room,* for example, harks to the mid-1800s, when the Kayser family owned the home. It has a magnificent carved New York State four-poster Empire canopy bed draped with creamy damask and accented with teal blue. There's a two-tier crystal chandelier and an ornate mantelpiece with columns carved to match the bed. The mantel is topped by a late Victorian pier mirror. The *Holt Room* is furnished in colonial Revival style, reflecting the taste of the Holt family, who lived here in the 1920s. The fireplace is surrounded by blue-and-white Delft tile; the four-poster mahogany bed and a matching highboy date to the 1930s. The room is lavishly swagged in cream-and-blue French toile. Thoroughly modern bathrooms include pedestal sinks; in *Tam's Room* the original brass-and-glass towel bars are still in place. Although most rooms have decorative mantels, the fireplaces are not functional, alas.

The dining room is furnished with a spectacular mid-19th-century Duncan Phyfe pedestal table, a Sheraton sideboard, and Chippendale chairs that date from 1760. In this grand setting, breakfast is served on antique Royal Doulton china, with family sterling and Waterford crystal. The Grand Marnier soufflé pancakes with strawberry sauce, accompanied by country sausage and homemade breads, are a popular way to start a day.

The inn is located in the Shenandoah Valley, near historic sites, golf, tennis, swimming, hiking, horseback riding, and skiing.

SAMPSON EAGON INN 238 E. Beverley St., Staunton, VA 24401 (phone and fax: 540-886-8200; 800-597-9722). This antebellum mansion has five guestrooms and suites with private baths, queen-size beds, TV sets with VCRs, and air conditioning. Open year-round. Rate for a double room (including full breakfast): $85 to $99.

Two-night minimum stay in May, October, and on certain holiday weekends. No credit cards accepted. Not appropriate for children under 12. No pets. Jeepers Creepers, a Cairn terrier, in residence in the family quarters. No smoking. Frank and Laura Mattingly, innkeepers.

DIRECTIONS: From I-81 take Exit 222 and follow Route 250 west to Staunton. Turn right onto Route 11 (Coalter Street) and continue past the traffic light. The inn is on the left, at the corner of Coalter and Beverley Streets.

PROSPECT HILL PLANTATION INN

TREVILIANS, VIRGINIA

Nestled into the rural countryside of Virginia, *Prospect Hill Plantation Inn* offers a 20th-century look at life on an 18th-century Southern plantation. With a reverence for the land and its history, Bill and Mireille Sheehan, who have owned the 40-acre property since 1977, converted the stately *Manor House* (ca. 1732) and its charming outbuildings into 13 spectacular guestrooms. The conversions were accomplished one by one and strictly adhered to the historic character of each building. The plantation is now listed on the National Register of Historic Places.

Prospect Hill is believed to be the oldest continuously occupied wood-frame plantation house in America. In 1699, Roger Thompson built the first log cabin; in 1720 he started construction on the *Manor House.* At one time 20 slaves tended the crops, the livestock, and the occupants of the *Manor House* on this self-sustaining plantation. The Overton family added several wings and began taking in guests after the Civil War. Today, the restored buildings surrounding the *Manor House* include *Sanco Pansy's Cottage* (last used as a henhouse); the *Coach House,* dating from 1880; the *Carriage House and Grooms Quarters* from 1850; *Uncle Guy's House* (the former slave quarters), ca. 1796; the *Overseer's Cottage,* the *Smokehouse,* and the *Summer Kitchen* (which still contains its brick fireplace) from 1720; and the *Boy's Cabin* (the original log cabin) from 1699.

Painted buttercup yellow with forest green shutters and white trim, the inn is a model of gracious hospitality. The living room, with its fireplace and plush sofas, opens to a verandah furnished with wicker and brightly colored cushions. The three dining rooms, which occupy the oldest part of the house, are rich in atmosphere. Old wide-plank floors are polished to a soft luster. Oriental rugs, a fireplace, Federal-style chairs, French toile wallpaper, and such antiques as a polished sideboard complete the decor. Downstairs, the brick-floored wine cellar displays the inn's impressive collection of vintages. Adjacent to the wine cellar is the *Board Room,* where leather chairs are pulled up to a fireplace for evening reading. Outside, a gazebo looks out over rolling pastureland, clipped hedges border flower beds, and a pool is surrounded by chaises, ready for sunny days.

Furnishings in the guestrooms include antiques compatible with their style. Some *Manor House* rooms, for example, have four-poster beds with lacy canopies and Federal antiques. The *Boy's Cabin,* with its beamed ceiling, log walls, and brick fireplace, has a simple bed with a quilt coverlet. All rooms have working fireplaces, and most have Jacuzzis.

For years, Mireille Sheehan, who was raised in Provence, France, was the chef at *Prospect Hill,* creating dinners that reflected her heritage. Today, her son Michael is both executive chef and innkeeper. In his first role, he oversees a full staff that continues to prepare robust Provençal dinners (also open to non-guests). The Sheehans take pride in serving local specialties, and wine is no exception. Guests find a half bottle of Virginia wine in their rooms, and there's a Virginia wine tasting before dinner every evening. A full breakfast, which might include a soufflé, is delivered to rooms every morning.

Located 15 miles east of Charlottesville, the inn is near the *University of Virginia, Monticello, Ashlawn,* and recreational activities such as hiking, golf, ballooning, and biking.

PROSPECT HILL PLANTATION INN Rte. 3, PO Box 430, Trevilians, VA 23093 (phone: 703-967-0844; 800-277-0844, reservations; fax: 703-967-0102). This plantation inn has 13 guestrooms with private baths, double, queen-, or king-size beds, and air conditioning. Open year-round; restaurant closed December 24 and 25. Rate for a double room (including full breakfast and dinner): $245 to $325; bed and breakfast: $155 to $235. Discover, MasterCard, and Visa accepted. Children welcome. No pets. Horses on property. Smoking permitted except in the dining room. Sheehan family, owners; Michael and Laura Sheehan, innkeepers.

DIRECTIONS: From Charlottesville take I-64 east to Exit 136, and follow Route 15 to Zion Crossroads. Turn left onto Route 250 east. Go 1 mile to Route 613; turn left and drive 3 miles to the inn, which is on the left. From Washington, DC, take I-66 west to Gainesville. Take Route 29 south to Culpeper, then Route 15 south through Orange and Gordonsville to Zion Crossroads. Turn left onto Route 250 east and follow the directions above.

INN AT LITTLE WASHINGTON

WASHINGTON, VIRGINIA

This little inn neatly approximates the fine country-house hotels of England, yet for all its elegance, it is remarkably free of pretension.

Constructed as a nondescript garage, the building served as a country store, before owners Patrick O'Connell and Reinhardt Lynch turned it into a restaurant in 1978. Word of their exceptional fare spread, attracting diners from afar, so they added rooms to accommodate them.

If the decor and furnishings seem a bit dramatic, it's no accident. They were designed by Joyce Conway-Evans, a London theatrical designer, whose charming sketches for each of the rooms are framed in the upstairs hallway. Unusual touches include wallpaper where borders are trimmed with hand-cut paper flowers; the entryway ceiling is covered with a similarly spectacular collage. Fabric—used lavishly in window treatments and on canopy beds—swags the rooms. The bathrooms are a medley of brass and marble. Fresh flowers sit by the bed, on the desk, and in the bathroom, and a bowl of fruit awaits guests' arrival. Museum-quality antiques are found throughout.

The restaurant's decor is as stunning as that in the guestrooms, and since the restaurant was the raison d'être for the *Inn at Little Washington,* it would be a crime to miss dinner here. Self-taught Patrick is the acclaimed chef; Reinhardt the host. For first-time visitors, the tasting menu is an excellent choice, offering small portions of a broad variety of appetizers and entrées. On the other hand, since the menu changes every night to reflect the freshest local ingredients, it's impossible to go wrong. The cuisine can be described as classical French, but with the chef's own interpretations. An award-winning wine cellar contains more than 9,000 bottles. The pretty little flower garden, with a terrace and reflecting pool, is a wonderful place for an aperitif or after-dinner coffee.

Continental breakfast is served to guests either in the garden or on an enclosed side verandah. It starts with juice, followed by a bowl of fresh fruit (strawberries or raspberries in season, topped with *crème fraîche)* and a basket of fresh-baked breads. For an additional charge a hot entrée is available.

The inn is located in the foothills of the Blue Ridge Mountains, an hour from Washington, DC. Hiking, horseback riding, wineries, and art galleries are all nearby.

INN AT LITTLE WASHINGTON PO Box 300, Middle and Main Sts., Washington, VA 22747 (phone: 703-675-3800; fax: 703-675-3100). This country inn has 12 guestrooms with private baths, queen- or king-size beds, telephones, and air conditioning. Restaurant is wheelchair accessible. Closed *Christmas;* restaurant also closed Tuesdays from June through September and November through April. Rate for a double room (including continental breakfast and afternoon tea): $240 to $490; $125 additional Saturday nights; $100 additional Friday nights, selected holidays, and in October. MasterCard and Visa accepted. Not appropriate for children under 10. Pets accepted by prior arrangement only; they must stay in a separate building. Two dalmatians, Rose and Desoto, in residence. Smoking permitted in guestrooms and lobby but not in the dining room. Patrick O'Connell and Reinhardt Lynch, innkeepers.

DIRECTIONS: From Washington, DC, take I-66 west for 22 miles to Exit 43A (Gainesville). Follow Route 29 south for 12 miles to Warrenton. In Warrenton take Route 211 west for 23 miles to Washington. Turn right onto Business Route 211 in Washington. The inn is a half mile down on the right, in the center of the village.

L'AUBERGE PROVENÇALE

WHITE POST, VIRGINIA

Tucked into Virginia's Shenandoah Valley, this little French *auberge* is just like the ones found in the countryside near Avignon—and that is no coincidence. Innkeeper Alain Borel was raised in Avignon, where he began acquiring his considerable culinary expertise at the age of 13 in his grandfather's restaurant. The inn's ambience is so thoroughly French that it's hard to believe it's really only 90 minutes from Washington, DC, and in a rural village with an all-American history: White Post got its name when a young surveyor, tramping these parts in the mid-18th century, set up a white marker post in town. His name was George Washington, and several other remnants of his early activities can be found nearby.

Set on nine acres and surrounded by flower and vegetable gardens, the inn occupies a stone manor house built as a private home in 1753. Borel's wife, Celeste, is responsible for the stunning French decor. Country French antiques are accented by bright, printed Provençal fabrics in the sitting area, the three dining rooms, and the guestrooms. There are pine canopy beds with turned posts, sleigh beds, and an antique cannonball bed; five rooms have fireplaces. The three guestrooms in the original 1753 manor house are among the largest, and all have fireplaces; the other rooms are in two wings that were added in 1983 and 1993. Guests find a platter of fresh fruit, homemade cookies, and chocolates awaiting their arrival.

Everyone looks forward to mealtimes at the inn—with good reason. One of Alain's fantastic breakfasts might start with a berry crêpe with *crème fraîche,* followed by poached eggs in a spinach nest. His dinners (also open to non-guests) are elaborate and inventive, using the freshest local ingredients and distinctive seasonings. Dinner is served in one of the manor house's three dining rooms, all of which are decorated with bright Provençal fabrics and French oils and prints. Be sure to note the original Picasso and Bernard Buffet.

The inn runs a gift shop stocked with unusual items from Provence, including hand-carved animals, dolls, and other collectibles, as well as jam, honey, and vinegars made on the premises. It's also near golf, horseback riding, vineyards, and White Post Restorations, a high-quality restorer of classic cars.

L'AUBERGE PROVENÇALE Rte. 340, PO Box 119, White Post, VA 22663 (phone: 703-837-1375; 800-638-1702; fax: 703-837-2004). This country French inn has 10 guestrooms with private baths, double or queen-size beds, and air conditioning. Closed January except for *New Year's* weekend; restaurant also closed Monday and Tuesday dinner. Rate for a double room (including full breakfast): $155 to $225. Major credit cards accepted. Not appropriate for children under 10. No pets. One husky, Sergeant Preston of the Yukon II, in residence. Smoking permitted in sitting room only. Alain and Celeste Borel, innkeepers.

DIRECTIONS: From Washington, DC, take I-66 west to Exit 23. Follow Route 17 north for 9 miles to Route 50. Turn left onto Route 50 and continue to the first traffic light—the intersection of Route 50 and Route 340. Turn left onto Route 340; the inn is on the right after 1 mile.

COLONIAL HOUSES AND TAVERNS

WILLIAMSBURG, VIRGINIA

From 1699 to 1780, Williamsburg was the political, social, and cultural center of Virginia. Today, thanks to the support of John D. Rockefeller, the restoration of some 88 original structures and the reconstruction of 50 others have made the streets of Williamsburg look and feel much as they did in colonial days. Here 20th-century visitors can experience 17th- and 18th-century history by staying in some of the original structures in the heart of the historic district, becoming part of the scene of passing carriages, militiamen hurrying to Market Square, and shopkeepers returning home after a day at work.

In the true sense of the word, this is not an inn. You will find no innkeeper spinning tales around the breakfast table or providing a plate of hot cookies in the parlor. But few places in America can boast such unique character and setting, or provide such a complete escape to an earlier age.

The 84 guest accommodations, which are managed by the *Williamsburg Inn,* are scattered among three taverns and 26 houses. Decor in the *Colonial Houses* authentically reflects each building's original use (you'll find histories of the buildings in the rooms). Handsome homes such as *Brick House, Lewis House,* and *Orrell House* offer canopy beds, fireplaces, sitting rooms, and brick courtyards or private walled gardens. Others, such as those in the *Market Square Tavern* (where Thomas Jefferson and Patrick Henry once stayed) and *Chiswell-Bucktrout Tavern,* are more informal. (The quaint *Quarter House* was home to Cary Grant during the 1940 filming of *The Howards of Virginia.*) Throughout, authentic Williamsburg restoration furnishings are used, and polished wood floors are topped by Oriental or braided rugs. However, every comfort for today's guests has been considered, including air conditioning and modern baths.

A variety of dining options is available in the historic quarter, including several of the taverns—the *King's Arms, Christiana Campbell's, Josiah Chowning's,* and *Shields*—or visitors may choose to eat in the dining room of the *Williamsburg Inn.* No meals are included in the room rates.

Guests who want to revisit the 20th century will find golf, tennis, swimming, and a fitness center.

COLONIAL HOUSES AND TAVERNS **Frances St., PO Box 1776, Williamsburg, VA 23187 (phone: 804-229-1000; 800-HISTORY; fax: 804-221-8797). This collection of historic buildings offers 84 guestrooms with private baths, twin, double, queen-, or king-size beds, telephones, and air conditioning. Open year-round. Rate for a double room: $99 to $175. Major credit cards accepted. Children welcome. No pets. Smoking permitted in designated rooms only. Colonial Williamsburg, owner; Brian O'Day, manager.**

DIRECTIONS: Traveling east on I-64, take Exit 238. Go a half mile and turn right onto Route 132 south. Follow the signs for the Williamsburg business district and *William and Mary College.* Route 132 becomes Henry Street. After the railroad tracks, turn right at the traffic light onto Lafayette Street. Take Lafayette to Virginia Avenue (the fourth street on the left) and turn left. Registration is at the *Williamsburg Inn,* which is on the corner of Richmond Road, two blocks down.

COUNTRY INN

BERKELEY SPRINGS, WEST VIRGINIA

Berkeley Springs is the nation's oldest spa, noted for its healing mineral waters as early as the 1750s. To this day, visitors come to enjoy the baths and the numerous other restorative spa services. There are Roman soaking tubs, massage therapies, swimming pools, and health clubs at *Berkeley Springs Spa State Park.* Berkeley Springs water is bottled and sold throughout the country and is piped directly into each of the guestrooms at the *Country Inn.*

The inn itself has been welcoming guests since 1932; Jack and Alice Barker have owned the place since 1972, and they continue to provide the same hands-on care for which they have long been known. Accommodations are in the original gracious, columned, brick colonial house and in the newer *Country Inn West,* a separate building connected by a covered walkway. Rooms in both are decorated with colonial-style furnishings, brass beds, and prints of country scenes.

Berkeley Springs State Park is just next door, but guests can enjoy spa treatments right at the inn. Its *Renaissance Spa* offers private whirlpool baths, deep-muscle massages, Thai massages, hot-oil treatments, and European facials, along with traditional beauty salon services such as manicures, pedicures, hairstyling, and makeup. After taking the waters, guests may walk through the flower gardens, relax on a bench beside the splashing fountain, or rock gently on the front porch.

The inn has two restaurants: the skylighted *Garden Room,* with its country French decor, and the smaller *West Virginia Room,* where a colonial look predominates. The menu offers some 20 "country fare" entrées, including crab cakes and New York strip steaks and dessert selected from a tray piled high with tempting sweets. On Saturday nights, there's live music and dancing in the *Garden Room.* The inn has conference and banquet facilities, as well.

Located 100 miles west of Washington, DC, the inn is near *Cacapon State Park,* with its 18-hole Robert Trent Jones Sr. golf course, fishing lake, and riding stables. Rafting trips are available through the inn, as are rides on the *Potomac Eagle Scenic Railroad.* A drive to a scenic overlook for a three-state view, antiquing, and cultural events are also nearby.

COUNTRY INN 207 S. Washington St., Berkeley Springs, WV 25411 (phone: 304-258-2210; 800-822-6630; fax: 304-258-3986). This inn has 70 guestrooms (56 with private baths) with twin, double, or queen-size beds, telephones, TV sets, and air conditioning. Wheelchair accessible. Open year-round. Rate for a double room: $37 to $145. Two-night minimum stay on weekends and holidays from April through November. Major credit cards accepted. Children welcome; no charge for children under 12. No pets. Smoking permitted except in the *Garden Room* and designated nonsmoking rooms. Jack and Alice Barker, innkeepers.

DIRECTIONS: From Washington, DC, take I-70 west to Exit 1B (Hancock). Stay in the left lane and follow Route 522 south for 6 miles to Berkeley Springs. The inn is on the village green.

HILLBROOK INN

CHARLES TOWN, WEST VIRGINIA

At the *Hillbrook Inn*, you can drink water from the same springhouse that slaked George Washington's thirst. Its 17 pastoral acres were originally part of Washington's *Rock Hall* estate, and the springhouse still captures the crystal waters of Bullskin Run.

A half-mile drive leads to an English rock garden skirting the front walk that leads to the manor house, a rambling wood-frame and stucco Tudor. Built to resemble a small hillside village, the house was constructed in seven sections on 15 levels. From a picturesque limestone ridge, it overlooks rolling lawns and English gardens. The property contains two streams, each spanned by a bridge. The 12-foot-wide Bridge of Sighs, in a Chinese Chippendale design with ornate lions' heads, is particularly romantic.

In contrast to the dark woodwork and white walls of most Tudor houses, *Hillbrook*'s common rooms, with their 20-foot ceilings, offer the reverse—bright white woodwork set against deep terra cotta walls. Antique wooden tables, tapestry-covered easy chairs, and richly colored Oriental rugs are complemented by innkeeper Gretchen Carroll's eclectic collection of primitive and modern pottery and art treasures, which she gathered on her travels to Italy, Vietnam, Turkey, Thailand, and the Ivory Coast.

The house was built in 1922, around the frame of a 1700s log house, creating intriguing nooks and crannies, twists and turns in the guestroom configurations. The most sought-after room is *The Point,* with its mysterious tunnel entrance. Paisley linen on the double bed and dramatic wallpaper complement the European and Asian paintings and prints on the walls. *The Lookout,* tucked under a steeply slanted roof, has windows on three sides and overlooks the verdant countryside. A miniature teak Thai spirit house ensures safety and good luck.

Dinner (also open to non-guests) is served in the atmospheric dining room, with its brass chandelier made from antique oil lamps, and candles that cast romantic shadows on the fine crystal and antique tables. The seven-course meal might include sherried mushroom soup, grilled marlin with tarragon butter, and chocolate decadence. Generally, the morning meal—which may include pecan pancakes with ginger butter—is served on the glass-enclosed porch or on the terrace, as is lunch.

The inn is near *Harpers Ferry National Historic Park,* the *Antietam Battlefield,* whitewater rafting, the Charles Town races, and antiquing.

HILLBROOK INN Rte. 2, Box 152, Charles Town, WV 25414 (phone: 304-725-4223; fax: 304-725-4455). This Tudor-style mansion has six guestrooms with private baths, double or queen-size beds, and air conditioning. Closed December 24 and 25. Rate for a double room (including full breakfast and seven-course dinner with wine): $198 to $380. Discover, MasterCard, and Visa accepted. Not appropriate for children under 15. No pets. One cat, Princess Fuzzy Butt, in residence, plus ducks and geese on property. Smoking permitted except in the dining room. Gretchen Carroll, innkeeper; Nadia Hill, manager.

DIRECTIONS: The inn is 70 miles west of Washington, DC. From Washington take I-270 to I-70 west, then Route 340 west past Harpers Ferry to the Charles Town bypass, which is marked Route 340 south/9 east (Berryville/Leesburg). Go 4 miles and exit onto Old Route 340. Make an immediate left onto Huyette Road and drive almost 3 miles to a stop sign. Turn left, following Route 13 for just over a mile. The inn is on the left.

Deep South

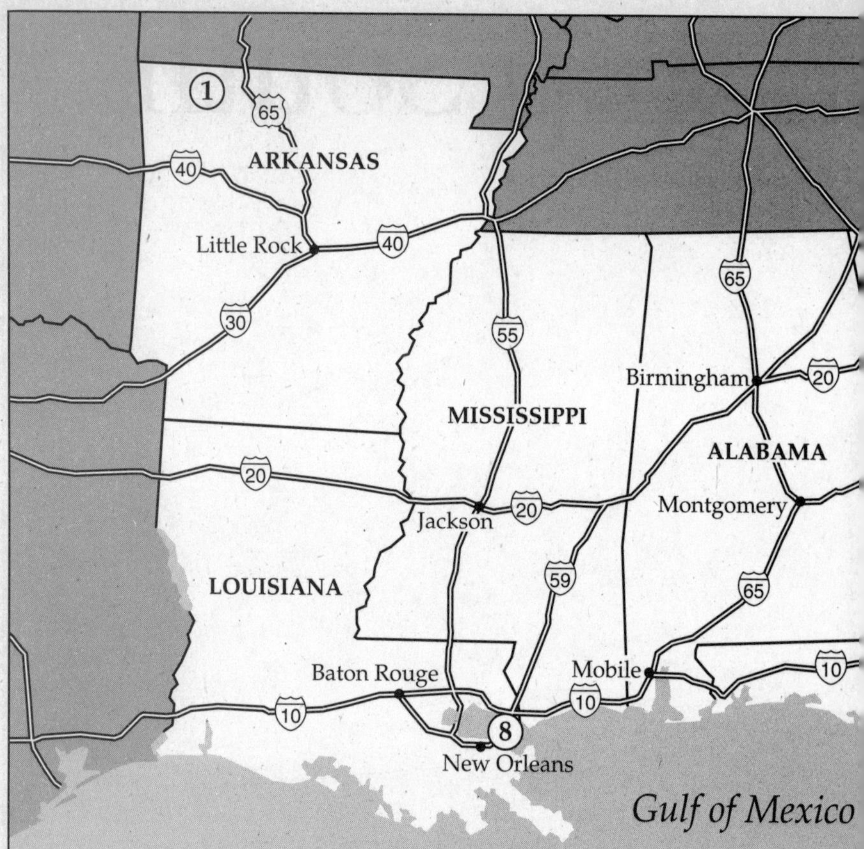

ARKANSAS
1. Eureka Springs: DAIRY HOLLOW HOUSE

FLORIDA
2. Apalachicola: GIBSON INN
3. Key West: MARQUESA HOTEL
4. Little Torch Key: LITTLE PALM ISLAND
5. Orange Park: CLUB CONTINENTAL SUITES

GEORGIA
6. Savannah: THE GASTONIAN
7. Senoia: THE VERANDA

LOUISIANA
8. New Orleans: HOTEL MAISON DE VILLE

SOUTH CAROLINA
9. Beaufort: RHETT HOUSE INN
10. Charleston: TWO MEETING STREET INN

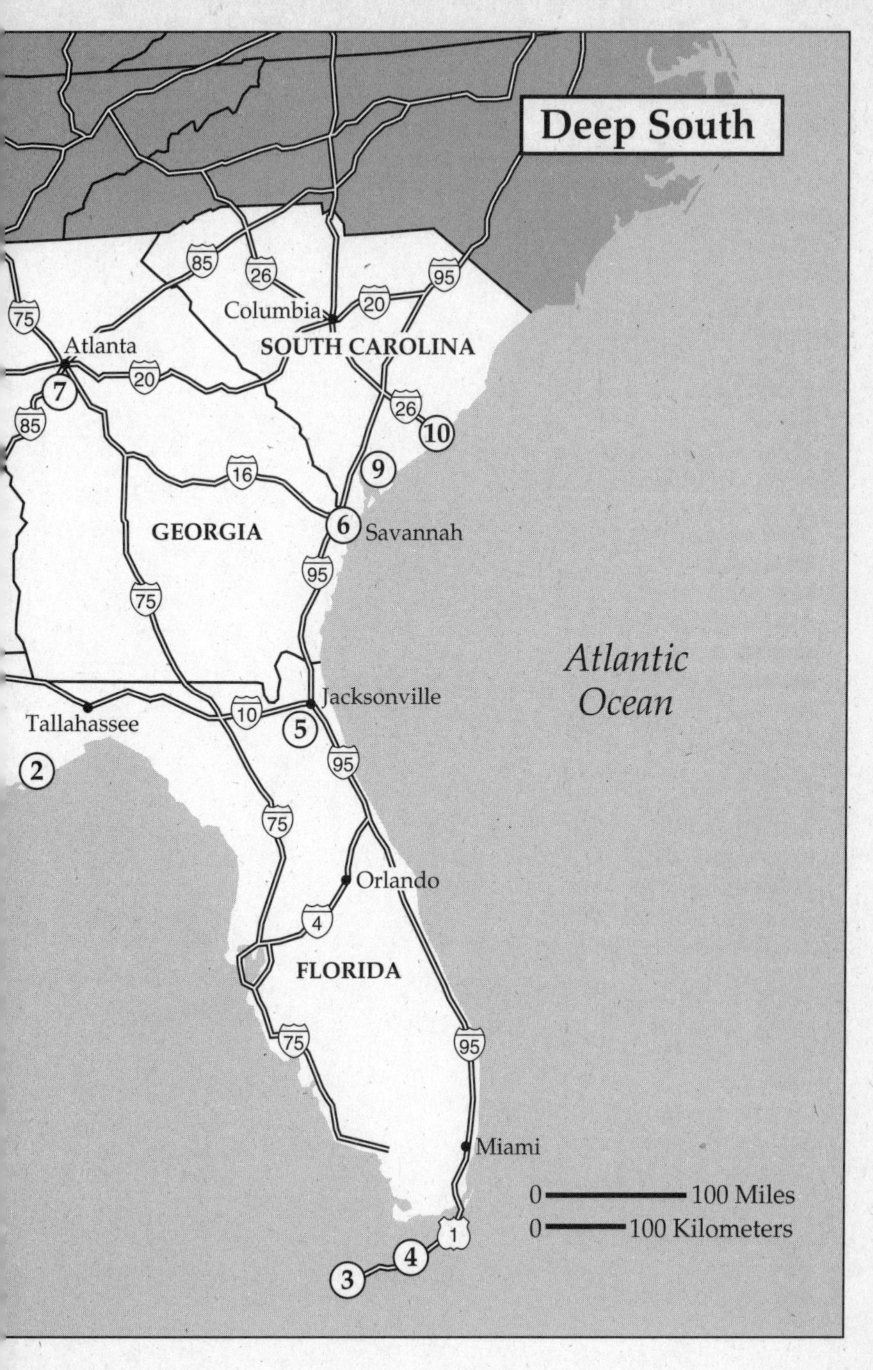

Deep South
85
26
95
20
Columbia
75
Atlanta
SOUTH CAROLINA
7
20
85
26
10
9
16
GEORGIA
6
Savannah
95
75
Atlantic
Ocean
Jacksonville
Tallahassee
10
5
2
95
75
Orlando
4
FLORIDA
75
95
Miami
0 100 Miles
0 100 Kilometers
1
4
3

Deep South

Arkansas

DAIRY HOLLOW HOUSE

EUREKA SPRINGS, ARKANSAS

It seems appropriate that Ned Shank and Crescent Dragonwagon (that really is her name) should have converted the last surviving dairy in Eureka Springs into the *Dairy Hollow House.* Ned was an intern with the *National Trust for Historic Preservation* when they met; Crescent was a chef and the author of children's books and cookbooks (there are now two *Dairy Hollow House* cookbooks). They combined their considerable skills to create a delightful inn with a restaurant that serves meals and special dinners five or six times a year.

The guestrooms are located in two separate buildings in the heart of Eureka's historic district: the *Main House* and the *Farmhouse.* The *Main House,* a 1940s bungalow, has three charming suites with fireplaces. *Spring Garden Suite,* decorated in yellow with blue and white accents, has a canopy bed, a stone fireplace, and a sunroom with white wicker furniture. *Summer Meadow Suite* feels like a mountain lodge, although the wood floors are covered with Oriental rugs. There's a stone fireplace and a built-in Dutch cupboard bed, a library filled with books, and a deck off the kitchen; sunlight streams through the skylights. *Peach Blossom Suite* has intricate stenciling throughout as well as a Victorian brass-and-wire bed, a stone fireplace, a kitchen, and a bath with a Jacuzzi.

The *Farmhouse* is a renovated 1880s farmhouse, decorated with quilts and local farmstead antiques in an "Ozark Vernacular" style. Its three guestrooms have fireplaces and antique beds. One is decorated in Eastlake Victorian style, with ornate, intricately carved furniture. There's a claw-foot tub in one bath, a Jacuzzi in another. An easy walk from Spring Street, Eureka's main street, the *Farmhouse* is a secluded hideaway, complete with a hot tub hidden among the dogwoods. For breakfast (included in the room rate), a full "Breakfast in a Basket" is served to guests in both houses.

There's lots to do in the area. Eureka Springs is rich in Victorian architecture and once was renowned for its mineral baths. Located in the dramatically beautiful heart of the Ozarks, this resort town has numerous crafts, art, and antiques shops, and hosts a passion play, summer opera, a fall jazz festival, and a summer blues festival.

DAIRY HOLLOW HOUSE 515 Spring St., Eureka Springs, AK 72632 (phone: 501-253-7444; 800-562-8650; fax: 501-253-7223). This inn has six guestrooms with private baths, double or queen-size beds, and air conditioning; restaurant open for occasional special dinners. Closed January. Rate for a double room (including full breakfast): $125 to $155 ($20 more on holidays and in October). Two-night minimum stay on weekends. Major credit cards accepted. Children welcome in one suite. No pets. No smoking. Crescent Dragonwagon and Ned Shank, innkeepers.

DIRECTIONS: From Fort Smith travel north on Route 71 to Fayetteville, then take Route 62 east to Eureka Springs. Turn left and follow the Historic Loop (Old Route 62B/Highway 23 north) to downtown Eureka Springs. Remain on the Historic Loop (it becomes Spring Street) as it winds through town for 1½ miles. The *Main House* is next to *Harmon Park*.

GIBSON INN

APALACHICOLA, FLORIDA

Apalachicola was once a bustling Gulf port, with ships carrying lumber to far-flung shores; today it's a sleepy village on the Florida panhandle where oysters and shrimp are the primary catch. Through the years, the town's varying economic fortunes have left it with a smorgasbord of architectural styles, and many of its buildings are now on the National Register of Historic Places—among them the *Gibson Inn.*

On the waterfront overlooking the harbor and St. George Island beyond, the three-story, blue-and-white Victorian confection was built in 1907, during Apalachicola's glory days. Still boasting much of its former splendor, the *Gibson* was fully restored in 1983 by Michael Koun and his brothers. From its rocking-chair porches to its widow's walk, the inn stylishly encourages visitors to stay a while and explore this seafaring town—part of old Florida at its best.

The interior displays interesting features as well. There's an old polished cypress bar, hand-carved newel posts flanking a mahogany stairway, tongue-and-groove wainscoting, as well as pine paneling. The dining room is decorated with marvelous old photos of the town and the inn, that provide a local history lesson along with meals.

Upstairs, the guestrooms are furnished with a mix of antiques and reproductions—four-poster or iron beds, armoires, and pine or mahogany chests. Ceiling fans augment the air conditioning. Bathrooms are finished in period style right down to pedestal sinks and claw-foot tubs with brass and porcelain fixtures.

Not surprisingly, fresh seafood is the specialty of the restaurant (which serves three meals a day and is open to non-guests). Dinner might include grouper en papillote or shrimp, scallop, and crab Dijon; it will definitely end with authentically rich, tart Key lime pie. Leave your dressy clothes at home: This is a laid-back place where shorts and sandals are just fine.

Located 75 miles west of Tallahassee and 65 miles east of Panama City, the *Gibson Inn* is near beaches, fishing, boating, tennis, the *St. Vincent National Wildlife Refuge,* and state parks.

GIBSON INN 100 Market St., PO Box 221, Apalachicola, FL 32320 (phone: 904-653-2191 or 904-653-8282). This Victorian hotel has 30 guestrooms with private baths, twin, queen-, or king-size beds, telephones, TV sets, and air conditioning. Open year-round. Rate for a double room: $65 to $115. Major credit cards accepted. Children welcome. Pets allowed for an additional $5 charge per stay. Four lazy cats in residence. Smoking permitted. Michael Koun, innkeeper.

DIRECTIONS: From Tallahassee travel south on Route 319 to the Gulf of Mexico, then follow Route 98 along the shore to Apalachicola. From Panama City follow Route 98 east to Apalachicola. The inn is in the village on the corner of Route 98 and Avenue C, at the foot of the high bridge.

MARQUESA HOTEL

KEY WEST, FLORIDA

If your image of Key West comes from steamy novels, you'll be disappointed with the *Marquesa Hotel.* There's still plenty of action along the streets, and museums capture the nuances of the key's somewhat shady past, but the *Marquesa* is a model of gentility.

Built in 1884, the hotel spent most of its first hundred years as a blowsy boardinghouse. In 1987, however, partners Erik deBoer and Richard Manley invested $2 million and untold hours converting it to a small hotel. They were so successful that it's now listed on the National Register of Historic Places. Erik's wife, Carol Wightman, is the innkeeper, and Richard's wife, Pamela, a floral designer, is responsible for the fantastic flower arrangements found throughout the establishment. In 1993, deBoer and Manley purchased several adjacent Victorian houses and converted them to 12 more rooms and suites. They have porches furnished with overstuffed chairs and breakfast tables, and they're surrounded by lush gardens with brick walkways and a lattice wall with a profusion of orchids and flowering vines.

The *Marquesa* is stylishly sophisticated, with antique and high-quality reproduction furnishings in a potpourri of styles. Common areas such as the lobby, verandah, and sitting room have a Caribbean ambience, with wicker tables and chairs. Audubon prints and vintage photos of Key West adorn the walls. Many of the guestrooms have small balconies overlooking the little pool in back. All bathrooms are modern, with Italian chrome fixtures and Art Deco sconces. Nightly turndown service includes Godiva chocolates.

The grounds are a riot of color, planted with bougainvilleas, impatiens, and bromeliads. The location is ideal—on a quiet side street within easy access of all the action.

The *Café Marquesa* (which is open to non-guests at dinner) presents elegant meals in an airy, bistro setting with 15-foot-tall windows, yellow plaster walls, and a grand mahogany-and-brass bar. A trompe l'oeil mural along one wall incorporates windows to the kitchen. Fresh local seafood is the specialty: Grilled shrimp in roast banana–red curry sauce comes with sweet-potato fritters and fresh mango relish; pan-seared yellowfin tuna in sun-dried tomato beurre blanc is accompanied by horseradish potatoes and roast green beans.

In the heart of Key West's historic district, the hotel is near many major attractions: the *Key West Aquarium, Audubon House,* the *Hemingway House Museum,* and the *Key West Lighthouse Museum.* Bicycling, ocean and gulf beaches, tennis, scuba diving, and fishing are among the recreational options.

MARQUESA HOTEL 600 Fleming St., Key West, FL 33040 (phone: 305-292-1919; 800-UNWIND-1; fax: 305-294-2121). This small hotel has 27 guestrooms with private baths, queen- or king-size beds, telephones, TV sets, and air conditioning. Wheelchair accessible. Open year-round. Rate for a double room: $125 to $285. Two-night minimum stay on weekends; three nights on holidays. Major credit cards accepted. Children welcome. No pets. No smoking in restaurant; smoking permitted in guestrooms. Carol Wightman, innkeeper.

DIRECTIONS: From US Route 1 turn right onto Simonton Street and continue for six blocks to Fleming Street. The inn is on the corner of Simonton and Fleming.

LITTLE PALM ISLAND

LITTLE TORCH KEY, FLORIDA

If Tahiti or Bora Bora are out of the question right now, you might want to consider *Little Palm Island.* Though not an inn in the traditional sense of the word, this place offers many of the amenities found at its mainland cousins—with a delightful difference: Guests stay on a private island off the Florida Keys, accessible only by a 15-minute boat ride. The island comes complete with coconut palms, hibiscus, orchids, and flamboyant bougainvilleas, and the air is perfumed with the sweet scent of plumeria.

In the late 1980s, developer Ben Woodson and his partners purchased five-acre Little Palm Island off Little Torch Key and began construction of their dream resort, modeling it after secluded retreats in the Caribbean. Today, in addition to the *Great House,* where the dining room is located, there are 14 bungalows, each containing two luxurious suites, as well as a *Houseboat Suite* and a *Poolside Suite.*

The thatch-roofed bungalows sit on stilts, surrounded by private decks. Inside, the ambience is tropical: Palmetto ceilings, wood-slat blinds to filter the sun, ceiling fans that gently stir the air, and wispy mosquito netting draped from the ceilings over king-size beds. Each bungalow is furnished with rattan furniture and a Jacuzzi, with an outdoor shower screened by bamboo poles. In true get-away-from-it-all spirit, there are no telephones or TV sets, but a hammock awaits on the deck.

Rich in atmosphere, with views across azure waters and an untrammeled private (although tiny) white sand beach, *Little Palm Island* feels like a page from a romance novel.

Dining is an exceptional treat here. Swiss-born chef Michel Reymond specializes in French cuisine with a Caribbean twist, offering local seafood dishes like sautéed grouper with artichoke hearts, olives, yellow tomatoes, and Pommery mustard sauce. The ethereal chocolate soufflé with bittersweet sauce is not to be missed.

Small boats are available for guests' use, and the marina can accommodate craft up to 110 feet. There's also fishing, windsurfing, scuba diving, and snorkeling to keep guests active. The reef just off the Florida Keys is home to brightly colored tropical fish, sea anemones, and brilliant coral formations. The inn arranges excursions and provides instruction for scuba-diving certification. There's also a pool for lazing away sunny afternoons, as well as an exercise room and a sauna.

LITTLE PALM ISLAND Rte. 4, PO Box 1036, Little Torch Key, FL 33041 (phone: 305-872-2524; 800-343-8567; fax: 305-872-4843). This luxury resort off the Florida Keys has 30 suites with private baths, king-size beds, and air conditioning. Wheelchair accessible. Open year-round. Rate for a double room: $330 to $495; breakfast, lunch, and dinner an additional $95 per person per day; breakfast and dinner an additional $75 per person per day. Two-night minimum stay on weekends; three nights on holidays; seven nights at *Christmas* and *New Year's.* Major credit cards accepted. Not appropriate for children under 12. No pets. Smoking permitted. Ben H. Woodson, innkeeper; Terri Marble and Barry Smith, managers.

DIRECTIONS: The island is 150 miles southwest of Miami and 28½ miles east of Key West. From Miami take the Florida Turnpike south to its end, then take US Route 1 for approximately 120 miles to Little Torch Key at mile marker 28.5 (the markers start at Key West). Look for the "Little Palm Island Ferry" sign. Turn left into the *Dolphin Marina* to the Little Palm Island Shore Station.

CLUB CONTINENTAL SUITES

ORANGE PARK, FLORIDA

In 1923, Caleb Johnson, founder of the Palmolive Soap Company, built a Mediterranean-style villa he called *Mira Rio.* Set on 17 acres on the banks of the St. Johns River, it was constructed of limestone and adorned with filigree ironwork, ornamental archways, and tile floors. In 1966, the estate was opened as a bed and breakfast establishment. Today, the property comprises six acres and is run as the *Club Continental Suites*—part secluded inn, part private country club. Despite the many changes over the years, the villa has been owned continuously by the Johnson family, and Caleb's great-great-grandchildren Caleb and Karrie Massee are the current innkeepers.

Guestrooms are furnished with antiques acquired by family members on their round-the-world travels. There are five rooms and two suites in the mansion, with 15 additional guestrooms located in *River House,* a pre–Civil War cottage that was moved from a local plantation to this site in 1976. All have magnificent views through trees to the river. The decor is variously English, country French, Mexican, and continental; the furnishings, eclectic. Guests will find carved Italian beds (some with theatrical canopies), a Jacobean sideboard, and one bathroom hung with Jamaican paintings. Elaborately swagged drapes frame three pairs of windows in the *French Room.*

Hidden behind huge cypress, hickory, and palm trees and bordered by impatiens and wildflowers, *River House* also contains the inn's dining room and a charming pub. The former is decorated with a medley of Italian elements. A row of fanlight windows offers views across the lawn, which stretches beneath towering oaks to the stone balustrades that rim the river. A buffet-style continental breakfast of juice, fresh-baked muffins and pastries, fruit, cereal, coffee, and tea is served here daily; lunch and dinner, which may include such local specialties as sautéed soft-shell crabs on a bed of fried spinach, also are available Tuesday through Friday; Sunday brunch also is served.

Guests may use the country club's facilities, including the marina, seven tennis courts, and three swimming pools (one for adults, one reserved for teens, and one for children); bicycling and jogging trails extend into the adjacent property. The club is close to Jacksonville, with its museums, theater, symphony, and shopping, and a golf course is nearby. St. Augustine, the country's oldest city, is 30 minutes away.

CLUB CONTINENTAL SUITES 2143 Astor St., PO Box 7059, Orange Park, FL 32073 (phone: 904-264-6070; 800-877-6070; fax: 904-264-4044). This retreat has 22 guestrooms with private baths, double, queen-, or king-size beds, telephones, TV sets, and air conditioning. Wheelchair accessible. Open year-round. Rate for a double room (including continental breakfast): $60 to $150. Major credit cards accepted. Children welcome. Pets allowed by prior arrangement. Smoking permitted in all but five rooms. Caleb Massee and Karrie Massee, innkeepers.

DIRECTIONS: From Jacksonville travel south on I-295, exiting onto US Route 17 south to Kingsley Avenue. Turn left toward the river, then right onto Astor Street. The gatehouse is a block and a half down on the left.

Georgia

THE GASTONIAN

SAVANNAH, GEORGIA

Laughter and music spill from the open windows. It is 1868, and a brilliant party is in progress at the opulent townhouse of insurance broker R. H. Footman. Next door, the equally lavish house of wholesale grocer Aaron Champion and his wife is dark; they are visiting the Footmans. The Civil War has been over for three years, and Savannah society, spared General Sherman's wrath, is returning to life.

Guests staying at this pair of old Southern townhouses, which comprise *The Gastonian,* find that such images are almost inevitable because the two houses, today, appear so similar to the way they were in their heyday. Hugh and Roberta Lineberger, who began restoration in 1984, have polished them to a fine patina. The Linebergers joined the two townhouses with an elevated walkway at parlor level that spans a portion of the garden, fragrant with myrtle and flowering dogwood. In the landscaped courtyard is a sun deck with a hot tub.

Inside the mansion, the pine floors, high ceilings, decorative moldings, and Scalamandre wallpapers (in an original Savannah pattern) make a marvelous background for the exceptional antiques (there are no reproductions here). A 1780s broken-pediment Chippendale secretary, an 1810 two-tier round mahogany table, and a 1780s Sheraton tilt-top table decorate the parlor. In the guestrooms, Charleston canopy beds and four-posters with a rice-grain pattern sit on Oriental rugs before working fireplaces. The baths are as opulent as the rooms. Several have Jacuzzis; one, in the *Caracalla Suite,* has an eight-foot round whirlpool on a platform placed before one of the suite's two fireplaces. Sheer floor-to-ceiling curtains enhance the theatrical effect. There's also a honeymoon suite in the converted carriage house.

The inn exudes Southern charm. Guests are greeted with a basket of fresh fruit, a split of wine, and fresh flowers in their room. Evening turn-down service includes Savannah pralines and peach schnapps. A full breakfast is served in the parlor, or a continental breakfast can be delivered to the room.

Located in the heart of Savannah, *The Gastonian* is surrounded by Civil War memorials, churches, gardens, townhouses, quaint shops, and restaurants. The Savannah River is within walking distance, as are the city's many cultural and historic attractions. Golf, a fitness center, tennis, and deep-sea fishing are nearby.

THE GASTONIAN 220 E. Gaston St., Savannah, GA 31401 (phone: 912-232-2869; 800-322-6603; fax: 912-232-0710). This historic inn has 13 guestrooms with private baths, double, queen-, or king-size beds, telephones, TV sets, and air conditioning. Wheelchair accessible. Open year-round. Rate for a double room (including full breakfast): $125 to $285; 15% additional for one-night weekend stays; two-night minimum stay on holidays; corporate rate available. Major credit cards accepted. Not appropriate for children under 12. No pets. A small dog, Calio, in residence. No smoking. Hugh and Roberta Lineberger, innkeepers.

DIRECTIONS: Traveling south on I-95, take Exit 17 to I-16 east into Savannah. From I-16 take the Martin Luther King Jr. Boulevard exit and continue straight. This boulevard becomes Gaston Street. The inn is on the corner of Lincoln Street and has ample off-street parking.

THE VERANDA

SENOIA, GEORGIA

The sleepy little town of Senoia (pronounced Se-*noy*) could have been taken straight from the pages of *Gone With the Wind.* Broad oak-lined streets and dignified old mansions are preserved in a setting of Southern gentility. Most of the town is included on the National Register of Historic Places, including *The Veranda.*

Originally the *Hollberg Hotel,* the inn was built in 1906, when Senoia was still a prosperous cotton town. Over the years, numerous famous people have graced its doorstep. In 1908, William Jennings Bryan stayed here while campaigning for the presidency against William Howard Taft. Margaret Mitchell visited to interview Civil War veterans when she was writing her great American novel. In 1985, Jan Boal and his wife, Bobby, purchased and refurbished the hotel, adding private baths, air conditioning, and other amenities. It was after this restoration that Jessica Tandy and Kathy Bates were guests while filming *Fried Green Tomatoes* in town.

The inn is a white clapboard plantation-style house, its Doric-columned, wraparound verandah lined with rocking chairs and swings. Several rooms have original pressed-tin ceilings and stained glass windows. This was one of the first commercial establishments in the area to use electricity, and many of the original light fixtures are still in use. The common rooms are historic and numerous. The most notable is the *Front Parlor,* where a pair of antique bookcases that once belonged to President William McKinley dominate the room. They contain a priceless collection of books, including such rare volumes as a 1789 10-volume commentary on the Old Testament and *Hume's History of England,* published in 1795. This room also contains old newspapers, sheet music, and a 1923 Estey pump organ, while the downstairs hall has a collection of antique hats, hairpieces, and beaded purses. The inn is famous for its collection of more than 350 kaleidoscopes. Impressive examples will be found in every room of the house, and smaller ones are sold in the inn's gift shop. A kaleidoscope is even placed on each guest's pillow during the nightly turndown service.

The guestrooms are furnished with family heirlooms and antiques based on given themes. The *Walking Stick Room,* for example, contains more than a hundred canes collected by Bobby's father (and some made by him). The *Historic Room* is notable for its original bathroom with its claw-foot tub and pedestal sink, as well as the dollhouse and furniture made by Jan for the couple's daughters. The *Mystery Room* contains several hundred paperback mysteries.

A complimentary full breakfast is offered to inn guests, and a five-course, prix fixe dinner is available at an additional charge. Bobby's meals win raves, and it's no wonder. Breakfasts are so extensive that lunch is generally unnecessary, if not impossible. Dinner might begin with a fresh seasonal fruit salad accompanied by homemade crackers, followed by French onion soup with Swiss cheese under a puff pastry dome, then seafood cocktail. Entrées might be baked sesame chicken served with rice, or veal Ione with a sweet-potato puff. Desserts are equally inventive.

Guests may stroll the grounds, with a rock garden, flagstone pathways, and the *Hollberg Hotel*'s original fountain. And don't miss the old-fashioned hardware/country store or the *Buggy Shop Museum* just across the street. Golf, tennis, fishing, historic walking tours, festivals, and antiquing are all nearby.

THE VERANDA 252 Seavy St., PO Box 177, Senoia, GA 30276 (phone: 770-599-3905; fax: 770-599-0806). In a village 36 miles south of Atlanta, this inn has seven guestrooms with private baths, queen- or king-size beds, and air conditioning. Wheelchair accessible. Open year-round. Rate for a double room (including full breakfast): $95 to $115. Major credit cards accepted. Children welcome with prior permission. No pets. Smoking permitted on the verandah only. Jan and Bobby Boal, innkeepers.

DIRECTIONS: From Atlanta take I-85 south to Exit 12 and turn left onto Route 74. Drive approximately 16½ miles, then turn right onto Rock-a-Way Road. Follow Rock-a-Way Road into Senoia. Turn left at the traffic light onto Seavy Street. *The Veranda* is on the left.

HOTEL MAISON DE VILLE

New Orleans, Louisiana

The historic preservation movement in the United States first flowered in the Vieux Carré (the French Quarter) of New Orleans. Once a neighborhood of gracious homes with iron-lace balconies and hidden gardens and courtyards, the section had deteriorated, becoming overrun by honky-tonk bars and fortune-tellers' storefronts. In 1936, the historic district was created, showcasing the advantages of preserving America's heritage.

The 1742 *Hotel Maison de Ville* is in the heart of the Vieux Carré, yet it's a world apart. It was here that onetime owner Dr. Peychaud added a dash of bitters to bourbon and stirred the drink with a rooster's quill, thereby inventing the cocktail. And Tennessee Williams rewrote *A Streetcar Named Desire* on the wrought-iron tables in the sequestered courtyard with its three-tier splashing fountain. Perhaps he was thinking about the *Maison de Ville* when he wrote that Blanche Dubois loved her languid "afternoons in New Orleans when an hour isn't just an hour—but a little piece of eternity dropped in your hands." Another visitor was John James Audubon, who stayed in one of the cottages when he painted the Louisiana portion of *Birds in America.*

Guestrooms in the original townhouse are formal and plush, decorated with antique canopy and four-poster beds, marble fireplaces, needlepoint chairs, gilt-framed mirrors, and swagged silk draperies with matching bedcovers. French doors lead to balconies overlooking a flower-filled stone courtyard, cooled by overhanging palm trees. Four more guestrooms are in the converted slave quarters on one side of the courtyard. These actually predate the main building by about 50 years, making them (along with the *Ursuline Convent*) the oldest buildings in New Orleans. They have beamed ceilings, brick walls, and fireplaces, and are less formal than those in the mansion.

The seven *Audubon Cottages* are about a block away, secluded behind a stucco wall. A brick pathway, lined with greenery and gaslights, leads from the gate to the cottages, each with its own private courtyard and kitchen. High beamed ceilings, brick walls, and floors of brick or slate covered by Oriental rugs characterize the interiors. Antiques are used throughout, and the gentility of the Old South is perfectly preserved. The center of the cottage complex is a pool overhung by fruit trees.

Continental breakfast and fresh flowers arrive at guestroom doors on a silver tray. Guests are welcome to carry it to the courtyard. *The Bistro,* a popular French restaurant under the same ownership, is next door.

The inn is close to the city's many museums, shops, restaurants, and galleries.

HOTEL MAISON DE VILLE 727 Toulouse St., New Orleans, LA 70130 (phone: 504-561-5858; 800-634-1600; fax: 504-528-9939). This historic inn has 23 guestrooms with private baths, double, queen-, or king-size beds, telephones, TV sets, and air conditioning. Open year-round. Rate for a double room (including continental breakfast, sherry, and port): $175 to $270. Two-night minimum stay on weekends. Major credit cards accepted. Not appropriate for children under 13. No pets. Smoking permitted. Jean-Luc Maumus, manager.

DIRECTIONS: In New Orleans's Veaux Carré, Toulouse Street is between Royal and Bourbon Streets.

South Carolina

RHETT HOUSE INN

BEAUFORT, SOUTH CAROLINA

Southerners appreciate the finer things in life: Good architecture, fine food, good drink—and trees. One realizes the respect accorded old trees when swaying in a hammock on the upper verandah of the *Rhett House Inn* and watching the breeze nudge the Spanish moss draped from the mammoth oak above, thought to be 300 years old.

The inn, originally the home of Thomas Rhett and his wife, Caroline Barnwell, is typical of the grand plantation houses built during the 1820s. Corinthian columns support a classic two-story verandah that loops around both sides of the house. The gardens are rich with pink and red azaleas, roses, and salvias growing beside a splashing fountain.

The mansion has been artistically decorated by owners Steve and Marianne Harrison, refugees from fashion and textile careers in New York City. Polished pine floors and pristine white walls are complemented by Oriental rugs, antique furnishings, floral fabrics, and original artwork. In the sun-drenched living room guests relax on sofas before the Adam-style mantelpiece. Family photographs add a personal touch. There are fresh flowers throughout, and classical music or jazz plays softly in the background.

The spacious guestrooms are furnished with English and American antiques, carved walnut and Charleston rice beds (four-posters with a rice-grain pattern) and crystal chandeliers among them. Some have fireplaces, and there's a Jacuzzi in one bath.

Afternoon tea and cookies are served in the parlor, as is an evening snack of fruit and cheese. A full breakfast of fresh fruit, hot-from-the-oven muffins, and perhaps French toast made with cinnamon-raisin bread and topped with fresh strawberries is included in the room rate. Dinner (also open to non-guests) features regional items such as crab cakes and fresh fish, accompanied by vegetables and herbs from the inn's gardens.

A stay at the *Rhett House Inn* will always be memorable, but several people are still talking about Barbra Streisand's visit in 1991, when she was scouting locations for her movie *The Prince of Tides,* based on the novel by local author Pat Conroy.

The inn is in downtown Beaufort near historic sites and the Intercoastal Waterway. Bicycles are provided to guests who want to tour the town. Swimming, golf, fishing, and tennis are nearby.

RHETT HOUSE INN 1009 Craven St., Beaufort, SC 29902 (phone: 803-524-9030; fax: 803-524-1310). This elegant antebellum mansion has 10 guestrooms with private baths, queen- or king-size beds, telephones, TV sets, and air conditioning. Open year-round; restaurant closed Sundays through Tuesdays. Rate for a double room (including full breakfast, afternoon tea, and evening fruit and cheese): $125 to $200. Major credit cards accepted. Not appropriate for children under five. No pets. Smoking permitted on porches only. Steve and Marianne Harrison, innkeepers.

DIRECTIONS: Traveling south on I-95, take Exit 33, then follow the signs to Beaufort. In Beaufort follow Bay Street along the waterfront, turning right onto New Castle Street. The inn is on the corner of New Castle and Craven Streets.

TWO MEETING STREET INN

CHARLESTON, SOUTH CAROLINA

A lavish Queen Anne Victorian mansion with fish-scale shingles on the turrets, bay windows, and a broad, curved porch supported by double-columned arches, *Two Meeting Street Inn* was built in 1892 as a father's wedding present to his daughter. The exceptionally beautiful stained glass windows by Louis Comfort Tiffany in the parlor were yet another present from the bride's father. There are nine stained glass windows in the house, including a sunburst design in the dining room that measures six feet across at the bottom. The entrance hall has carved English oak paneling, 12-foot ceilings, a Czechoslovakian cut-crystal chandelier, and seating around a fireplace.

The house was purchased from the original family in 1946 by the Spell family, which has run it as an inn ever since. The inn is furnished with family antiques and photographs, original artwork, and fine silver. In the guestrooms are Charleston rice canopy beds as well as armoires, marble-top chests, and Oriental rugs. All rooms are spectacular but the *Blue Room* is particularly notable. It was the original master suite and has a balcony overlooking the gardens, a window seat in the bay window, a wood-burning fireplace, and an ornate mahogany secretary. Oriental rugs cover the polished oak floors, and fabric in various shades of blue lavishly drapes the bed and windows. The bath in the *Pink Room,* originally the mother-in-law room, retains its original ornate marble sink with its attached mirror and the ball-and-claw tub.

Continental breakfast is served in the dining room, in the courtyard, or perhaps on the verandah—and always on family china and silver. Guests can expect giant homemade muffins (peach yogurt and pineapple with rum glaze are among the varieties), juice, and luscious, locally grown fresh fruit. Afternoon tea also is served, and may include cheese biscuits, poppyseed bread, pecan pralines, toffee, cream cheese brownies with fresh strawberries, and a spot of sherry.

From rockers on the porch, guests look across to *White Point Gardens* and the harbor on Charleston's historic Battery. Located in the historic district, the inn is close to all the city's main attractions, including the *Dock Street Theatre* and the *Spoleto Festival.* Nearby are the *Middleton Place* and *Magnolia Gardens* plantations, beaches, tennis, and golf.

TWO MEETING STREET INN 2 Meeting St., Charleston, SC 29401 (phone: 803-723-7322). This inn has nine guestrooms with private baths, double or queen-size beds, TV sets, and air conditioning. Closed December 24 through 26. Rate for a double room (including continental breakfast and afternoon tea): $130 to $225. Two-night minimum stay on weekends; three nights on holidays. No credit cards accepted. Not appropriate for children under 12. No pets. Smoking permitted outside only. Spell family, owners; Karen Spell Shaw, innkeeper.

DIRECTIONS: From I-26 traveling south, take the Meeting Street exit south. The inn is on the corner of Meeting Street and South Battery at *White Point Gardens.*

Midwest

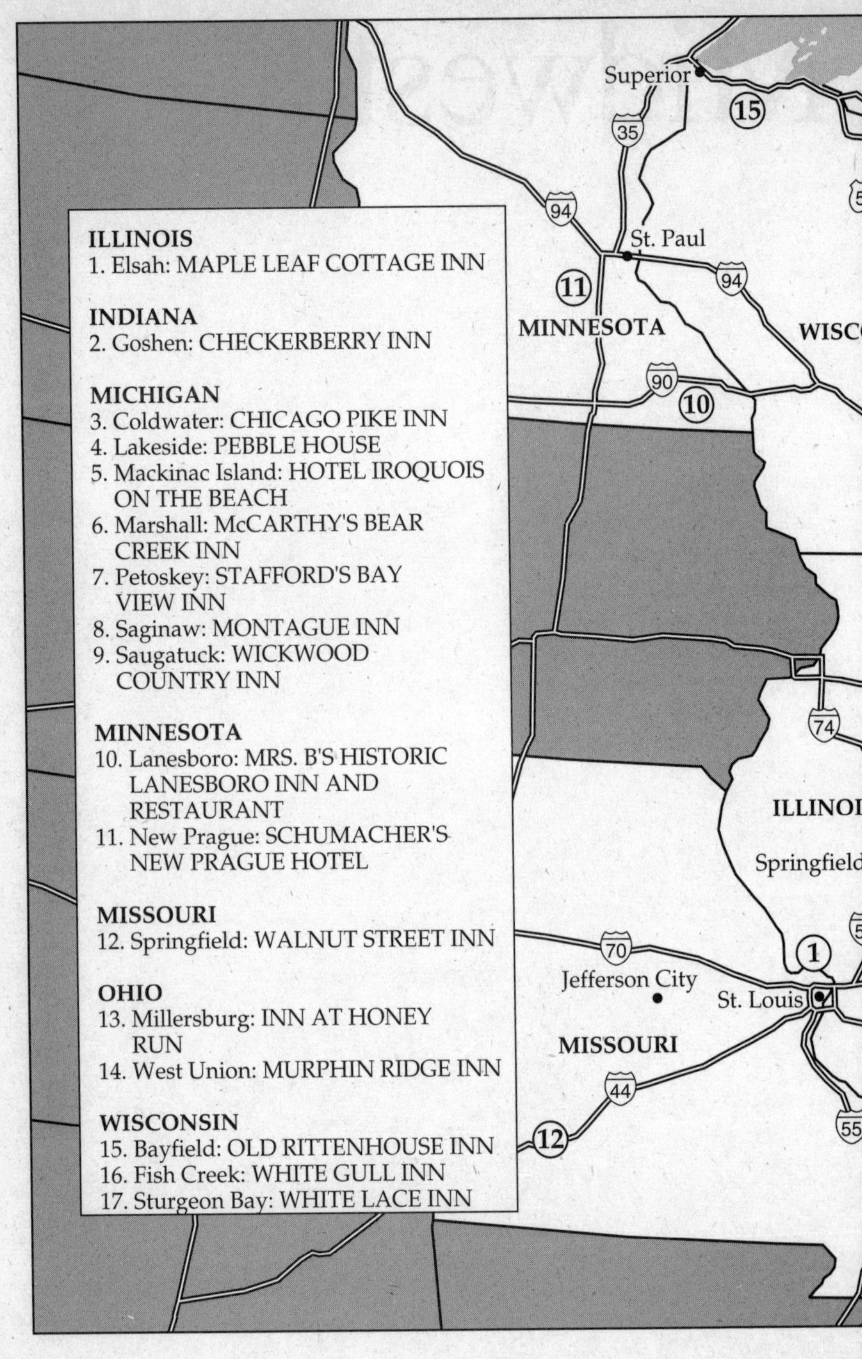
ILLINOIS
1. Elsah: MAPLE LEAF COTTAGE INN
INDIANA
2. Goshen: CHECKERBERRY INN
MICHIGAN
3. Coldwater: CHICAGO PIKE INN
4. Lakeside: PEBBLE HOUSE
5. Mackinac Island: HOTEL IROQUOIS ON THE BEACH
6. Marshall: McCARTHY'S BEAR CREEK INN
7. Petoskey: STAFFORD'S BAY VIEW INN
8. Saginaw: MONTAGUE INN
9. Saugatuck: WICKWOOD COUNTRY INN
MINNESOTA
10. Lanesboro: MRS. B'S HISTORIC LANESBORO INN AND RESTAURANT
11. New Prague: SCHUMACHER'S NEW PRAGUE HOTEL
MISSOURI
12. Springfield: WALNUT STREET INN
OHIO
13. Millersburg: INN AT HONEY RUN
14. West Union: MURPHIN RIDGE INN
WISCONSIN
15. Bayfield: OLD RITTENHOUSE INN
16. Fish Creek: WHITE GULL INN
17. Sturgeon Bay: WHITE LACE INN
Superior
15
35
94
St. Paul
11
94
MINNESOTA
90
10
74
ILLINOIS
Springfield
70
1
Jefferson City
St. Louis
MISSOURI
44
12
55

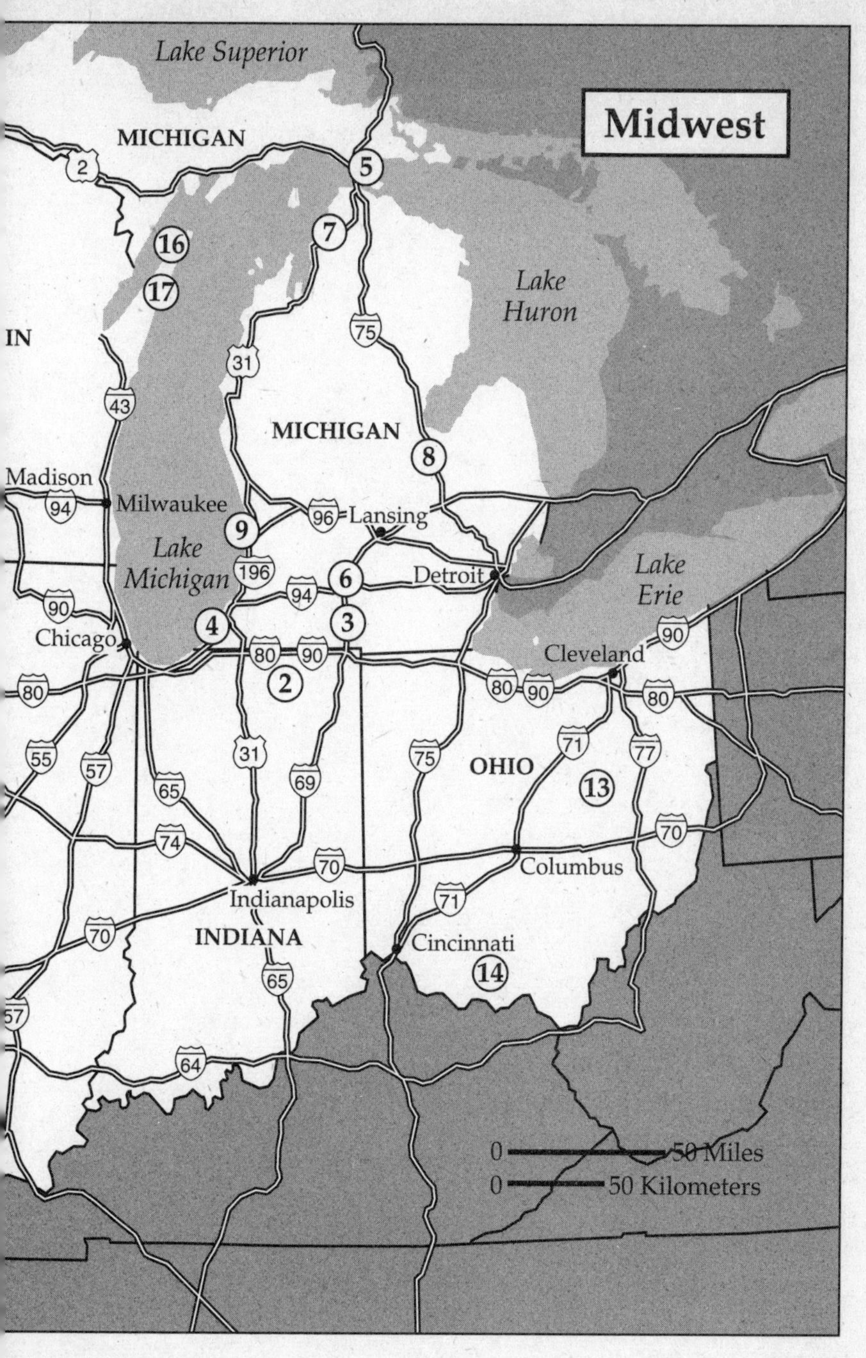
Midwest
Lake Superior
MICHIGAN
Lake Huron
MICHIGAN
IN
Madison
Milwaukee
Lake Michigan
Lansing
Detroit
Lake Erie
Chicago
Cleveland
OHIO
Columbus
Indianapolis
INDIANA
Cincinnati
0 50 Miles
0 50 Kilometers

Midwest

Illinois

MAPLE LEAF COTTAGE INN

ELSAH, ILLINOIS

In the days when St. Louis was the "great frontier" and steamboats plied the Mississippi, Elsah was a bustling little town. Founded in 1853, it flourished briefly as an important shipping center and then languished—only lightly touched by the growth that shaped so many other midwestern towns. As a result, Elsah's streets today echo the 19th century: stone houses with sprawling gardens, a ruined ivy-covered icehouse, an 1887 village hall. The original village (about a mile square) is listed on the National Register of Historic Places, and in the midst of this historic district stands the *Maple Leaf Cottage Inn.* It's actually a collection of four cottages that are joined by interior patios and herb, wildflower, and perennial gardens and together cover a city block.

The main house, originally built in 1880, was destroyed by fire in 1918 and rebuilt in a grander style, with a front verandah and wide windows. The *Maple Leaf* has been an inn since 1930 and has been owned by Patricia and Jerry Taetz since 1984.

Patty has decorated the inn with charm, imagination, and an endless collection of her "discoveries" from the past. The *Attic Room,* for example, contains trunks filled with antique treasures and memorabilia uncovered during the renovation, as well as a four-poster bed and lace curtains. It has a view of the garden. The *Wash House,* which was originally the summer kitchen and then the laundry, is a tiny cottage with an antique white iron bed, plus an old wooden washing machine, flatirons, washboards, and even an old clothesline to remind guests of its past. *The Gables* has headboards made from Gothic gables rescued from a demolished Elsah house. *The Maples* is the site of Patty's cleverest decorating scheme. She had a local artisan make wooden cutouts of Elsah's historic buildings. She then painted them, attached them to the walls, and placed in front of them portions of the original picket fence that surrounded the property. Stay here and you'll feel as if you are on the streets of Elsah.

A full breakfast is served in the dining room. The entrée might be Belgian waffles or extra-thick French toast. For groups of six to 20 people, the inn will cater lunch, a seven-course dinner, or a tea party. The Victorian "gilded tea," served in the evening and accompanied by entertainment, is especially popular.

Guests may explore historic Elsah and enjoy nearby antiques shops, theater, boating, and bicycling along the 14-mile Vadalabene Bike Trail.

MAPLE LEAF COTTAGE INN 12 Selma St./38-44 LaSalle St. (mailing address: PO Box 156), Elsah, IL 62028 (phone: 618-374-1684). This collection of cottages offers six guestrooms with private baths, double beds, TV sets, and air conditioning. Wheelchair accessible. Open year-round. Rate for a double room (including full breakfast): $80. No credit cards accepted. Not appropriate for children under 12. No pets. No smoking. Patricia and Jerry Taetz, innkeepers.

DIRECTIONS: From St. Louis take the McKinley Bridge to Illinois and follow Route 3 north for 60 miles to Alton. In Alton take Route 100 (Great River Road) southwest to Elsah. Turn right into the village on Mill Street. At the first stop sign turn left onto Maple Street. After one block turn left onto LaSalle Street. The inn is between Selma and Maple Streets on the left.

Indiana

CHECKERBERRY INN

GOSHEN, INDIANA

Located on a 100-acre farm in Indiana's Amish country, the *Checkerberry Inn* offers sheer tranquillity. Along the 6-mile road from Goshen to the inn, the only other travelers you're likely to pass will be driving simple Amish buggies.

John and Susan Graff decided to open an inn after renovating the 1880s farmhouse here, but rather than expanding the house (which had become their residence) they built a three-story, butter-colored Georgian house across the road. Black shutters frame the windows, and an expansive verandah with white wicker furniture extends the length of the building. Tennis courts, a pool, and a croquet lawn are incorporated into the gardens, which are vibrant with colorful blooms. At the inn's entrance, purple chrysanthemums and pink and red geraniums spill from earthenware pots.

Inside, the inn has a European feel, enhanced by John's photographs of the Bordeaux region of France. An interior decorator, Susan has used both traditional and contemporary furnishings, from country French to Amish and from rustic to Chippendale. There's a pine-paneled library with a fireplace that invites curling up with a good book and French doors that lead to the gardens. All the spacious guestrooms, named for flowers found in the yard, have views across the farmland. One has a fireplace in the sitting room and a Jacuzzi; another contains a secretary from the 1850s. Still another room has black Amish hats hanging over the bed. All the baths are well appointed.

The continental breakfast served buffet-style might include Susan's special blend of granola or fresh-baked muffins. Lunch (served Wednesdays June through August) and dinner are offered as well, and the dining room is a favorite of non-guests as well as those staying at the inn. One of the most popular luncheon dishes is tomato pie: beefsteak tomatoes layered with cheese and baked in a pastry crust. For dinner Amish chicken breast is stuffed with prosciutto, pine nuts, and goat cheese and served with a roasted lemon and pesto sauce.

The inn is near *Notre Dame University, Amish Acres* (a re-created village), antiques and crafts shops, theaters, and museums.

CHECKERBERRY INN 62644 County Rte. 37, Goshen, IN 46526 (phone and fax: 219-642-4445). This country inn has 14 guestrooms with private baths, twin, queen-, or king-size beds, telephones, TV sets, and air conditioning. Wheelchair accessible. Closed January; dining room closed for dinner from Sunday through Thursday in February and March, Sunday and Monday from April through December; lunch served Wednesdays from June through August. Rate for a double room (including continental breakfast): $90 to $325. Major credit cards accepted. Not appropriate for children under 12. No pets. No smoking. John and Susan Graff, innkeepers; Sheila Reed and Linda Vicary, assistant innkeepers.

DIRECTIONS: The inn is 10 miles from I-80/90 (Indiana Toll Road). Take Exit 107 (Middlebury) south onto State Route 13. Drive through Middlebury west to Route 4. Turn right (west) onto Route 4 and travel a half mile to County Route 37. Turn south onto County Route 37 and travel 1 mile. The inn is on the right.

CHICAGO PIKE INN

COLDWATER, MICHIGAN

Four American flags fly from massive columns at the entrance to the *Chicago Pike Inn.* Located on the old Chicago Turnpike (now US 12), the well-traveled route between Chicago and Detroit, the 1903 mansion served for many years as the home of the Clarke family. Intricate gingerbread trim and a wide verandah across the front of the house contrast with the clean lines of the clapboard exterior.

The Schultz family, which has owned the house since 1987, has lavished attention on its renovation and decor. The reception room contains a spectacular, sweeping, polished cherry stairway and fireplace, said to have been fashioned from trees cut from the Clarkes' orchard. The room has been decorated in a canine theme, with a collection of Staffordshire dogs on the mantel and an overstuffed chair with dog heads carved into the arms.

There are parquet floors and stained glass windows throughout, and fine fabrics by Schumacher and Waverly cover the walls. In the library, the white woodwork of the bookshelves contrasts with the dark paneling in the rest of the house. A Victorian love seat near the fireplace provides a rainy-day retreat, and Jane Schultz's three-tiered Victorian candy table is always filled with delectable goodies. Tea and scones are served here, in the afternoon.

The guestrooms are named for Clarke family members. *Charles's Room* has a Chinese theme and a sleigh bed with a wall canopy; *Ned's Room* has the feel of a gentlemen's club, with a brass bed, a green leather wing chair, and red and paisley wallpaper. There are lace curtains in all the rooms.

The dining room boasts cherry-paneled walls, a built-in cherry buffet, and a large walnut table with elaborately carved chairs and needlepoint cushions. Breakfast is served here and may include an apricot Victorian (a frozen mix of apricot purée and preserves) and wine-and-cheese *strata.* A set dinner menu (served Fridays from January through March and Thursdays from June through August) might include mandarin salad, marinated chicken with wild rice, and a dessert of raspberry trifle. Guests may bring their own wine.

Bicycles are available for guests who want to pedal around the village. Other activities in the area include *Tibbitts Summer Stock Theater,* fishing, boating, swimming, and cross-country skiing. The inn is located near Allen, an antiques center.

CHICAGO PIKE INN 215 E. Chicago St., Coldwater, MI 49036 (phone: 517-279-8744; fax: 517-278-8597). This Victorian inn has eight guestrooms with private baths, twin or queen-size beds, telephones, and TV sets. Wheelchair accessible. Open year-round; dinner served Fridays January through March, Thursdays June through August. Rate for a double room (including full breakfast): $80 to $165. Major credit cards accepted. Not appropriate for children under 12. No pets. Smoking permitted in the library and reception room only. Harold and Jane Schultz, owners; Rebecca Schultz, innkeeper/manager.

DIRECTIONS: Coldwater is midway between Chicago and Detroit on the old Chicago Turnpike. From I-94 take the exit for I-69 south. Follow I-69 to Exit 13 onto US Highway 12, which is Chicago Street. Turn right and go through the second traffic light. The inn is on the next right-hand corner.

PEBBLE HOUSE

LAKESIDE, MICHIGAN

In the early 1900s, the Arts and Crafts movement influenced architecture, furnishings, fabrics, pottery, jewelry, book design, and the fine arts. It rejected Victorian excess and the cookie-cutter designs made possible by the Industrial Revolution. The movement is considered the first truly American style—one that reflects unadorned functionalism.

The *Pebble House* incorporates the best of this movement, as well it might: Owners Jean and Ed Lawrence, authorities in the field, are writing a book on the subject and operate an antiques shop that specializes in Arts and Crafts pieces; they seek out the finest examples for their personal collection and for their inn. Jean, herself an artist, has taught a course on the Arts and Crafts movement at *Indiana University* and regularly conducts seminars. With Ed, she founded the *Midwest Arts and Crafts Society,* and they sponsor special weekends at the inn, to discuss the philosophy of the period.

Set on a one-acre plot directly across from Lake Michigan, the inn's main building is a 1912 Arts and Crafts–style house that had been abandoned before the Lawrences purchased it in 1983. The outside walls, as well as the fence posts at the entrance to the driveway, are constructed of blocks embedded with thousands of beach pebbles, giving the inn its name. Wooden walkways connect the *Main House* to the outbuildings: the *Coach House,* with two suites and a guestroom, and the *Blueberry House,* a separate cottage. Jean designed everything in the inn–from its dried arrangements (made from herbs and wildflowers from her gardens) to the rooms themselves. Each has either a deck or a balcony. One is decorated with Victorian pieces, but the rest are furnished in American or European Arts and Crafts style, as are the common rooms. For example, the living room features a Stickley buffet and a Charles Limbert settle, gateleg table, and buffet.

The bountiful Scandinavian-style buffet breakfast, served in the dining room, includes juice, fruit, breads, cereal, and a hot entrée—perhaps Finnish pancakes with a fresh fruit sauce or baked apple pancakes. There's often a big bowl of oatmeal, studded with apples, raisins, nuts, brown sugar, and cinnamon.

The inn, which has a tennis court, is 90 minutes north of Chicago on Lake Michigan, with the beach just across the street and two marinas nearby. Also in the area are *Warren Dune State Park,* Warren Woods, art galleries, and antiques shops.

PEBBLE HOUSE 15093 Lakeshore Rd., Lakeside, MI 49115 (phone: 616-469-1416; fax: 616-469-5995). This Craftsman-style inn has seven guestrooms and suites with private baths (one is across the hall), queen- or king-size beds, and air conditioning. Wheelchair accessible. Open year-round. Rate for a double room (including full breakfast): $90 to $140. Two-night minimum stay on weekends; three nights on holiday weekends. MasterCard and Visa accepted. Not appropriate for children under 10. No pets. One cat in residence. Smoking permitted on decks and balconies only. Jean and Ed Lawrence, innkeepers.

DIRECTIONS: **From Chicago take I-94 north to Exit 6 (Union Pier) and turn left at the end of the ramp. Go about 200 feet to the stop sign and turn left onto Lakeside Road. Continue for 1½ miles, crossing over the Red Arrow Highway and passing through the town of Lakeside, to the stop sign at Lakeshore Road. Turn left and travel about half a mile. The inn is on the left. From Detroit take I-94 to Exit 12 (Sawyer Exit) and turn left at the end of the ramp. Turn left onto Red Arrow Highway and travel 5 miles to Lakeside Road. Turn right onto Lakeside Road and follow the directions above.**

HOTEL IROQUOIS ON THE BEACH

MACKINAC ISLAND, MICHIGAN

To visit Mackinac Island is to step back to the age before automobiles. Cars have been banned from Mackinac since the 1930s, so no fumes or motor noises foul the air (although there is a marina and a small airport). Ferry service to the island is available from either Mackinaw City on the south peninsula or St. Ignace on the north peninsula; once there, bicycles are the preferred means of transportation (the island has several rental shops).

Mackinac Island is merely 3 miles long and 2 miles wide, and most of it is preserved in state parks. The village, however, has drawn summer residents for many years. They built fantastic homes with broad verandahs, manicured lawns, and formal gardens to take advantage of the cooling breezes that blow off the Straits of Mackinac, which connects Lakes Huron and Michigan.

The *Hotel Iroquois,* a Victorian confection of gables and turrets built in 1902, occupies an enviable spot directly on the beach with spectacular views across the harbor. Its broad windows and porches allow for panoramic vistas from anywhere in the house. The dining room feels as if it's cantilevered right over the water. The sunny common rooms are filled with light and decorated with Victorian wicker and abundant fresh flowers.

The hotel has been owned and operated by the McIntire family since 1954, and their continuing personal attention is evident. The 47 rooms and suites, all with private baths and ceiling fans, offer old-fashioned comfort. Victorian patterned wallpaper and wall-to-wall carpeting grace the rooms, most of which are decorated in bright colors of pink, green, yellow, and blue. Some of the lakeside rooms have private porches.

The hotel's dining room serves breakfast, lunch, and dinner. Luncheon specialties include a seafood-salad sandwich made with grilled crab, lobster, and shrimp. The dinner menu also reflects the bounty of nearby lakes, with fresh broiled whitefish one favored entrée. Also popular are grilled shrimp with Iroquois barbecue sauce and tiny pop-in-the-mouth corn muffins.

Many activities take place on the island in season, when the hotel is open. There's a *Lilac Festival* in June, fireworks in July, a horse show, a footrace, and much more. Also available are golf, tennis, swimming, bicycling, horseback riding, carriage tours, and shopping.

HOTEL IROQUOIS ON THE BEACH 298 Main St., PO Box 456, Mackinac Island, MI 49757 (phone: 906-847-3321 or 906-847-6511, May through October; 616-247-5675, November through April). This island resort hotel has 47 rooms and suites with private baths, queen- or king-size beds, and telephones. Closed mid-October through mid-May. Rate for a double room: $78 to $340. Two-night minimum stay on weekends. Discover, MasterCard, and Visa accepted. Children welcome. No pets. Smoking permitted in designated areas. Margaret D. McIntire, innkeeper; Mary K. McIntire, general manager.

DIRECTIONS: Take I-75 north to Mackinaw City or to St. Ignace. Frequent ferry service runs from both towns. The hotel porter meets all boats and takes luggage to the hotel. It's a short walk or buggy ride from the dock to the hotel.

MCCARTHY'S BEAR CREEK INN

MARSHALL, MICHIGAN

High on a hill, a mile outside Marshall, *McCarthy's Bear Creek Inn* is surrounded by fieldstone fences, its 14 acres encompassing green lawns, rolling meadows, and fields whose mowed paths are ideal for hiking in summer and cross-country skiing in winter. There's also a footbridge crossing a tiny creek. The cream-colored brick, Cape Cod–style *Main House* was built in 1948 by Robert Maes, a wealthy agricultural inventor, who obtained the first patent for an automatic milker. In back is a 1930s slate-roofed, stone-and-wood dairy barn, called the *Creek House.* The property was purchased in 1986 by Beth and Michael McCarthy, who converted it to an inn.

Michael is a woodcraftsman, and examples of his work are found throughout the inn. His Shaker-style pencil-post and log beds—as well as several blanket chests and numerous accent pieces—are featured in the *Creek*

House, which has a cupola, also built by Michael. The rooms here have balconies overlooking the creek. Rooms in the *Main House* are decorated with iron, brass, four-poster, and Jenny Lind beds (twins with spindles on the head- and footboards). Watercolors by local artist Maureen Reed brighten the walls.

The inn offers several comfortable common rooms. In the *Main House*, reading chairs are set by the living room fireplace. The enclosed porch in the *Creek House* has a fieldstone floor and a view of the fields and creek. Deer, black squirrels, raccoons, and even a fox or a blue heron might be spotted.

A breakfast buffet is set up in the dining room. On the menu are fresh fruit, cereal (from the nearby Kellogg plant), breads (including chocolate bread and Michael's fresh-baked blueberry or raspberry muffins), and a baked egg-and-cheese dish.

Marshall's downtown is a National Landmark Historic District with more than 1,200 homes built before 1900 and five museums describing its history. The inn is also near quaint antiques, crafts, and gift shops.

MCCARTHY'S BEAR CREEK INN 15230 C Dr. N., Marshall, MI 49068 (phone: 616-781-8383). This country inn has 14 guestrooms with private baths, twin, double, or queen-size beds, and air conditioning. Closed December 23 through *Christmas Day.* Rate for a double room (including breakfast): $65 to $98. Major credit cards accepted. Children welcome. No pets. A black labrador and two cats reside in their own building. Smoking permitted in some guestrooms. Beth and Michael McCarthy, innkeepers.

DIRECTIONS: From I-69 take Exit 36 to Marshall and turn west onto Michigan Avenue. The inn is a quarter mile down on the left, at the junction of Michigan Avenue and C Drive North.

STAFFORD'S BAY VIEW INN

PETOSKEY, MICHIGAN

Petoskey is located on Little Traverse Bay, south of the Straits of Mackinac. The section of town known as Bay View was founded as a Chautauqua summer campground in 1876 (Helen Keller and William Jennings Bryan were once guests). Some 500 Victorian cottages and campus buildings remain, and Bay View is now on the National Register of Historic Places.

Stafford and Janice Smith met as college students while working at the old *Bay View Inn.* Just before their wedding day, the winter hotel where Stafford worked was sold, and he lost his job. Aware that the old *Bay View Inn* was for sale, he boldly inquired about buying it, and the owner agreed to set him up in business. At 22 years of age, Stafford and Janice Smith found themselves the proud owners of a 63-room summer hotel with only seven baths. Now, more than three decades and three children later, they have pared down the inn through careful renovation to 31 rooms, all with private baths and many with such luxurious appointments as gas fireplaces and whirlpool tubs. Today a new generation of Smiths carries on the family innkeeping tradition, including Reg and his wife, Lori, who are now the innkeepers at the *Bay View Inn,* and Mary Kathryn, who is at *Stafford's Perry Hotel* in downtown Petoskey.

Constructed in 1886, *Stafford's Bay View Inn* is a High Victorian building with a mansard roof, turret, and grand front porch. The interior is embellished with gingerbread woodwork and fireplaces. In the forest green sunroom, guests can relax on the family's extensive heirloom collection of antique wicker, while sipping early-morning coffee. A library on the second floor offers board games and a cozy spot for reading.

The guestrooms contain a variety of antiques, with a full range of beds: two- and four-posters, canopy, brass, and sleigh. Amish quilts gathered on family outings to Ohio and Pennsylvania, accent the modest cottage-style furnishings in the *Primrose Cottage* rooms. The *Trillium* rooms are larger and have views of the manicured ladeside gardens, while the popular *Forget-Me-Not Spa* rooms have fireplaces and whirlpool tubs; three also have decks and some have views.

Stafford's is a full-service inn, offering breakfast, lunch, and dinner daily, in the summer, and weekend dining in the winter. A full breakfast is complimentary to inn patrons; the popular buffet-style Sunday brunch attracts between 600 and 700 people each week. *Stafford's* roast turkey, smoked ham, and famous malted waffles are favorites. The dinner menu features such local specialties as Great Lakes whitefish and local brook trout. Bay View, located on "Methodist land," is a dry community by tradition; the inn observes the local custom and does not sell alcohol, although it provides a bottle of wine for guests to enjoy in their rooms or with dinner in the dining room.

Take a walk along the many trails that wind through here, or borrow a bicycle for a ride along the shore. Play a game of croquet, badminton, or *bocci* on the inn grounds, or walk across the street to watch the spectacular sunset across Little Traverse Bay. In winter, there's skiing, ice fishing, and rides on sleighs pulled by the inn's matched Percheron horses. Chautauqua programs continue to attract visitors to Bay View, with lectures, Sunday worship services, adult education, and a variety of recreational activities in July and August. The *Bay View Conservatory* holds concerts almost daily and noted artists come to perform and teach. The gaslight shopping district of Petoskey is nearby. Sports enthusiasts will find golf, boating, tennis, fishing, hiking, and swimming in the area as well.

STAFFORD'S BAY VIEW INN 613 Woodland Ave., PO Box 3, Petoskey, MI 49770 (phone: 616-347-2771; 800-456-1917; fax: 616-347-3413). This lakefront hotel has 31 guestrooms with private baths, twin, double, queen-, or king-size beds, and air conditioning. Wheelchair accessible. Closed mid-March to *Mother's Day;* restaurant closed weekdays November through March. Rate for a double room (including full breakfast): $79 to $195. Major credit cards accepted. Children welcome. No pets. Smoking permitted in main lobby and on the front porch only. Stafford and Janice Smith, owners; Reginald and Lori Smith, innkeepers.

DIRECTIONS: From Detroit take I-75 north to the Gaylord exit, then follow Michigan Route 32 to Route 131 north to Petoskey. In Petoskey take Route 31 north to Bay View, where the road becomes Woodland Avenue. The inn is on the right.

MONTAGUE INN

SAGINAW, MICHIGAN

After settling comfortably into one of the love seats in the library at the *Montague Inn* with an aperitif in hand, glance around the book-lined walls to see if you can locate the hidden panel. When the fine old mansion was built by Robert Montague in 1929, Prohibition was the law of the land and many citizens went to elaborate lengths to conceal their contraband alcohol. One of the bookcases still opens to reveal a closet where liquor was stored.

Robert Montague, a Saginaw community leader, experimented with sugar beet by-products and developed a thriving industry manufacturing soaps and cosmetics, a business he eventually sold to the Jergens Company. After Mrs. Montague died, the house stood empty for several years before being appropriated by the city of Saginaw for its municipal offices, which moved out in the mid-1970s. In the ensuing years, the house was almost hidden by overgrown bushes and ivy. Finally, in 1986, a group of local couples purchased it, restored it to its former beauty, and opened it as an inn.

Today, the *Montague Inn* sits on eight acres of lawns and gardens that sweep down to Lake Linton, a lagoon that separates it from *Ojibway Island,* a city park. The paneled front doors, decorated with leaded glass, lead to a semicircular foyer with a majestic curved staircase. Furnished with Oriental rugs, oil paintings, and fine Georgian-style antiques, the richly appointed common rooms have numerous fireplaces and bay windows, and there are inviting nooks tucked into stair landings. The guestrooms contain antique furnishings too, and several have four-poster or canopy beds. Original Art Deco tiles and fixtures have been preserved in the bathrooms.

The inn has a well-deserved reputation for fine fare, and the dining room is an inviting place with a large bay window overlooking the lawns to the lake beyond. A buffet breakfast is available daily. Lunch and dinner (also open to non-guests) are prepared Tuesdays through Saturdays. Dinner entrées include rack of lamb with pesto cream and baked Norwegian salmon filled with shrimp and brie and served with an orange beurre blanc.

The inn is in a parklike setting in the Grove area of Saginaw, with fishing and ice skating nearby. *Hoyt Park* is across the avenue, and the *Children's Zoo* is just south.

MONTAGUE INN 1581 S. Washington St., Saginaw, MI 48601 (phone: 517-752-3939; fax: 517-752-3159). This Georgian mansion has 18 guestrooms (16 with private baths) with twin, double, queen-, or king-size beds, telephones, TV sets, and air conditioning. Wheelchair accessible. Closed *Christmas* and *New Year's Day;* dining room also closed on Sundays and Mondays for lunch and dinner. Rate for a double room (including breakfast): $72 to $165. MasterCard and Visa accepted. Children welcome. No pets. Smoking permitted in the library only. The Kinney, Acker, Tincknell, Kiefer and Ideker families, owners; Willy Schipper, innkeeper.

DIRECTIONS: From I-75 take the Route 46 exit (Holland Avenue), bearing right onto Remington Avenue. Turn left onto Washington Avenue and continue to the inn, which is on the right a half block down.

WICKWOOD COUNTRY INN

SAUGATUCK, MICHIGAN

Can you take a cookbook author out of the kitchen? Not unless it's to run a country inn, and even then, Julee Rosso Miller, innkeeper of the *Wickwood Country Inn,* has managed to write yet another book.

Julee's saga began in 1977, when she and Sheila Lukins opened a tiny food shop called the *Silver Palate* on Manhattan's Upper West Side. Soon, they were bottling and packaging their sauces, vinegars, and chutneys (eventually 150 items) and distributing them to some 5,000 outlets across the United States. The culinary duo followed up with a cookbook in 1982, another in 1985, and a third in 1989. Eventually, however, they sold the business, and Julee returned home to Michigan. There she became reacquainted with, and later married, Bill Miller.

In 1991, the couple purchased the *Wickwood Country Inn,* the first bed and breakfast in Saugatuck—a village on the shores of Lake Michigan that now calls itself the "bed and breakfast capital of the Midwest." Julee's verve and decorating savvy have added spice to what was already a successful establishment. She began her career in New York by working for several textile designers, and her use of color, texture, and design throughout the inn are inspired. Floral chintzes, bold checks, and tartan plaids combine to create an eclectic but sophisticated decor. There are paneled walls and cozy fireplaces, accented by an abundance of original paintings and sculptures. Beds are dressed with stunning canopies, or have brass-and-iron headboards. The *Master Suite,* for example, has a cherry canopy bed with drapes and a duvet of navy-and-white Fragonard French toile, plus a bedskirt and pillow shams in red, white, and blue plaid taffeta. It's piled high with antique lace pillows.

And true to form, Julee's seldom out of the kitchen. While working on her fourth cookbook, *Great Good Food,* which came out in 1993, she frequently would zip through the common rooms, dispensing samples of cookies or candies to guests. Breakfast includes fresh juices and fruit, homemade granola, and fresh-baked berry muffins or cinnamon-pecan coffee cake; on weekends, there's often ham-and-pesto *strata,* a baked egg dish. Every evening, an array of hors d'oeuvres is set out in the library, which looks like an English gentlemen's club. Guests may bring their favorite wine along (the inn doesn't serve liquor).

The inn is in the heart of town, with golf, tennis, boating on Lake Michigan, and crafts and art galleries nearby.

WICKWOOD COUNTRY INN 510 Butler St., PO Box 1019, Saugatuck, MI 49453 (phone: 616-857-1465; fax: 616-857-1552). This bed and breakfast establishment has 11 guestrooms with private baths, queen- or king-size beds, and air conditioning. Wheelchair accessible. Open year-round. Rate for a double room (including continental breakfast weekdays, brunch weekends, plus evening hors d'oeuvres): $96 to $185. Two-night minimum stay on weekends. MasterCard and Visa accepted. Not appropriate for children under 12. No pets. Smoking permitted. Bill and Julee Rosso Miller, innkeepers.

DIRECTIONS: From I-196 take Exit 41 and go west on A2 (also called Blue Star Highway). Follow "Saugatuck Business Route" signs to Butler Street. Turn left onto Butler; the inn is one block down, on the corner of Mary Street.

MRS. B'S HISTORIC LANESBORO INN AND RESTAURANT

LANESBORO, MINNESOTA

Set amid Minnesota's farm country, Lanesboro village is also surrounded by 400,000 acres of hardwood forests and high bluffs. A fork of the Root River meanders through the center of town, where trees and 19th-century buildings line both sides of wide streets.

Mrs. B's is a native limestone structure built as a furniture shop in 1872, and the storefront exterior looks just the same, except for the awning shading the entrance. Inside, the ceilings are high; the decor, country Victorian. In the lobby, where afternoon coffee and tea are served, overstuffed chairs and a sofa are grouped near the piano. Stenciled borders line the hallway to the 10 guestrooms. The rooms feature canopy beds, pine furniture, and quilts that create a cozy feeling, rather than one of elegance. Two of the rooms have fireplaces; all have either balconies or decks.

Food at *Mrs. B's* is one of the highlights of a stay here. A full breakfast–perhaps including oatmeal-buttermilk pancakes with blueberries and hot syrup–is served to guests in the cheerful breakfast room. Dinner (also open to non-guests) is a five-course meal that changes daily and uses fresh vegetables, herbs, and raspberries from the garden in season. Popular specialties include a wildflower salad with honey-rhubarb vinaigrette, a warm vegetable strudel appetizer, and pork loin stuffed with dried-fruit compote and crusted with peppercorns. Desserts tempt even the diet-conscious, and

"Mrs. B's Bedtime Bump," a concoction of milk, eggs, brandy, chocolate, and "secret ingredients," sends even the stress-ridden off to a sound sleep.

To work off some of those calories, head for the 30-mile Root River Trail, which passes the inn. This outstanding bicycle, hiking, and cross-country ski route parallels soaring limestone bluffs and crosses 48 bridges along the serpentine Root River. Also nearby are guided cave tours, wineries, Amish tours, canoeing, and—for those on the lookout for something unusual—a tour of a commercial shiitake mushroom operation.

MRS. B'S HISTORIC LANESBORO INN AND RESTAURANT 101 Parkway N., PO Box 411, Lanesboro, MN 55949 (phone: 507-467-2154). This inn has 10 guestrooms with private baths, twin or queen-size beds, and air conditioning. Wheelchair accessible. Open year-round; dining room closed Monday and Tuesday for dinner. Rate for a double room (including full breakfast and afternoon tea, coffee, and sherry): $50 to $95. No credit cards accepted. Children welcome with prior permission. No pets. No smoking. Bill Sermeus and Mimi Abell, innkeepers.

DIRECTIONS: From Minneapolis/St. Paul traveling south, take Minnesota Route 52 through Rochester to Fountain. Turn onto County Road 8 to Lanesboro. Once in town turn north onto Parkway and proceed to the inn.

SCHUMACHER'S NEW PRAGUE HOTEL

NEW PRAGUE, MINNESOTA

The *New Prague* was a very fashionable edifice when it was built in 1898. Cass Gilbert, who also designed the *Woolworth Building* in New York City, the *Supreme Court Building* in Washington, DC, and the Minnesota *State Capitol*, was one of the finest Beaux Arts architects of his day. When he did the *New Prague,* then called the *Broz Hotel,* he created a relatively straightforward building, quite unlike some of his frothier confections.

After John and Kathleen Schumacher purchased the hotel in 1974, they masterminded its conversion into a Central European–style inn. There are ornately carved Bavarian cuckoo clocks, 150-year-old Bavarian pine wainscoting imported from Europe, and carved German chairs. Bavarian folk artist Pipka painted the distinctive furniture throughout the inn.

The guestrooms, which have the same Old World ambience, are named for the months of the year (since there are only 11, there is no July). *August* has an elaborately hand-painted armoire and a gas fireplace. *May* has a canopied bed with a hand-painted design. Each of the rooms has a double whirlpool tub, and a complimentary bottle of wine awaits guests.

People come from miles around for the food. John is a master chef, having received his initial training at the *Culinary Institute of America.* He serves a distinctive Central European cuisine that has earned numerous awards. It borrows heavily from Czech, Austrian, and German dishes, but with John's personal twist. There's Wiener schnitzel, sauerbraten in gingersnap sauce, and such accompaniments as *spätzle, knedlicky* (a Czech potato dumpling), and red cabbage. For dessert, don't miss John's torte, made with meringue, whipped cream, nuts, and chocolate, or the *kolache* bread pudding, made with Czech sweet rolls. In the hunting-style pub, German and Czech beers are on tap, and additional brands are available by the bottle. Breakfast, which is not included in the room rate, features a special omelette of the day.

The inn's extensive gift shop specializes in handcrafted imports, particularly unusual *Christmas* nutcrackers and ornaments. Guests will find a casino, golf, tennis, and cross-country skiing nearby. The *Mall of America* is 42 miles from the hotel.

SCHUMACHER'S NEW PRAGUE HOTEL 212 W. Main St., New Prague, MN 56071 (phone: 612-758-2133; fax: 612-758-2400). This Central European–style hotel has 11 guestrooms with private baths, double, queen-, or king-size beds, telephones, and air conditioning; most have TV sets. Restaurant is wheelchair accessible. Closed *Christmas Eve* and *Christmas Day.* Rate for a double room: $107 to $165. Major credit cards accepted. Not appropriate for children under 18. No pets. Smoking permitted in bar only. John and Kathleen Schumacher, innkeepers.

DIRECTIONS: From Minneapolis/St. Paul take I-35 south to Exit 76 (Elko/New Market), then County Road 2 west for 10 miles to Highway 13. Turn south onto Highway 13 and follow this road for 2 miles to the New Prague exit (Highway 19 west). The hotel is 4 miles farther along, on the south side of Main Street.

WALNUT STREET INN

SPRINGFIELD, MISSOURI

Built in 1894 by Charles McCann for his 18-year-old bride, the *Walnut Street Inn* features 21 hand-painted Corinthian columns, delicate leaded-glass windows, a grand verandah, and Victorian roof gables. Today, it is owned by Nancy and Karol Brown, a mother-daughter team who, after orchestrating a decorator show house here, turned it into a romantic bed and breakfast establishment.

When the Browns purchased the property in 1987, there were dirt floors and horse stalls in the separate carriage house; these have been replaced by luxurious suites, complete with four-poster beds, European antiques, double Jacuzzi tubs, fireplaces, and fully stocked bars. The *Rosen Room,* for example, has burgundy paisley-print wallpaper and white lace curtains, a forest green chaise with colorful pillows tucked into its corners, and a gilt-framed mirror. On the antique bureau are faded snapshots of Karol's great-grandfather. The guestrooms also boast skylights, private gardens, balconies, or fireplaces.

The common rooms are as charming as the guestrooms. The *Living Room* has pale peach walls accented with touches of teal and gold, a rosewood piano, and leaded-glass windows. In the *Gathering Room* a fireplace warms those who nestle in the wing chairs with a book from the room's shelves. The *Walnut Street Inn* may be located in the heart of the Springfield Historic District, but the amenities are thoroughly up-to-date. There's a computer, a fax machine, a spacious writing desk, and other services required by business travelers.

Breakfast, which is served in the dining room, on the deck, or in the guestrooms, might include Ozark "feathercakes" or raspberry blintzes, a fresh-fruit soup, and black-walnut bread or persimmon muffins.

Guests enjoy tennis, golf, boating, and spelunking nearby. Also in the area is *Wilson's Creek National Park.* The music shows in neighboring Branson are particularly popular.

WALNUT STREET INN 900 E. Walnut St., Springfield, MO 65806 (phone: 417-864-6346; 800-593-6346; fax: 417-864-6184). This Victorian inn has 14 guestrooms with private baths, double or queen-size beds, telephones, TV sets, and air conditioning. Wheelchair accessible. Open year-round. Rate for a double room (including full breakfast and wine and cheese): $80 to $150. Major credit cards accepted. Not appropriate for children under 10. No pets. No smoking. Karol Brown and Nancy Brown, innkeepers; Jennifer Branstetter, manager.

DIRECTIONS: From I-44 take Highway 65 south. Turn west onto the Chestnut Expressway and drive for about 2 miles. Turn left onto Sherman Avenue (John Q. Hammons Parkway). Go three blocks to Walnut Street. The inn is on the southeast corner of Hammon and Walnut. Off-street parking is located behind the inn.

INN AT HONEY RUN

MILLERSBURG, OHIO

Innkeeper Marge Stock's dream was to create an inn that would complement the forest and fields surrounding it, and she has succeeded. The *Inn at Honey Run*–60 acres of pastures and woods, laced with nature trails—is a treasure. Though relatively new, it blends beautifully into the forest of maple, ash, oak, poplar, black walnut, butternut, and hickory trees.

The goal of the inn is to enhance guests' enjoyment of nature. The decks actually reach into the forest, and there are bird feeders everywhere. A six-acre orchard has been planted with 450 trees—14 varieties of apple, peach, cherry, and plum. Floor-to-ceiling windows bring the outdoors inside.

The main house has 25 contemporary rooms decorated with furniture made nearby in Holmes County, as well as local art. This is Amish country, and many of the colorful quilts that cover the walls and beds were made by local craftspeople. The spectacular freestanding fireplace in the living room is made of native sandstone.

Some of the most popular accommodations are in the *Honeycomb,* a building tucked into the hillside so discreetly that azaleas, junipers, and heather almost hide it. The *Honeycomb*'s lobby soars 30 feet, and skylights add to the sense of spaciousness. Marge believes this is the first earth-sheltered building with public accommodations in the country. As in the rest of the inn, the furnishings are contemporary: In each guestroom a massive fireplace wall of native sandstone has a niche for a TV. Beyond the sliding doors, the private patio is literally in the forest—wildflowers are so close you can touch them, and birds feed nearby. These rooms face west, so guests are treated to fantastic sunsets.

Two additional cottages are hidden in the woods. Each has a stone fireplace, a living room with a skylight, and a pullman kitchen, with the bedroom up a short flight of stairs.

Lunch and dinner (open to non-guests) are prepared using regional bounty such as trout and chicken. The drink of choice is local grape or peach juice. ("Respecting the religious beliefs of the Honey Run Valley, the innkeeper does not allow alcoholic beverages in the public areas of the inn.") A bountiful continental breakfast served buffet-style is complimentary to inn guests; a full breakfast also is available.

The *Inn at Honey Run* is much more than a place to stay and eat. Marge cares deeply about the environment, wildlife, and local crafts, and on Sunday nights, when the dining room is closed, she sponsors a "raid the kitchen supper," followed by a fireside talk or a symposium. Sometimes the speaker will discuss Amish recipes, or there may be a musical program, a nature slide show, or a photography demonstration.

The inn is in north-central Ohio, where the world's largest Amish population is said to live. Local crafts shops specializing in quilts and cheese are especially popular with visitors. Also nearby are golf, canoeing, and performances of the *Ohio Light Opera* in Wooster.

INN AT HONEY RUN 6920 Country Rd. 203, Millersburg, OH 44654 (phone: 216-674-0011; fax: 216-674-2623). This contemporary inn has 41 guestrooms with private baths, twin, queen-, or king-size beds, telephones, TV sets, and air conditioning. Wheelchair accessible. Closed the first two weeks of January. Rate for a double room (including continental breakfast): $79 to $150. Two-night minimum stay on weekends. Major credit cards accepted. Not appropriate for children under 18. No pets. Two cats, three dogs, sheep, goats, ducks, and geese on the property. Smoking permitted in designated guestrooms and all public areas except the dining room. Marjorie Stock, innkeeper.

DIRECTIONS: From Millersburg take East Jackson Street (Routes 39 and 62) past the courthouse and gas station on the right. At the next corner turn left onto Route 241. After almost 2 miles turn right immediately around the small hill onto Route 203 (it's not well marked). After about 1½ miles turn right at the inn sign. (Beware of slow-moving Amish buggies on the road in this area.)

MURPHIN RIDGE INN

WEST UNION, OHIO

Surrounded by towering maples, the *Murphin Ridge Inn*—with its unique combination of old and new architecture—presides over 717 acres of woods and farmland. Only an hour east of Cincinnati, this quiet haven offers not only serenity and comfort, but excellent regional cuisine as well.

In 1990, owners Bob and Mary Crosset began serving food in the original 1810 brick farmhouse that serves as the inn's *Dining House.* Four months after the restaurant opened, the new, separate guesthouse was completed, and the Crossets were in business.

The three small dining rooms in the *Dining House* are simply furnished with Shaker-style polished tables and plank chairs. Borrowing from the local Amish culinary heritage and adding some Swiss and Southern-style dishes, Bob and Mary created what they call "folk cuisine." Murphin Ridge meat loaf, a hearty mix of pork, beef, onions, and spices served with orange-tomato mayonnaise, is especially appealing, as is the Cedar Run salmon—grilled salmon with a cracked black pepper–and–orange juice sauce. The full breakfast may include homemade Danish and scones, fresh fruit, and cottage-cheese pancakes with local maple syrup.

The simple guesthouse was built of materials compatible with the custom-designed, Shaker-inspired furniture of David T. Smith, a local craftsman specializing in 19th-century reproductions. Two of its 10 guestrooms have fireplaces, several have porches with views of the woods and fields, and most are furnished with trundle beds.

The inn's common rooms include a *Gathering Room* in the guesthouse and two galleries in the *Dining House,* which display the work of local artists. Among the items exhibited, and for sale, are paintings, sculpture, furniture, baskets, dolls, quilts, and ceramics. The inn also sponsors a popular *Art Fair.*

Extensive gardens, a patio, and porches are welcome spots to relax, while a pool and a tennis court beckon more energetic guests. The inn maintains eight miles of hiking trails and has shuffleboard, croquet, horseshoes, and a basketball court. Amish farms, shops, quilt auctions, *Nature Conservancy* preserves, and the *Serpent Mound Historic Site* are all nearby.

MURPHIN RIDGE INN 750 Murphin Ridge Rd., West Union, OH 45693 (phone: 513-544-2263). This inn has 10 guestrooms with private baths, queen-size beds, telephones, and air conditioning. Wheelchair accessible. Closed Mondays, Tuesdays, and January through mid-February. Rate for a double room (including full breakfast): $79 to $89. No credit cards accepted. Children welcome. No pets. A dog, Honey, and five cats on the property. No smoking. Robert and Mary Crosset, innkeepers.

DIRECTIONS: From Cincinnati take Ohio Route 32 east to Unity Road (about 60 miles). Turn right onto Unity, go under a grove of maple trees and continue on Unity to the left and up the hill to Wheatridge Road in the village of Unity. Turn left onto Wheatridge Road and travel 3 miles to Murphin Ridge Road. Turn left onto Murphin Ridge Road and continue for less than 1 mile to the inn, which is on the right.

OLD RITTENHOUSE INN

BAYFIELD, WISCONSIN

The quaint village of Bayfield is tucked away on a little wing of land that extends into Lake Superior, in the northernmost reaches of Wisconsin. Nearby is the *Apostle Island National Lakeshore,* a group of 22 islands teeming with birds, including Canada geese, loons, and eagles; here, too, deer, bear, raccoon, and beaver make their homes. A fisherman's and a boater's paradise, whitefish and lake trout are plentiful.

Sleepy Bayfield was originally a fishing and logging port, and many Victorian homes built in its heyday still grace its streets. The *Old Rittenhouse Inn* is an impressive Queen Anne Victorian mansion that sits high on a knoll above the town and shoreline. The house has four stories of decorative gingerbread and a wide verandah that wraps around the front and side. Hanging baskets spilling over with flowers and white wicker tables and chairs add to the charm. Owners Jerry and Mary Phillips also have added two additional historic houses to the inn complex, *Le Château Boutin* and the *Grey Oak Guest House,* both nearby.

Jerry and Mary pride themselves on the fine antiques that fill the inn's common areas and guestrooms. There are walnut, cherry, and mahogany dressers and beds, brass beds, and Victorian tables and lamps. All the rooms have romantic touches, including wood-burning fireplaces. There is a Victorian *Parlor Room* in the *Grey Oak Guesthouse,* and the entire first floor of *Le Château Boutin* is a sitting area, also furnished with Victorian pieces.

The *Old Rittenhouse Inn* offers fine dining in three intimate, interconnected rooms, each with a fireplace. A six-course dinner (also open to non-guests) starts with a choice of three soups or, in summer, a fruit salad of homegrown raspberries, blueberries, or apples. Local whitefish or trout might be on the menu, accompanied by fiddlehead ferns or mushrooms. In the fall, the Phillipses stage concerts featuring the *Rittenhouse Chamber Singers,* who entertain dinner guests with choral chamber music.

In addition to their innkeeping endeavors, the Phillipses have a thriving gourmet food business. Jams, jellies, marmalades, candies, and fruitcakes are among the items sold at the inn's shop and by mail.

From the porch of the *Old Rittenhouse Inn,* guests may enjoy magnificent views of Lake Superior. They also may play croquet on the two-acre grounds of *Le Château Boutin* or sit in its formal fountain garden. Hiking, sailing, and bicycling are available, and many festivals are held in the vicinity.

OLD RITTENHOUSE INN 301 Rittenhouse Ave., Box 584, Bayfield, WI 54814 (phone: 715-779-5111). This Victorian inn has 20 guestrooms with private baths and double, queen-, or king-size beds. Wheelchair accessible. Open year-round. Rate for a double room (including continental breakfast): $99 to $199; with full breakfast: $5 additional. Two-night minimum stay on weekends. MasterCard and Visa accepted. Children welcome. No pets. Smoking permitted in guestrooms only. Jerry and Mary Phillips, innkeepers.

DIRECTIONS: This inn is approximately 85 miles east of Duluth. From Duluth take Route 53 south across the bridge to Superior, Wisconsin. Turn east onto Route 2 and travel some 60 miles to Ashland. Turn north onto Highway 13 to Bayfield. Highway 13 becomes Rittenhouse Avenue in Bayfield. The inn is right in the town, which is only 5 blocks long.

WHITE GULL INN

FISH CREEK, WISCONSIN

The Door Peninsula, which thrusts into Lake Michigan some 80 miles north of Green Bay, offers miles of shoreline and is a popular summer recreational magnet for boaters and fisherfolk. On the west bank of the peninsula is Fish Creek, a village with a turn-of-the-century flavor.

The *White Gull Inn* has been hosting visitors here since 1896, when it was part of a bustling summer resort run by local doctor Herman Welker. Welker created the property by having houses moved intact across ice-covered Green Bay—a less expensive procedure than constructing new ones. The complex catered to guests who came by steamboat from Chicago and Minneapolis. Andy and Jan Coulson have been running the place since 1972.

The white clapboard, New England–style inn is informal—a place to kick off your shoes and relax. The Coulsons have improved the main lodge over the years, adding to the many antiques that were in the house when they bought it. In addition, there are five cottages with one to four bedrooms each. These are rented to families or groups. *Cliffhouse,* yet another building, has four suites. Eight of the guestrooms and all the cottages have fireplaces. One of the suites has a whirlpool.

The inn has long been famous for its Door County fish boil—the local version of a New England clambake—which takes place every Wednesday, Friday, and Saturday in summer, Wednesdays and Saturdays in winter. Master boiler Russ Ostrand starts a wood fire outside under a cauldron filled with water, then places chunks of fresh whitefish (probably caught only hours earlier) and new potatoes in the pot. At just the right moment he tosses kerosene on the flame, and the sudden burst of heat causes the water to boil over. This eliminates the fish oil from the water's surface and adds a dramatic finale to the cooking. In the dining room, guests eat the light, flaky fish with melted butter, coleslaw, and fresh Swedish *limpa* bread, while Russ entertains with songs on his old-fashioned accordion. A piece of Door County cherry pie, and the meal is complete.

A more traditional dinner is served the rest of the week; breakfast and lunch are served daily (all meals are open to non-guests). Among the interesting breakfast items are cherry-stuffed French toast and scrambled eggs flavored with morsels of green pepper, onions, and mushrooms and topped with Wisconsin cheddar. Locally raised produce and products made in Wisconsin are used liberally in all the inn's dishes. Among other thoughtful touches, hot cider, popcorn, and cookies are set out in the lobby on winter afternoons.

The inn will mark its centennial this year with a number of special events and activities, but its location near Lake Michigan means guests can enjoy swimming, boating, and fishing every year. Also available are music festivals, summer-stock theater, antiques shops, arts and crafts stores, golf, and cross-country skiing.

WHITE GULL INN 4225 Main St., PO Box 160, Fish Creek, WI 54212 (phone: 414-868-3517; fax: 414-868-2367). This village inn has 14 guestrooms and cottages with private baths, twin, double, or queen-size beds, telephones, TV sets, and air

conditioning. Restaurant is wheelchair accessible. Closed *Thanksgiving* and *Christmas*. Rate for a double room: $89 to $165. Two-night minimum stay on weekends; three nights for cottages in July and August. Major credit cards accepted. Children welcome. No pets. Smoking permitted on porches and patio only. Andy and Jan Coulson, innkeepers.

DIRECTIONS: From Milwaukee take I-43 north. Before reaching Green Bay, take Highway 57 north in Manitowoc to Sturgeon Bay. In Sturgeon Bay take Highway 42 north to Fish Creek. Once in the village turn left at the bottom of the hill. Drive three blocks; the inn is on the left.

WHITE LACE INN

STURGEON BAY, WISCONSIN

When Bonnie and Dennis Statz purchased the turreted *Main House* of the *White Lace Inn* in 1982, it was decidedly down-at-the-heels. After repairing, painting, and decorating it, however, they created one of the most delightful Victorian inns in Wisconsin. And this energetic couple never slowed down. The inn now has rooms in two other houses, all connected by brick pathways bordered by colorful flower beds.

The *Main House* was built in 1903 and is notable for its broad porch and ornate oak interior, a highlight of which is the mantelpiece in the parlor. The exterior is done in tints of rose, ivory, and raspberry. The *Garden House* next door, an 1880s country Victorian with long, inviting porches, is painted different shades of green, while the *Washburn House* is butter yellow with white gingerbread trim.

Guestrooms in all three buildings are furnished with lovely antiques or high-quality reproductions. There are handsome four-poster canopy beds, brass beds, and a spectacular 1880s Victorian Renaissance bed. Fabrics are coordinated with wallpapers in Laura Ashley or Ralph Lauren prints. All of the rooms in the *Garden House* have fireplaces, and several in the *Main House* have double whirlpool tubs; those in the *Washburn House* have both. Every guest comfort has been anticipated. The baths are tiled; the towels are thick; the linen is of high quality; and games, puzzles, and books about local history are available.

The continental breakfast features fresh-baked breads such as cherry-orange-walnut scones, lemon-herb bread, or bran muffins, supplemented by a Scandinavian fruit soup or creamy rice pudding with apricots. In the afternoon, Bonnie fixes lemonade, iced or hot tea, and cookies.

More than 5,000 daffodils bloom in the garden, in spring, and from early spring to late fall the perennial gardens are full of lilacs, phlox, peonies, and mums. A Victorian gazebo and Adirondack chairs placed about the garden are scenic spots for relaxation.

The inn is near Sturgeon Bay's historic district, the *Door County Historical Museum,* cultural events, boating, fishing, beaches, cross-country skiing, and unique crafts, art, and gift shops.

WHITE LACE INN 16 N. Fifth Ave., Sturgeon Bay, WI 54235 (phone: 414-743-1105). This Victorian inn has 15 guestrooms with private baths, double or queen-size beds, and air conditioning. Wheelchair accessible. Open year-round. Rate for a double room (including continental breakfast and afternoon refreshments): $75 to $170. Two-night minimum stay on weekends; three nights on holiday weekends and weekends during the fall festival (late September to early October). Major credit cards accepted. Not appropriate for children under six. No pets. Smoking permitted on porches only. Bonnie and Dennis Statz, innkeepers.

DIRECTIONS: From Milwaukee take I-43 north. Before reaching Green Bay, take Highway 57 north in Manitowoc to Sturgeon Bay. In Sturgeon Bay follow Business Route 42/57 across the bridge into town. You will be on Michigan Street. Follow Michigan to Fifth Avenue and turn left. The inn is on the right.

Southwest, Plains, and Rocky Mountains

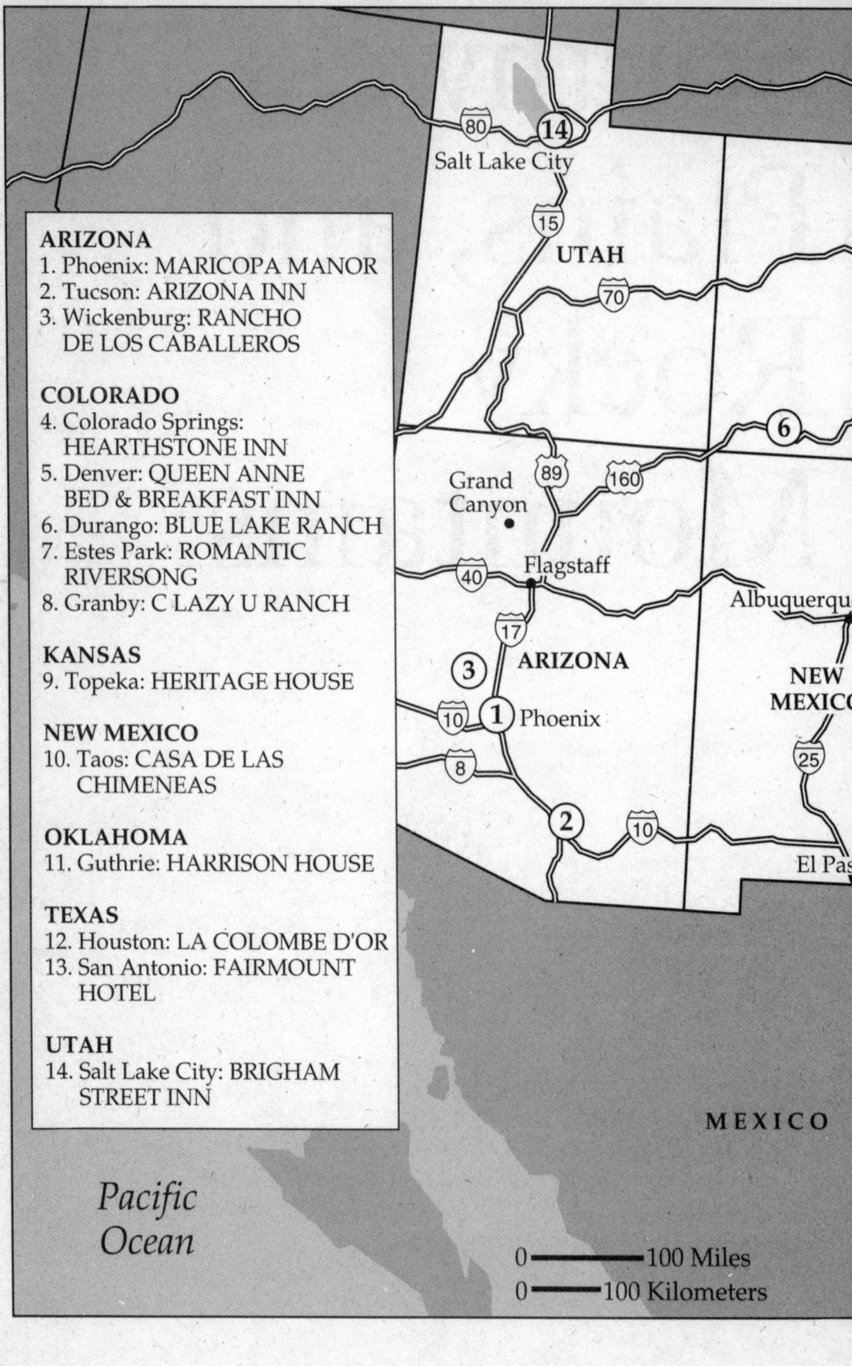

ARIZONA
1. Phoenix: MARICOPA MANOR
2. Tucson: ARIZONA INN
3. Wickenburg: RANCHO DE LOS CABALLEROS
COLORADO
4. Colorado Springs: HEARTHSTONE INN
5. Denver: QUEEN ANNE BED & BREAKFAST INN
6. Durango: BLUE LAKE RANCH
7. Estes Park: ROMANTIC RIVERSONG
8. Granby: C LAZY U RANCH
KANSAS
9. Topeka: HERITAGE HOUSE
NEW MEXICO
10. Taos: CASA DE LAS CHIMENEAS
OKLAHOMA
11. Guthrie: HARRISON HOUSE
TEXAS
12. Houston: LA COLOMBE D'OR
13. San Antonio: FAIRMOUNT HOTEL
UTAH
14. Salt Lake City: BRIGHAM STREET INN
80
14
Salt Lake City
15
UTAH
70
6
89
160
Grand Canyon
40
Flagstaff
Albuquerque
17
ARIZONA
3
NEW MEXICO
10
1
Phoenix
25
8
2
10
El Paso
MEXICO
Pacific Ocean
0 100 Miles
0 100 Kilometers

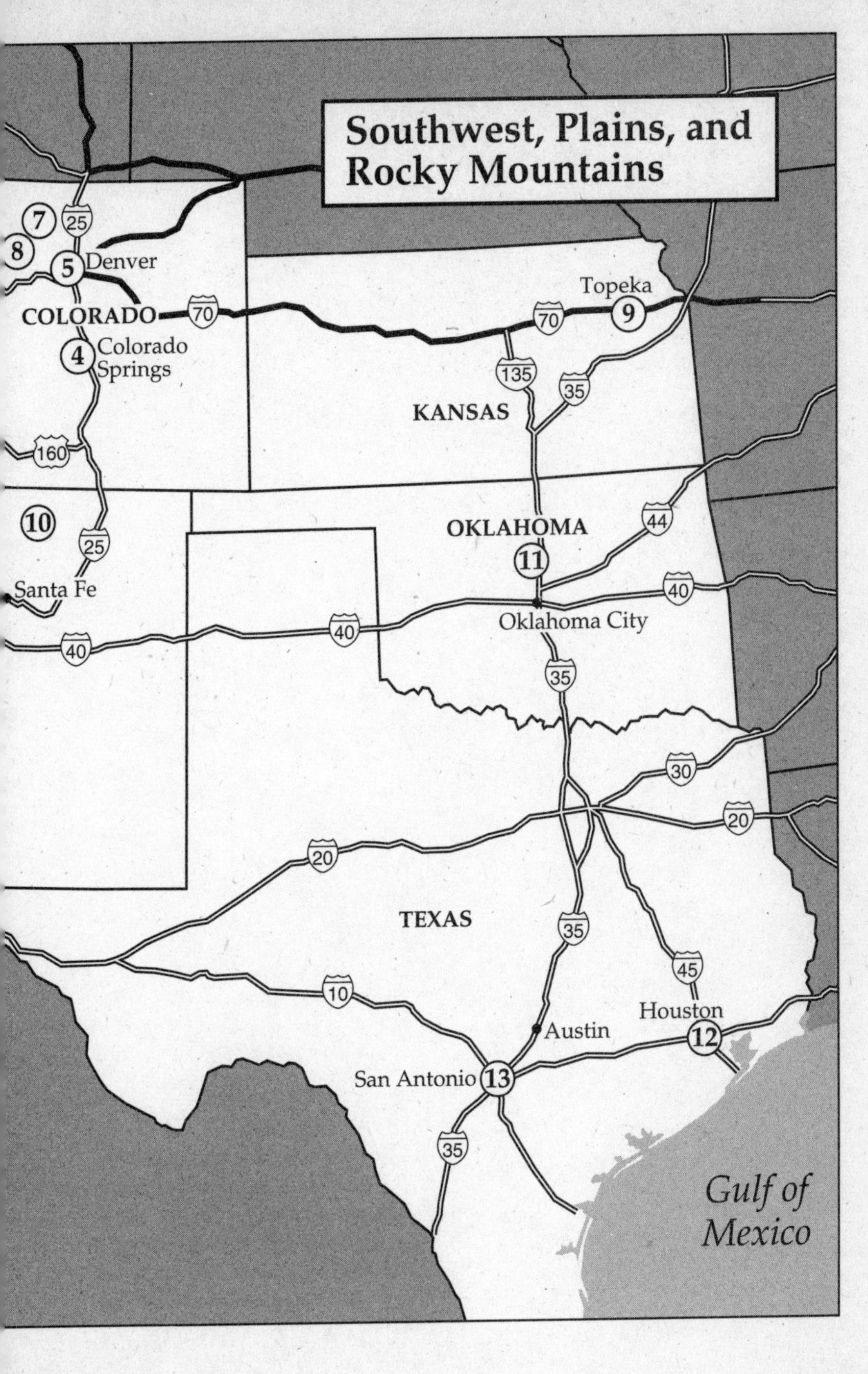

Southwest, Plains, and Rocky Mountains
7
25
8
5
Denver
Topeka
COLORADO
70
70
9
4
Colorado Springs
135
35
KANSAS
160
10
OKLAHOMA
44
25
11
Santa Fe
40
Oklahoma City
40
40
35
30
20
20
TEXAS
35
45
10
Houston
Austin
12
San Antonio
13
35
Gulf of Mexico

Southwest, Plains, and Rocky Mountains

Arizona

MARICOPA MANOR

PHOENIX, ARIZONA

In 1970, Paul and Mary Ellen Kelley purchased the one-acre compound, now known as *Maricopa Manor* (named for the Maricopa Indians who once lived here), because it was large enough to house their three children, eight foster children, and visiting exchange students, as well as Mary Ellen's mother and Aunt Jeannette. Aunt Jeannette is still living there, but as the last of the fledglings left the nest, the Kelleys expanded their hospitality to the general public, opening their home as an inn in 1990.

When the buildings were constructed in 1928, they were beyond the city limits. In the ensuing years the city spread out, so now the inn is close to many attractions. Built in Spanish Revival style, the main house and adjacent casita have been renovated and modernized. Red tile roofs and white stucco walls reflect the intense Arizona sun. In the courtyard, water splashes in the fountain. An outside hot tub is surrounded by a latticed gazebo and palm trees, and there are lovely gardens beside the brick patios.

The inn has five suites, each decorated in a different style. In the main house, the *Library Suite* has a king-size bed with a brilliant blue canopy. Bookshelves are filled with some of the Kelleys' leather-bound collection. The *Victorian Suite* evokes romance with its antique mirrored armoire and accents of satin and lace. The two-bedroom *Palo Verde Suite* has antique furniture, including a carved spool bed with a lace canopy in one room and a king-size canopy bed and Franklin stove in another. The guesthouse has two more suites. *Reflections Past,* whose name comes from its wall of antique mirrors, has a canopy bed, rich tapestries, and a fireplace. *Reflections Future* is in contemporary black and white with Art Deco touches and a sunroom.

The common rooms in the main house are equally inviting. The *Gathering Room* has white sofas and wing chairs; a massive antique hutch occupies one wall. The *Music Room,* with its dark oak floors and a pale blue Oriental rug, boasts an Irish harp, a dulcimer, and an organ. The more formal living room has a fireplace and antique love seats.

Breakfast—fresh juice, fruit, homemade breads, and an egg dish (perhaps a potato or three-cheese quiche)—is delivered to each suite in a basket.

The inn is near tennis, golf, horseback riding, museums, theaters, and shopping.

MARICOPA MANOR 15 W. Pasadena Ave., PO Box 7186, Phoenix, AZ 85013 (phone: 602-274-6302; 800-292-6403; fax: 602-266-3904). This Spanish-style inn has five suites with private baths, queen- or king-size beds, telephones, TV sets, and air conditioning. Open year-round. Rate for a double room (including full breakfast): $89 to $159. Major credit cards accepted. Children welcome. No pets. No smoking permitted in guestrooms. Paul and Mary Ellen Kelley, innkeepers.

DIRECTIONS: The inn is located in north-central Phoenix. From I-17 take the Camelback Road exit to Third Avenue. Turn left onto Third and travel one block, turning right onto Pasadena Avenue. The inn is on the right.

ARIZONA INN

Tucson, Arizona

The *Arizona Inn* has an unusual history. Shortly after World War I, when many veterans moved to Arizona for their health, philanthropist Isabella Greenway opened a furniture factory to provide employment. The furniture they crafted by hand, which included spool beds and spindle-back chairs with rush seats, was sold through major outlets in New York. When the Great Depression came along, the retail market dried up, but rather than close the factory, Greenway started buying the furniture herself. Soon, she had warehouses full of it. Then she had another idea: Her East Coast friends loved to visit Arizona, so she built an inn for them, giving her furniture a permanent home. Today her granddaughter Patty Doar is the innkeeper.

When Isabella built the inn, she gave it a typical southwestern look with pink adobe walls. Despite the heat, the 14 acres of landscaped grounds are lush with green lawns, stone fountains gushing water, and flower gardens bright with bougainvilleas, zinnias, lilianthus, and daisies.

The 83 rooms at the *Arizona Inn* are noted for their privacy. Most have patios secluded by trees, creating personal hideaways. Several also have fireplaces for the cool months. The original furniture remains, maintained by a carpenter shop on the grounds.

The common rooms, decorated with ornate family antiques, include a classics-filled library with a beamed cathedral ceiling and hand-pegged mahogany floor; the *Audubon Lounge,* where bird lithographs hang on the walls and piano music is played nightly; and two dining rooms, one of which is decorated with lithographs by George Catlin. There's also an outside terrace. Dining is traditional at the inn, which specializes in filet mignon and broiled salmon. Both a continental and a full breakfast are available to guests; dinner also is open to non-guests.

The inn offers a 60-foot swimming pool, bordered by snapdragons, poppies, and anemones, Ping-Pong, croquet, an exercise room, and tennis on two clay courts. Thanks to its location near downtown Tucson, there are many things to do and places to go. Golf, horseback riding, hiking in the Sabino Canyon, skiing, the *Arizona-Sonora Desert Museum,* the *Tucson Museum of Art,* the *Saguaro National Monument,* and Colossal Cave are all nearby.

ARIZONA INN 2200 E. Elm St., Tucson, AZ 85719 (phone: 520-325-1541; 800-933-1093; fax: 520-881-5830). This luxury hotel has 83 guestrooms with private baths, twin, double, queen-, or king-size beds, telephones, TV sets, and air conditioning. Wheelchair accessible. Open year-round. Rate for a double room: $85 to $204. Major credit cards accepted. Children welcome. No pets. Smoking permitted except in the lobby and library. Patty Doar, president and general manager.

DIRECTIONS: From I-10 take the Speedway exit. Travel 2 miles east on Speedway to Campbell Avenue. Turn left onto Campbell and proceed to the first traffic light. Turn right onto Elm Street and travel three blocks. The inn is on the right.

RANCHO DE LOS CABALLEROS

WICKENBURG, ARIZONA

The very name *Rancho de los Caballeros* (Ranch of the Gentlemen on Horseback) conjures up romantic images, and the setting—20,000 acres in Arizona's high country north of Phoenix—doesn't disappoint. A working cattle ranch when the Gants began welcoming guests in 1948, this elegant guest ranch (we used to call them dude ranches) is still run by the same family.

So many horseback-riding trails wind through here, that it's possible to go out twice a day for a week and never take the same one. In addition to riding, there are four tennis courts, an 18-hole golf course, a pool, and a range for skeet and trap shooting. Baby-sitters are provided for infants, and counselors will supervise children ages five through 12 on daytime rides, swims, and hikes and keep them occupied with games in the evening. They even accompany children to all three meals in a special dining room, if desired. For families who'd rather play together, the inn will arrange family rides or a friendly game of tennis with the resident pro.

Most of the accommodations are built around a cactus garden and putting green. Each of the brick casitas has two or three guestrooms and a private patio. The *Sunset* and *Bradshaw Mountain Rooms* have wood-burning fireplaces and views of either the Sonora Desert (with spectacular sunsets) or the golf course with its Bradshaw Mountain backdrop. The decor reflects the colors of the desert: Soft earth tones of beige, brown, and yellow accented with bright Southwestern colors and dark wood furniture.

Dinner is served in the dining room, where gentlemen are asked to wear jackets or Western vests. Meals typically begin with a green salad, followed by such entrées as chicken cordon bleu or fresh sea bass. For dessert there might be mocha fudge cake or raspberry pie. Wednesday is generally cook-out night, and there's a buffet lunch every day.

RANCHO DE LOS CABALLEROS **1551 S. Vulture Mine Rd., Wickenburg, AZ 85390 (phone: 520-684-5484; fax: 520-684-2267). This guest ranch in the Sonora Desert has 72 guestrooms with private baths, double, queen-, or king-size beds, telephones, TV sets, and air conditioning. Wheelchair accessible. Closed mid-May through September. Rate for a double room (including breakfast, lunch, dinner, and most facilities): $284 to $396; supplemental charge for golf, horseback riding, and skeet shooting. No credit cards accepted. Children welcome. No pets. Smoking permitted except in the dining room. Dallas Gant family, owners; Dallas Gant and Rich Keily, innkeepers.**

DIRECTIONS: Exit *Phoenix Airport* westbound via the 24th Street exit and follow signs to I-17. Take I-17 north for 29 miles to State Route 74 (Carefree Highway). Continue on State Route 74 for 30 miles to US Route 60. Turn right (northwest) onto Route 60 and travel 12 miles through Wickenburg to the second traffic light, which is at the intersection with Vulture Mine Road. Go south on Vulture Mine Road for 1½ miles to the ranch. The trip takes about one and a half hours.

Colorado

HEARTHSTONE INN

COLORADO SPRINGS, COLORADO

The two charming houses that comprise the *Hearthstone Inn* are colorful delights: The 1885 building is painted gray with plum and magenta trim, while its 1918 sister is plum with lilac and persimmon trim. Both feature gabled roofs, gingerbread porches, bay windows, and rectangular and oval shingles. A pretty fence of hand-forged cast iron, velvety lawns, and abundant flower gardens complete the picture. Although the houses were originally two distinct entities, they are now linked by a more recent carriage house that today contains a sitting room with a pump organ and a banquet room accommodating up to 40 people.

Dot Williams and Ruth Williams (who are not related) bought the properties in 1977 and opened one as Colorado Springs's first bed and breakfast establishment. After several years, they restored the other house and began taking in guests there as well. Today, the inn has 25 guestrooms decorated in period style–brass, iron, carved walnut, or oak beds; oak or walnut armoires; working fireplaces with elaborate mantels; window seats; and private porches. Several rooms have mountain views.

Common areas include a comfortable parlor and a sitting room, both of which have fireplaces. A piano, board games, and puzzles provide indoor entertainment. Outdoors guests can relax in one of the Tennessee oak rocking chairs on the verandah or try out the croquet set.

Breakfast at the inn is worth lingering over. Start the day with such delicacies as fresh-baked spicy apple cake or hot pumpkin fritters, fresh fruit, and eggs baked in a tomato shell topped with cheddar cheese, or baked French toast *strata* (French toast layered with cream cheese and served with hot apple-cinnamon syrup). Guests may enjoy their meal in the dining room, with its old-fashioned pressed-back oak chairs and a fireplace, or on the porch.

The *Christmas* season is particularly festive here. Every December, the inn throws its doors open to the entire town for a tree-trimming party, complete with cider and cookies. Trees in both the dining room and parlor are decorated with traditional popcorn strands as well as hundreds of handmade ornaments donated by guests from around the world—each sporting a tiny tag identifying its place of origin.

Golf, tennis, skiing, and jogging are available nearby. Area attractions include Pikes Peak, the *Garden of the Gods,* and the *US Air Force Academy.*

HEARTHSTONE INN 506 N. Cascade Ave., Colorado Springs, CO 80903 (phone: 719-473-4413; 800-521-1885; fax: 719-473-1322). This inn has 25 guestrooms (23 with private baths) with twin, double, queen-, or king-size beds and air conditioning. Wheelchair accessible. Open year-round. Rate for a double room (including full breakfast): $78 to $150. Two-night minimum stay during some weekend events at nearby *Colorado College.* Major credit cards accepted. Children welcome. No pets. Smoking permitted outside only. Dot Williams and Ruth Williams, owners; Mark Mitchell, innkeeper.

DIRECTIONS: From I-25 take Exit 143 (Uintah Street) and travel east to the third light. Turn right onto Cascade Avenue. The inn is seven blocks down on the right, at the corner of St. Vrain Street.

QUEEN ANNE BED & BREAKFAST INN

DENVER, COLORADO

In Denver's Clements Historic District, these two Queen Anne–style houses (dating to 1879 and 1886) with a pretty garden between them are listed on the National Register of Historic Places. Built by noted architect Frank Edbrooke (who also designed Denver's *Brown Palace* hotel), the 1879 property has stained glass windows, a grand oak staircase, and a three-story turret. In 1992, Tom King purchased it, and the following year acquired and restored the 1886 house with its 35-foot turret.

Guestrooms in both houses are furnished with Victorian antiques—a canopied four-poster bed in one; a carved king-size bed and cherry armoire in another; a walnut-and-ash armoire in a third. One tiled bathroom has a gilt-fixtured stall shower and a window seat. The highlight of the *Aspen Room* is a hand-painted wraparound mural of an aspen grove that extends 12 feet into the turret peak, making the room itself a work of art. Four spectacular suites are named for King's favorite artists—Alexander Calder, Frederic Remington, Norman Rockwell, and John James Audubon—each featuring original artworks by its namesake. The *Frederic Remington Suite* has a claw-foot cast-iron tub, a barbershop-style wash basin, and a small porch with a hot tub; the *Norman Rockwell Suite* features a sitting-room view of pretty *Benedict Fountain Park* just across the street and large bay windows in the bedroom. Two of the rooms have Jacuzzis, and all have fresh flowers and speakers that pipe in soothing classical music. Most of the guestrooms overlook the mountains, the Denver skyline, or the garden.

A buffet breakfast is laid out each morning: Juice, fruit, muffins, croissants, granola, and a hot entrée such as spinach-mushroom quiche or perhaps an apple or strawberry strudel. In the afternoon, Colorado wine and cheese are served in the dining room.

Sitting in the quiet interior courtyard, it's hard to believe that you're in the heart of one of America's largest cities. In fact, this inn's location near Denver's business district and many of its major attractions makes it a popular choice with both businesspeople and vacationers. Nearby are a fitness center, golf, tennis, and the *Denver Art Museum, Museum of Western Art, Colorado History Museum* and *Governor's Mansion.*

QUEEN ANNE BED & BREAKFAST INN 2147-2151 Tremont Pl., Denver, CO 80205 (phone: 303-296-6666; 800-432-INNS, outside Colorado; fax: 303-296-2151). Near Denver's business district, this inn offers 14 guestrooms with private baths, twin, double, queen-, or king-size beds, telephones, TV sets, and air conditioning. Wheelchair accessible. Open year-round. Rate for a double room (including full breakfast and afternoon wine and cheese): $75 to $165. Two-night minimum stay on holiday weekends. Major credit cards accepted. Not appropriate for children under 12. No pets. No smoking except on the porch or in the garden. Tom King, owner; Chris King, innkeeper.

DIRECTIONS: From *Denver International Airport,* turn right (west) onto I-70. Take the Colorado Boulevard exit and travel south to 17th Avenue. Turn right (west) onto 17th Avenue, then right (north) onto Logan. Drive to the end of Logan, to *Benedict Fountain Park.* Turn left and immediately right onto Tremont. The inn is on the left. There's plenty of on- and off-street parking.

BLUE LAKE RANCH

DURANGO, COLORADO

Homesteaded by Swedish immigrants in the early 1900s, *Blue Lake* remained a ranch until 1982, when David and Shirley Alford bought the place and turned it into a flourishing bed and breakfast inn. Surrounded by an Indian reservation and a 6,000-acre agricultural station, the 100-acre grounds include a lake filled with rainbow trout and a magnificent, uninterrupted view of La Plata Mountains, part of the Rockies. In spring and summer, bright colors blanket the hills–purple lupines; pink, red, and yellow Indian paintbrush; and blue columbine.

Today the original homestead, painted yellow with white trim and green shutters, has four charming guestrooms filled with family antiques. The *Garden Room* contains a Louis XV armoire and is accented by a green carpet and curtains in a pink-and-green floral fabric. A French chaise and sofa snuggle beside the fireplace, and French doors lead to a private deck overlooking the lake. The elegant bath has double sinks set into a green marble counter, a soaking tub, and a "living wall" of cedar with clusters of small orchids growing out of it. A spiral staircase leads to the lovely *Rose Room,* where the highlight is a marvelous 360° view of the inn's hills and gardens. The walls here are faux terra cotta, and a mural depicting a garland of flowers held by two birds is painted over the bed.

The inn also offers a variety of accommodations in five cottages. *Cabin on the Lake* was designed to resemble a Swiss chalet. Geranium-filled window boxes line the exterior, and there's a little balcony overlooking Blue Lake. Located on La Plata River, *River House* is an old Indian hunting lodge that has been turned into a two-bedroom, one-bath cottage—ideal for families. *Mountain View Suite* overlooks the iris field and has uninterrupted mountain views. It has two bedrooms and two baths. *Cottage in the Woods* has a hot tub and its own picnic area by the lake.

Several large flower gardens surround the main house—the source of the brilliantly colored arrangements throughout the inn. Adirondack chairs are scattered on the grounds to encourage quiet communion with nature.

A buffet breakfast, consisting of hot croissants, tamales, corn bread, various cheeses, cereals, and fresh fruit, is served in the main house; afternoon tea is served on the patio in summer.

Blue Lake Ranch is about 16 miles west of Durango in the San Juan Range of the Rocky Mountains. Trails leading from the ranch can be used for hiking in warm weather and cross-country skiing in winter. Nearby, in *Mesa Verde National Park,* the *Mesa Verde Cliff Dwellings* reveal intriguing artifacts left by the Anasazi, who occupied these cliffs more than 1,200 years ago.

BLUE LAKE RANCH 16919 Hwy. 140, Hesperus (Durango), CO 81326 (phone: 303-385-4537; fax: 303-385-4088). This inn offers nine guestrooms and cottages with private baths, twin, double, queen-, or king-size beds, telephones, and TV sets. *Cottage in the Woods* is wheelchair accessible. Open year-round. Rate for a double room (including buffet breakfast and summer afternoon refreshments): $85 to $225. Two-night minimum stay. No credit cards accepted. Children welcome. No pets. Inn's pets reside outside. No smoking. David and Shirley Alford, innkeepers.

DIRECTIONS: From Durango take Highway 160 west for 12 miles. Turn right at Highway 140 in Hesperus and travel about 6 miles south. The entrance to the ranch is on the right.

ROMANTIC RIVERSONG

ESTES PARK, COLORADO

In 1986, Gary and Sue Mansfield traded their house in Denver for a 30-acre estate in this Rocky Mountain region of Colorado. They also exchanged their careers (Sue had been a wholesale tour operator, Gary a real-estate broker) for the challenging task of running an inn. *Romantic RiverSong* is aptly named: Its warm, intimate ambience and lovely nature setting make this a perfect love nest. (You even can get married here—Gary, a mail-order minister, has officiated at many wedding ceremonies at the inn itself or on a nearby mountaintop.)

Elegant comfort and rustic charm characterize the inn's atmosphere and decor. The massive living room has a floor-to-ceiling river-rock fireplace and a wall of windows affording a splendid view of the Continental Divide. Many guests like to spend an afternoon or evening in this room, thumbing through the diverse selection of books on the shelves.

Family heirlooms and antiques grace both the guestrooms and common areas. For example, the eight-foot headboard in *Forget-Me-Not* once belonged to Sue's grandmother. The *Chiming Bells* suite has a brass bed, a rock fireplace, a skylit cathedral ceiling, and a bath with a recessed tub in sapphire blue and a redwood-paneled shower with another skylight. The most unusual guestroom, however, is the *Indian Paintbrush,* a separate cottage ringed by pine trees and decorated in a Southwestern theme. A rose tiled fireplace warms the room, Indian pottery and baskets provide accents, and there's a swinging bed suspended from the ceiling by heavy white chains.

A full breakfast is served each morning. It might include fresh peaches with banana blizzard (yogurt and bananas spiked with lemon zest), Irish potato pancakes with garlic and green peppers, a fresh pineapple-banana smoothie (a drink made with yogurt, juice, and fruit), or John Wayne chili pepper–cheese casserole served with apple-cinnamon tortillas. Dinner is available by prior arrangement.

The inn's surroundings are unsurpassed in their natural beauty, and there are plenty of opportunities for outdoor activity. The house sits amid a cluster of pines, with the Big Thompson River running alongside the road. A gazebo by the river, with an old stone fireplace, is a romantic place to sit and enjoy the peace and quiet. The fly-fishing is excellent, both in the river and the many ponds on the grounds. Guests also can hike the trails around the inn and in nearby *Rocky Mountain National Park,* with its abundance of wildflowers and mountain peaks that are snow-capped throughout the year. Deer, bighorn sheep, chipmunks, squirrels, and raccoons frequently can be seen, and if you're lucky, you may spot an elk. Cultural events in the area include several art and music festivals in summer and the popular *Irish-Scottish Festival* in September.

ROMANTIC RIVERSONG 1765 Lower Broadview Rd., PO Box 1910, Estes Park, CO 80517 (phone: 303-586-4666). This mountain retreat offers nine guestrooms with private baths and double or queen-size beds. Wheelchair accessible. Open year-round. Rate for a double room (including full breakfast): $135 to $205. Two-night minimum stay; three nights on holidays. Not appropriate for children under 12. No pets. Smoking permitted outside only. Sue and Gary Mansfield, innkeepers.

DIRECTIONS: From Denver take Highway 36 north through Boulder to Estes Park. In Estes Park turn left at the fourth light onto Moraine Avenue, then left again at the next light onto Mary's Lake Road. Cross the bridge and turn right at the *RiverSong* mailbox onto a gravel road. The inn is at the end of the road.

C LAZY U RANCH

GRANBY, COLORADO

Visitors here can be as lazy as they want, but the ranch hands have plenty to keep them busy. This is a full-service guest ranch with lots of activities for young and old alike, and a veritable army of staff members works very hard to ensure that guests have everything they could possibly want. Located in Colorado's Willow Creek Valley, the *C Lazy U Ranch* has been welcoming guests since 1925.

The rambling native pine log *Lodge* houses a cozy library with leather chairs and a working fireplace, and several other public areas, including a bar, a card room, and a dining room. Off the dining room an inviting verandah with wooden chairs offers spectacular views over Willow Creek to craggy Trail Peak. The *Patio House,* directly across from the *Lodge,* is where cookouts, staff talent shows, square dancing, and lessons in Western swing dancing take place.

The spacious guestrooms, located in separate two-unit buildings near the *Lodge,* have a rustic elegance, with native stone and wood plank walls. They are furnished with sturdy oak furniture, sheer curtains, and fluffy comforters; many also have fireplaces and verandahs.

Meals, all of which are included in the room rate, are bountiful, to say the least. At breakfast, guests may choose from a varied menu that includes juice, fresh fruit, cereals, eggs, pancakes, waffles, ham, sausage, bacon, toast, and rolls. Lunch is organized around a different theme each day, perhaps Mexican fare or a barbecue; dinner is more elegant, featuring entrées like rack of lamb and grilled salmon.

Horseback and trail riding are the ranch's primary attractions; more than 100 miles of trails wind through the 5,000-acre grounds. Each guest is assigned a horse suited to his or her ability for the duration of the visit. Nonequestrians won't have any trouble keeping busy, though, as the ranch boasts a heated pool, a whirlpool, a sauna, exercise equipment, a racquetball court, two tennis courts, paddleboats for excursions on the pond, nature hikes, and trout fishing. In winter, there's skiing, ice skating, sleigh rides, sledding, and horseback riding either on the trails or in the indoor arena. During select weeks, the ranch organizes separate activity programs for teenagers and young children, including lunch and dinner with their counselors.

C LAZY U RANCH 3640 Colorado Hwy. 125, PO Box 379, Granby, CO 80446 (phone: 970-887-3344; fax: 970-887-3917). A modern guest ranch near *Rocky Mountain National Park,* it offers 41 guestrooms with private baths and twin or king-size beds. Wheelchair accessible. Closed April to mid-May, October, and November. Weekly rate per person (based on six people per unit, including all meals and use of all facilities except skeet shooting range): $1,350 summer; $1,300 fall; $675 winter; $1,450 holidays. One-week minimum stay June through *Labor Day;* three nights in September; packages available January through March. No credit cards accepted. Children welcome except in September. No pets. Smoking permitted (no cigars or pipes in the dining room). Clark and Peg Murray, owners; John H. Fisher, manager.

DIRECTIONS: From Denver take I-70 west about 40 miles to Exit 232 (Empire Junction). Travel north on Highway 40 to Granby (about 45 miles) and continue another 3 miles to the junction of Highway 125. Turn right (north) onto Highway 125, go another 3½ miles, then turn right through the ranch's main gate.

Kansas

HERITAGE HOUSE

TOPEKA, KANSAS

Built around the turn of the century, this white wood-frame building was purchased in 1925 by C. F. Menninger and two of his sons, Will and Karl, to house the famous Menninger Clinic. Almost 60 years later, in 1982, the clinic moved to a new location, and the house lay empty until 1988, when it was renovated to house the Topeka Designers' Showhouse. Later that year, the building attracted the attention of Don and Betty Rich, who turned it into a country-style inn.

The house was built of the highest quality materials, and the extensive renovation—both by the interior decorators who took part in the showcase and the Riches—restored all of its fine craftsmanship, including the original hardwood floors. The highlights of the parlor (once the site of the clinic's afternoon staff meetings) are the walls, painted to look like marble, and a fabulous fireplace of green Italian ceramic tile. The guestrooms are furnished and decorated in widely varying styles. One, formerly Dr. Will's office, retains its knotty-pine paneling and has a Southwestern flavor. Another room, done in various shades of blue, boasts an elegant mahogany four-poster bed. The decor of other guestrooms ranges from Kansas country style (with pine furniture and ruffled curtains) to Oriental (including a lacquered four-poster bed and an elevated Jacuzzi).

The dining room, considered by some to be the finest in the city, is open to the general public as well as to guests. A full breakfast may include the inn's version of French toast, made by coating bread with crushed multigrain cereal before grilling it. The menu for lunch and dinner features such dishes as Atlantic salmon with dill sauce, red snapper with ginger and honey, and blackened tuna with a three-mustard sauce; on occasion Colorado buffalo is served. Amaretto cheesecake and a three-chocolate torte are among the luscious desserts.

A large, bustling city, Topeka has many interesting attractions, including the *Kansas Museum of History* and the *Topeka Zoo*. Local festivals include the *Sunflower Music Festival* and *Fiesta Mexicana* in summer, *Railroad Days* and *Cider Days* in fall.

HERITAGE HOUSE 3535 SW Sixth St., Topeka, KS 66606 (phone: 913-233-3800; fax: 913-233-9793). This country inn has 11 guestrooms with private baths, twin, double, queen-, or king-size beds, telephones, TV sets, and air conditioning. Open year-round; restaurant closed for lunch on Saturdays and Sundays and for dinner Sundays. Rate for a double room (including full breakfast): $79 to $159. Major credit cards accepted. Not appropriate for children under 10. No pets. Smoking permitted in the parlor and lobby only. Linda Roberts, manager.

DIRECTIONS: From I-70 take Route 40 to Exit 358B (Gage Boulevard). Travel south on Gage to Sixth Street and turn left. The inn is the third building on the right.

CASA DE LAS CHIMENEAS

TAOS, NEW MEXICO

In Spanish, *chimeneas* means "chimneys," and true to its name, the adobe *Casa de las Chimeneas* has at least one kiva fireplace in each room (some have two). The beehive-shaped kivas, based on a centuries-old Pueblo Indian design, are embellished with hand-painted Mexican *talavera* tiles, as are the elegant bathrooms. The four spacious guestrooms also have beamed ceilings, hand-carved furniture, and luxurious extras such as sheepskin mattress pads, lacy blanket covers, and down pillows. Tiled counters serve as bars, and mini-refrigerators are stocked with juices and mineral water. Each guestroom has a private entrance off the terrace.

Framed by dark wooden beams and pillars, the airy common rooms are accented with plants and illuminated by skylights. A comfortable sitting area surrounds the living room fireplace. The white adobe walls throughout display exceptional regional artwork.

Innkeeper Susan Vernon has created a garden oasis surrounding the inn, with seasonal blooms of irises, tulips, daffodils, roses, daisies, pansies, columbine, lilies, and poppies. A manicured lawn and a seven-foot-high wall separate the property from the street. Cottonwoods, elms, and a massive willow ring the one-acre grounds. Two fountains serve as playgrounds for neighborhood birds, and there are paths for strolling.

A full breakfast includes enchiladas, blue-corn pancakes, or French toast made with whole-wheat–orange–date-nut bread; pears baked with maple syrup and cinnamon in a pastry crust or an individual strawberry-rhubarb cobbler; and an iced fruit frappé. In the late afternoon, guests snack on hors d'oeuvres or sweets, perhaps while soaking in the outdoor hot tub. One favorite is moonshine cake, filled with fruit that has been steeped in liquor for a month.

In the heart of Taos, the inn is a short drive from the *Pueblo de Taos,* which is a thousand years old and still occupied. Hiking, skiing, fishing, excellent museums, and numerous art galleries and shops are also in the area.

CASA DE LAS CHIMENEAS 405 Cordoba Rd., Box 5303, Taos, NM 87571 (phone: 505-758-4777; fax: 505-758-3976). This luxurious adobe inn has four guestrooms with private baths, twin, queen-, or king-size beds, telephones, and TV sets. Limited wheelchair accessibility. Open year-round. Rate for a double room (including full breakfast and afternoon snack): $120 to $145. MasterCard and Visa accepted. Children welcome. No pets. A cat in residence. Smoking permitted outside only. Susan Vernon, innkeeper.

DIRECTIONS: From Santa Fe travel north on Paseo del Pueblo Sur to Taos. The inn is in the heart of town, two blocks south of the Plaza. At the traffic light at the intersection of Paseo del Pueblo Sur and Los Pandos Road, turn right onto Los Pandos. Go two blocks and turn right again onto Cordoba Road. Look for the inn sign on the adobe wall on the left.

Oklahoma

HARRISON HOUSE

GUTHRIE, OKLAHOMA

When the Oklahoma Territory was opened to homesteaders in 1889, some 50,000 people flooded in, many of them clustering around Guthrie, then the capital of the territory. Numerous Victorian buildings were erected to handle the influx. The town retained its political status until 1910, when the capital was moved to Oklahoma City. The town then languished, but fortunately no one bothered to tear down the old structures; today, there are more than 2,000 in the Guthrie Historic District.

In the heart of it all, stands *Harrison House,* which is not a house at all, but a complex of three adjacent commercial-residential buildings dating from 1893 through 1904. The Late Victorian tone in the common rooms is captured so well that guests may be surprised they haven't sprouted a handlebar mustache or a bustle.

Guestrooms are named for figures who lived in town or contributed to its history and legends. Tom Mix, for example, once worked right up the street in a saloon, and O. Henry wrote some of his short stories in Guthrie. The rooms are furnished with comfortable pieces—carved oak and iron beds, mirrored armoires, and brass chandeliers—that reflect the days when Guthrie was a frontier town. Every room is different: Some are lacy and romantic; others have patchwork quilts.

Owners and innkeepers Jane and Claude Thomas preside over breakfast with down-home hospitality. Claude serves, while Jane stays in the kitchen, cooking up fluffy waffles and muffins.

The inn is near golf, fishing, bicycling, museums, theater, rodeos, and historic tours.

HARRISON HOUSE 124 W. Harrison St., Guthrie, OK 73044 (phone: 405-282-1000; 800-375-1001; fax: 405-282-4304). This hotel has 30 guestrooms with private baths, twin, queen-, or king-size beds, telephones, and air conditioning. Wheelchair accessible. Open year-round. Rate for a double room (including full breakfast): $57 to $102. Major credit cards accepted. Children welcome. Pets allowed. Kodi, a black German shepherd, in residence. Smoking permitted. Claude and Jane Thomas, innkeepers; Randy Thomas, manager.

DIRECTIONS: From Oklahoma City take I-35 north for 20 miles to Guthrie. The inn is on the corner of West Harrison and First Streets.

LA COLOMBE D'OR

HOUSTON, TEXAS

In a cosmopolitan city of glass-sheathed skyscrapers, *La Colombe d'Or* is a pleasant departure. Located about five minutes from downtown Houston, on a full city block in a residential area near the *Museum of Fine Arts* and *Rice University,* this former mansion has been restored and converted to a fine inn and restaurant. With only six exquisitely appointed suites, *La Colombe d'Or* is a jewel.

When owner Steve Zimmerman first saw this splendid but run-down home, he knew it had possibilities. It had been built in 1923 by the founder of Esso (now Exxon) and offered spacious rooms with oak floors, high ceilings, dark woodwork, numerous fireplaces, plus a regal stairway. Today, the main floor contains four luxurious dining rooms, a European-style bar, and a library. The bar is especially lively on weekends, when it attracts those visiting the nearby museums. Outside are a terrace and sculpture garden.

Each of the suites is furnished with either Victorian or contemporary pieces, and original art decorates the walls. Oriental rugs cover the floors, and vases of fresh flowers seem to be everywhere. The *Penthouse Suite* occupies the entire top floor and has a Jacuzzi with an expansive treetop view. The baths, finished in marble and brass, are almost as large as the bedrooms. One unusual feature is the private dining room in each suite, where guests frequently entertain friends; they are also romantic spots for special-occasion dinners.

Some people compare *La Colombe d'Or,* a member of the prestigious Relais & Châteaux group, to an *auberge* in the south of France; certainly, the acclaimed restaurant compares favorably with that country's finest. It has received many awards for its distinctive cuisine—the rack of lamb is a favorite—and is renowned for its "Oil Barrel Baron Special," a three-course lunch which costs the same as the day's price for a barrel of West Texas crude. Breakfast is available to guests; both the restaurant and bar are open to non-guests for lunch and dinner.

The inn is in the heart of Houston's museum district, not far from the *Astrodome.*

LA COLOMBE D'OR 3410 Montrose Blvd., Houston, TX 77006 (phone: 713-524-7999; fax: 713-524-8923). The inn has six suites with private baths, king-size beds, telephones, TV sets, and air conditioning. Open year-round. Rate for a double room: $195 to $575. Major credit cards accepted. Children welcome. Small pets allowed. Smoking permitted. Steve Zimmerman, innkeeper; Patrice Huart, manager.

DIRECTIONS: From downtown Houston take Main Street north to Elgin Street. Go west on Elgin, which becomes Westheimer after two blocks. At Montrose Boulevard turn left and travel one and a half blocks to the inn.

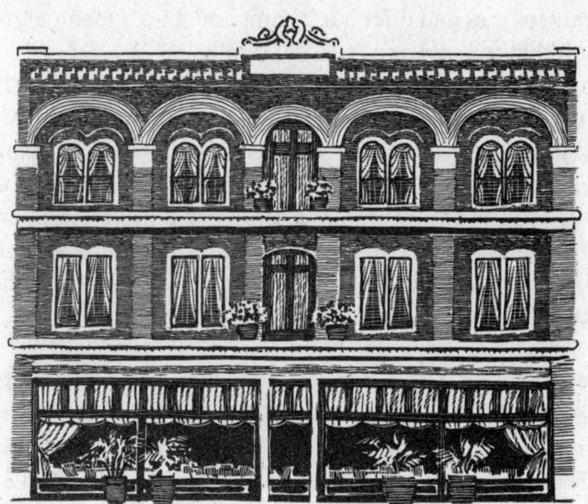

FAIRMOUNT HOTEL

SAN ANTONIO, TEXAS

The *Fairmount* has the distinction of being the heaviest building ever moved, an achievement documented in the *Guinness Book of World Records.* Built in 1906 as a hotel for travelers on the city's new railroad, the Italianate Victorian building was rescued from demolition and moved through the streets of San Antonio and across the river in 1985. The move took six days and cost $650,000. When excavating the new site, archaeologists from the

University of Texas unearthed cannonballs, muskets, and bayonets from the Battle of the Alamo. Apparently, the hotel's new site had been the preparation area for the army of Mexican General Santa Anna.

Most of the interior and exterior of the hotel was intact, including the front verandahs and back porches. Although 10 new rooms and a porte cochère were added, the work was done so well that it's indiscernible from the original. Today the interior—with its high ceilings, stone and marble finishes, and rich woods–is a shining example of historic preservation.

The entire inn is furnished in an elegant Southwestern theme. The lobby contains Mexican marble floors accented by textured rugs with Native American motifs. Warm desert colors on the plush sofas and chairs are enlivened by peach walls. There are stone lamps, and contemporary abstract art graces the walls. The theme continues in *Polo's at The Fairmount,* the hotel's full-service restaurant, which has bleached oak floors and ivory banquettes. Dinner entrées might include grilled chicken stuffed with proscuitto and jalapeños and served with cranberry chutney, or grilled rack of lamb with a peppered crust, sliced and served with a blackberry-sage sauce.

The 20 guestrooms and 17 suites all have lofty ceilings and expansive windows for a light, airy feeling. Some have canopy beds. In-house movies are available at no additional charge. The baths are done in Italian marble with brass fixtures and offer a full complement of amenities, including terry robes and lighted makeup mirrors.

The *Fairmount* is in San Antonio's historic district, across the street from the *Convention Center* and near the *Governor's Palace* and *Hemisfair Park.* It's also near *Riverwalk,* San Antonio's unique walking street that stretches for 2 miles along both sides of the lazy San Antonio River, which twists and turns through town. The walk crosses back and forth over little arched bridges and leads past the numerous boutiques and restaurants housed in tile-roofed adobe buildings with courtyards full of bright hibiscus and azaleas and shady oak and pecan trees.

FAIRMOUNT HOTEL 401 S. Alamo St., San Antonio, TX 78205 (phone: 210-224-8800; 800-642-3363; fax: 210-224-2767). The hotel has 37 units with private baths, queen-size beds, telephones, TV sets, and air conditioning. Wheelchair accessible. Open year-round. Rate for a double room: $185 to $475. Two-night minimum stay on weekends. Major credit cards accepted. Children welcome. No pets. Smoking permitted only in designated guestrooms and the bar. Linda Finger, manager.

DIRECTIONS: From the airport follow Route 281 south for approximately 10 miles to downtown San Antonio. Take the Commerce Street exit, and get into the far left lane. At the third traffic light turn left onto Alamo Street. Go through two traffic lights; the hotel is on the right, at the corner of Alamo and Nueva.

Utah

BRIGHAM STREET INN

SALT LAKE CITY, UTAH

In 1982, Nancy Pace was looking for a house to use as a designers' showhouse to benefit the *Utah Heritage Foundation,* on whose board she served at the time. She came across a red brick Victorian mansion, built in 1896 by a wool merchant and located on the same street where Mormon leader Brigham Young had lived. Although the house was extremely dilapidated, Nancy recognized its potential. She bought the place, and after the showhouse was over, she gave it new life as the *Brigham Street Inn.*

The common rooms reflect the character of a grand, late-19th-century mansion. There are eight working fireplaces, some with original tile facings; warm woods are found throughout. Golden oak wainscoting highlights the entry, and bird's-eye maple was used for the mantel of the tiled fireplace in the parlor. Nancy's extensive collection of paintings by local artists can be seen throughout the inn. Guests may play the Steinway grand piano in the gracious music room, with its dramatic black walls, white woodwork, and richly carved mantel. A 17th-century Tibetan tapestry graces one wall of the dining room, where guests enjoy the continental breakfast each morning.

Each of the nine guestrooms was decorated for the showhouse by a different local designer in a different style—Victorian, colonial, Asian, contemporary, and so on. Several have fireplaces, and one room (No. 4) has a balcony.

Salt Lake City has all of the historical and cultural attractions of a state capital. *Temple Square,* the heart of the Mormon church, is near the inn, as are the *University of Utah,* performances by the *Mormon Tabernacle Choir, Ballet West,* and the *Utah Symphony,* and several museums. In addition, several ski areas are within a half-hour drive of the city. If you need guidance, Nancy, who now works for the *Salt Lake County Convention and Visitors Bureau,* has plenty of information.

BRIGHAM STREET INN 1135 E. South Temple, Salt Lake City, UT 84102 (phone: 801-364-4461; 800-417-4461; fax: 801-521-3201). An elegant bed and breakfast mansion in the heart of downtown Salt Lake City, it offers nine guestrooms with private baths, twin or queen-size beds, telephones, TV sets, and air conditioning. Open year-round. Rate for a double room (including continental breakfast): $115 to $175. Major credit cards accepted. Not appropriate for children under 18. No pets. Smoking permitted in guestrooms only. Nancy Pace, innkeeper; Jeffrey R. Pace and Susan Scott, managers.

DIRECTIONS: From the airport travel east on North Temple Street to *Temple Square* (where North Temple intersects South Temple). From there turn right and travel 11 blocks on South Temple to the inn.

California

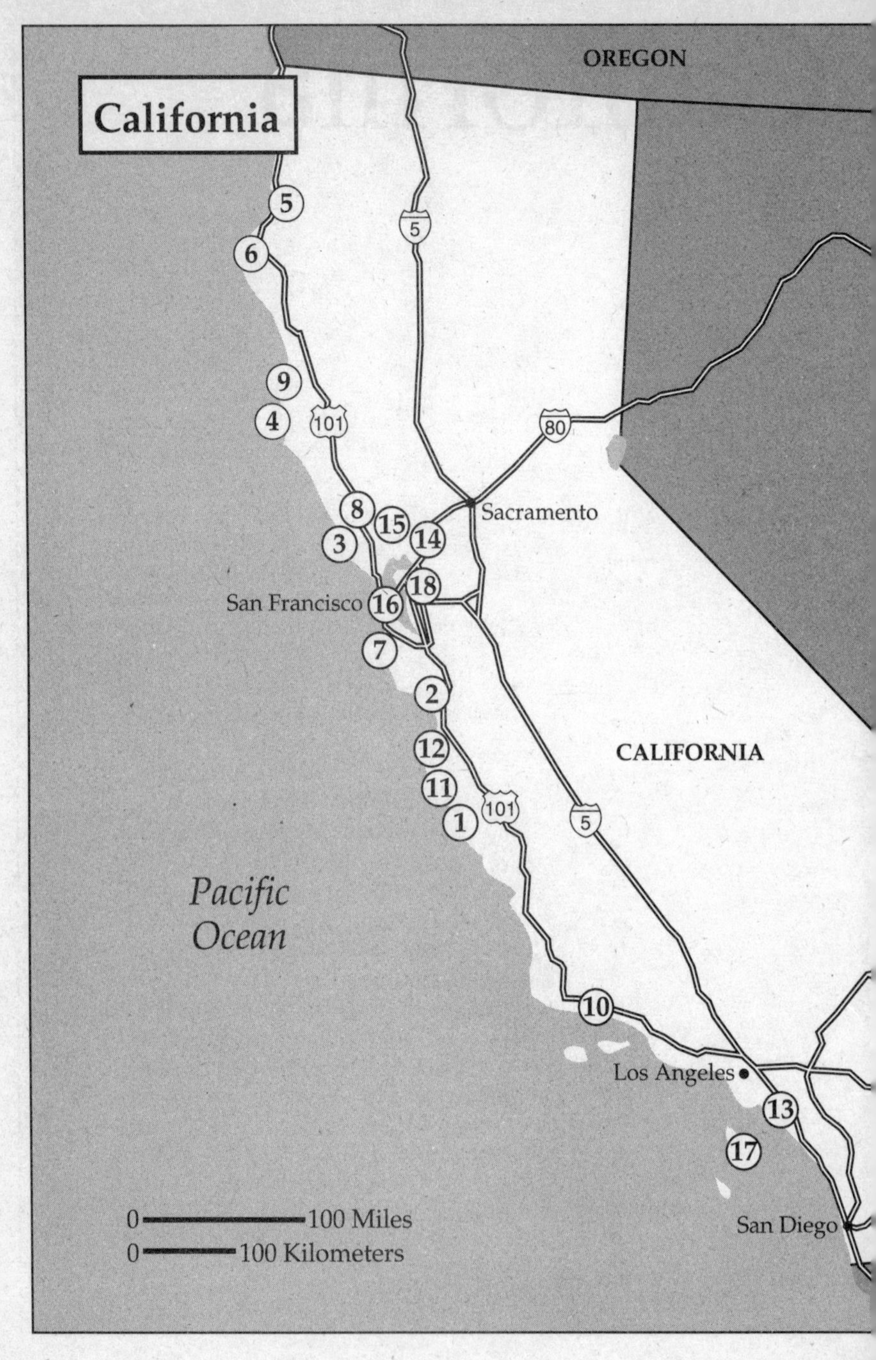
California
OREGON
CALIFORNIA
Sacramento
San Francisco
Los Angeles
San Diego
Pacific
Ocean
5
101
80
1
2
3
4
5
6
7
8
9
10
11
12
13
14
15
16
17
18
0 100 Miles
0 100 Kilometers

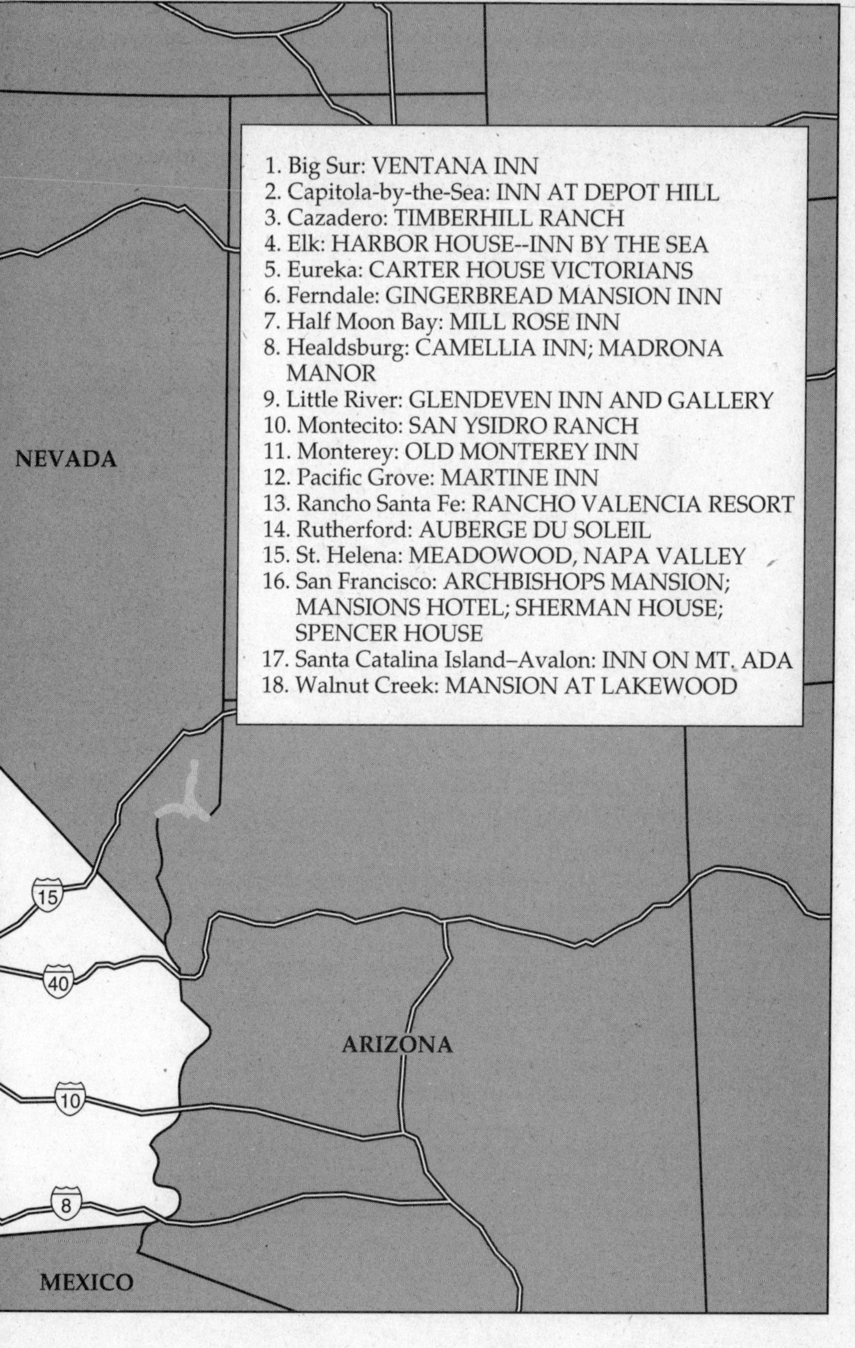
1. Big Sur: VENTANA INN
2. Capitola-by-the-Sea: INN AT DEPOT HILL
3. Cazadero: TIMBERHILL RANCH
4. Elk: HARBOR HOUSE--INN BY THE SEA
5. Eureka: CARTER HOUSE VICTORIANS
6. Ferndale: GINGERBREAD MANSION INN
7. Half Moon Bay: MILL ROSE INN
8. Healdsburg: CAMELLIA INN; MADRONA MANOR
9. Little River: GLENDEVEN INN AND GALLERY
10. Montecito: SAN YSIDRO RANCH
11. Monterey: OLD MONTEREY INN
12. Pacific Grove: MARTINE INN
13. Rancho Santa Fe: RANCHO VALENCIA RESORT
14. Rutherford: AUBERGE DU SOLEIL
15. St. Helena: MEADOWOOD, NAPA VALLEY
16. San Francisco: ARCHBISHOPS MANSION; MANSIONS HOTEL; SHERMAN HOUSE; SPENCER HOUSE
17. Santa Catalina Island–Avalon: INN ON MT. ADA
18. Walnut Creek: MANSION AT LAKEWOOD
NEVADA
ARIZONA
MEXICO
15
40
10
8

California

VENTANA INN

BIG SUR, CALIFORNIA

The surf pounds against the rocks and salt spray fills the air as guests drive along Highway 1 toward the *Ventana Inn,* 28 miles south of Carmel. On the other side of the road, rolling hills are covered with oak, redwood, and bay laurel trees, and meadows are blanketed in wild poppies.

Located on 243 acres atop a bluff overlooking the perpetual drama of the ocean (*ventana* means "window" in Spanish), the inn was built in 1975. Preservation of the natural environment has been a keystone of the *Ventana* philosophy from the beginning, and although the inn is now owned by the Transamerica Corporation, that philosophy remains an important part of the operation. It has a complete recycling program, practices organic gardening, encourages water and energy conservation, and features indigenous plants on its grounds.

The inn's 12 cedar-sided buildings boast 59 guestrooms; there is also one private cottage. On entering the main lodge, new arrivals may find a fire crackling in the massive stone fireplace, as guests gather for afternoon wine, fruit, and cheese. Picture windows overlook mountains meeting the sea.

Ventana is a casual, relaxed resort, and in keeping with the informality, furnishings are simple yet stylish. Rattan chairs are cushioned in striped fabrics; headboards, end tables, and chests are custom-made of cedar. Walls are finished in cedar as well, giving them a fresh-from-the-woods smell. Most of the rooms have stone fireplaces, with an ample supply of logs provided. All have large, private decks; some feature private hot tubs. Windows overlook either the ocean, the Santa Lucia Mountains, or the forest.

The inn is also a spa. Its complete fitness center is equipped with treadmills, bicycles, and weights, and there are two heated swimming pools, a sauna, and communal Japanese hot tubs. Trained practitioners offer a variety of massages. The screened sun deck is a clothing-optional area.

With a romantic view of the coast, the restaurant (also open to nonguests) is decorated with red tile floors and redwood tables. The food is California style, with an emphasis on fresh local seafood prepared in an uncomplicated manner. Whole rainbow trout may be accompanied by a salad of baby chicory; vegetarian plates are made to order. A buffet breakfast of fruit and fresh-baked breads is available to inn guests in the lobby or delivered to the room.

Pathways lead from the inn through the woods, down to the beach, and across the meadows. Nearby are boutiques and hiking.

VENTANA INN Hwy. 1, Big Sur, CA 93920 (phone: 408-667-2331; 800-628-6500, reservations; fax: 408-667-0513). This oceanfront resort has 59 guestrooms with private baths, queen- or king-size beds, telephones, TV sets, and air conditioning. Wheelchair accessible. Open year-round. Rate for a double room (including continental breakfast and afternoon wine and cheese): $175 to $400. Two-night minimum stay on weekends and holidays. Major credit cards accepted. Not appropriate for children under 18. No pets. Smoking permitted in 12 guestrooms only. Randy Smith, general manager; Lisa Mitchell, inn manager.

DIRECTIONS: The inn is 152 miles south of San Francisco. From San Francisco take Highway 101 south to Salinas, then follow Route 68 to Monterey. In Monterey take Highway 1 south for 32 miles to the inn.

INN AT DEPOT HILL

Capitola-by-the-Sea, California

At one time, this Southern Pacific depot, a 1901 train station on the bluffs above the village of Capitola and Monterey Bay, was a stop on the "Suntan Special" route from San Francisco to Salinas. In 1990, innkeepers Suzie Lankes and Dan Floyd transformed the structure into Capitola's first bed and breakfast establishment.

The inn retains much of the old railway station's romantic aura. Doric columns (some new ones hand-milled to match the originals) support the eaves surrounding the simple tan-and-white building, and the bay window in the dining room was originally the ticket window. The parlor/library has a baby grand piano, a gilded Venetian glass chandelier, a fireplace, and an abundance of railroad memorabilia; books about trains fill the bookcases.

A wrought-iron gate opens to a red brick courtyard and, around back, a garden patio is bordered by beds of climbing roses, trumpet vines, and azaleas.

In keeping with the travel theme, the eight guestrooms are named after locations around the world and decorated accordingly. The *Delft Suite,* for example, is decorated with delftware and has a fireplace faced with blue-and-white tiles, a wrought-iron bed with floor-to-ceiling drapes in blue-and-white chintz, and lace curtains at the windows. Planted with pink and white tulips, the suite's private garden boasts an outdoor Jacuzzi. All of the guestrooms have fireplaces, and most have either four-poster or canopy beds and balconies or patios. In-room extras include a VCR (there's a lending library of tapes), dual shower heads, and fresh flowers.

A full breakfast—juice, fruit, croissants, cinnamon rolls, and an entrée—is served to inn guests on a unique three-legged, paw-footed table in the dining room. Entrées, also based on the fare of different countries (such as Belgian waffles or Mexican quiche), change daily. In the afternoon, hors d'oeuvres and wine are set out, and following dinner at a local restaurant, guests may indulge in one of the inn's desserts—coconut-nut tart and lemon-yogurt cake head the list.

Inn at Depot Hill is near beaches, golf, shops, art galleries, and museums.

INN AT DEPOT HILL **250 Monterey Ave., Capitola-by-the-Sea, CA 95010 (408-462-3376; 800-572-2632; fax: 408-462-3697). This inn has eight guestrooms with private baths, queen- or king-size beds, telephones, and TV sets. Wheelchair accessible. Open year-round. Rate for a double room (including full breakfast, wine and hors d'oeuvres, and evening dessert): $165 to $275. Two-night minimum if stay includes Saturday night. Major credit cards accepted. Not appropriate for children under 14. No pets. Smoking permitted outside only. Suzanne Lankes and Dan Floyd, innkeepers; Inez Marshall, manager.**

DIRECTIONS: From Highway 101 or I-280 traveling south, take the exit to Highway 17/880 toward Santa Cruz. Pass the Soquel/Capitola exit and take the Monterey/Watsonville exit onto Highway 1, which parallels the coast. Leave Highway 1 at the Park Avenue/New Brighton Beach exit and proceed 1 mile to the T-intersection with Monterey Avenue. Turn left and immediately left again into the driveway of the inn, which is located on the corner of Park and Monterey Avenues.

TIMBERHILL RANCH

CAZADERO, CALIFORNIA

Winding up the coastal highway toward *Timberhill Ranch* and then wandering through its 80 acres, you'll pass meadows peppered with wild iris, bluebells, and forget-me-nots and groves of blood-red madrona, oak, and fir trees standing beside majestic, spicy-scented redwoods. Horses, llamas, sheep, and goats graze contentedly beside the road. The ranch sits in a clearing set 1,000 feet above the Pacific Ocean's coastal fog and wind. Although located in Sonoma County, it is separated from the Sonoma Valley by a range of low mountains. In the 1800s, the Pomo Indians chose this sheltered slice of northern California coast for their winter home. Today, the serenity, here, is a balm for modern jangled nerves.

On arrival at the ranch, you will be met by one of the four owners, Tarran McDaid, Michael Riordan, Barbara Farrell, or Frank Watson, all of whom left high-pressure corporate jobs in San Francisco for the peace and quiet of these hills. They live on the ranch and share many of the innkeeping duties.

A working ranch in the 1930s, then a school, the main house was restored in 1984. Its cedar-shake exterior may look rustic, but the interior will immediately dispel any worries about "roughing it." Beneath a vaulted ceiling guests relax on comfortable sofas before a large fieldstone fireplace. Books, magazines, puzzles, cards, and games offer entertainment when night masks the spectacular views across the meadows.

Each guestroom is located in a separate cedar-clad cottage with a wood-burning fireplace. The air is infused with the heady smell of warm cedar, and nothing disturbs the tranquillity. The furniture is hand-crafted in pine and walnut; colorful quilts, handmade by local artisans, cover the beds. A private deck affords views of the surrounding landscape, spectacularly enhanced in the evening by sunsets. Privacy is paramount at *Timberhill,* and even turndown service, which includes a small bouquet of flowers and chocolates placed on each pillow, will be withheld on request.

In the morning, continental breakfast is delivered to each door (a full breakfast is available for a supplemental charge). Lunch, which some guests choose to take in a picnic basket, also is available daily for an additional fee. In the candlelit dining room, the six-course evening meal (open to non-guests by reservation only) begins with a selection of appetizers and progresses through soup, salad, sorbet, entrée, and dessert. The menu might include roast Petaluma duckling with sun-dried figs or grilled Pacific salmon with tomatillo *coulis.* All breads and desserts are made on the premises, and there's a fine selection of California wines.

Bordered by the 317-acre *Kruse Rhododendron Reserve* and 6,000-acre *Salt Point State Park,* the ranch offers miles of hiking trails that traverse the park and the inn property. Also on the grounds are a heated swimming pool, a hot tub, and two tennis courts. Ocean beaches, golf, and art galleries are only 4 miles away; a 60-mile drive leads to the marvelous Sonoma Valley wineries.

TIMBERHILL RANCH 35755 Hauser Bridge Rd., Cazadero, CA 95421 (phone: 707-847-3258; fax: 707-847-3342). This ranch has 15 cottages with private baths and twin or queen-size beds. Wheelchair accessible. Closed weekdays in January. Rate for a double room (including continental breakfast and dinner): $325; weekends: $350. Two-night minimum stay on weekends; three nights on holidays. Major credit cards accepted. Not appropriate for children under 14. No pets. Dogs, cats, llamas, sheep, goats, and horses on the property. Smoking permitted in designated cottages only. Tarran McDaid, Michael Riordan, Barbara Farrell, and Frank Watson, innkeepers.

DIRECTIONS: The ranch is 96 miles north of San Francisco. From San Francisco take Highway 101 north for 5 miles past Santa Rosa. Turn west onto River Road and continue through Russian River to Jenner. Follow Highway 1 north for 5 miles beyond Jenner, then turn right onto Meyers Grade Road and ascend to the ridge. Continue on this road for 13¾ miles (its name changes to Seaview, then to Hauser Bridge Road). Continue three-quarters of a mile past Seaview Plantation Road to the ranch.

HARBOR HOUSE—INN BY THE SEA

Elk, California

In this part of the world the sea in its many moods dominates the scenery. Waves wash ashore in a never-ending rhythm, great rock formations seem to have been thrown helter-skelter across the headlands, and depending on the season, sea otters or whales play just offshore. Sea stacks and blowholes, arches, caves, and islands are all part of the scene, and guests at *Harbor House* have a perfect vantage point from which to view the spectacle.

Built in 1916 by the Goodyear Redwood Lumber Company, the inn was constructed entirely of virgin redwoods cut from the nearby Albion Forest. It was used as a retreat and entertainment facility for company executives and guests and as a showcase for redwood construction. Fashioned after the "Home of Redwood" exhibit at the 1915 *Panama-Pacific International Exposition* in San Francisco, the inn has numerous fireplaces, a living room with a hand-carved redwood ceiling, and walls that originally were coated with hot beeswax to preserve their rich red color.

Located in both the main lodge and four cottages on the grounds, the 10 guestrooms offer either ocean or garden views; many have private decks. Fireplaces warm nine of the rooms, and each is furnished with antiques. For example, the *Redwood Room,* which is paneled in virgin redwood, contains a massive French armoire. There's a sleigh bed in the *Greenwood Room;* the *Lookout Room* and *Shorepine* and *Seaview Cottages* have iron-and-brass beds; and *Oceansong Cottage* has a queen-size four-poster. Thoughtful touches include a gift of potpourri, made from flowers grown in the gardens, in each guestroom.

A stay at *Harbor House* includes both breakfast and dinner (the latter is open to non-guests by reservation only). Extensive vegetable and herb gardens provide many of the staples, and eggs from the inn's chickens are served for breakfast. The emphasis is on fresh ingredients and uncomplicated preparations. Meals built around regional fish and meat are accompanied by fresh-baked breads and desserts. Dinner might be grilled salmon with mustard-dill sauce, followed by lemon pudding or a fresh peach crisp.

A croquet set stands ready for guests to use, and tennis, golf, hiking trails, wineries, antiques shops, art galleries, and a botanical garden are all nearby.

HARBOR HOUSE—INN BY THE SEA 5600 S. Hwy. 1, Elk, CA 95432 (phone: 707-877-3203). This redwood lodge on the Pacific Ocean has 10 guestrooms with private baths and queen- or king-size beds. Open year-round. Rate for a double room (including full breakfast and dinner): $170 to $265. Two-night minimum stay on weekends. No credit cards accepted. Not appropriate for children under 12. No pets. Two outdoor cats. No smoking. Helen and Dean Turner, innkeepers.

DIRECTIONS: From San Francisco either travel north on Highway 1 all the way, or take Highway 101 to Cloverdale, then Highway 128 west, then Highway 1 south for 6 miles to the inn.

CARTER HOUSE VICTORIANS

EUREKA, CALIFORNIA

Innkeeper Mark Carter came by his love of Victorian architecture naturally. He was born in Eureka, a logging and fishing town overlooking Humboldt Bay in the heart of the "redwood empire," where lumber barons built magnificent Victorian mansions to showcase their wealth. To this day, Eureka has some of the most spectacular examples of Victorian architecture in America. Mark became a builder, and by the time he was 30, he had renovated more than 20 of Eureka's Victorian jewels, developing a lasting appreciation for the craftsmanship that went into their creation.

The finest examples of the period were the work of San Francisco architects Samuel and Joseph C. Newsom, who designed the *Carson Mansion* and the *Pink Lady,* both in Eureka, for lumber king William Carson. When Mark found a book of original Newsom plans, he was intrigued by an 1884 mansion they had designed for a San Francisco banker; it had been destroyed in the 1906 earthquake and fire, but, in 1981, Mark decided to rebuild it as his family's dream home. Sixteen months and $700,000 later, they had a vintage extravaganza, authentic down to the marble fireplaces.

Although the exterior looks as if it had been built in 1884, there are amenities inside (such as Jacuzzis), unimaginable in those days. Using the house as a bed and breakfast inn hadn't been the Carters' original intent, but it had such a welcoming air that they began taking in guests. Today, the *Carter House,* with its marble entry, glowing woodwork, and lofty ceilings, offers five guestrooms.

But the Carters didn't stop there. In 1986, they built the 23-room *Hotel Carter* across the street, a re-creation of the *Old Town Cairo Hotel,* one of Eureka's boom-era hostelries. The lobby, with a marble fireplace, massive ceramic urns, Oriental rugs, and antique pine furniture, is a sophisticated blend of the Old World and the New. In 1990, the Carters restored a neighboring house they call the *Bell House,* creating three more suites, all with marble bathrooms.

The rooms in all three Carter properties feature a blend of antiques and modern amenities. TV sets are tucked away in antique armoires, and original local art decorates the walls. Ten of the rooms have fireplaces, many have balconies, and there are views of the bay and the *Carson Mansion.* Most of the thoroughly modern baths have dual shower heads.

Fine food is wife Christi Carter's forte—another good reason to visit *Carter House Victorians.* Classically trained, she has attracted a loyal following with her creative cooking. More than 50 types of lettuce and more than a hundred herbs flourish in the extensive kitchen gardens. In fact, the homegrown produce is so important to the hotel's menus that the Carters employ a master gardener, who also gives interpretive garden tours, classes, and seminars. Herb starts and seed packets are for sale at the inn, and there's an extensive wine room, with a broad selection of California vintages for sale.

A four-course breakfast (served to inn guests only) consists of a fruit course, fresh-baked muffins or sweet rolls, an egg dish or pancakes, and dessert–perhaps Christi's spectacular tart made with buttered phyllo layers, sautéed apples, and almond paste. In the afternoon, wine, hors d'oeuvres, tea, and cookies are served. With the presentation as carefully planned as the menu, dinner in the restaurant (also open to non-guests) is in a class by itself. Entrées might include sautéed sea scallops, curried chicken breast, or Long Island duckling with seasonal fruit.

The inn is near theaters, art and antiques shops, the *Redwood National Park,* and the *Salmon-Trinity Alps Wilderness Area.* Carriage rides and architectural tours of Eureka also are available.

CARTER HOUSE VICTORIANS 301 L St., Eureka, CA 95501 (phone: 707-444-8062; 800-404-1390; fax: 707-444-8067). This inn, comprising three Victorian buildings, has 31 guestrooms with private baths, double, queen-, or king-size beds, and telephones; most have TV sets. Wheelchair accessible. Open year-round. Rate for a double room (including full breakfast and afternoon refreshments): $125 to $275. Major credit cards accepted. Children welcome. No pets. No smoking. Mark and Christi Carter, innkeepers; Brent Critch and Bob Graves, managers.

DIRECTIONS: The hotel is approximately 280 miles north of San Francisco. Take Highway 101 to Eureka, where it becomes Broadway. At L Street turn left. The inn is on the corner.

GINGERBREAD MANSION INN

FERNDALE, CALIFORNIA

Ferndale is a small village off the beaten tourist trail amid the redwoods of northern California. Settled originally by Scandinavians, the town's primary occupation was, and remains, dairy farming. As the farmers prospered, they built resplendent homes in the Eastlake, Carpenter Gothic, and Queen Anne styles of architecture with the fortunes they amassed. Probably due to Ferndale's hideaway location, many of these "butterfat palaces" remain, making this one of the finest Victorian villages in America. The entire town is a state historic landmark, and Main Street is on the National Register of Historic Places.

The *Gingerbread Mansion Inn* is itself a showplace of Victorian architecture, and it's frequently touted as the most photographed house in

California. Built in 1899 as a doctor's residence, it was expanded in the 1920s to become *Ferndale General Hospital.* In 1983, innkeeper Ken Torbert enlarged the rooms, added bathrooms, and opened a bed and breakfast inn. A fantasy of Victoriana, it has turrets, bay windows, and an entire catalogue of fanciful trim, all highlighted by a peach and butter yellow color scheme.

The inside is as elaborate as the façade. There are parlors with fireplaces where guests can read or work on a jigsaw puzzle depicting the inn. All 11 guestrooms are furnished with Victorian antiques and have fantastic bathrooms. The *Fountain Suite,* for example, has a bonnet-canopy bed and side-by-side claw-foot tubs for romantic bubble baths. A mirrored wall reflects the flames from the bathroom's tiled corner fireplace. The *Rose Suite* has a fireplace in the bedroom, as well as in the bathroom, which also features a claw-foot tub and wallpaper that calls to mind a garden. The *Empire Suite* has Victorian stained glass entry doors, Ionic columns surrounding a king-size bed, and a massive marble-clad bathroom with a shower and an over-size porcelain tub placed before a fireplace. There's another fireplace in the living room.

A full breakfast, perhaps featuring eggs Benedict or French toast stuffed with cream cheese and blueberries, is served in the dining room. Afternoon tea–small sandwiches, cake, cookies, fruit with clotted cream, and petits fours–is offered daily.

The surrounding English gardens include neatly trimmed boxwoods, three-story fuchsias, gigantic camellia trees, and a fountain. The inn is 5 miles from the beach (a nice bicycle ride). Also nearby are the *Redwood National Park,* village tours, theater, museums, and art galleries.

GINGERBREAD MANSION INN 400 Berding St., PO Box 40, Ferndale, CA 95536 (phone: 707-786-4000; 800-952-4136; fax: 707-786-4831). This Victorian mansion has 11 guestrooms with private baths and twin, queen-, or king-size beds. Open year-round. Rate for a double room (including full breakfast and afternoon tea): $130 to $375. Two-night minimum stay on weekends and holidays. Major credit cards accepted. Not appropriate for children under 10. No pets. Smoking permitted outside only. Ken and Sandie Torbert, innkeepers.

DIRECTIONS: From Highway 101 take the Ferndale exit and proceed west 5 miles to Ferndale. From Main Street turn left at the Bank of America building and continue one block to the inn.

MILL ROSE INN

Half Moon Bay, California

Hidden away on a quiet street within walking distance of the ocean and the shops of Half Moon Bay, the *Mill Rose Inn* is set amid spectacular gardens that could compete with the finest in the English countryside. Bursting with color all year, this oasis is the creation of Terry Baldwin, innkeeper and landscape contractor. He has planted hundreds of perennials, annuals, and more than 200 rosebushes. Inside the inn, a profusion of fresh-cut bouquets and bowls of dried flowers grace each of the guestrooms.

The six elegant and comfortable guestrooms were decorated by Terry's wife, Eve. The *Bordeaux Rose Suite* is done in shades of peach, crimson, and ivory, and is furnished with Georgian antiques and a lace-canopied featherbed; it has a fireplace and doors leading to the rose garden. The bath has a marble double whirlpool and a marble shower. In the *Renaissance Rose Suite* are a brass-and-porcelain bed, a hand-painted fireplace, and an oversize bathroom with hand-painted sinks. Other rooms boast antique claw-foot tubs for two or showers with plant-filled bay windows. All rooms feature European antiques, original watercolors, Japanese robes in the armoires, featherbeds, and VCRs (there's a video lending library).

Among the special treats here is the Jacuzzi. Tucked inside a garden gazebo, it's surrounded by a charming brick courtyard with Australian tree ferns, abundant impatiens beds, and a cascading fountain. There's room for seven people, but it can be reserved as a private escape for two.

Breakfast is a lavish affair that starts with champagne and continues with juice, fresh fruit, apple-cranberry crunch, homemade breads and pastries, and perhaps a frittata made with locally grown artichokes. Afternoon wine and cheese are served before the fireplace in the front parlor and the library. In the evening, a selection of pastries and coffees, accompanied by brandies and sherries, is offered.

San Francisco is just a half hour to the north. Activities in the immediate vicinity include tennis, golf, horseback riding on the beach, sailing, and whale watching tours. Also in the area are myriad art galleries; jazz and classical concerts often are held nearby.

MILL ROSE INN 615 Mill St., Half Moon Bay, CA 94019 (phone: 415-726-8750; 800-900-ROSE; fax: 415-726-3031). This secluded Victorian inn has six guestrooms with private baths, queen- or king-size beds, telephones, and TV sets. Open year-round. Rate for a double room (including full breakfast and afternoon and evening refreshments): $165 to $285. Two-night minimum if stay includes Saturday night. Major credit cards accepted. Not appropriate for children under 10. No pets. Two standard poodles and a blind Siamese cat in residence. Smoking permitted outdoors only. Eve and Terry Baldwin, innkeepers.

DIRECTIONS: From San Francisco travel south on Highway 101 or I-280, then follow Highway 92 west to Half Moon Bay. Turn left onto Main Street, then right onto Mill Street. The inn is on the corner of Mill and Church Streets. Or take Highway 1 from San Francisco, turn left in Half Moon Bay onto Highway 92 and right onto Main Street.

CAMELLIA INN

HEALDSBURG, CALIFORNIA

This lovely inn on a quiet side street in Healdsburg, in the Russian River Valley, has an interesting history. Built in 1869, the house was purchased in 1892 by the Seawells, whose son obtained a medical degree and returned to establish his practice in his family's home. The story is that Dr. Seawell's good friend Luther Burbank, the renowned plant breeder, gave him some of the camellia plants that now highlight the gardens. Although Dr. Seawell died in 1938, his widow continued to live in the home and tend the gardens until 1969.

When Ray and Del Lewand and their daughter Lucy purchased the house in 1981, it was in nearly perfect condition. Guests at the *Camellia Inn* therefore have the rare opportunity to stay in a 127-year-old house that has never undergone major renovations.

The interior is painted peach with white trim to reflect the many camellia bushes outside. The common rooms have numerous fireplaces, polished hardwood floors, decorative friezes, and sparkling Victorian chandeliers. In the double parlors at the front of the house are elaborate twin marble fireplace mantels. With its period antiques and Oriental rugs, the house has a gracious ambience similar to that which the Seawells enjoyed when they lived here.

Each of the guestrooms (except the *Tower Rooms*) is named for a variety of camellia and decorated with antiques. The *Memento Room,* for example, is furnished with a brass bed, Victorian lamps, and wicker chairs; there's a claw-foot tub with brass fixtures in the bath. On display are treasures that belonged to Del's grandmother, including photo albums and old dance cards. The centerpiece of the *Moonglow Room* is a four-poster canopy bed. The two *Tower Rooms* have canopy beds and enormous whirlpool tubs.

In the elaborate dining room, a full breakfast buffet is served from a mahogany sideboard. The menu consists of fresh fruit, cereal, granola, yogurt, fresh-baked sourdough bread, a sweet pastry such as berry coffee cake ring or almond croissants, and perhaps sausage-and-potato pie or Mexican fiesta biscuit bake. An afternoon social hour in the parlors includes cheese, crackers, iced tea, and lemonade.

The inn sponsors numerous activities, including special teas for *Mother's Day, Valentine's Day,* and a children's fashion tea. One of the most popular events is the annual supper in honor of Scottish poet Robert Burns (the Lewands trace their ancestry to Scotland). Naturally, there's a reading or two, as well as the playing of Scottish folk tunes.

Beyond the formal gardens behind the house are a fishpond and a heated swimming pool. Here, guests relax after visiting some of the many wineries in the area, or spending the day bicycling or playing golf or tennis nearby.

CAMELLIA INN 211 North St., Healdsburg, CA 95448 (phone: 707-433-8182; 800-727-8182; fax: 707-433-8130). This Italianate Victorian inn has nine guestrooms with private baths and double or queen-size beds. Wheelchair accessible. Open year-round. Rate for a double room (including full breakfast and afternoon refreshments): $70 to $145. Two-night minimum if stay includes Saturday. Major credit cards accepted. Children welcome. No pets. Smoking permitted outside only. Ray, Del, and Lucy Lewand, innkeepers.

DIRECTIONS: Driving north on Highway 101, take the Central Healdsburg exit. Follow Healdsburg Avenue to North Street and turn right. The inn is 2½ blocks on the left.

MADRONA MANOR

HEALDSBURG, CALIFORNIA

Madrona Manor is a three-story, High Victorian mansion set on eight acres amid spectacular landscaped gardens. To reach this Sonoma Valley inn, one passes through an impressive archway flanked by flowers and follows the long, winding drive up a hill—from which vantage point it is possible

to survey Healdsburg, the Sonoma Valley, and the mountains beyond. The house was built in 1881 by San Francisco financier John Paxton, who lived here with his wife and 10 servants. In 1983, it was purchased by John and Carol Muir, who have made of it one of the finest inns and restaurants in California.

Listed on the National Register of Historic Places, the inn is furnished in a style that matches the exuberance of the architecture. In the parlor is an array of massive carved walnut and mahogany furniture and an Oriental rug. A hundred-year-old square grand piano dominates the music room.

Five of the nine guestrooms in the *Main House* are decorated with furniture that once belonged to the original owner. Room No. 301 boasts a High Victorian carved walnut bed with matching nightstands and dresser, as well as a fireplace. Another of the rooms has a 10-foot-high canopy bed (ceilings in the *Main House* reach 14 feet) and a matching armoire. Dripping with Gothic gingerbread trim, the *Carriage House,* which John converted to nine guestrooms, sits just beyond the pool and is furnished with hand-carved rosewood pieces. Room No. 503 has a fireplace and a large private deck with a view of the surrounding treetops and the vineyards beyond. Suite 400 is the pièce de résistance, with a king-size bed, a fireplace, and a bath that has Greek marble tiles and a Jacuzzi. The most private accommodation is in the *Garden Cottage,* with its private gardens and sheltered deck.

The restaurant meanders through three formal parlors, all with fireplaces, overlooking the flower gardens. The tables are set with fine china, silver, linen, and crystal, as well as elaborate English silver candlesticks, each one different. The inn is renowned for its food, thanks to son Todd Muir, who trained at the *California Culinary Academy* and has been the executive chef since opening day. The menu reflects his interpretation of California cooking and his love of fresh Sonoma County produce. Dinner (also open to non-guests) may include corn chowder, goat-cheese salad, roast local squab, and a cream puff for dessert. Breakfast may include Carol's homemade marmalade or raspberry or kiwi jams.

Guests can visit the many wineries of the Sonoma Valley, browse through nearby antiques shops, or explore the area on bicycles.

MADRONA MANOR 1001 Westside Rd., Healdsburg, CA 95448 (phone: 707-433-4231 or 707-433-6831; 800-258-4003; fax: 707-433-0703). This country inn has 21 guestrooms with private baths, twin, double, queen-, or king-size beds, telephones, and air conditioning. Wheelchair accessible. Open year-round. Rate for a double room (including full breakfast): $140 to $240. Two-night minimum stay from April through October in the *Main House* rooms and suites. Major credit cards accepted. Children welcome in designated rooms. Pets allowed in some rooms with prior permission only (a deposit is required). Three cats—Tiger, Tux, and Little Bit—in residence. Smoking permitted outside only. John and Carol Muir, innkeepers.

DIRECTIONS: Driving north on Highway 101, go 12 miles past Santa Rosa and take the Central Healdsburg exit. Follow Healdsburg Avenue north to Mill Street and turn left. Mill Street becomes Westside Road. The inn is three-quarters of a mile down on the right.

GLENDEVEN INN AND GALLERY

LITTLE RIVER, CALIFORNIA

The lure of the Mendocino section of California's coastline—a craggy strip of high bluffs and rocky promontories punctuated by tiny coves—is its rugged scenery. The breathtaking views are made for photographers and romantics. On the ocean, 1½ miles south of the historic town of Mendocino, *Glendeven* sits on a headland meadow overlooking Little River Bay. Built in 1867, the inn complex includes the *Farmhouse,* the *Barn,* and the *Stevencroft Building.*

Innkeeper Jan deVries, an architect and furniture designer, and his wife, Janet, an interior designer, have been part of the local arts and crafts scene, since they renovated the inn in 1977. In a gallery in the *Barn,* they show the work of local artists—jewelry, pottery, etchings, and paintings, as well as Jan's furniture.

The parlor in the *Farmhouse* is the inn's social center, especially when a guest decides to pick out a tune on the baby grand piano. Overstuffed chairs are gathered around the fireplace, a necessity in this area where the cool morning mists sometimes last until noon. Picture windows face the garden and a distant view of the bay. A pathway leads down to the beach.

The 10 guestrooms are furnished with country French antiques plus Jan's modern upholstered furniture, with its curves and clean lines. Most rooms have fireplaces and views of Van Damme Bay; many have private decks. The *Barn* has been converted into a two-story suite with two bedrooms, a sitting room, a full kitchen, and a sun deck.

A continental breakfast—juice, fresh fruit, muffins, and quiche—is delivered to guestrooms on a tray or in a basket. Coffee, tea, and cookies are available in the kitchen round-the-clock.

The town of Mendocino is a terrific shopping destination, with numerous art galleries, crafts shops, and restaurants. Also nearby is *Van Damme State Park,* hiking, tennis, and golf.

GLENDEVEN INN AND GALLERY 8221 N. Hwy. 1, Little River, CA 95456; mailing address: Box 252, Mendocino, CA 95460 (phone: 707-937-0083; 800-822-4536; fax: 707-937-6108). This inn has 10 guestrooms with private baths and queen-size beds. Open year-round. Rate for a double room (including continental breakfast and snacks): $90 to $220. Two-night minimum stay on weekends. Major credit cards accepted. Children welcome in designated rooms. No pets. Smoking permitted outside only. Jan and Janet deVries, innkeepers.

DIRECTIONS: The inn is located on the inland side of Highway 1 between Little River and Mendocino. To travel part of the way by freeway, take Highway 101 from San Francisco north to Cloverdale. Then take Highway 128 north for 65 miles to Highway 1. Continue north on Highway 1 for 10 miles to Little River. The inn is three-quarters of a mile north of Little River, just past the entrance to *Van Damme State Park.*

SAN YSIDRO RANCH

Montecito, California

In the late 1700s, the area where *San Ysidro Ranch* now stands was a stopping place for Franciscan monks on their trek along the Spanish Mission Route. Tomas Olivera, a Mexican rancher, built the oldest building on the property, the *Adobe,* for his bride in 1825. By 1893, the cottage-style bungalows had been built and the ranch was accepting guests. In 1935, matinee idol Ronald Colman purchased the inn, and it soon became an exclusive hideaway for celebrities. Bing Crosby, Jack Benny, and Katharine Hepburn were frequent guests. Vivien Leigh and Laurence Olivier were married in the *Rose Garden.* John and Jacqueline Kennedy visited in 1953. Somerset Maugham wrote on the terrace of the *Geranium Cottage,* and John Huston completed his script for *The African Queen* here.

After years of acclaim, the ranch slipped into disrepair. It was purchased by new owners in 1976, and with extensive renovation and the addition of some much-needed amenities, *San Ysidro* was again reaping national renown and awards. Today, the 540-acre ranch is owned by Claude Rouas and Bob Harmon (Auberge Associates), who have infused it with their own sophisticated style.

High in the hills above Santa Barbara, *San Ysidro* enjoys spectacular views of the ocean on one side and of the Santa Ynez Mountains on the other. Surrounded by herb, flower, and vegetable gardens, wisteria-covered arches, and ancient, gnarled oak, acacia, and sycamore trees, the ranch's 21 cottages possess a rustic simplicity. With names such as *Jasmine, Magnolia, Lilac,* and *Rose,* the rooms are evocative of their surroundings.

In the cottages are 44 guestrooms and suites, each with a private terrace, a wood-burning fireplace, and a wet bar. Many have private Jacuzzis. All rooms are furnished with antiques that include armoires, buffets, and chests—those in the *Willow Suites* are refinished pieces that have been at the inn since it was built; Oriental rugs cover the polished hardwood floors. When guests arrive at their cottages, they find wooden signs bearing their names hanging outside.

The *Stonehouse* restaurant (also open to non-guests) serves award-winning meals, including spa cuisine. There's also a pub, the *Plow and Angel,* carved out of the space that was used as a wine cellar in 1893. Every Thursday and Friday night jazz concerts are held here. Other nights there's dancing to the tunes on the 1952 Wurlitzer jukebox.

Recreational opportunities at the ranch are numerous. Tennis, swimming, a fitness center, *bocci,* horseshoes, mountain biking, and hiking are available. Numerous body and beauty treatments are offered in the privacy of guests' rooms. These include Swedish and sports massage and aromatherapy. Guests also can go to the beach, play golf, or frequent boutiques, all of which are nearby. In addition, extensive facilities are available for children, including a petting zoo and a play area. *Camp SYR* (offered to children ages five to 12 during the summer and on major holidays) keeps the younger set busy panning for gold, learning about Indian lore, and riding ponies. There's even a program for visiting pets.

SAN YSIDRO RANCH 900 San Ysidro La., Montecito, CA 93108 (phone: 805-969-5046; 800-368-6788; fax: 805-565-1995). This sophisticated ranch resort has 44 guestrooms with private baths, queen- or king-size beds, telephones, TV sets, and air conditioning. Wheelchair accessible. Open year-round. Rate for a double room (including use of pool, tennis courts, and other ranch facilities): $235 to $850. Two-night minimum stay on weekends; three nights on holidays. Major credit cards accepted. Children welcome. Pets allowed ($45 extra per stay). Smoking permitted except in the *Stonehouse* restaurant and the common room. Auberge Associates, owners; Janis Clapoff, manager.

DIRECTIONS: The ranch is approximately 5 miles south of Santa Barbara. Traveling south on Highway 101, take the San Ysidro exit and head east, toward the hills. Follow San Ysidro Road to San Ysidro Lane, which ends at the ranch.

OLD MONTEREY INN

MONTEREY, CALIFÓRNIA

A gracious half-timbered, English Tudor–style home sits on a quiet residential street in the heart of historic Monterey. Ivy covers the front, and wisteria climbs up two stories and wraps around the arched windows. The grounds are studded with majestic oak, pine, and redwood trees; baskets of colorful impatiens hang from the trees; rhododendrons bloom brightly; and the rose garden is a riot of color all summer. This is the *Old Monterey Inn.*

Built in 1929, the house is the longtime residence of Ann and Gene Swett, who raised their six children here. In 1978, they opened their home as an inn and have been offering warm hospitality ever since. The eight guestrooms, a delightful suite, and a garden cottage are all furnished with choice antiques; featherbeds are dressed with fine antique linen and down comforters. Special features include skylights and stained glass windows, and all but two rooms have fireplaces.

One of the rooms, the *Rookery,* brings to mind Monet's gardens at Giverny. It's a whimsical room with a garden theme and a delightful assortment of white wicker and hand-painted furniture. Moonlight streams down from the skylight over the queen-size bed, and a fireplace warms the room in winter. The *Garden Cottage,* down a cobblestone path lined with impatiens, has skylights, a fireplace, a canopy bed, and a window seat for gazing at the private garden. The *Library,* on the other hand, is a masculine retreat, with book-lined walls, a large stone fireplace, and a private deck that affords panoramic views of the gardens below.

The high-ceilinged living room offers a variety of comfortable seating, a fireplace, and a garden view. Afternoon tea is served here, as are wine and hors d'oeuvres in the evening. A full breakfast is offered to guests in their rooms, the dining room, or, if the weather is nice, the rose garden. It usually includes juice, fruit, homemade muffins, and perhaps *strata* soufflé with artichokes and mushrooms or orange-blossom French toast, served with marmalade-maple syrup.

The inn is located near Carmel, *Cannery Row,* the *Monterey Bay Aquarium,* 17-Mile Drive, and Pebble Beach; shopping, theater, and symphony concerts are in the area as well.

OLD MONTEREY INN 500 Martin St., Monterey, CA 93940 (phone: 408-375-8284; 800-350-2344; fax: 408-375-6730). This English country-house inn has 10 guestrooms with private baths and double, queen-, or king-size beds. Closed *Christmas.* Rate for a double room (including full breakfast, afternoon tea, and evening wine and hors d'oeuvres): $170 to $240. Two-night minimum stay on weekends; three nights on holidays. MasterCard and Visa accepted. Not appropriate for children under 12. No pets. A German shepherd, Liza, in residence. No smoking except in rose garden. Ann and Gene Swett, innkeepers; Patti Kreider, manager.

DIRECTIONS: Traveling south on Highway 1, take the Soledad/Munras exit. Follow Soledad Drive, cross Munras Avenue, and turn right onto Pacific Street. Continue a half mile to Martin Street on the left. Traveling north on Highway 1, take the Munras Avenue exit. Make an immediate left onto Soledad Drive and then turn right onto Pacific Street. Proceed as above.

MARTINE INN

PACIFIC GROVE, CALIFORNIA

Located in the charming village of Pacific Grove, the *Martine Inn* is a grand old mansion perched high on the cliffs overlooking Monterey Bay's spectacular coastline. The epitome of elegance and luxury, the huge (29-room) house was built in the 1890s, for James and Laura Parke, of Parke-Davis Pharmaceuticals.

Originally, the building was a full-blown Victorian with a cupola and dormers, but these features were removed in the 1920s, when it was transformed into a Mediterranean villa with a stucco exterior. Purchased in 1972 by Marion and Don Martine, the structure underwent additional renovations, though its authentic turn-of-the-century features were retained. The house is now painted rose, and careful attention has been paid to restoring the interior Victorian details. Marion and Don opened the inn to guests in 1984.

Although larger than most bed and breakfast establishments, the *Martine Inn* offers an intimate atmosphere, and each of its 19 guestrooms is distinctive. A unique 1850s American walnut bedroom suite—with busts of Jenny Lind carved in the mirror frame, armoire, and headboard—dominates one room, while another is furnished with a suite that once belonged to costume designer Edith Head. Thirteen rooms, many of which have fireplaces and views of the bay, are located in the *Main House;* there are six more in the *Carriage House,* overlooking the courtyard pond and Oriental fountain.

An 1890s billiards table, an antique piano and slot machine, and a six-person Jacuzzi are found in the conservatory, which previously served as the estate's greenhouse. The library, with its beautiful inlaid oak bookcases, offers a comfortable place to read by the fire. Be sure to ask Don about his collection of MGs, which he drives in vintage-car races. Three are on display in a small auto museum on the grounds.

Breakfast is served in the dining room on a French walnut table, part of a 14-piece suite that includes three sideboards with elaborate finials and beveled mirrors. Marion sets out her finest Victorian china, crystal, and her 1896 Lancaster Rose–pattern sterling silver. The menu always includes fresh-baked muffins and a hot entrée such as Monterey eggs (eggs and cottage cheese baked with green chilies and cheddar cheese). Afternoon wine and hors d'oeuvres also are served.

The views of Monterey Bay from the dining and sitting rooms can yield some delightful surprises. Binoculars are placed along the window ledges so guests may scan the water for whales, dolphins, and pelicans. Watch carefully, and you'll be treated to a show by the clown of the sea, the brown sea otter. Through the open windows, over the crash of the waves, you may hear the barking of sea lions as they sun themselves on the craggy rocks.

The inn is four blocks from the *Monterey Bay Aquarium* and within walking distance of *Cannery Row;* also nearby are the Monterey Peninsula Recreational Trail, 17-Mile Drive, and excellent shopping.

MARTINE INN 255 Ocean View Blvd., Pacific Grove, CA 93950 (phone: 408-373-3388; 800-852-5588; fax: 408-373-3896). This mansion inn has 19 guestrooms with private baths, double, queen-, or king-size beds, and telephones. Wheelchair accessible. Open year-round. Rate for a double room (including full breakfast and afternoon wine and hors d'oeuvres): $125 to $230. Two-night minimum if stay includes Saturday night. Major credit cards accepted. Children welcome. No pets. Smoking permitted in guestrooms with fireplaces only. Don and Marion Martine, innkeepers; Tracy Harris, manager.

DIRECTIONS: From Highway 1 exit onto Highway 68, staying in the right lane and traveling west to Pacific Grove. Once in town continue on Forest Avenue to the beach. Turn right onto Ocean View Boulevard and continue to the inn, which is on the right between Fifth and Third Streets.

RANCHO VALENCIA RESORT

RANCHO SANTA FE, CALIFORNIA

This sun-splashed resort sits high on a 40-acre plateau overlooking the San Dieguito Valley. Nearby, the seaside villages of La Jolla and Del Mar offer sophisticated shops and restaurants, but *Rancho Valencia* is such a peaceful retreat that guests find few reasons to leave.

Climbing the hill to the canyon plateau, a series of sloping lawns are bordered by beds of bright impatiens, agapanthus, hibiscus, and geraniums. The resort's 2,000 citrus trees provide shade as well as a steady supply of Valencia oranges, lemons, and limes.

Although *Rancho Valencia Resort* was built in 1989 (as *John Gardiner's Tennis Camp*), it is reminiscent of the grand old haciendas built in Rancho Santa Fe in the 1920s and 1930s, with typical Spanish colonial architecture: earth-toned stucco walls, red tile roofs, terra cotta patios, and custom-made Mexican tiles. The 43 suites are in casitas, each with a cathedral ceiling and whitewashed beams, a tiled fireplace, a ceiling fan, a private patio, a wet bar, a refrigerator, and a VCR. The luxuriously appointed baths offer dressing rooms and oversize walk-in showers. The *Hacienda,* with its own pool and secluded gardens, is an ultraprivate three-suite retreat.

Meals (also open to non-guests) are a highlight of any stay at the resort, where the fare is a sophisticated blend of California and Mediterranean styles. A salad, for example, might feature thin slices of mango and seared salmon with a citrus dressing; entrées include veal sweetbreads sautéed with oyster mushrooms, asparagus, and a madeira reduction. The *Rancho Valencia* orange cake is a medley of orange custard and chocolate mousse. For the health-conscious, a spa menu provides a delicious alternative. No meals are included in the room rate, but a carafe of juice—freshly squeezed from oranges grown on the property—is delivered to guestrooms each morning with a newspaper.

Tennis is still a draw here, with 18 courts that are in regular use. In addition, there are two outdoor swimming pools, bicycles, a regulation croquet lawn, a full-scale fitness center, and a spa featuring a wide array of services, from manicures and Swedish massages to aromatherapy and reflexology. Spirited sunrise walks and scenic hikes prepare guests for the day. Activities especially for children include the *Junior Tennis Academy,* a special amenity package and menu, and a playground.

Located in the hills above the Pacific, the resort is 10 miles north of La Jolla and 24 miles north of San Diego. Also nearby are *Del Mar Racetrack, Balboa Park, Sea World, San Diego Zoo,* golf (the inn has privileges at three courses), hot-air ballooning, and boutique shopping.

RANCHO VALENCIA RESORT **5921 Valencia Circle, PO Box 9126, Rancho Santa Fe, CA 92067 (phone: 619-756-1123; 800-548-3664; fax: 619-756-0165). This luxury resort has 43 suites with private baths, queen- or king-size beds, telephones, TV sets, and air conditioning. Wheelchair accessible. Open year-round. Rate for a double room (including tennis and fitness facilities): $325 to $800 ($2,000 for the *Hacienda*). Two-night minimum stay on weekends; three nights on holidays. Major credit cards accepted. Children welcome. Pets permitted ($75 charge per night, per pet). Smoking permitted except in dining room. Michael Ullman, general manager.**

DIRECTIONS: From Los Angeles take I-5 south to Del Mar. Turn left onto Via de la Valle and then right onto El Camino Real. Turn left at San Dieguito Road. Proceed for 3 miles to the first traffic light and turn right at Rancho Diegueno Road. Turn left immediately onto Rancho Valencia Road. Rancho Valencia Drive is on the left; drive up two blocks to Rancho Valencia Circle and the inn. From San Diego take I-5 north to Del Mar Heights Road east. Follow this road to El Camino Real and turn left. Turn right onto San Dieguito Road and follow directions above.

AUBERGE DU SOLEIL

RUTHERFORD, CALIFORNIA

In 1981, Claude Rouas opened the *Auberge du Soleil* (Inn of the Sun), a fine French restaurant on a 33-acre hillside, surrounded by an ancient olive grove and overlooking the Napa Valley. As the restaurant and its food began winning praise, patrons requested a similarly luxurious place to stay. In response, Rouas opened the first of the inn's romantic guestrooms in 1985; the number has since grown to 50.

The guestrooms, each of which has a private terrace, a fireplace, and a fabulous view of the valley, are located in a series of one- and two-story Mediterranean-style villas named for French provinces. With their wood-shingled roofs, they look for all the world as if they've just arrived from

France. The rooms inside have exposed-beam ceilings and terra cotta floors; tiles decorate both the custom-made headboards and the fireplace surrounds. The chairs are made of soft stretched leather; original paintings hang on the walls; fresh flowers brighten the soft earth tones. Illuminated by skylights, many of the large baths have Jacuzzis as well as separate stall showers. The in-room refrigerator is stocked with Napa Valley wines and gourmet snacks, and a big bowl of fresh and dried fruits awaits guests' arrival.

The dining rooms at the *Auberge* (open to non-guests) continue to serve exceptional fare, a mix of classic French and nouveau California styles using the freshest local meat, seafood, produce, and herbs. Dinner might feature grilled Pacific salmon with caramelized pearl onions or pan-seared veal chop with crisp polenta and Napa ham-sage-apple sauce. The setting and ambience reflect California's distinctive casual style. Decorated in stucco and tile, the dining rooms have fireplaces, a terrace with breathtaking views, and seating areas divided by massive stone pots filled with flowers and greens. Original art adds color to the walls. A bar with a fireplace leads to a wisteria-covered terrace and an open deck.

Facilities include a full-size pool, a fitness center, a beauty salon, three tennis courts, and meeting rooms. A sculpture garden featuring work by local artists can be viewed from the nature trail that has been cut into the hillside. Guests can pursue bicycling, ballooning, gliding, golfing, and horseback riding nearby. With more than 200 of California's finest wineries in the area, wine touring is one of the most popular activities.

AUBERGE DU SOLEIL 180 Rutherford Hill Rd., PO Drawer B, Rutherford, CA 94573 (phone: 707-963-1211; 800-348-5406; fax: 707-963-8764). This inn has 50 guestrooms with private baths, twin or king-size beds, telephones, TV sets, and air conditioning. Wheelchair accessible. Open year-round. Rate for a double room: $200 to $1,000. Two-night minimum stay on weekends; three nights on holiday weekends. Major credit cards accepted. Not appropriate for children under 18. No pets. Smoking permitted in guestrooms and bar but not in the restaurant. Claude Rouas, owner; George A. Goeggel, general manager.

DIRECTIONS: From San Francisco, take Highway 101 north through Marin County to the Highway 37 cutoff south of Novato. Follow Highway 37 to Highway 121 and turn toward Sonoma. South of Sonoma bear right (east) onto Highway 12 toward Napa. Turn left onto Highway 29 and continue north through Napa, Yountville, and Oakville. At Rutherford turn right onto Highway 128. Drive 3 miles to the stop sign at the Silverado Trail and turn left. Go 200 yards and turn right at Rutherford Hill Road. The inn will be on the right up the hill.

MEADOWOOD, NAPA VALLEY

St. Helena, California

The road twists and turns past acres of trim vineyards as it climbs through the Napa Valley hills before turning into the driveway of *Meadowood.* Set on 250 acres, the inn is surrounded by oak and madrona forests and sunny meadows, offering guests a welcome sense of seclusion.

Meadowood was built as a private club and golf course in the mid-1960s. After considerable renovation and expansion, it was converted to an elegant but relaxed inn and resort in 1985. Designed in an understated New England style with gabled windows, tan shingles, and white trim, it has 85 rooms and very private suites located in cottages scattered throughout the property. Some overlook the golf course, some offer views across the hills, others sit near the pools, still others are tucked into the woods. All are spacious and decorated in simple country style with hand-carved beds and comfortable wood and wicker furniture. They have private porches, lofty beamed ceilings, cream-colored walls, and abundant windows; many boast flagstone fireplaces as well.

The food at *Meadowood,* which has won numerous awards, emphasizes local ingredients and changes with the seasons. Dinner (which is open to non-guests) might include langoustines with seared foie gras, roast lamb accompanied by potatoes and tomatoes wrapped in red onion, and warm passion-fruit mousse with raspberry *coulis.* The inn's wine tutor, an expert who regularly conducts seminars and classes (by reservation only), is available to answer questions at the complimentary wine tastings for guests held on Friday nights in the comfortable common room. The resort is also the site of the annual *Napa Valley Wine Auction.*

In addition to the golf course, there are seven tennis courts, two tournament-quality croquet lawns, two swimming pools, 3 miles of hiking trails, and a luxurious health spa—and a tennis pro, a spa director, a golf pro, and even a croquet pro are all on hand to assist. Off the property, guests can visit the many Napa Valley wineries, nearby art galleries, and historic homes.

MEADOWOOD, NAPA VALLEY 900 Meadowood La., St. Helena, CA 94574 (phone: 707-963-3646; 800-458-8080; fax: 707-963-3532). This resort has 85 guestrooms with private baths, twin, double, queen-, or king-size beds, telephones, and TV sets. Wheelchair accessible. Open year-round. Rate for a double room: $320 to $1,875. Two-night minimum stay on weekends. Major credit cards accepted. Children welcome. No pets. Smoking permitted in guestrooms. Jorg Lippuner, managing director.

DIRECTIONS: From San Francisco take I-80 east toward Sacramento. Five miles north of the Carquinez toll booth, take Napa Highway 37 to Highway 29. Turn right (north) onto Highway 29 and travel 25 miles to the Napa Valley, following signs for Calistoga. Travel through Napa, Yountville, Oakville, and Rutherford. One mile after Rutherford, turn right onto Zinfandel Lane, then turn left onto the Silverado Trail and drive 1 mile to Howell Mountain Road and turn right. Continue 500 feet to Meadowood Lane, turn left, and proceed 1 mile to the inn.

ARCHBISHOPS MANSION

SAN FRANCISCO, CALIFORNIA

One of the most opulent inns in San Francisco—or anywhere—the *Archbishops Mansion* was built in 1904 as the private residence of the Catholic Archbishop of San Francisco. As much a retreat for visiting clerics as a home, it was designed with 15 bedrooms and suites, all with private baths and many with sitting rooms and fireplaces. Before it was purchased by Jonathan Shannon and Jeffrey Ross in 1980, it had survived the 1906 earthquake, served as a refugee center during the fires that followed, and weathered 35 years as a boys' school. There was considerable work to do, but Shannon and Ross were no neophytes (having previously created an inn in the old *Spreckles Mansion*), and their two-year renovation produced spectacular results.

The inn is a study in grandeur—from the hand-painted ceiling in the parlor to the three-story redwood stairway crowned by a 16-foot stained glass dome. French antiques, gilded mirrors, crystal chandeliers, Oriental rugs, and a marvelous 1904 Bechstein grand piano once owned by Noël Coward adorn the downstairs common rooms. Carved mantelpieces cap the magnificent fireplaces.

The mansion is only nine blocks from the *San Francisco Opera House,* so the guestrooms are all named for famous operas. Each is distinctive and lavishly romantic, with a carved bed as the centerpiece. In the *Don Giovanni Suite,* an 18th-century canopy bed from a château in southern France is carved with life-size angels. This suite also has a fireplace in the bedroom, another massive fireplace in the grand parlor, and views of Alamo Square and the "Painted Ladies" on Steiner Street (the most photographed row of Victorians in San Francisco). Rich fabrics drape the bed and windows. The playful *Carmen Suite* has a claw-foot tub placed before the fireplace in the bedroom, as well as a carved antique French canopy bed and a view of *Alamo Square Park.*

A continental breakfast is served downstairs in the dining room or delivered to the room. Afternoon wine is offered in the parlor, where guests listen to selections on the programmed player piano.

The friendly staff sees to all guest needs: A limousine can be hired to whisk visitors around the city, dinner reservations secured, dry cleaning attended to, and business services arranged.

ARCHBISHOPS MANSION 1000 Fulton St., San Francisco, CA 94117 (phone: 415-563-7872; 800-543-5820; fax: 415-885-3193). This mansion has 15 guestrooms with private baths, double, queen-, or king-size beds, telephones, and TV sets. Open year-round. Rate for a double room (including continental breakfast and afternoon wine): $129 to $385. Two-night minimum stay on weekends. Major credit cards accepted. Children welcome. No pets. No smoking in guestrooms. Jonathan Shannon and Jeffrey Ross, innkeepers; Rick Janvier, manager.

DIRECTIONS: From the airport follow Highway 101 north to the Fell/Laguna exit. Follow Fell Street for five blocks to Steiner Street and turn right. Take Steiner for two blocks to Fulton Street and turn left; the inn is on the corner.

MANSIONS HOTEL

San Francisco, California

Whimsical and wacky, *Mansions Hotel* is an out-of-the-ordinary place that guests long remember. Part fine arts museum, part P. T. Barnum's *American Museum,* and part *Old Curiosity Shop,* it reflects owner Robert Pritikin's far-ranging interests and eclectic tastes: There's a surprise around every corner.

Located in a prestigious neighborhood that includes some of San Francisco's most splendid homes, the hotel is composed of two houses: an 1887 twin-turreted Victorian and a 1903 Greek Revival. Magnificently restored, the two are connected by an interior corridor and a sculpture garden displaying work by Benjamino Bufano.

The grand foyer, with its golden oak paneling and massive crystal chandelier, sets the stage for drama and quirky humor. An inventive mural tells the story of the houses' former residents. To the right, past a huge dollhouse plucked from the stage of Edward Albee's *Tiny Alice,* is the entry to the *International Pig Museum;* it displays thousands of little porkers, from a sculpture that once was part of a turn-of-the-century French carousel to a massive mural of "pignicking" in *Golden Gate Park.* In the common areas treasures of times past and present—tapestries, museum-quality paintings (there's an original Turner), and sculptures—surround you. Historical documents signed by Abraham Lincoln and John Hancock hang beside notes from Barbra Streisand and Eddie Fisher.

The 21 guestrooms at *Mansions Hotel* are spectacular in dimension and style. Many have fireplaces, several have rooftop balconies and Jacuzzis, and all are furnished with antiques: four-poster and canopy beds, French armoires, and inlaid desks and tables. The beds are swathed in velvet or silk, as are the windows.

And then there are Pritikin's dinner-theater productions. Guests gather in the living room to sip champagne while waiters unobtrusively take dinner orders. Then, to the strains of Bach's "Invention in C-Major," a large multicolored macaw screeches from his perch—and it's show time. Everyone is ushered into the cabaret (complete with a grand piano painted with winged pigs), where Pritikin tells corny jokes and performs corny magic tricks before playing the saw, amusing guests with his renditions of "Moonlight Sawnata" and "The Last Time I Sawed Paris." It's all great fun.

Dinner (also open to non-guests) includes four courses with a choice of entrées in a remarkable setting. Two walls of the dining room are lined with a 32-foot stained glass mural, a turn-of-the-century masterpiece from a villa in Barcelona. Continental breakfast is served to inn guests daily in another dining room overlooking the sculpture garden.

In addition to the in-house entertainment, the city of San Francisco has much to offer just outside the door.

MANSIONS HOTEL 2220 Sacramento St., San Francisco, CA 94115 (phone: 415-929-9444; 800-826-9398; fax: 415-537-9391). This inn has 21 guestrooms with private baths, queen- or king-size beds, and telephones. Open year-round. Rate for a double room (including continental breakfast): $129 to $350. Major credit cards accepted. Children welcome. Pets accepted. One macaw and doves in residence. Smoking permitted. Robert Pritikin, innkeeper.

DIRECTIONS: From the Golden Gate Bridge follow signs to downtown and exit at Lombard Street. Go east on Lombard to Van Ness and turn right. From Van Ness, turn right onto Sacramento. The inn is on the right between Laguna and Buchanan. Coming from the east or south, follow signs to the Golden Gate Bridge but exit at Van Ness. Follow Van Ness north to Sacramento and turn left. The inn is on the right.

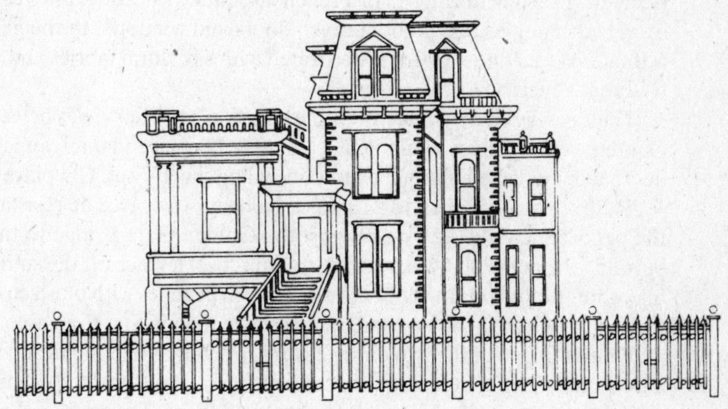

SHERMAN HOUSE

San Francisco, California

Don't be surprised if you hear ghostly sounds of music echoing through the hallways of *Sherman House.* Built in 1876, this magnificent mansion in tony Pacific Heights originally was the home of Leander Sherman, founder of the Sherman Clay Music Company. For 50 years, he lavishly entertained artistic, literary, and musical stars, including such greats as Enrico Caruso,

Lillian Russell, Ernestine Schumann-Heink, and Ignacy Jan Paderewski. In 1901, he added a music room the size of a ballroom so that his guests might better enjoy the impromptu concerts he hosted.

After Sherman died, the building served variously as a restaurant, a ballet school, and a sculptor's studio, but even after a stint as a decorator show house, it seemed destined for demolition until a group of public-spirited citizens were successful in having it designated a San Francisco landmark. In 1982, Manou and Vesta Mobedshahi (he a San Francisco hotelier, she an art historian) bought the building and began its restoration.

Today, the Italianate mansion reflects the grace of a bygone era. Hardwood floors are covered with Oriental rugs, the spectacular double stairway has been extended to the top floor, ornate plaster friezes have been repaired and painted, and crystal chandeliers hang from ornate ceiling medallions. Priceless antiques are found throughout. A Coromandel screen and a Flemish tapestry are focal points in the lobby. Afternoon tea is served in the sitting room, with its Louis XVI–style commode and a Regency-style table.

All but one of the 14 guestrooms have fireplaces, and most feature canopied featherbeds. They also offer views, often from private decks or plush window seats, either of San Francisco Bay and the Golden Gate Bridge or of the English gardens in back. Guestrooms in the mansion are richly furnished with English or French antiques. Brocade fabrics cascade from bed canopies and across French doors and windows. In the gardens is the *Carriage House,* which is decorated with silk floral fabrics and country French furniture.

The *Leander Sherman Suite,* on the mansion's top floor, has beige walls painted to resemble raw silk, a black marble fireplace mantel, an antique desk, and a polished antique chest concealing the TV set, CD player, and VCR. French doors open to a tiny side balcony. The pièce de résistance is the panoramic view—it extends past the Golden Gate Bridge to the bay beyond—from the 800-square-foot, treetop-level terrace off the suite's living room. Abundant flower boxes and built-in benches with plush cushions make this one of the most romantic places to dine in San Francisco.

Dinner in one of the two dining rooms (also open to non-guests) is also a treat. Entrées might include rack of lamb with thyme-scented onion marmalade or seared salmon on a bed of braised leeks. The setting, the food, the excellent wine list, and the friendly, helpful staff make the *Sherman House* one of San Francisco's favorite restaurants. Breakfast is also served, although it's not included in the room rate. A house specialty is brioche French toast with apple wood–smoked bacon.

The inn is near the sophisticated shops and restaurants on Union Street, *Fisherman's Wharf, Ghirardelli Square,* the *Cannery,* museums, and historic walks.

SHERMAN HOUSE **2160 Green St., San Francisco, CA 94123 (phone: 415-563-3600; 800-424-5777; fax: 415-563-1882). This luxury mansion has 14 guestrooms with private baths, twin or queen-size beds, telephones, and TV sets. Wheelchair accessible. Open year-round. Rate for a double room: $250 to $825. Two-night minimum stay on major holiday weekends. Major credit cards accepted. Children welcome. No pets. Boots, a calico cat, in residence. Smoking permitted in one public room only. Manou and Vesta Mobedshahi, proprietors/managers.**

DIRECTIONS: Traveling north on Highway 101, follow signs to the Golden Gate Bridge but exit onto Fell Street. Travel a half mile and turn right onto Webster Street. Continue for approximately 2 miles and turn left onto Green Street. *Sherman House* is on the right.

SPENCER HOUSE

SAN FRANCISCO, CALIFORNIA

Located in the Haight-Ashbury section of San Francisco, *Spencer House* is an 1887 Victorian beauty, built by a milliner named Spencer. It has a round tower, Palladian windows, marble stairs, a triple-arched main entry porch, elaborate stained glass windows with faceted crystals, and a profusion of exterior ornamentation. Numerous gables crown the graceful roof. They didn't build many like this, and certainly there aren't many left.

Barbara and Jack Chambers purchased *Spencer House* in 1984, embarked on a major restoration project, and opened it as a bed and breakfast establishment in 1985. The results of their work are spectacular.

The Chamberses surrounded the property with an ornate wrought-iron Victorian fence, accented with gilt and designed to complement the arched windows. Inside, they retained the original plaster walls but covered those in the double parlor in silk. The main floor also features vaulted 12-foot ceilings and fanciful hand-painted Bradbury and Bradbury wallpapers. The front parlor is cozily elegant with down-filled couches, a Kirman rug, and spectacular antiques—the player piano is especially popular.

A grand staircase of hand-carved oak leads to the six guestrooms. Here, the hallway retains the original gilded Lincresta Walton wallpapers, and oversize, solid-wood doors open into enormous rooms with bay windows. The featherbeds have down comforters; Barbara traveled to England to select the special bed linen. Three rooms have glorious views of *Buena Vista Park,* the inn's gardens, or the Golden Gate Bridge; all are furnished with antiques. The *French Room,* for example, contains a delightful antique French Eastlake bed and a matching armoire, an Oriental rug, hand-stenciled walls, and a "notorious" Victorian chandelier–it once belonged to a madam. As exquisite as the furnishings are, the decor is not fussy. It's as if the Spencers had returned to town and invited you for the weekend.

A full breakfast is served in the formal dining room, where elegant fine china and sterling silver are used. The entrée might be cheese blintzes with brandied cherry sauce and *crème fraîche.*

The inn is near *Golden Gate Park, Buena Vista Park,* museums, and the many interesting shops on Haight and Union Streets.

SPENCER HOUSE 1080 Haight St., San Francisco, CA 94117 (phone: 415-626-9205; fax: 415-616-9230). This Victorian mansion has six guestrooms with private baths, queen- or king-size beds, and telephones. Open year-round. Rate for a double room (including full breakfast): $105 to $165. Major credit cards accepted. Not appropriate for children under 12. No pets. Two cocker spaniels, Percy and Perry, and a macaw, Carmen, in residence. No smoking. Barbara and Jack Chambers, innkeepers; Chrysanthe Soukas, manager.

DIRECTIONS: Traveling north on Highway 101, follow signs to the Golden Gate Bridge but exit onto Fell Street. Follow Fell Street to Baker Street and turn left. The inn is on the left, at the corner of Baker and Haight Streets.

INN ON MT. ADA

Avalon, Santa Catalina Island, California

Catalina is just an hour from Los Angeles, yet it's light-years away in ambience and attitude. Reached by ferry from the mainland, this serene island enchants with spectacular sunrises and sunsets, accompanied by the soft sounds of birds, the sea, and ocean breezes. No cars are permitted (people get around by walking, bicycling, or driving golf carts—the inn provides guests with their own golf cart for the duration of their stay), so noise and fumes are minimal.

High atop the hills overlooking Avalon Harbor, the *Inn on Mt. Ada* was formerly the summer home of chewing-gum magnate William Wrigley Jr. The large, stately Georgian home, listed on the National Register of Historic

Places, is ornamented with elaborate columns in the foyer and hand-carved moldings throughout. About 25 years after Wrigley last used the house (he died in 1932), it was donated to the *University of Southern California* for use as a marine institute. Eventually, the property came to the attention of the Mt. Ada Inn Corporation, a group of local residents intent on saving it from further deterioration. In 1985, the corporation signed a lease with the university, and the inn was born. Today, the mansion and the five-and-a-half-acre grounds are jointly owned by the university and the Santa Catalina Island Conservancy.

The inn's numerous common rooms, including a den, a sun-room, a living room, and dining room, are decorated with Chippendale and Hepplewhite antiques and local crafts, including several examples of rare Catalina pottery made in the 1920s. All the rooms afford ocean or harbor views. The four guestrooms and two suites also are decorated with Old World antiques, including canopy and four-poster beds with lavish curtains.

The hearty breakfast may consist of juice, bran muffins, poached pears with strawberry sauce, and banana-pecan pancakes with sausage. Hot and cold appetizers and fresh-baked cookies are served in the afternoon, along with wine, sherry, port, beer, and champagne. Both a deli-style lunch and a complete dinner—which might feature filet of beef or pork tenderloin—are included in the rate as well. All meals are available to non-guests.

Santa Catalina Island offers many outdoor activities, such as swimming, tennis, golf, snorkeling, parasailing, and hiking. There's good shopping, too.

INN ON MT. ADA 398 Wrigley Rd., PO Box 2560, Avalon, CA 90704 (phone: 310-510-2030; fax: 310-510-2237). This mansion inn has six guestrooms with private baths, queen-size beds, and TV sets. Closed *Christmas Eve* and *Christmas.* Rate for a double room (including breakfast, lunch, afternoon refreshments, and dinner):

$350 to $650. Two-night minimum stay on weekends. MasterCard and Visa accepted. Not appropriate for children under 14. No pets. No smoking permitted. Marlene McAdam and Susie Griffin, innkeepers.

DIRECTIONS: Ferries leave from San Pedro, Long Beach, and Newport Beach; the crossing takes an hour. The inn is also accessible by helicopter from Long Beach and Newport Beach; the ride takes 15 minutes. Guests are met at the dock and the heliport.

MANSION AT LAKEWOOD

WALNUT CREEK, CALIFORNIA

Through the white wrought-iron gates of the *Mansion at Lakewood* lies a world of sweeping verandahs and lush lawns skirted by colorful flowers. The three-acre estate, shaded by hundred-year-old oaks, magnolias, and redwoods and featuring a cactus garden and a pond where *koi* slide beneath the water lilies, is a tranquil oasis only a quarter-mile from downtown Walnut Creek and 25 miles from San Francisco.

The rambling, two-story Victorian mansion was constructed in 1861 with tongue-and-groove siding and raised verandahs. The 8,000-square-foot structure still has an etched glass transom over the door, showing a flag with 34 stars, the full complement in those days. Mike and Sharyn McCoy were charmed by the house when they toured it, in 1986, and thought it would be ideal for an inn. They purchased the property, launched a major renovation, and opened their bed and breakfast establishment in 1988.

The main floor boasts a majestic library with arched 14-foot ceilings, redwood bookshelves, and a black marble fireplace. The parlor, decorated with wallpaper in shades of teal, mauve, and burgundy, also has a fireplace. A cherry table and two matching buffets grace the dining room. Toy bunnies, part of Sharyn's collection, peek around corners throughout the inn.

Country-fresh charm pervades the five guestrooms and two suites, which are decorated with fine antiques. The unusual *Summerhouse* has hand-painted floors and a claw-foot tub on an enclosed porch. All rooms have private baths (one suite has a black marble bath with a double Jacuzzi), and the suites include fireplaces.

After a breakfast of fresh-baked croissants, apple crêpes, or Mexican quiche, guests might enjoy a game of croquet or stroll on one of the nature paths. A formal high tea (open to non-guests) is served from Friday through Sunday in the *Secret Garden Tea Room.*

The *Regional Center for the Arts,* a playhouse and performing arts center, and a summer Shakespeare festival are both nearby. Also in the area is *Mt. Diablo State Park* for hiking.

MANSION AT LAKEWOOD **1056 Hacienda Dr., Walnut Creek, CA 94598 (phone: 510-945-3600; 800-477-7898; fax: 510-945-3608). This secluded Victorian inn has seven guestrooms with private baths, queen- or king-size beds, and telephones. Wheelchair accessible. Open year-round. Rate for a double room (including full breakfast): $135 to $300; corporate rates available. Major credit cards accepted. Children welcome. No pets. Smoking permitted on outdoor balconies or terrace only. Sharyn and Mike McCoy, innkeepers; Angie and John Senser, managers.**

DIRECTIONS: From San Francisco cross the Oakland Bay Bridge and then take I-580 east to Route 24. Follow Route 24 through the Caldecott Tunnel to Walnut Creek. Bear left when the highway forks and get onto I-680 north to Ygnacio Valley Road. Continue to the seventh traffic light and turn right onto Homestead Avenue. Proceed three blocks, then turn left onto Hacienda Drive. The house is just down the street behind white wrought-iron gates.

Pacific Northwest, Alaska, and British Columbia

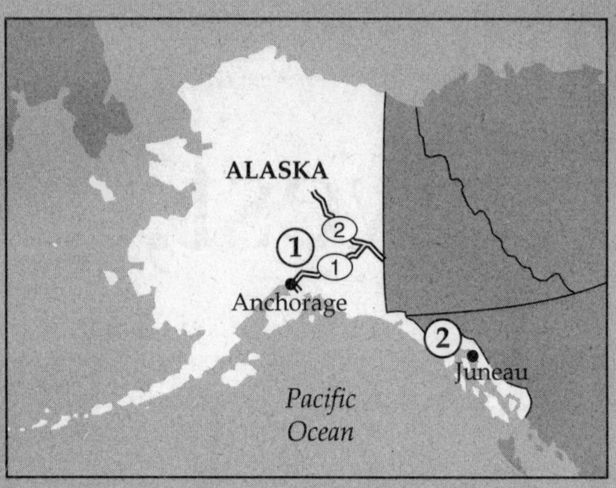

ALASKA

1. Denali National Park: NORTH FACE LODGE/ CAMP DENALI
2. Gustavus: GLACIER BAY COUNTRY INN

OREGON

3. Ashland: MT. ASHLAND INN
4. Cannon Beach: STEPHANIE INN
5. Gold Beach: TU TU' TUN LODGE
6. Portland: HERON HAUS

WASHINGTON

7. Bremerton: WILLCOX HOUSE
8. Orcas Island-Eastsound: TURTLEBACK FARM INN
9. Port Townsend: OLD CONSULATE INN/ F.W. HASTINGS HOUSE
10. Poulsbo: MANOR FARM INN
11. Seaview: SHELBURNE INN
12. Seattle: INN AT THE MARKET
13. Whidbey Island–Langley: INN AT LANGLEY

BRITISH COLUMBIA, CANADA

14. Mayne Island: OCEANWOOD COUNTRY INN
15. Sooke: SOOKE HARBOUR HOUSE INN AND RESTAURANT
16. Victoria: ABIGAIL'S BED AND BREAKFAST HOTEL; BEACONSFIELD INN

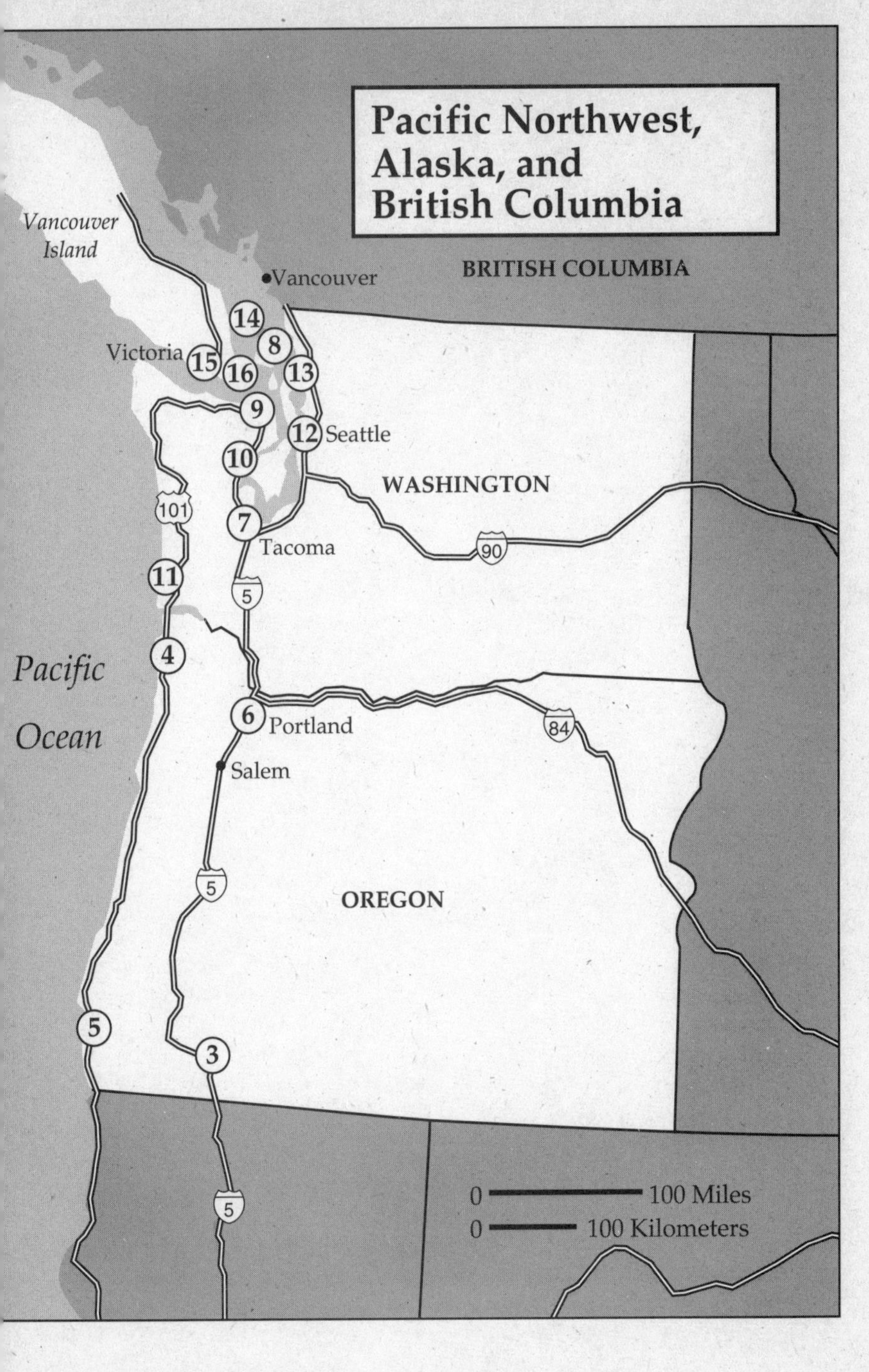

Pacific Northwest, Alaska, and British Columbia
BRITISH COLUMBIA
Vancouver Island
Vancouver
Victoria
Seattle
WASHINGTON
Tacoma
Pacific Ocean
Portland
Salem
OREGON
101
90
5
84
14
8
15
16
13
9
12
10
7
11
4
6
5
3
0 100 Miles
0 100 Kilometers

Pacific Northwest, Alaska, and British Columbia

Alaska

NORTH FACE LODGE/CAMP DENALI

DENALI NATIONAL PARK, ALASKA

The rising sun casts a golden glow across the jagged white peaks of Mt. McKinley (the highest mountain in North America). Beneath it, a moose and her calf amble across a field strewn with wildflowers to drink at the lake. The air is crystal clear; the scent of pine is on the breeze; and the only sound is the buzz of a bee seeking nectar from a flower.

This awesome spectacle begins the day for the privileged guests at *North Face Lodge/Camp Denali,* two separate properties in the heart of *Denali National Park.* Owned and operated by Wallace and Jerryne Cole for a number of years, the two properties offer distinctly different experiences.

Camp Denali, on a mountain ridge with breathtakingly beautiful views, seems almost of another world. It offers a true taste of Alaska's rugged, wild nature. The camp's 17 log cabins were built on land acquired in 1951 through the Alaska homesteading grant. The accommodations are rustic, although certainly not primitive. Each of the cabins can accommodate from two to six people and has a potbelly wood stove (with a wood box that's refilled daily), propane lights, a hot plate for making coffee and tea, and a porch. The country decor includes handmade quilts (made by staff members) on comfortable pine beds and pretty blue calico curtains at the windows.

Nearby, three common buildings each house showers and restrooms, a living room, and a dining room, where all meals are served at communal tables to give guests the chance to share notes. (For those who want to get away from civilization altogether, there also are two separate homestead cabins in the wilderness. They have neither electricity nor running water; an outhouse is nearby, and guests use the showers at *Camp Denali,* 1½ miles away.)

North Face Lodge is almost luxurious by comparison. In a modern motel-like building, it has 14 small guestrooms and one suite, all with electricity and private baths. The guestrooms fill one wing of the building, and a living room with a massive stone fireplace and a dining room are in another wing. Hors d'oeuvres are set out every evening, and meals are served at communal tables.

At both facilities, the day begins early with a full breakfast, perhaps pineapple muffins and green chili soufflé or asparagus quiche. Lunch is served buffet style, or sandwiches, fresh fruit, drinks, and dessert can be packed for a day's journey into the wilderness. A typical dinner might feature barbecued salmon with black bean sauce, homemade bread, and "mud cake" for dessert.

The variety of activities in this naturalist's paradise is staggering, including organized programs to explore the birds of Alaska, the tundra, the geology, and the Aurora Borealis, as well as nature expeditions with professional photographers. There also are self-guided hiking trails, flightseeing, canoeing, biking, rafting, fishing, and panning for gold. Visitors are likely to see moose, elk, caribou, grizzly bear, mountain sheep, beaver, fox, and wolf, but there's plenty of time to commune with other humans, too, since twilight lingers until 10 PM during Alaskan summers.

NORTH FACE LODGE/CAMP DENALI PO Box 67, Denali National Park, AK 99755 (phone: 907-683-2290; fax: 907-683-1568), mid-May through mid-September; PO Box 369, Cornish, NH 03746 (phone: 603-675-2248; fax: 603-675-9125), mid-September through mid-May. These rustic properties offer 17 cabins (sleeping two to six people) with shared baths and twin, double, or queen-size beds and 15 guestrooms with private baths and twin beds. Closed early September through early June. Rate for a double room (including breakfast, lunch, dinner, transportation to

and from railroad, and many activities): $480 to $550. Two-night minimum stay at *North Face Lodge;* three nights at *Camp Denali.* No credit cards accepted. Not appropriate for children under 10. No pets. One dog in residence at the camp. Smoking permitted outdoors only. Wallace and Jerryne Cole, innkeepers.

DIRECTIONS: Guests arrive by railroad; the station is at the entrance of *Denali National Park,* 90 miles (a four-hour drive) from the properties. A van transports guests to and from the station.

GLACIER BAY COUNTRY INN

GUSTAVUS, ALASKA

Those hardy pioneers who trekked across the United States by covered wagon had nothing on Al and Annie Unrein. After graduating from college in Colorado in the 1970s, Al accepted a teaching job in Alaska. Then, in the 1979 annual state land lottery, they won the right to buy a 160-acre parcel of land on Glacier Bay. Suddenly the Unreins were homesteaders.

Starting with nothing but the raw land, they bought a tractor and began building roads, bridges, and finally a house. At first they farmed the land, but soon found that it cost too much to transport the produce to market. By then Glacier Bay had become a prime tourist attraction, so they decided to open a country inn. In 1986 they welcomed their first guests.

The rustic inn, which can be reached only by boat or air, is located in a spectacularly beautiful spot overlooking fields of wildflowers. In the distance is a rain forest, and beyond that, craggy, snow-covered mountains. From the inn's dining room window, it's not unusual to watch black bears as they amble across a field, or to see bald eagles soaring overhead.

Built of spruce, hemlock, and pine logs that were cut and milled on the land, the lodge boasts many attractive architectural features. Some units have floor-to-ceiling windows, some have cathedral ceilings, and others have a built-in window seat or a gambrel roof. The *Nest,* a guestroom (without a private bath) at the top of a three-story tower, is reached by a handcrafted log-and-rope spiral staircase.

The living room, with its overstuffed sofa and rocking chair, is a favorite gathering place, as is the *Potbelly Lounge,* where a stove warms the room and windows overlook the mountains. There's also an inviting library off the living room, with shelves of books and a cabinet full of games.

Furnishings at the inn are a mix of antiques and newly hand-crafted pieces, but all the guestrooms are country-fresh and appealing. One has a bentwood rocker, another an antique washstand, still another, walnut Jenny Lind beds. In other rooms are a pine armoire, a brass bed, and an oak dresser. Tables are topped with gingham, and the walls are hung with quilts made by Annie, her mother, or her grandmother, as well as watercolors by Alaskan artists.

Breakfast, lunch, and dinner are served at common tables in the dining room; dinner also is open to non-guests. Breakfast and lunch are served family style (or the inn will pack a lunch for guests who wish to go exploring). There's a set menu for each meal, but selections and portions are bountiful. Specialties of the house are fresh local seafood—halibut, Dungeness crab, salmon—plus produce from the gardens, including a wide variety of herbs and edible flowers. All breads and desserts are homemade, as are the cookies served with tea in the afternoons.

The natural wonders of *Glacier Bay National Park* are only 7½ miles away, and the staff arranges transportation for those who want to participate in the programs there. In addition, the inn has its own fleet of charter boats for fishing and whale watching. Kayak excursions enable guests to see dolphins and seals up close and to paddle up Glacier Bay. Hiking, flightseeing, bird watching, and biking also are possible.

GLACIER BAY COUNTRY INN PO Box 5, Gustavus, AK 99826 (phone: 907-697-2288; fax: 907-697-2289), May through September; PO Box 2557, St. George, UT 84771 (phone: 801-673-8480; fax: 801-673-8481), October through April. This rustic lodge has nine guestrooms (eight with private baths) with twin or queen-size beds. Closed October through April. Rate for a double room (including breakfast, lunch, afternoon tea, dinner, transportation to and from airport, and some activities): $238. No credit cards accepted. Children welcome. No pets. Smoking permitted outdoors only. Al and Annie Unrein, innkeepers.

DIRECTIONS: The nearest large airport is in Juneau, 50 miles west of Gustavus. *Alaska Airlines* makes the connecting flight to *Gustavus Airport,* where the inn meets guests.

Oregon

MT. ASHLAND INN

ASHLAND, OREGON

Former Bostonians Jerry and Elaine Shanafelt are modern-day pioneers. They packed up and moved to Ashland with all their belongings and a dream: to own a mountaintop and make a living on it.

The 160 acres the Shanafelts purchased in 1975 are in the Siskiyou Mountains at an elevation of 5,500 feet. The Pacific Crest Trail—a hiking path that extends some 2,500 miles from the Canadian border to Mexico—crosses the property. In 1987, they built a two-story, 4,200-square-foot inn on their mountain, using cedar logs cut by Jerry (who has a background in building).

The multitalented couple added their own artwork to their dream house. Jerry made stained glass windows and a spiral staircase. He also hand-carved a panel for each of the guestroom doors. Jerry's beds and bathroom cabinets complement the Early American antiques and Oriental rugs Elaine has collected. And in the *Sky Lakes Suite* is a two-person whirlpool tub and a wet bar.

Elaine has earned awards for her impressive breakfasts, and her recipes have been featured in several cookbooks. A typical menu starts with her "best-ever" granola, fresh juice, and freshly ground coffee. Next come bananas baked in orange-rum sauce with blueberry gingerbread, then an entrée, perhaps eggs and Swiss cheese baked over tiny shrimp, along with whole-wheat biscuits and locally produced honeys and jams.

The Shanafelts have poured so much of themselves into their inn that a visit here feels like a stay with friends. For stay-at-homes they've provided a selection of books, games, and videocassettes; for outdoorsy types, hiking and cross-country trails lead from the front door, and downhill skiing is just 3 miles away.

For some 50 years the tiny town of Ashland has been the home of the famed *Oregon Shakespeare Festival,* which runs from February through October. Historic Jacksonville and Crater Lake are also nearby.

MT. ASHLAND INN 550 Mt. Ashland Rd., PO Box 944, Ashland, OR 97520 (phone: 503-482-8707; 800-830-8707). This log-cabin inn in the Siskiyou Mountains has five guestrooms with private baths and twin, queen-, or king-size beds. Open year-round. Rate for a double room (including full breakfast): $85 to $130. Two-night minimum stay on weekends from June through September and all holiday weekends. Major credit cards accepted. Not appropriate for children under 10. No pets. Smoking permitted outside only. Elaine and Jerry Shanafelt, innkeepers.

DIRECTIONS: The inn is located 25 minutes south of Ashland. Take I-5 to the Mt. Ashland exit and follow signs to the *Mt. Ashland* ski area. The inn is about 6 miles away.

STEPHANIE INN

CANNON BEACH, OREGON

Highway 101 twists and turns up the Oregon coast between California and Washington, offering breathtaking views of the crashing Pacific Ocean from craggy promontories. It's one of nature's great spectacles, with blowholes spouting water into the air like geysers, calm sandy inlets, and massive rocks rising from the sea.

The *Stephanie Inn,* built in 1993 by Steve and Jan Martin, is well positioned to take in all this grandeur. Set on a broad stretch of sandy beach, its windows look out on one of Oregon's favorite monuments, Haystack Rock, a monstrous boulder that juts some 800 feet heavenward. It's a bird sanctuary and off-limits for climbing, but at low tide, pools at its base reveal a wealth of sea life, including starfish and purple and green anemones.

The inn's exterior design combines the sharp angles of Pacific Northwest architecture and the shingled façades associated with New England. Inside, the lobby features beamed old-growth fir ceilings and pillars, a polished oak floor, and a river-rock fireplace. The *Chart Room and Library* has another fireplace, a leather sofa, and bay windows that seem to pull in the ocean. Binoculars are provided to watch the changing scene, which is particularly fascinating when the gray whales are migrating. There's a nightly nibble hour here, with Pacific Northwest wines, cheese, and crackers, that gives guests an opportunity to become acquainted.

The spacious guestrooms are named for women who have contributed to Oregon history and for family friends (the inn itself is named for the owners' daughter). All have ebony four-poster beds strategically placed before a fireplace, an abundance of upholstered seating, and a private deck. Each room has a wet bar, a refrigerator stocked with soft drinks and gourmet snacks, and a VCR for watching movies from the inn's extensive library. Every bath in this romantic retreat features a two-person Jacuzzi.

The full breakfast features such entrées as pancakes with bacon or homemade biscuits with a sausage-mushroom gravy. The prix fixe dinner (which is open to non-guests) is served in elegant surroundings, with a view toward the coastal mountains. Guests are seated at 7PM, when the chef, who specializes in local produce, fish, and meat, enters the dining room and describes the components and preparation of each course. Entrées might be Pacific rockfish wrapped in parchment paper or roasted rack of Ellensberg lamb with parsnip purée. Desserts include an almond Florentine basket filled with fresh berries and served with vanilla-bean sauce or raspberry-chocolate cake.

Amenities include the services of an in-house masseuse and complimentary use of the *Cannon Beach Athletic Club.* In addition to walking along the misty beach, attractions include the *Coaster Theater* for performing arts, bicycling, and horseback riding nearby.

STEPHANIE INN 2740 S. Pacific St., PO Box 219, Cannon Beach, OR 97110 (phone: 503-436-2221; 800-633-3466; fax: 503-436-9711). This inn on the Oregon coast has 46 guestrooms with private baths, queen- or king-size beds, telephones, TV sets, and air conditioning. Wheelchair accessible. Open year-round. Rate for a double room (including full breakfast): $129 to $370. Two-night minimum stay if Saturday is included, for all weekends in July, and throughout August; three and four nights for some holiday and special-event weekends. Major credit cards accepted. Not appropriate for children under 12. No pets. No smoking. Steve and Jan Martin, owners; Sharon Major, manager.

DIRECTIONS: From Portland take Highway 26 west for 75 miles to Highway 101 in Seaside. Follow Highway 101 south for 3 miles to Cannon Beach. Take the third exit for Tolava Park. At the end of the ramp turn right, go 100 feet, and turn right again onto Hemlock Street. Continue on Hemlock about seven blocks and turn left onto Mantanuska. The inn is straight ahead, one block down the hill.

TU TU' TUN LODGE

GOLD BEACH, OREGON

A breeze whispers through the trees, and fresh pine, cedar, and salt scent the air. A river flows gently by, while deer graze in the apple orchard and a bald eagle soars overhead. *Tu Tu' Tun* (the accent is on the second syllable) is not so much a guest lodge as it is an attitude—a serene and tranquil retreat from the workaday world.

Dirk Van Zante's stepfather, an architect, built this spacious cedar-plank lodge in 1970; in 1977, Dirk and his wife, Laurie, were married in front of the floor-to-ceiling, river-rock fireplace in the inn's living room; today, they are the innkeepers. They have created a unique hideaway beside the Rogue River, 6 miles east of Oregon's spectacular coast.

The lodge is a linear building, its architecture reminiscent of Frank Lloyd Wright. It would be a mistake to call the guestrooms rustic, although they have log beds; with their clean lines and comfortable furniture, the interiors are recall Wright's Prairie style. Each of the rooms has a private deck or balcony with a six-foot-wide door that brings the outdoors in. Five rooms are equipped with outdoor tubs, and eight have fireplaces. Floral and geometric cottons and woolens adorn the beds and upholstered furniture. The walls are decorated with old fishing gear and mining equipment (nearby Gold Beach got its name from a flurry of mining activity in the mid-1800s) and scenic watercolors by local artists.

Breakfast and dinner are offered to guests (for an additional fee) as well as to non-guests. The full buffet-style breakfast is served in the dining room and includes juice, fruit, fresh-baked breads, and two entrées. (A breakfast basket with coffee appears at the door of those who plan an early-morning guided fishing trip.) At dinnertime, everyone assembles in the living room for hors d'oeuvres and Oregon wine; then guests are seated in the dining room at five round tables with views of the setting sun across the river. Fires in two stone pits on the terrace add to the drama. Dinner features the bounty of the nearby river, ocean, and forests: fresh salmon, mesquite-grilled meat, baked cod, and desserts made with local berries. Following the meal, guests may linger on the terrace, sipping a sweet wine and conversing with new friends. On returning to their rooms, they'll find the beds turned down and a plate of homemade cookies.

The inn's wooded setting offers a heated lap pool, a four-hole pitch-and-putt golf course, horseshoes, and croquet. Inside are an antique player piano, a pool table, and a variety of games and books. The Rogue is a designated National Wild and Scenic River: A jet boat makes the trip to its whitewater section from the inn's dock. Fishing for salmon and steelhead trout is a popular pastime, and ocean beaches, hiking, and bird watching are nearby.

TU TU' TUN LODGE 96550 N. Bank Rogue Rd., Gold Beach, OR 97444 (phone: 503-247-6664; fax: 503-247-0672). This lodge has 19 guestrooms with private baths, twin, double, queen-, or king-size beds, and telephones. Wheelchair accessible. Open year-round; dining room closed November through April. Rate for a double room (including evening hors d'oeuvres): $125 to $275; breakfast and dinner: $37.50 per person per day. Two-night minimum stay from July through September. Discover, MasterCard, and Visa accepted. Children welcome. No pets. One black labrador in residence. No smoking. Dirk and Laurie Van Zante, innkeepers.

DIRECTIONS: From Highway 101 take North Bank Rogue Road, which starts at the north end of the bridge over the Rogue River in Gold Beach. Travel 7 miles to the inn.

HERON HAUS

PORTLAND, OREGON

Julie Keppeler's years in Hawaii are reflected not only in the overall airiness of her spacious three-story home, but also in the names of the guestrooms: *Kanui, Kulia, Ko, Manu,* and *Makua.* Despite her love of the islands, she was drawn back to the Northwest, where her grandfather was an early settler.

Heron Haus, a magnificent 7,500-square-foot English Tudor mansion, was built in 1904 by a cranberry grower, but when Julie discovered it, in 1986, it was in sorry shape. Nevertheless, she couldn't resist its beautiful hilltop site with expansive views of Portland and the Cascade Mountains. Today, with her renovations completed, guests enjoy the ultimate in luxurious quarters and scenery: Mt. St. Helens is visible from the living room and the mahogany-paneled library. From the enclosed sunroom, which overlooks the pool, guests enjoy a garden that displays a profusion of blooms from spring through fall.

The house has leaded-glass windows, intricate ceiling moldings, and parquet floors. Ballast stones from an old sailing ship were used to build walls at the entrance and around the pool. There's also a small orchard of pear, apple, and cherry trees.

The spacious guestrooms, decorated in soft shades of blue, lavender, and rose, also have spectacular views. For example, *Kulia* boasts a raised spa on a porch with a view of the city, Mt. St. Helens, and Mt. Rainier. *Kanui* looks eastward and has a view of Mt. Hood. *Ko*'s bath contains the original seven-nozzle shower stall. The three guestrooms on the top floor, in the former servants' quarters, all have brass beds. The room rate includes continental breakfast, which is served in the dining room and included fresh fruit and pastries.

The inn is located in Portland's Northwest Hills, a residential district studded with fine homes and only blocks from a bustling shopping area. Because of the inn's popularity with business travelers, Julie offers a computer, fax, and work area for guests. Boutiques, fine restaurants, the *Oregon Museum of Science and Industry,* and *Washington Park,* with its rose gardens, are nearby.

HERON HAUS 2545 NW Westover Rd., Portland, OR 97210 (phone: 503-274-1846; fax: 503-243-1075). This bed and breakfast establishment has five guestrooms with private baths, queen- or king-size beds, telephones, TV sets, and air conditioning. Open year-round. Rate for a double room (including continental breakfast): $85 to $250. MasterCard and Visa accepted. Not appropriate for children under 10. No pets. No smoking. Julie Keppeler, innkeeper.

DIRECTIONS: Traveling on I-405, take the Everett Street exit onto Glisan (a one-way street). Turn right on 24th Street and travel three blocks to Johnson Street. Turn left onto Johnson, then right onto Westover. Proceed half a block up the incline and look for the address on the rock wall.

WILLCOX HOUSE

BREMERTON, WASHINGTON

Despite its Bremerton address, *Willcox House* is actually located about 17 miles from town on Hood Canal. A long private road dips past glades of lush ferns and around massive cedar trees for more than a mile before reaching the gatehouse. The arched log-and-stone structure that spans the roadway used to be the servants' quarters.

The massive house was built in 1936 by noted Northwest architect Lionel Pries for a retired Marine Corps colonel, Julian Willcox, and his wife, Constance. Pries's clean, linear design evidences a Frank Lloyd Wright influence. No expense was spared, and the 10,000-square-foot mansion reportedly cost a quarter of a million dollars, an astronomical figure in a Depression-era economy.

After retirement, Willcox became a war consultant to the movie industry, and his celebrity visitors lent a glamorous cachet to the new home. Locally the house was called the "grand entertainment capital of Hood Canal," and records indicate that Clark Gable, Errol Flynn, Spencer Tracy, and Ernest Hemingway all stayed here. Mrs. Willcox continued to live in the house until 1971, but by the time Phillip and Cecilia Hughes purchased it in 1988, it had also been a boys' boarding school and a conference center.

The large entry hall is clad in faux marble panels. There are oak parquet floors throughout. The massive *Great Room,* with its burnished walnut walls, copper fireplace, and overstuffed sofas, overlooks the restored gardens and the unheated saltwater swimming pool. The adjacent dining room and terrace beyond, afford spectacular views across Hood Canal to the Olympic Mountains. A favorite with guests, however, is the clubby library, where walnut shelves are stocked with books on everything from cooking to local history. In winter, the leather chairs in front of the fireplace encourage immersion in a Hemingway novel. Downstairs, a clock that runs backward hangs over the mahogany bar, and a gameroom provides pool, boardgames, puzzles, and darts. Be sure to ask to see the "secret" room–a closet camouflaged within a closet—and the hidden passages between bedrooms.

The spacious guestrooms are decorated in English country style. Many retain features original to the house. In *Constance's Room,* for example, the marble Art Deco fireplace and the built-in vanity are reminders of the many years Mrs. Willcox spent here. *Julian's Room,* however, contains luxuries of which the owner never would have dreamed: a king-size bed and a Jacuzzi. *Clark Gable's Room* has a balcony overlooking the rose garden.

In addition to the garden, the grounds offer wisteria-covered terraces, goldfish ponds with water lilies, an Oriental pond surrounded by Japanese sculptures, and a path to the beach, where visitors tie up their boats at the 300-foot pier.

Cecilia prepares breakfast (as well as lunch and dinner upon request)—perhaps cream cheese–stuffed French toast or apple pancakes. In the afternoon, wine, cheese, and fruit are served. The set dinner includes seasonal produce and fish or shellfish. A salmon steak with chive-and-lime butter might be followed by a peach-and-ginger cobbler.

Hiking trails lead from the inn across the surrounding hills; golf, fishing, and biking are nearby.

WILLCOX HOUSE 2390 Tekiu Rd. NW, Bremerton, WA 98312 (phone: 360-830-4492; fax: 360-830-0506). This mansion on Hood Canal has five guestrooms with private baths and queen- or king-size beds. Wheelchair accessible. Open year-round. Rate for a double room (including full breakfast and afternoon wine and cheese): $120 to $185. Two-night minimum stay on weekends. Discover, MasterCard, and Visa accepted. Not appropriate for children under 16. No pets. A dog and cat outdoors. Smoking permitted outside only. Cecilia and Phillip Hughes, innkeepers.

DIRECTIONS: From Seattle take the ferry from Colman Dock to Bremerton (one hour). In Bremerton drive west on Sixth Street, which becomes Kitsap Way; continue for about 1½ miles to Northlake Way and bear left at the fork. Drive 1 mile and bear left again onto Seabeck Highway. Drive almost 3 miles and turn left onto Holly Road. After another 5 miles (past *Camp Union*), turn left at the stop sign onto Seabeck-Holly Road. Drive 5 miles to Old Holly Hill Road and bear right at the fork. Go 200 yards and turn right at the mailboxes onto Tekiu Road. Follow the paved road for just over 1 mile, turning left at the cabin and driving through the gatehouse.

TURTLEBACK FARM INN

EASTSOUND, ORCAS ISLAND, WASHINGTON

Orcas Island, a jewel in the string of enchanting islands in the San Juan archipelago, is snuggled into the elbow of Puget Sound, protected, on the west, by Vancouver Island and, on the east, by the mainland. Access to the islands is via ferry from Anacortes, 75 miles north of Seattle. Bring a camera, as the trip through narrow, glistening channels with lush, forested islands on either side is a shutterbug's delight. The views are one of the things that make the journey worthwhile. *Turtleback Farm* is another.

When Susan and Bill Fletcher purchased their 80-acre farm in 1985, it was run-down and overgrown. Built in the 1870s, it had been a dairy farm and later a cattle ranch. Bill was a real-estate broker from San Francisco when they began looking for a summer cottage. Thoughts of operating an inn hadn't crossed their minds, but when they saw the farm, they changed their career paths.

Today *Turtleback Farm* is still a farm—the Fletchers raise Suffolk sheep, chickens, geese, bees, and pigeons—but after years of painstaking work and the addition of a new wing, they also have created a cozy retreat in a handsome setting overlooking acres of pastureland.

The original shallow Rumford fireplace still stands in the living room, where there's also a corner game table. Furnished with antiques and contemporary pieces, the seven guestrooms are simple and uncluttered, with hardwood floors and floral duvets. Several rooms have private decks; nearly all have claw-foot tubs in the bathrooms.

A full breakfast is served either on the broad deck in warm weather or in the dining room. It features homemade granola, home-baked breads, and a main course using fresh eggs.

The San Juan islands are breathtakingly beautiful and enjoy a relatively mild climate. Guests will find golf, tennis, fishing, boating, sailing, kayaking, hiking in *Moran State Park,* and bicycling nearby.

TURTLEBACK FARM INN **Crow Valley Rd., Rte. 1, Box 650, Eastsound, WA 98245 (phone: 360-376-4914). This country inn has seven guestrooms with private baths and double, queen-, or king-size beds. Wheelchair accessible. Open year-round. Rate for a double room (including full breakfast): $80 to $160. Two-night minimum stay from May through October, weekends, and holidays. MasterCard and Visa accepted. Not appropriate for children under eight. No pets. Two dogs and farm animals on property. Smoking permitted outside only. William and Susan Fletcher, innkeepers.**

DIRECTIONS: From Seattle take I-5 north for 65 miles to Route 20, just beyond Mt. Vernon. Follow Route 20 for 10 miles to Anacortes and the ferry. From the ferry dock on Orcas Island go north on Horseshoe Highway for almost 3 miles. Take the first left turn toward Deer Harbor and travel almost 1 mile. Turn right onto Crow Valley Road and continue about 3 more miles to the inn.

OLD CONSULATE INN/F. W. HASTINGS HOUSE

PORT TOWNSEND, WASHINGTON

Port Townsend occupies an enviable site on Admiralty Inlet at the entrance to Puget Sound beside the Straits of Juan de Fuca. Settled by Loren Hastings in 1850, its history predates Seattle's. It soon became the main port of entry to the sound, and a fine customshouse was built. Increased trade also attracted consulates from such far-flung countries as Chile and Sweden, and grand houses were built for their representatives.

In the 1880s, speculators thought Port Townsend was going to be the terminus for the *Union Pacific Railroad* and believed their town would become the New York City of the West. In anticipation of this, a clutch of impressive brick buildings was erected along the waterfront. On the bluff above, elaborate gingerbread Victorians rivaled houses in San Francisco.

The railroad didn't come, however, and the prosperous little boom evaporated. Fortunately there was no reason to modernize, so the buildings have remained, now forming a National Historic District of some 70 structures, thought to be the best remaining example of a Victorian seacoast town north of San Francisco.

The *Old Consulate Inn* is a prime remnant of that impressive era. Built in 1889 by Frank Hastings, son of the town's founder, it served for a time as the German Consulate. Nicknamed the "Red Victorian on the Hill" and the most photographed house in town, it is a soufflé of turrets, gables, chimneys, and gingerbread trim, its wraparound porch complete with a swing.

When innkeepers Joanna and Rob Jackson purchased the house in 1987, it was sorely in need of an overhaul, but the Jacksons were undaunted (Rob is a building contractor). They rebuilt the ornate carved oak staircase and the front porch, installed a private bathroom for each guestroom, and painted the exterior burgundy with deep green, pale green, charcoal, and black trim. In back, they fashioned an octagonal gazebo to match the style of the house and installed an eight-person hot tub that affords soakers a spectacular view of the bay.

The common rooms on the main floor have 10½-foot ceilings and include an entrance foyer where guests have morning coffee; there's also a formal parlor with a wood-burning fireplace, a grand piano, and an antique organ. In the library, with another fireplace, numerous books and jigsaw puzzles provide diversions and, in the gameroom, a pool table and a VCR with an extensive video library round out the indoor entertainment options. The most popular tape is *An Officer and a Gentleman,* which was filmed in Port Townsend. Joanna's collection of glamorous dolls decorates tables in the common rooms (an elegantly clad "madam" presides over the gameroom) and fills a glass-enclosed cabinet in the foyer.

Guestroom furnishings include antique Victorian pieces such as marble-topped dressers, a four-poster rice bed, as well as brass, iron, and wicker beds. Every room has a view of the Olympic Mountains, the marina, or the inlet. One suite has a sitting room in the rounded turret, a claw-foot tub in the bath, and a sweeping view from Admiralty Inlet to the mountains.

The seven-course breakfasts served in the ornate dining room are legendary, with juice and fruit, an egg dish with meat, potatoes and vegetables, a cheese platter, freshly baked sweet breads and biscuits, and a dessert such as apricot-amaretto-almond cheesecake. In the evening wine, sherry, and brandy are available.

There are interesting shops and restaurants downtown; theater, concerts, festivals, and seminars are available in nearby Ft. Warden. Tennis facilities are in the area as well.

OLD CONSULATE INN/F. W. HASTINGS HOUSE 313 Walker St., Port Townsend, WA 98368 (phone: 360-385-6753; 800-300-6753; fax: 360-385-2097). This Victorian inn, in the historic town of Port Townsend, has eight guestrooms with

private baths and queen- or king-size beds. Open year-round. Rate for a double room (including full breakfast, afternoon tea, and evening refreshments): $79 to $190. Major credit cards accepted. Not appropriate for children under 12. No pets. Fred, a German shorthaired pointer, in residence. No smoking permitted indoors. Joanna and Rob Jackson, innkeepers.

DIRECTIONS: From Seattle take the Winslow ferry from Colman Dock to Bainbridge Island (35 minutes) and follow the signs to the Hood Canal Bridge. After crossing the bridge, follow Route 104 for 5 miles to Highway 19. Turn right (north) and continue for 20 miles to Port Townsend. Watch for the *Port Townsend Motel* on the left and drive up the hill beside it (Washington Street). The inn is on the left at the top of the hill, on the corner of Washington and Walker Streets.

MANOR FARM INN

POULSBO, WASHINGTON

The *Manor Farm Inn* is full of surprises. In a pastoral landscape of hay fields and dairy farms, far removed from urban life, you wouldn't expect to find such a high level of sophistication. But, then, you probably don't know innkeeper Jill Hughes.

After completing her education at *Stanford,* majoring in psychology, she moved to the Pacific Northwest and, in 1975, purchased what was then a working dairy farm. Its collection of old buildings still remains. The farmhouse, built in 1886, now houses an enormous kitchen and two dining rooms. The barn and chicken house in back, continue to serve their original purpose. The adjacent fields, dotted with Coopworth sheep, are neatly bordered by white rail fences.

In 1982, Jill added a wing of seven spacious guestrooms plus a drawing room with fireplace. The latter is a favorite late-day gathering place. In the center of the U-shaped inn, a courtyard contains a profusion of flowers, and roses climb the posts to the roof of the verandah.

Guestrooms are furnished with natural pine pieces. Fresh flowers add bright touches to the neutral carpets and upholstery. Several rooms have wood-burning fireplaces or private porches or gardens. The *Farm Cottage* across the street provides more seclusion, plus a hot tub and a fireplace. Another house, the *Beach Cottage,* also with a hot tub on the deck and a fireplace, is 2 miles away on Hood Canal.

Here, morning begins with a gentle knock on the door announcing the arrival of fresh-squeezed orange juice and hot-from-the-oven scones with fresh raspberry jam. This tasty wake-up call is followed, in the dining rooms, by a three-course breakfast, which might include French toast or an apple crêpe.

Fishing in the inn's trout pond is popular, as are hiking the 25 acres of fields and woods, playing croquet, badminton, or horseshoes, or taking a ride on the inn's bicycles—but simply reading a book under the vine-covered trellis beside the courtyard is just as tempting. The tiny Scandinavian community of Poulsbo is interesting to visit, and the inn is near boating and golf.

MANOR FARM INN 26069 Big Valley Rd. NE, Poulsbo, WA 98370 (phone: 360-779-4628; fax: 360-779-4876). This country inn on the Kitsap Peninsula has nine guestrooms with private baths and queen- or king-size beds. Open year-round. Rate for a double room (including full breakfast or Sunday brunch and afternoon tea): $100 to $200. MasterCard and Visa accepted. Not appropriate for children under 16. No pets. Farm animals on property. Smoking permitted outdoors only. Jill Hughes, innkeeper.

DIRECTIONS: From Colman Dock in Seattle, take the Winslow ferry to Bainbridge Island (35 minutes). Follow Route 305 across the Agate Pass Bridge to Poulsbo. Turn right onto Bond Road and go a quarter mile; turn left onto Big Valley Road. The inn is 3½ miles down on the left.

SHELBURNE INN

SEAVIEW, WASHINGTON

David Campiche grew up on the 29-mile expanse of beach called the Long Beach Peninsula; he met Laurie Anderson, a native Seattleite, when she was visiting her parents nearby. When the old *Shelburne Inn* was put up for sale in 1977, they bought it, and now operate it as a very special retreat.

The *Shelburne Inn* was built in 1896 and soon became a popular summer resort for Portland folks, who reached it by traveling the Columbia River by sternwheeler, then continuing the journey by narrow-gauge railway. They made the trek to walk the gray sand beaches, go clamming at low tide, fish, and climb over the rocks at *North Head Lighthouse,* where the Columbia River empties into the Pacific Ocean (near the spot where Lewis and Clark completed their cross-country expedition).

The inn was moved across the street in 1911, and attached to another structure, but many of its original features remain: the tongue-and-groove wood paneling, the brick fireplace in the living room, the ceilings with exposed beams, and the brass chandeliers. Some of the spectacular Art Nouveau stained glass windows were rescued by David and Laurie from a church in England that was being demolished.

Listed on the National Register of Historic Places, the inn is now filled with antiques the couple picked up on their travels. There are oak dressers, spectacular walnut bedroom suites, Oriental rugs on the hardwood floors, and brass beds with quilts. Fresh flowers from the inn's extensive gardens scent the rooms. Room No. 15 has a massive English armoire, an octagonal table inlaid with an intricate pattern, an elegant bed dressed with a crocheted spread, and a balcony overlooking the herb and flower garden. The tile baths are handsomely appointed with brass and porcelain fixtures.

Breakfasts, cooked by both David and Laurie, are so delicious and so popular that the recipes have been assembled into a cookbook. Fresh herbs, berries, and edible flowers from the gardens enhance the local seafood. Perhaps a seafood frittata or asparagus crêpes with sweet curry sauce will be the day's offering.

The inn's outstanding restaurant, *Shoalwater's,* is operated as a separate business by friends Tony and Ann Kischner. Its Victorian decor includes oak chairs, interior pillars, and stained glass windows. It has won numerous awards for its imaginative cuisine. Oysters, for example, might be paired with champagne, brie, and saffron. Local produce and an extensive cellar of Northwest wines figure prominently.

Beachcombing, shops, the *Lewis and Clark Interpretive Center,* museums, and a bird sanctuary are all nearby.

SHELBURNE INN **PO Box 250, Seaview, WA 98644 (phone: 360-642-2442; fax: 360-642-8904). This country inn on the Long Beach Peninsula has 15 guestrooms with private baths and double or queen-size beds. Wheelchair accessible. Open year-round; restaurant closed for two weeks following *Thanksgiving.* Rate for a double room (including full breakfast): $95 to $170. Two-night minimum stay on weekends and holidays. Major credit cards accepted. Children welcome. No pets. No smoking. Laurie Anderson and David Campiche, innkeepers.**

DIRECTIONS: From Portland take Highway 26 north for 75 miles to Highway 101 in Seaside. Follow Highway 101 north for 22 miles across the Columbia River into Washington. Continue on Highway 101 north for 10 miles to Seaview. Continue to the flashing yellow light and turn right onto Highway 103. The inn is five blocks ahead on the left. From Seattle take I-5 south through Olympia to the Aberdeen/Port Angeles exit to Highway 12. Follow signs for Aberdeen. Follow Highway 12 for 37 miles to Montesano and turn south onto Route 107, which leads in 8 miles to Highway 101 south. Follow Route 101 for 62 miles to Seaview, then follow the directions above.

INN AT THE MARKET

SEATTLE, WASHINGTON

Seattle's *Pike Place Market* has changed little since the 1800s, when farmers drove their trucks into town on Saturday mornings and people gathered to buy the fresh seafood, fruit, vegetables, flowers, and livestock. Today, the market stretches some five blocks above Elliott Bay, spilling down four levels in a warren of shops and restaurants reached by rickety stairs and tucked into improbably tiny spaces. From vantage points throughout the market are awesome views of the busy harbor, with Mt. Rainier as a backdrop.

The *Pike Place Market* is Seattle's heart. It's also where the *Inn at the Market* welcomes guests.

On the way to the discreet lobby door, guests cross a small brick courtyard with benches, café tables, and chairs; in the center is a cherry tree beside a fountain ringed with geraniums and lobelia. In the lobby, where guests gather for morning coffee and evening cider, a crackling fire and overstuffed sofas in paisley prints create a gracious country French ambience.

All guestrooms have floor-to-ceiling bay windows; those on the water side have breathtaking views of sunsets across the water, while others overlook the city or the courtyard. A charming rooftop deck with chairs and tables is open to all guests. The rooms are furnished with custom-made pine armoires, beds, and nightstands, and are decorated in earth and sea tones. Several incorporate Laura Ashley fabrics, but most feature plaids or checks. With everything from good-size desks to spacious tiled baths, the guestrooms are well appointed—there's even a snack basket of Northwest products, including ground coffee, excellent cookies, chips, and local chocolates.

Three restaurants share the courtyard with the inn, although meals are not included in the room rate. *Bacco* prepares excellent breakfasts that can be delivered to the room. *Campagne,* an award-winning eatery, features innovative French fare and is open for lunch and dinner. *Café Campagne* is a more informal French bistro. During the summer months lunch and dinner are served in the courtyard.

The inn is only two blocks from Seattle's shopping district, and the *Seattle Art Museum* is nearby as well. Guests are advised to leave their cars in the inn's garage and walk or use the city's excellent transit system. For those who like to pedal, a bicycle path runs 7 miles along the waterfront from *Myrtle Edwards Park* to *Pioneer Square,* past seafood restaurants, the *Seattle Aquarium,* and colorful working piers.

INN AT THE MARKET **86 Pine St., Seattle, WA 98101 (phone: 206-443-3600; 800-446-4484; fax: 206-448-0631). This inn at *Pike Place Market,* overlooking Seattle's waterfront, has 65 guestrooms with private baths, double, queen-, or king-size beds, telephones, TV sets, and air conditioning. Wheelchair accessible. Open year-round. Rate for a double room: $125 to $300. Two-night minimum stay on some holidays. Major credit cards accepted. Children welcome. No pets. Smoking permitted in designated guestrooms only. Market Group Management, owners; Joyce Woodard, general manager.**

DIRECTIONS: From I-5 traveling north, take the Seneca Street exit and continue down Seneca to First Avenue. Go four blocks north to Pine Street and turn left. The entrance to the inn is in the middle of the block on the right.

INN AT LANGLEY

LANGLEY, WHIDBEY ISLAND, WASHINGTON

Owners Paul and Pam Schell have created a retreat woven of earth and sky and trees. The inn has a spectacular waterfront view of the Saratoga Passage, where freighters with goods bound for the Orient slip by, and the Cascade Mountains in the background. Every room has a window wall with doors leading to a tiled deck. A broad, greenery-filled planter serves as a divider between the deck and the view.

The building has a cedar-shake exterior; inside, rough-plank cedar walls impart that heady aroma that makes you feel as if you're deep in the woods. Made of logs, glass, and slate, the furniture is of solid, Craftsman-style construction in soothing shades of brown and gray. The bathrooms, done in quarry tile, have open showers (without walls) and two-person Jacuzzis strategically placed to capture views of both the water and the flicker of the fire in the bedroom hearth.

Continental breakfast—juice, fruit, granola, and muffins—is set out on the counter in the stunning open kitchen/dining room, with its double-sided river-rock fireplace. The plank tables and wrought-iron chandelier were made by local artists. Dinner is served here on Friday and Saturday nights for an additional charge. Chef Steve Nogal (who is co-manager with his wife, Sandy) first gathers guests for sherry beside the fireplace, where he describes the evening's set menu and the wines that will be served. The group then moves to the dining room. The preparations are creative yet simple, perhaps using oysters from nearby Penn Cove, freshly caught salmon, or mushrooms or loganberries gathered in the woods. The relaxed, convivial evening ends with a glass of port.

The inn's location on Whidbey Island in Puget Sound is convenient for beachcombing, fishing, and shopping.

INN AT LANGLEY **400 First St., PO Box 835, Langley, WA 98260 (phone and fax: 206-221-3033). This inn has 24 guestrooms with private baths, queen-size beds, telephones, and TV sets. Wheelchair accessible. Open year-round; dinner served Fridays and Saturdays year-round, plus Sundays in summer. Rate for a double room (including continental breakfast): $169 to $249. Two-night minimum stay on weekends. Major credit cards accepted. Not appropriate for children under 12. No pets. No smoking. Paul and Pam Schell, innkeepers; Steve and Sandy Nogal, managers.**

DIRECTIONS: The inn is 32 miles north of Seattle, accessible by ferry from the south and by the Deception Pass Bridge from the north. From Seattle the trip takes approximately 90 minutes: Take I-5 north to Exit 189 (Whidbey Island/Mukilteo Ferry), following signs to the ferry landing, where boats depart every half hour. Arriving in Clinton, follow Highway 525 north to Maxwelton Road. Turn right and proceed to the end of the road; bear left onto Langley Road and continue on to Cascade Street, which becomes First Street. The inn is on the right. From the north take I-5 south to Anacortes and Deception Pass; cross the bridge to Whidbey Island. Driving south on Highway 20/525, turn left onto Maxwelton Road and follow directions above.

OCEANWOOD COUNTRY INN

MAYNE ISLAND, BRITISH COLUMBIA

The Gulf Islands are a string of lush green emeralds stretching some 150 miles north from Sidney, through the Straits of Georgia, to the Campbell River. With charter boats available for salmon fishing and sailboats skittering through the channels, the area is a veritable paradise for recreational boaters and fisherfolk.

Mayne Island, part of the Gulf Island chain, is a pastoral 8-square-mile spot dotted with orchards and sheep farms. It's rugged, remote, and wildly beautiful, yet it can be reached by ferry in one hour from either Vancouver Island or the mainland.

Marilyn and Jonathan Chilvers pursued careers in advertising and public relations in Vancouver until 1990, when they decided to trade city for country life. They made an inn of the Tudor-style house that had been their summer retreat on this island getaway. The house, located on 10 acres with spectacular views of Navy Channel, was renovated and expanded and now boasts 12 luxurious guestrooms, as well as several elegant common rooms.

Reminiscent of a fine English country home, the *Living Room* has polished oak floors, Oriental rugs, and floral sofas before the fireplace. The *Library,* a cozy nook with an abundance of books, a window seat, and another fireplace, also contains an outstanding video collection for viewing in the small conference room. The inviting, sunny *Garden Room* is filled with plants and a multitude of books about gardens and gardening. The *Gameroom* contains tables for bridge, chess, backgammon, and boardgames, as well as puzzles. A hot tub is perched on a secluded deck that affords outstanding views of the channel; there's a sauna as well. Plus, eight of the guestrooms have fireplaces and nine have soaking tubs; most have water views.

Each of the guestrooms is named for a flower and has ceiling borders fancifully stenciled in that flower's motif. The *Rose Room,* for example, has a white wicker bed with an arched headboard and a stenciled garland of roses above it. This room also contains a marble-faced fireplace, French doors opening onto a private balcony, stairs leading down to the gardens, and a whirlpool tub with a view of the water. The *Lavender Room* has a marine blue carpet and a spectacular four-poster canopy bed, lavishly draped with blue-and-white striped fabric and accented with blue-and-rose floral chintz. The bed's raised platform provides unobstructed views of the water. Down three steps is a sofa placed before a fireplace and a two-person soaking tub with its own unobstructed view. A private deck completes the picture.

Guests are served a full breakfast—always with a hot entrée and delicious home-baked goods. Afternoon tea, served on fine china with silver spoons, features homemade pastries. Dinner (also open to non-guests) is a major attraction here. The waterfront restaurant has wraparound windows that capture the ever-changing scene on Navy Channel, yet the presentations and the food are as spectacular as the setting. The prix fixe menu offers a choice of two entrées each night and features the bounty of the Pacific Northwest, from fish and shellfish to produce and herbs from the garden. It might include roast free-range quail served on basil polenta or trout with spinach and blackberries. The Chilverses are very knowledgeable about local wines and provide a marvelous selection of California and Northwest vintages, by both the bottle and glass.

Mayne Island is laced with lanes for bicycling, cliff-edge footpaths for walking, and vest-pocket beaches for sunning. The Chilverses provide bicycles and will arrange kayak excursions to explore the coves and watch the harbor seals at play. Golf is available on nearby Pender Island, and hiking and tennis also are in the vicinity. Mayne Island is noted for its crafts shops, especially those selling goods woven from locally spun wool.

OCEANWOOD COUNTRY INN 630 Dinner Bay Rd., Mayne Island, BC V0N 2J0, Canada (phone: 604-539-5074; fax: 604-539-3002). This country inn in the Gulf Islands has 12 guestrooms with private baths and twin or queen-size beds. Closed December through February. Rate for a double room (including full breakfast and afternoon tea): CN $120 to $295 (US $95 to $233 at press time). MasterCard and Visa accepted. Not appropriate for children under 16. No pets. Smoking permitted in the library and outside only. Marilyn and Jonathan Chilvers, innkeepers.

DIRECTIONS: From the Village Bay ferry terminal, turn right onto Dalton Drive. At the junction with Mariner's Way, turn right and then immediately left onto Dinner Bay Road. Continue on Dinner Bay Road for half a mile until you see *Oceanwood*'s sign on the left. For those who arrive by boat, a mooring buoy is located just off the inn's beach.

SOOKE HARBOUR HOUSE INN AND RESTAURANT

SOOKE, BRITISH COLUMBIA

Sinclair and Frederique Philip have created an idyllic retreat with luxurious guestrooms and outstanding food on a remote rocky promontory called Whiffen Spit, 23 miles west of Victoria on Vancouver Island. Seldom will you find innkeepers more enthusiastic about their chosen calling or more knowledgeable about how to make it successful. Indeed, Sinclair has been credited with substantially increasing tourism on Vancouver Island.

As you walk toward the entrance of the inn, the raised beds containing more than 200 varieties of vegetables, herbs, and edible flowers give the first hint of the serious attention paid to food here. Sinclair also considers the sea to be an important part of his "garden"—he not only reaps fish and shellfish from the inn's tidal tank, but harvests more than 60 kinds of seaweed.

The inn's chefs have won the admiration of food writers from around the world for their imaginative use of local fresh and organic ingredients. Much of what is on your plate may have been picked from the inn's garden only moments before. The full breakfast, which changes daily, might include juice, fruit, muffins, and pancakes or French toast; lunch also is served to guests.

Dinner (open to non-guests) is a truly memorable experience. The menu changes daily, but a meal might begin with an appetizer of local beach runner oysters on the half shell with day lily sauce. The entrées—frequently featuring locally raised organic meat or locally caught salmon, halibut, skate, or black cod—are equally impressive. The evening's bill of fare might include roasted veal with a crust of coriander, tarragon, carraway, and pine nuts, served with chive flower and cremini mushroom sauce, or roasted yellowtail rockfish filet with an island ale, horseradish, and rosemary cream sauce, accompanied by a pinto bean and cilatro pancake. Be sure to order the house salad of organic garden greens tossed with bright nasturtium and pansy blossoms and splashed with a hazelnut oil dressing. As flavorful as it is colorful, the salad is served on piece of slate. Among the dessert choices might be the unique and delicious wild rose crêpes filled with warm rhubarb and fir-infused honey compote and served with tarragon ice cream. The excellent wine list includes California, Washington, and Oregon brands, as well as Canadian vintages.

Vying with the inventive food for your attention is the spectacular view from the inn's dining room. A wall of windows overlooks the Strait of Juan de Fuca and the snow-capped peaks of the Olympic Mountains beyond. Guests can watch the seals frolicking on the rocks beyond the garden and may even see a bald eagle soaring above the water. Vines of passion fruit cascade past the windows, and a clump of lavender adds a touch of color to the patio. The light and airy room is decorated with Frederique's imaginative flower and herb arrangements and unusual Native American artwork.

In fact, the entire inn is a showcase of British Columbian art. Each of the guestrooms has a fireplace and a name that reflects its decor. In the *Victor Newman Longhouse Room,* for example, are masks, paintings, and drawings by local Kwakiutl artist Victor Newman (who even painted a grouping of sacred native symbols on the red cedar surrounding the tub); there's also a vaulted ceiling with a skylight, a Jacuzzi with an ocean view, and a four-poster bed. The *Underwater Orchard Room* has stained glass windows that depict deep-sea life, plus a hot tub for two on a private deck.

Sports fishing, beachcombing, and bird watching are all nearby, as is hiking on the West Coast Trail, which extends more than 62 miles.

SOOKE HARBOUR HOUSE 1528 Whiffen Spit Rd., RR4, Sooke, BC V0S 1N0, Canada (phone: 604-642-3421; 800-889-9688; fax: 604-642-6988). This inn has 13 guestrooms with private baths, queen- or king-size beds, and telephones. Wheelchair accessible. Closed January. Rate for a double room (including full breakfast and lunch): CN $225 to $295 (US $178 to $233 at press time). Major credit cards accepted. Children welcome. Pets allowed with advance permission only (and a $20 charge per day). Smoking permitted outside only. Frederique and Sinclair Philip, innkeepers.

DIRECTIONS: Sooke is on Vancouver Island, approximately 23 miles (37 km) from Victoria. From Victoria take Highway 1 west to Highway 14. Continue west on Highway 14 to the village of Sooke. Approximately 1 mile (1.6 km) past the traffic light, turn left onto Whiffen Spit Road and continue to the end. The inn is on the right, next to the water.

ABIGAIL'S BED AND BREAKFAST HOTEL

VICTORIA, BRITISH COLUMBIA

Bill McKechnie, a builder/lawyer/architect, has a knack for reworking dilapidated heritage homes into charming, modern-day hostelries. His latest project is *Abigail's.* On a cul-de-sac in a quiet residential area, the English

Tudor building, with its forest green and burnt-orange trim, is surrounded by flower beds full of petunias, marigolds, and pansies.

Bill's concept for the hotel's interior was inspired by a Rodin sculpture of a young woman with flowers in her hat (a copy rests on a table near the front door); for him, it embodies the charm and gentility of the late 19th century. Using floral wallpapers and antique furnishings, he has tried to re-create the look of that era.

The spacious entrance hall, with its archways and vaulted ceiling, is decorated in soft peach, rose, teal, and ivory. To the left, is a pretty library with burgundy couches placed before a granite fireplace, which becomes the social center in the evening. Stemmed glasses, a decanter of sherry, and a selection of hors d'oeuvres are set out on the library table. Guests compare notes on their days' activities and review the book of menus from local restaurants.

Eight of the charming guestrooms have Jacuzzis and fireplaces; all are decorated with a combination of antiques and period reproductions. The *Abby Rose,* for example, has a rose-colored carpet, pink walls, a crown-canopied queen-size bed, two comfortable chairs, and a double-sided fireplace that faces both the bedroom and the bathroom, so you can soak in the giant Jacuzzi and watch the flickering flames.

The oak-floored breakfast room has an open kitchen, so the aroma of fresh-baked bread permeates the room. There's also a brick fireplace, and fresh flowers brighten the tables. Guests are seated either at one large oak table or at smaller ones. Breakfast begins with fresh-squeezed orange juice and homemade sweet rolls; the gingerbread pancakes with lemon syrup, served with bacon and fresh fruit, are especially popular.

Abigail's is within an easy walk of downtown Victoria and its many attractions, including the outstanding *Provincial Museum* (with an excellent Northwest Coast Indian collection that includes numerous totems, and recreated historical street scenes so complete that the smell of baking bread wafts from the ovens) and the *Houses of Parliament. Butchart Gardens,* several miles outside of town, is well worth the trip.

ABIGAIL'S BED AND BREAKFAST HOTEL 906 McClure St., Victoria, BC V8V 3E7, Canada (phone: 604-388-5363; fax: 604-388-7787). This European-style inn has 16 guestrooms (all with private baths) with double or queen-size beds. Open year-round. Rate for a double room (including full breakfast and evening sherry): CN $120 to $225 (US $95 to $178 at press time). MasterCard and Visa accepted. Not appropriate for children under 18. No pets. No smoking. Bill McKechnie, innkeeper; Julie Usher, manager.

DIRECTIONS: From the Inner Harbour travel north on Government Street. Take a right onto Humboldt Street and continue four blocks to Vancouver Street. Turn left onto Vancouver and travel four and a half blocks, then turn left onto McClure Street. *Abigail's* is on a cul-de-sac at the end of the street.

BEACONSFIELD INN

VICTORIA, BRITISH COLUMBIA

This little Edwardian-era jewel even takes its name from a favorite haunt of King Edward VII—*Beaconsfield* was a pre–World War I English hotel. With its abundant flower gardens, turn-of-the-century charm, and air of serenity and ease, this inn would also please a king—or anyone in search of a gracious retreat.

The house was built in 1905 by R. P. Rithet, a former mayor of Victoria, as a wedding gift for his daughter. He hired the popular Victoria architect Samuel McClure, who fashioned the house with 11-foot beamed ceilings, wainscoted walls, mahogany floors, and exquisite stained glass.

From the moment you enter the front door, you know you're in for a treat. The inviting plant-filled sunroom boasts stained glass windows with a subtle peacock-feather motif, wicker furniture with floral cushions, Oriental rugs on a black-and-white tile floor, and a softly splashing fountain. The entrance hall has oak paneling and an extravagant mantel over the fireplace. In the library, where afternoon sherry, tea, and snacks are served, there's another fireplace and the walls are lined with dark oak bookcases.

Con and Judi Sollid, formerly an orthodontist and an attorney, respectively, have owned the *Beaconsfield Inn* since 1993. Possessing a warm sense of hospitality and a refined sense of style, they've decorated the nine guestrooms with interesting antiques, including canopy and brass beds. There are fluffy down comforters on all the beds, and most of the rooms have Jacuzzis and fireplaces. (They also have hair dryers and alarm clocks, but no telephones or televisions to disturb the peace.) All the rooms convey an air of comfort and understated elegance, without being fussy or ostentatious. There's a air of romance about them as well, underscored by the fireplaces, the Jacuzzis (complete with bathside candles), and complimentary champagne and chocolates.

Each of the rooms has its own personality and decor. The *Attic Room* takes up the entire top floor and offers a feeling of privacy and seclusion. It features an antique four-poster canopy bed, a cozy window seat, a love seat in front of the fireplace, a skylight, and a Jacuzzi. *Duchess* has a fox hunt theme and a regal air, with a teal and apricot color scheme, a wood-burning fireplace, and an antique "fainting chair." The large bathroom is embellished with an unusual Edwardian wood-canopied tub and a tapestry armchair.

Two new suites (fashioned from four existing rooms) were created in 1995. The charming *Gate Keeper's Suite* has a door leading out to a private garden patio area with two Adirondack chairs and a small wrought-iron table and chair set. Mosquito netting hangs over the brass bed, which is made up with floral Ralph Lauren linen and heaped high with pillows. The adjoining room has a gas fireplace with a stone mantlepiece and a Jacuzzi for two. The *Emily Carr Suite,* also newly created, is named for Victoria's most famous artist. Decorated with Ralph Lauren fabrics in hunter green and burgundy, it has a sitting room with a two-person Jacuzzi and a fireplace, and a shower for two in the bathroom.

Breakfast is served either in the dining room or the sunroom. Both are pleasant, but we recommend arriving for breakfast a few minutes early to secure a sun-splashed table in the latter. In the dining room, a built-in oak buffet, a cast-iron Inglenook fireplace, and antique English oak tables provide a country-house setting. Breakfast entrées might include French toast with apple topping and vanilla yogurt sauce, eggs Florentine, or baked egg with salsa. The meal also features juice, fresh fruit, freshly baked breads and muffins, and granola and other cereals.

The inn is three blocks from Victoria's downtown, with its museums and other attractions, and only one block from *Beacon Hill Park.*

BEACONSFIELD INN 998 Humboldt St., Victoria, BC V8V 2Z8, Canada (phone: 604-384-4044; fax: 604-721-2442). This Edwardian inn has nine guestrooms and suites with private baths and queen-size beds. Closed *Christmas.* Rate for a double room (including full breakfast and afternoon tea and sherry): CN $175 to $300 (US $138 to $237 at press time). MasterCard and Visa accepted. Not appropriate for children under 18. No pets. No smoking. Con and Judi Sollid, innkeepers.

DIRECTIONS: Traveling from the Inner Harbour on Government Street, turn right onto Humboldt Street and drive three blocks. The inn is on the left, on the corner of Vancouver and Humboldt.

Index

Inns

Maps

Notes